10/04

BY THE SAME AUTHOR

I Know Just What You Mean (with Patricia O'Brien)

Value Judgments

Making Sense

Keeping in Touch

At Large

Close to Home

Turning Points

The presenting symptom, the spokesman for the train company... reasons that we can't figure out, people chattering into their cell phones.

In fact, cell phones have become the boom box of the 1990s. Gray-flanneled men and women wouldn't be caught dead carrying a boom box onto the commuter train that disturbs the peace with equal disregard. The cell phone, however, has become a status symbol on par with the SUV. It's audible proof that you are too busy to waste a minute or a second, too essential to be out of reach for a second.

Anyone who's shared a park bench or an airplane with a phone abuser can tell you just how free he is. If, on the other hand, you turn sweetly and ask, "Why is your friend's wife leaving him?" you will be accused of eavesdropping.

I admire the guerrilla tactic of the New York commuter who sat beside so many lawyers conducting business that he finally made a tape recording that blared, "Your attorney-client privilege is no longer privileged!"

OK, cellular phones are great for emergencies, getting directions, ordering Chinese food to take home, and — oh, well, I admit it — calling my mother.

But if cell phone rage is a reaction to noise pollution, I think it's also and more commonly induced by public space pollution. Not long ago everyone was commenting on how the Walkman privatized the public world, turning people inward so they could waltz or rock through their community without being a part of it.

Well, the mobile phone promotes a verbal gated community; you can shut out everyone around you. It's become a personal accessory that allows the oblivious to live in their own world. Consider if you will a Bethesda, Md., man who talked away on his phone while his hair was being washed and cut. If I were the hairdresser, I would have tried my skills at a Mohawk.

Soon we are all going to be wired with a personal telephone number that allows us to be reached everywhere we go. The mobile phone, the... Remember someone... out and touch someone... we'll be looking for ways... May I suggest that the commuter train is just the... restaurants, they already... section with us...

Paper Trail

COMMON SENSE IN UNCOMMON TIMES

Ellen Goodman

Simon & Schuster

New York London Toronto Sydney

SIMON & SCHUSTER
Rockefeller Center
1230 Avenue of the Americas
New York, NY 10020

SIMON & SCHUSTER and colophon are registered trademarks
of Simon & Schuster, Inc.

For information about special discounts for bulk purchases,
please contact Simon & Schuster Special Sales:
1-800-456-6798 or business@simonandschuster.com

Designed by Liney Li

Manufactured in the United States of America

1   3   5   7   9   10   8   6   4   2

Library of Congress Cataloging-in-Publication Data
Goodman, Ellen.
Paper trail : common sense in uncommon times / Ellen Goodman.
p.   cm.
I. Title.
AC8.G7625 2004
081—dc22   2003066863
ISBN 0-7432-4919-4

To Logan and Cloe

Contents

Family Matters

At Large

Gender & Other Gaps

Bio & Other Ethics

Connections & Missed Connections

Close to Home

Rest Stop

Introduction

About halfway along this paper trail, I was invited to teach a course at Stanford on opinion writing, which I called, "Telling People What You Think."

This is the phrase my daughter came up with many years ago when a friend asked her what my job was. Katie said, "My mom is a columnist." Her friend then promptly followed up with: "What's a columnist?" At that point, Katie answered, "My mom gets paid for telling people what she thinks." I've never come up with a much better job description.

But when I arrived at Stanford and opened up the course catalog, I discovered my course had morphed into "Telling People What to Think."

After gagging a few times, I went down to the main office and explained the problem. The secretary was most apologetic and promptly sent out a campus-wide correction. When I opened up my e-mail, I discovered that I was teaching a course on "Telling People *How* They Think."

I had evolved from being a fascist to being a neurobiologist in one slip of the keyboard. I had gone from uttering dogma to reading minds.

Now I sit here with columns chosen from over the last decade—across a trail on which I was both a fellow traveler and an observer—and I think there was a tip in the typos.

Opinion-writing and opinion-speaking over the course of these years have become something closer to a combat sport: opinion-hurling. We moved into a time when politics became polarized and political debate became more like a food fight. The Olympic sport of opinion-hurling found a stadium on talk radio and cable TV, the playing fields of certitude.

Americans have felt ambivalent about many issues of the past decade—from abortion to gay marriage, from welfare reform to globaliza-tion—but rarely heard that ambivalence in the media. On the panels and round tables that dot TV, they only see two sides of an issue when people filled with certainty and untinged with doubt are invited to duke it out.

I confess that I've resisted lining up for the opinion food fights. I only agreed once to go on the *O'Reilly Factor.* That afternoon, as I raced to the car that would take me to the TV station, I literally ran into the glass door of my office building—a door that had been there for as many years as I had—and ended up with a black eye. That was God's way of telling me to give Bill O'Reilly a good leaving alone.

But generally I have found a less self-destructive way to avoid the opin-ion-hurling circuit. When the booker asks me for a quick view on assisted suicide or the death penalty or affirmative action, all I have to say is "well, that's complicated" or "I have mixed feelings about that." I can hear the phone heading back to the cradle.

On my travels back and forth to Maine in the summer, I listen to talk radio. The voices of the anchor and the call-in audience seem linked by anger as much as politics. I am not sure why certitude is so much the rage. And rage is the right word. I have on my desk books written by folks in the Telling People What to Think business: *Useful Idiots, Treason, Stupid White Men, Lies and the Lying Liars Who Tell Them.* You get the picture.

When I was testing out names for this collection of columns, a friend joked that to fit with the tenor of the times and baritone of the bestseller list, I should call it *I'm Right, You're Wrong,* or *Shut Up and Listen to Me.*

I've tried to stay on my own, somewhat separate trail through this in-creasingly noisy corridor. The columns on these pages were written for people who argue with both hands, the one and the other, and occasion-ally end up with them clasped together.

Most of these pieces began with curiosity rather than conclusion. I set about writing with a question for myself as well as readers: What's going on here? Do we really want to be putting human eggs for sale? What do we make of a world in which some folks hide women under chadors and oth-ers expose them on your laptop? Why, in the wake of the Columbine high school shooting or the Oklahoma City bombing or even September 11, do people talk about the need for closure? Do we really think the loss of a child or a homeland can be healed in time for dinner?

The other day after I gave a speech in Des Moines, a woman came up and said: "You're always writing what I'm thinking." I laughed and an-swered, "Well, we're both in trouble then." But I suspect that I write what she's thinking *about.* We both open up the morning paper or log on to the computer or turn on TV and say, "Oh no, now hormones cause

Alzheimer's?" "Now marriage is the national *anti-poverty* program?" "Hillary did *what?*"

But of course most people then go to work or to the cleaners or to pick up the kids from school. It's my odd business to figure out the promises and dangers of, say, cloning or zero tolerance or the search for the perfect mom.

The questions that most intrigue me take time, and time is the commodity in shortest supply. In the decade reprised here, our lives have gone on fast-forward. The one thing that typified this era beyond the polarization of debate was the speed.

News became 24/7. The Internet now has a new edition out every minute. A scandal is treated like a commodity to be marketed. A story becomes all the rage and disappears as quickly as the suitor in *Who Wants to Marry a Millionaire*. Or for that matter Princess Di.

I labeled one part the Speed Zone, because this is the neighborhood that we moved into. Multitasking became the norm. Our attention span shrank faster than the sound bite. Our learned attention deficit disorder is now so acute that we skip from Elian Gonzalez to Elizabeth Smart, from O.J. Simpson to Kobe Bryant, from one "trial of the century" to another "trial of the century," from one superstar and reality program to the next.

The op-ed page that's been my home for more than twenty-five years is one of the few places in the media reserved for those who want to resist that trend. It's the designated thoughtful corner of the newspaper.

It's always been a challenge to reflect on deadline, let alone in 750 words. It's been tricky to write with perspective from the inside of an ongoing story, whether it's a sex scandal in the White House or war in Iraq.

But I can see how much trickier it became during the time span covered in these pages, when I often worried that speed would trump thoughtfulness and the sell-by date on a commentary seemed shorter than ever.

I have been aware of this speed zone, been affected by it and resisted it as well. As I chose the columns for this book, I revisited the stories that came and went as quickly as Wayne Bobbitt. I left many columns by the wayside, especially the ones about political flaps that seemed so important—for a day or two. I included others as souvenirs from the trail, small pieces of paper to mark the way.

There are four columns in these pages on Hillary Clinton as she evolved from first lady to wronged wife to Senator—an incredible journey for a woman who has been an icon or perhaps a Rorschach test for her generation. There are as well a handful of pieces on the Lewinsky scandal. Remember when the feminist slogan was "the personal is political." Be careful what you wish for. In this decade the political became (too) personal.

In the time I have followed the women's movement—what I think of literally as the "movement of women"—there were arguments over everything from burqas to Botox. In the welfare reform debate, the right and the left, the Republicans and the Democrats, men and women signed on to a social change so radical that no one actually acknowledged it: A mother's place is in the workforce. Or should I say, a *poor* mother's place is in the workforce? We completed a huge transformation without answering the question that was asked at the outset: Who will take care of the children?

Meanwhile the family-values debates that once raged around working mothers raged with all the same intensity around the issues of gay rights and especially gay marriage. Abortion remained a flashpoint, but it also became the issue behind new bioethical debates from cloning to stem cells.

I cannot retrace my steps along this trail without stopping short a few times. A column from the 2000 presidential trail, a campaign of trivia and factoids that took place while in a soaring economy and a peaceful world, was eerily prescient. I worried in print that we'd forgotten how fragile the economy could be and how dangerous the world could become.

A year later, early on September 11, 2001, after sketching out a column on Serena and Vanessa Williams, I logged on to the Internet to send the outline to my office. There on AOL was the shocking image of a plane crashing into the World Trade Center. I rushed to the television in time to watch the twin towers come, incredibly, down, and then another plane hit the Pentagon and a fourth crash in the Pennsylvania soil.

I have included here the rawest of impressions from that day when I felt and wrote that "everything has changed." Did everything change? We still don't know exactly how much our world tilted. But the war on terrorism evolved into a war with Iraq in ways we are still unraveling. September 11 led all of us into a life of bag searches and homeland security alerts and the uncertain leadership of a photo op president in full gear on a flight deck.

My companions on this trail have been skepticism, the perspective that we call humor and, I guess, something in the DNA that says, "wait a minute." Did the President call it *preventive* war? Wait a minute. Did you say that Bill Bennett, the virtue monger, is a *gambler*? Wait a minute. Did you say the doctor offering to clone himself is named *Seed*? Whoa.

But these columns are not just about the wider world. When I first began as a columnist, I deliberately set out to write across the retaining walls that separated private life from public life. So I have written as someone on this trail as well. I've written as an insider—not to Capitol Hill battles but to everyday struggles with growing kids and aging parents, with culture wars and gender skirmishes.

At the beginning of this trail, cell phones were relatively rare, e-mail had not yet become universal, Spam was still in a can, and Google wasn't even a company, let alone a verb. Like all of us, I have been playing catchup to technology and questioning it. Like many, I have lived on a two-trail life, fast and slow. I have felt that tension between the pace of the Internet and the natural rhythms, especially those of a tidal cove in Maine.

Some of these columns are about the American family; others are about my family. Some are as universal as Thanksgiving and others as personal as my daughter's wedding. My "true confessions" are limited to a blushing admission of golf or coffee addiction.

I actually chose *Paper Trail* as the title for this book after hearing someone dismissed as a potential political candidate. "He'll never make it," said a colleague. "He has a paper trail a mile long."

A paper trail was a liability? I couldn't disagree more. I think of this trail as a record, a running commentary on these times and my times. This is my path tracked through the newspaper pages, to remind us of what we've been through, where and who we are.

Finally, these ten years have been surprising ones for me. This is the time of life we optimistically call "midlife," as if we were all going to live to be a hundred. It has been richer, less settled, more questing, than I ever imagined as a young woman.

For all the events of these years, the ones that have touched me the most have happened in the last months—the birth of a grandson in Montana and the arrival of a granddaughter from China.

There must be some pheromone, some chemistry that marks the entry into grandparenthood, opening up new emotional spaces. Logan was born three weeks early into a troubled world, a small life-affirming wonder. Our Cloe arrived, at a year old, the arc of her short life transformed from being abandoned to being treasured.

They have already taught me how small the world and how wide open the future. Their trail begins here and now.

American Scene

AMERICANS LIKE THINKING OF "US," NOT "US AND THEM."
THEY BELIEVE IN EQUALITY. THEY REJECT CLASS AND
PRIVILEGE. . . . THAT WOULD BE FINE IF EQUALITY WERE A
GUIDING PRINCIPLE, SOMETHING THAT REQUIRED RE-
NEWED COMMITMENT IN EVERY GENERATION. BUT IT'S A
SCAM IF WE THINK IT'S REALITY, A FANCIFUL SELF-
PORTRAIT THAT CAN'T BE CRITICIZED.

–FROM "CLASS WARRIORS," JANUARY 12, 2003

THE SELF-SERVICE GENERATION

I t is 8:30 in the morning, and I am standing at a gas station in a silk suit with an unusual fashion accessory dangling from my right hand. This metal and rubber accouterment looks exactly like a gasoline hose.

In fact, it is a gasoline hose.

I am poised (for disaster) at this petroleum establishment that boasts of self-service—which is to say, no service, because there is no longer any station on my corner that has "full service," which is to say, any service.

At precisely 8:33, as if on cue, the hose balks, the gas leaps from its point of destination and proceeds to decorate my skirt in a fashion familiar to Jackson Pollock fans.

The transfer of gas to silk is accompanied by expletives that will be deleted for the family newspaper. It is followed by a return home, a change of clothes, a trip to the cleaners and a delayed start of more than an hour.

Normally I would spare you the details of a gasoline-splattered morning. But this event was accompanied by a reverie about the brave, new economy.

We all know the now-classic joke about the job market. An economist exclaims about the millions of new jobs, and a worker counters, "I know, I have four of them." In my variation on this theme, another economist brags about jobs in the service industry, and the consumer says, "I know, I'm doing them all."

The fastest-growing part of the economy is not the service industry. It's the self-service industry. The motto of the new age is: Help Yourself.

The generic story is that of the company phone operator, whose job has been outsourced to customers. The great American gripe is about the endless minutes spent wending our way through multichoice listings before we get to the person or information we want. (Press 9 for Frustration.)

But that's just the beginning.

We now have a supermarket that not only allows us to pick our food from the shelves but scan it ourselves at the checkout counter. We have telephone companies where so-called "directory assistance" forces us to shout the town and name we are after into an electronic void.

Across the country, home delivery is increasingly replaced by pickup.

If you buy something, U-Haul. If you break it, U-Haul it back. And if it's a refrigerator, you sit home at the convenience of the truck driver.

Even in the world of alleged health care, once house calls went the way of milkmen, we learned to haul each body part to a separate specialist. But now we are sent home from hospitals with instructions on self-care that stop just short of a do-it-yourself appendectomy.

I am not opposed to the self-help ethic. I am still amazed and delighted that an ATM machine in Seattle will give $100 to a woman from Boston.

But I rebel at the casual ways corporations have downsized by replacing employees with consumers. Did anyone ask us if we want to moonlight for them?

Of course, this is all done, or so we are told, in the name of competition, lower prices and the American way. When Southwest Airlines initiated a policy of BYO food and had passengers transfer their own bags, the airline bragged of low fares. But sooner or later, competitors will pare down, fares will creep up, and we will be left toting the bag.

Where are the economists who tally up the cost-shifting of time and money and energy from them to us? When companies boast that we pay less for gas, do they include the cost of our labor, not to mention dry cleaning?

Do companies add up the wages lost while the country's on hold? (Press 8 for Outrage.) And do they include the cost to us of being hassled?

I hear that a modest rebellion is encouraging a few new businesses— even an oil company—to advertise their latest frill: people. But the whole trend of the new economy is some perverse play on the great American can-do spirit. That we can do everything on our own and without ever encountering another human being.

But before my gas tank runs dry again, may I suggest a rallying cry from those who only serve themselves: Help!

October 20, 1996

THE LATEST RAGE

When did I first come down with cell phone rage, you ask?

Oh, maybe you didn't ask, but as an advocate of free speech who has been sorely tried, I'll tell you anyway.

It came over me at lunch a few years ago when my companion's pocketbook rang. For the next ten minutes, this very, very busy woman talked to her office while I was left to study the leaf patterns on my arugula.

Then, of course, there was the day of my niece's college graduation when a very, very important father was seen talking his way through the baccalaureate.

Finally there was the evening when an utterly indispensable man seated near me at the theater could be heard doing his own dialogue over the phone to some absent co-star.

By now there is hardly a person in the country who hasn't experienced cell phone abuse and inner rage. There are 66 million phones bouncing off satellites and at any moment I am sure, 10 percent of them are offending someone.

So I was thrilled at the news that a New York commuter railroad company is considering a no-phone zone. It seems that the suburbanites who trek to the center of Manhattan every day did not suffer their phone rage silently. Surrounded by the chattering classes, they demanded the passenger's right to ride in a car without noise pollution.

The presenting symptom was volume control. As the spokesman for the train company said, "For reasons that we can't figure out, people are hollering into their cell phones."

In fact, cell phones have become the boom boxes of the 1990s. Gray-flanneled men and women who wouldn't be caught dead carrying a boom box onto the commuter train carry a mobile voice box that disturbs the peace with equal disregard. The cell phone, however, has become a status symbol on par with the SUV. It's audible proof that you are too busy to waste a minute and too essential to be out of reach for a second.

Anyone who's shared a park bench or an airplane with a phone abuser can tell you just how free he is with his speech. I have been bombarded with the details of business and other affairs. If, on the other hand, you turn sweetly and ask, "What did you say that stock was selling for?" or, "Why is your friend's wife leaving him?" you will be accused of eavesdropping.

I admire the guerrilla tactic of the New York commuter who sat beside so many lawyers conducting business that he finally made a tape recording that blared, "Your attorney-client privilege is no longer privileged!"

OK, cellular phones are great for emergencies. In my life, an emergency includes getting directions when I'm lost, ordering Chinese food to take home, and—oh, well, I admit it—calling my mother.

But if cell phone rage is a reaction to noise pollution, I think it's also and more commonly induced by public space pollution. Not long ago everyone was commenting on how the Walkman privatized the public world, turning people inward so they could waltz or rock through their community without being a part of it.

Well, the mobile phone promotes a verbal gated community; you can shut out everyone around you. It's become a personal accessory that allows the oblivious to live in their own world.

Consider if you will a Bethesda, Maryland, man who talked away on his phone while his hair was being washed and cut. If I were the hairdresser, I would have tried my skills at a Mohawk.

Soon we are all going to be equipped with one personal telephone number that goes with us everywhere we go. The mobile phone will be the phone. Remember the 1980s telephone ads: Reach out and touch someone. In the next millennium we'll be looking for ways to be out of reach.

May I suggest that the no-phone zone on the commuter train is just the beginning. In Hong Kong restaurants, they already ask you to check the phone with your coat. What about a restaurant with two sections: phone or no phone. And while we are on the subject, what about a no-phone lane on the highway?

So far the railroad is worrying about free speech issues. Can you ban talking? But the last time I looked at my bill, cell speech wasn't free. In any case, somewhere tonight you can be sure there's a cell phone yelling fire in a crowded theater.

March 21, 1999

I'm delighted that our commander in chief is warning the country to be wary of warmongers. It isn't what I expect from George W. Bush at this moment in time, but so it goes.

The problem is that the president is talking about domestic warfare, not international. He wants the role as peacemaker for civilian hostilities, not military.

The war games began even before he announced the $674 billion tax cut package. In a preemptive strike, he said that his opponents—those folks who think a tax break for the rich is, um, a tax break for the rich—would foment "class warfare."

Democrats then insisted that the president was the one who started it. Soon every kid in the political playground was accusing another of aggression and declaring their own pacifism.

There's something remarkable in the class-conflict consciousness. Class has become a dirty word in America unless it's "middle class"—a shrinking category in which most Americans swear they belong.

Through thick and thin, boom and bust, we tenaciously hold on to the belief that we are, fundamentally, a classless society. This self-image survives even though we have the most unequal distribution of wealth in the Western world. It survives even though 1 percent of us own 40 percent of the wealth. And even though there's less income mobility between generations in our country than in any other but South Africa and Great Britain.

The strength of that American belief in equality may sound like a delusion. Benjamin DeMott, who wrote *The Imperial Middle*, says, "It's a terrible thing that we won't face up to the fact that we have a class system." But, at the same time, he adds, "It's not a vice that makes people say 'no' to class, it's a kind of virtue."

He traces that virtue back to the country's origins. "When the founders were at their best, when they were thinking about the Revolution and the goodness of people who made a sacrifice for something beyond themselves, they realized that it had something to do with the fact that this wouldn't be a class society like the old world."

Talk of class warfare isn't always politically incorrect. During the last robber-baron era, Teddy Roosevelt spoke about the "malefactors of great wealth." Populists preached against "plutocrats," a moniker that doesn't trip off our lips a century later.

But we rarely hear anyone talk about the "ruling class" anymore. Al

Gore may have talked about the "people vs. the powerful." John Edwards now promises to be a "champion for regular people" against, presumably, irregular people. But Bush is considered to be a regular guy just for having a hamburger in Crawford, Texas. The only class he wants to talk about is the "investor class."

If politicians dodge charges of class warfare, Ralph Nader figures that it's because most citizens align themselves with the "haves." "So, they see the class warfare coming against them."

Never, he says, underestimate the power of television to sell the story of the poor guy who becomes a basketball star, the winner who takes all. When voters were asked where they belong on the income pecking scale, 19 percent said they were in the top 1 percent of income earners. Another 20 percent said they expected to be there.

And did you wonder about the popularity of repealing the estate tax? Thirty percent of Americans think they'd have to pay death taxes, even though only 2 percent of estates fall in the taxable range.

It's the wide-eyed optimism of "regular people" who play the lottery when the odds are a million to one. It reminds me of the man who was told that an earthquake would leave one survivor in his town. "Phew," he replied.

The Bush administration figures that the couple earning $40,000 who get a $1,333 tax cut won't begrudge a $10,244 tax cut to the couple earning $500,000. More to the point, they won't figure what they'll lose in federal programs. As for the folks too poor to pay taxes? These are, after all, the Americans that *The Wall Street Journal* called "lucky duckies."

Americans like thinking of "us," not "us and them." They believe in equality. They reject class and privilege. As DeMott says, that would be fine if equality were a guiding principle, something that required renewed commitment in every generation. But it's a scam if we think it's reality, a fanciful self-portrait that can't be criticized.

George W. describes himself as an opponent of class warfare. Well, of course he is. This plan would keep every, um, plutocrat in place. It's not peace at any price. It's peace at his price.

January 12, 2003

B less your heart, Neil.

Here we are in a sexual frenzy about the drug that is raising male spirits. On the joke circuit, Viagra has replaced Monica. On the cover of *Time,* the little blue pill has become the Man of the Year. In the newspaper, the word erection is now part of the hard news vocabulary. And double-entendres about this growth stock are spilling over the airwaves like water over Niagara.

Today, men who never talked about fear of failure are sharing. Phone lines to urologists are jammed by rising expectations. There are 150,000 prescriptions already written, the price of Pfizer stock is soaring higher than its product, and on the ever-tasteful Don Imus show, the host is passing out purloined pills to his pals in exchange for performance reports.

Meanwhile we have a hallelujah chorus singing praise to the restoration project and a patient telling *Nightline,* "The skies opened, a bolt of lightning came down, and God said, 'I love you.' " In short, the earth has moved.

But from deep in the heart of New York State comes our guy Neil Levin to remind us of our Puritan roots. In the midst of all the hype, the state insurance superintendent has announced that his department doesn't want to support the use of Viagra by anyone who wants to "just take it for fun."

Sex for the fun of it? Nooooooo.

Neil is not entirely alone in his anxiety. The man who headed the British studies of this drug also wants men to take Viagra seriously or not at all. Dr. Ian Osterlow has been everywhere telling folks that the pill that brings blood rushing to the rescue is not a "superstud" drug to be used by "regular guys" who want "a little extra performance."

Nevertheless, I am not surprised that the real cold shower on Viagra would come from folks in the health insurance industry. After all, Pfizer's magic little pills cost about $7 apiece, or $10 retail.

Insurance companies are not part of the sex industry. They are in the business of cost control. So they ask, in the charming words of Leslie Fish of Fallon Healthcare Systems: "How many erections does a health plan owe a patient?"

The fundamental question is the one posed so many years ago by James Thurber: "Is Sex Necessary?" Is a sex pill like thyroid medication or plastic surgery? Where's the line between a cure for impotence and a prescription for whoopee?

Insurance companies are deciding whether a man must prove he has a preexisting condition like diabetes to get free Viagra and whether, say, old age is or isn't a medical problem. They are calibrating how much sex is good for your health and how much is just for fun.

So far in this fairly bizarre conversation, at least one major insurer has decided to pay for six sex acts a month. There you have it. Insurers now control how often clients will have sex. This is truly managed care.

Now, I confess to being fascinated with this conversation piece. I can't help wondering why we got a pill to help men with performance instead of communication. Moreover, how is it possible that we came up with a male impotence pill before we got a male birth-control pill? The Vatican, you will note, has approved Viagra while still condemning condoms.

It also seems that in some places, we'll get health insurance coverage for male potency before we get it for female contraceptives. Hasn't anybody noticed that the chief sexual turnoff for women is fear of pregnancy? It's all enough to give a gal Viagra envy.

But at the risk of taking sex too seriously, may I offer a footnote about a nation of have and have-nots. We already have a two-tier health plan. From now on, it will also determine whether men have or have not sex.

Boston urologist Michael O'Leary says: "I'm not convinced it's a God-given right to have an excellent erection." Maybe not. But for some it's going to be an insurance-given right.

The wealthy man from LA who told a reporter that Viagra would be a trophy for his young trophy wife can buy all he wants. The un- or underinsured man without $10 to spare will get six tries and on the seventh day, he'll rest.

Who knows whether Viagra will yet sprout physical side effects. But we are already seeing some bizarre social side effects. As the beat goes on, listen for the strange sound of men trying to convince their insurers that sex is not for fun.

May 3, 1998

HURRYING HEALING

I don't remember when the words first began to echo in the hollow aftermath of loss. But now it seems that every public or private death, every moment of mourning is followed by a call for "healing," a cry for "closure."

Last month, driving home in my car just twenty-four hours after three Kentucky students were shot to death in a school prayer meeting, I heard a Paducah minister talk about "healing." The three teenagers had yet to be buried, and he said it was time to begin the healing process, as if there were an antibiotic to be applied at the first sign of pain among the survivors.

Weeks later, at a Christmas party, a man offered up a worried sigh about a widowed mutual friend. "It's been two years," he said, "and she still hasn't achieved closure." The words pegged her as an underachiever who failed the required course in Mourning 201, who wouldn't graduate with her grief class.

This vocabulary of "healing" and "closure" has spread across the postmortem landscape like a nail across my blackboard. It comes with an intonation of sympathy but an accent of impatience. It suggests after all, that death is something to be dealt with, that loss is something to get over—according to a prescribed emotional timetable.

It happened again when the Terry Nichols verdict came down. No sooner had the mixed counts of guilty and innocent been announced, than the usually jargon-free Peter Jennings asked how it would help the "healing" for Oklahoma City. Assorted commentators and reporters asked the families whether they felt a sense of "closure."

The implicit expectation, even demand, was that the survivors of 168 deaths would traverse a similar emotional terrain and come to the finish line at the same designated time. Was two-and-a-half years too long to mourn a child blown up in a building?

It was the families themselves who set us straight with responses as personal and diverse as one young mother who said, "It's time to move on," and another who described her heart this way: "Sometimes I feel like it's bleeding."

In the Nichols sentencing trial last week, we got another rare sampling of raw grief. Laura Kennedy testified that in the wake of her son's death in 1995, "I have an emptiness inside of me that's there all the time."

Diane Leonard said that since her husband's death her life "has a huge hole that can't be mended."

By the second day, however, the cameras had turned away, the microphones had turned a deaf ear, as if they had heard enough keening. Again, observers asked what affect a life-or-death sentence would have on, of course, "healing" and "closure."

I do not mean to suggest that the people who testified were "typical" mourners or the Oklahoma bombing a "typical" way of death. I mean to suggest that grief is always atypical—as individual as the death and the mourner.

The American way of dealing with it however has turned grieving into a set process with rules, stages and, of course, deadlines. We have, in essence, tried to make a science of grief, to tuck messy emotions under neat clinical labels—like "survivor guilt" or "detachment."

Sometimes, we confuse sadness with depression, replace comfort with Prozac. We expect, maybe insist upon, an end to grief. Trauma, pain, detachment, acceptance in a year—time's up.

But in real lives, grief is a train that doesn't run on anyone else's schedule. Jimmie Holland at New York's Sloan-Kettering Hospital, who has studied the subject, knows that "normal grief may often be an ongoing lifelong process." Indeed, she says, "The expectation of healing becomes an added burden. We create a sense of failure. We hear people say, 'I can't seem to reach closure, I'm not doing it fast enough.' "

Surely it is our own anxiety in the presence of pain, our own fear of loss and death, that makes us wish away another's grief or hide our own. But in every life, losses will accumulate like stones in a backpack. We will all be caught at times between remembrance and resilience.

So whatever our national passion for emotional efficiency, for quality-time parents and one-minute managers, there simply are no one-minute mourners. Hearts heal faster from surgery than from loss. And when the center of someone's life has been blown out like the core of a building, is it any wonder if it takes so long even to find a door to close?

January 4, 1998

THE GOSPEL OF ABSTINENCE

W ho would have believed that Christmas would provide a "teaching moment" for sex ed?

The folks at the Rapides Station Community Ministries of Louisiana bubbled with pride as they reported, indeed bragged, that "December was an excellent month" for abstinence class. "We were able to focus on the virgin birth," they wrote, "and make it apparent that God desires sexual purity as a way of life."

June, however, is probably not such an excellent month. The other day, the American Civil Liberties Union took Louisiana to court, claiming that the state was using public money to teach Christianity. Sex ed, they said, was really religious ed.

This court appearance also provided another "teaching moment": on constitutional law. The Louisiana providers didn't tiptoe across the line separating church and state. They ignored it.

Public funds went to one group that took field trips to abortion clinics for prayer vigils. Federal and state dollars paid for a "Passion 4 Purity" program that taught abstinence through "scriptural concepts." The state even funded the arts: a roving troop of "Just Say Whoa" players that told students that sex outside of marriage is "offensive to God."

Ah yes, your tax dollars at work. And don't forget the "fact sheet" that blamed sexually transmitted disease on the fact that "we removed God from the classroom." The solution: "It's time to restore our Judeo-Christian heritage in America."

In the courtroom, Dan Richey, the state program's administrator and former news director of a fire-and-brimstone radio station, admitted rather cavalierly that some programs may have promoted religion: "Those things will happen." He promised tighter controls in the future.

The ACLU has nevertheless asked the court for more accountability. They want to ensure that public dollars aren't translated into religious messages and/or handed out to contractors from religious institutions.

Whichever way the court eventually rules, the Louisiana case couldn't come at a better time. After all, the Bayou State has been teaching the gospel of sex education with money allocated under the 1996 welfare reform bill.

Now the Senate is about to take up a new welfare reform proposal—already passed by the House—that would up the ante. It would distribute $50 million a year to abstinence-until-marriage programs across the country. Indeed, if the Bush administration gets its way, there will be $135 million in three different federal pots dedicated to a sex ed curriculum that fits on the T-shirt worn by a star pupil in Louisiana: "Abstinent I will stay until my wedding day."

Now let it be said that most parents, in or out of Louisiana, favor abstinence . . . at least for their children. We want to push against the shove of the culture. Given our druthers, we also want our children to wait for sex at least until they are 18 or so, an age that coincides mysteriously with the time they are out of the house.

But by and large, American parents also have a realistic two-pronged approach to protecting children, especially teenagers. Today 70 percent of 18-year-olds have had intercourse. It's not a surprise that 82 percent of parents want sex ed to cover contraception as well as abstinence.

The problem with the abstinence-only classes isn't just that the groups receiving the dollars read like a Who's Who of the Religious Right. It's that programs preaching—excuse me, teaching—this are spreading fear, misinformation, and disinformation.

Under federal guidelines, this money can go only to a program that has "as its exclusive purpose teaching the social, psychological and health gains to be realized by abstaining from sexual activity."

The money is to teach, specifically, "that abstinence from sexual activity is the only certain way to avoid out-of-wedlock pregnancy, sexually transmitted disease, and other associated health problems."

And for extra measure, "that sexual activity outside the context of marriage is likely to have harmful psychological and physical side effects."

They can't talk about contraceptives, except to emphasize the failure rates. Call it the bad news gospel.

"This is a classic example of ideology trumping public health," says James Wagoner of Advocates for Youth. It isn't just inaccurate education. It's ineffective. There is no proof that the half-billion dollars already spent in abstinence-only lessons delays intercourse or prevents pregnancy.

Is it any wonder that the abstinence-only supporters in Congress have fought amendments that would require the lessons to be medically accurate? I guess we're supposed to take the value of abstinence-only education on, um, faith.

Faith-based politics? Faith-based sex education? Welcome to the United States of Louisiana.

June 23, 2002

A NEW "MODEST PROPOSAL"

N ow that we have repealed welfare, I have a modest proposal. Let's go all the way and rescind childhood.

Childhood has become far too burdensome for the American public to bear. It isn't good for the country. It isn't even good for children who are captured in an unwholesome and prolonged state of dependency.

The whole idea of childhood, it should be remembered, is nothing but an anachronistic leftover from the original liberals. Before the so-called Enlightenment, before Rousseau, before the left-wing conspiracy of 18th-century do-gooders, the young dressed, worked and were looked upon as short adults.

Children existed, but they didn't have their own 'hood—a place where they were supposed to be educated and nurtured until they reached maturity. Adolescence, for that matter, wasn't invented until the early 20th century. Nor was the concept of juvenile as in delinquency, nor the notion of teenage as in pregnancy.

But now we are stuck with this useless thing called childhood, a drain on the private and public exchequers. Not to mention a merciless drag on private and public conscience.

Consider what happened when Congress passed and the president approved the "Personal Responsibility and Work Opportunity Act of 1996" (a k a welfare reform). The only teensy-weensy reservations about cutting $56 billion from the poorest Americans, ending the federal guarantee of assistance to poor families and launching them into the unknown had to do with children.

There are still a handful of people troubled by the fact that America has the highest child poverty rates of any industrialized country and that when this "reform" clicks in, more children are expected to become poor.

Why not eliminate all this messy, counterproductive guilt? Why not apply the same principles of "personal responsibility" and "work opportunity" to our youngest citizens?

I am not alone in my plan, though perhaps I am the first to put it quite so baldly. But we are already erasing the line between childhood and adulthood whenever we want to.

At the Olympics, we had 14-year-old gymnasts on the "Women's Team." In the states, we now have plans to try 13-year-old lawbreakers as adults. In Congress they are considering doing away with juvenile jails and "mainstreaming" kids with older criminals. Across the world, the "new economy" is using kids as a way to meet global competition.

Most Americans already recognize that childhood is simply not cost-effective. If children were once economic assets, they are now deficits, unlikely to ever pay back our investments. So only a third of our households has anyone under 18 in them today. Communities which once felt a collective responsibility for the next generation now often regard children as private property to be exclusively maintained by their owners.

If we eliminated the entire notion of childhood we wouldn't have to worry about children having children. Or about child care. Or after school care. Or school. Child labor would become another "work opportunity."

Of course, we could retain childhood as a luxury item for those who could afford it. Sort of like an Ivy League college. The rest, the poor especially, will have to do without childhood the way they do without so much else.

It takes a village to raise a child, as the former Hillary Clinton—somebody file a missing person report on her—once wrote. But the village has now given instructions to the government: Everyone is on her own.

The last great evil in America today is dependency. The last remaining "culture of dependency" is, of course, childhood. Is it any wonder that it has to go?

If my modest proposal seems too harsh, may I remind you of the one Jonathan Swift offered in 1729: "A Modest Proposal for Preventing the Children of Poor People in Ireland from Being a Burden to Their Parents or Country and for Making Them Beneficial to the Public."

Swift proposed, modestly and satirically, that the Irish young be sold and eaten. They would be as well off as growing up in poverty under British policy.

I would never suggest such a thing. But come to think of it, this reckless "reform" is also cutting food stamps by about a fifth. Maybe Swift was just ahead of his time.

August 8, 1996

THE SUPERSIZING OF AMERICA

I work in a danger zone. Across the street from my office is a restaurant that sells bagels larger than my hand. Around the corner is a Ben and Jerry's that scoops an ice cream flavor that is "Phish food" for the whale-sized. This morning the local pizza place put up a sign announcing "all you can eat" night.

Life on this Boulevard of Broken Diets is not easy. After all, like most Americans I subscribe to the "just say no" school of weight control. This is a school that promotes theorists like Will and Power. It offers a school motto of Personal Responsibility.

Even as the ideal body has gotten slimmer and the real body has gotten wider, students of this philosophy react like our Puritan ancestors. We assume that what separates the saved from the damned is virtue.

Well, fat chance for virtue. The only part of our economy that seems to be expanding is the waistline. Sixty percent of Americans are overweight. Twice as many kids are overweight as a generation ago. And in the last few weeks we've had health warnings about fat that range from diabetes to Alzheimer's.

The only good news is that we are beginning to shift from describing obesity as a moral failing to describing it as a public health epidemic. We are beginning to shift at least some attention from self-control to environment-out-of-control.

This change is partly due to the collective, um, weight of scientific studies. Yale's Kelly Brownell, who coined the phrase "toxic environment," sums them up this way: "When the environment changes, weight changes." When, for example, immigrants from thinner countries come to America they gain weight while their cousins back home stay lean. When you give moviegoers a big box of popcorn instead of a small one, they eat about 50 percent more.

The change also comes from the discovery that there really were business plans for the fattening of America. We don't actually have much less willpower than we used to. In *Fat Land,* Greg Critser details the deliberate supersizing of servings from the Big Mac to the Big Gulp. Instead of expanding the number of customers, they expanded the existing customers.

At the same time, we have learned something from the campaigns against smoking. Yes, it's up to the smoker to stub out the last Marlboro. But personal responsibility is not a free pass for corporate irresponsibility. It's easier to just say no when you aren't being manipulated and marketed to say yes. Willpower is influenced by price, by advertising, and even lawsuits.

It's not an accident that Kraft, maker of Oreo cookies and macaroni and cheese, became the first Big Foodie to pledge to help the fight against obesity. The company is, after all, a subsidiary of the much-sued Philip Morris before it changed its name and image to Altria.

As Margo Wootan of the Center for Science in the Public Interest says, "Kraft belongs to a tobacco company that knows what the inside of a courtroom looks like." It didn't take a Ph.D., she adds, to realize that everyone would figure out that cookies and cheese contribute to obesity.

One of Kraft's pledges is to stop marketing in schools. Indeed, the public seems most willing to acknowledge the weight of the environment in the weight of kids.

The first step in downsizing Americans may be in the schools. Over the past decade, schools have said yes to soft drinks and junk food in hallway vending machines. Now some large school districts from Los Angeles to New York have banned the sale of sodas. There are bills in Massachusetts and Maine to get rid of junk food in those same machines.

But it's likely to be a long haul to get smaller portions, labeling in fast-food restaurants and to slim down advertising to kids. Wootan says, "People still haven't made the connection about how industry practices shape and influence their choices. Your child begs you for junk food, begs you to go to McDonald's and you think 'that's kids.' You don't think, 'shame on that food company.' "

Food is one part of a complex obesity problem that includes Game Boys instead of ball games and TV instead of track. Moreover, it's still tricky to attack fat as a health issue without attacking fat people, and we've had a big enough portion of that, thank you. But Brownell believes, "We are at a place where it no longer makes sense to blame people for a problem their environment is causing."

What do we need to change the environment? How about Will and Power?

July 27, 2003

T here is an old story about the time Jack Kennedy was campaigning in West Virginia. One day the senator was confronted by a coal miner with a question.

"Is it true," the man asked, "that you haven't done an honest day of hard labor in your life?"

The would-be president abashedly admitted as much and waited for the blow. But the coal miner shook his hand and replied, "Believe me, you haven't missed a thing."

The tale, apocryphal or not, has been repeated for forty years because of the punch line. In a country that shares one ethic—work—somebody offered a counterpoint from real life.

For the most part, the great American philosophy is "We work, therefore we are." Work is identity; the workplace is our community; production equals self-worth. But there are occasions when an alternate truth punches through the retaining wall of this shared religion.

What happens, for example, whenever a hard worker wins the lottery? When Johnnie Ely, the first big winner of the new millennium, checked the right numbers off on his $100 million New York lottery ticket—8, 23, 38, 39, 46, 14—he left the Java Shop kitchen where he'd worked for twenty years, never to return.

The first question his wife, a nurse, asked was, "Can I retire?" She swiftly cleaned out her locker.

I am thinking of the coal miner and the lottery winner because the president is about to sign a bill that will allow people on Social Security to work as much and earn as much as they want without losing any benefits. It's a bill Congress passed unanimously—unanimously—to end the penalty on earnings in retirement.

This won't make much difference to either the earners or the Social Security budget. The small penalty currently inflicted on those between 65 and 69 who earned more than $17,000 was credited to them at 70.

But the change is not just a cheap and popular way of offering more dollars to older workers and more older workers to a labor-starved economy. It's a piece of the one consistent message being put forth by politicians for whom "working with your hands" means gesturing during a speech. The policies they favor add up to one thing: It's off to work we go.

The most radical of these changes has been eliminating welfare. In the *Miami Herald* this week there was an ad featuring a small girl and her mother: "Need a hard worker? How about my mom? Moms coming off welfare are motivated, responsible employees. They have to be."

The social change behind welfare reform has been so dramatic that we don't often acknowledge it. It's a message that says, "A mother's place is in the work force."

But what of older Americans? Once, senior citizens, like mothers, were encouraged to get out of the work force. Now, as the country ages, as the Social Security population grows, are they too expected to stay in the work force? Or, to use the welfare analogy, to get out of the cart and pull their own weight?

We are gradually raising the age of Social Security from 65 to 67. Now we are also separating Social Security from retirement. We are making work a part of the "retirement" picture.

Senator Daniel Patrick Moynihan, who is leaving the Senate at 73, attributes it to changes in the work force. "Coal mines were no place for 70-year-olds. Computer terminals are. It's as simple as that."

Maybe so. I am sure that the good senator will retire to his memoirs and his keyboard. But some 29 percent of the elderly earners are now working in jobs that hover around the minimum wage. This tweaking of the rules does little for them. And it does nothing for the population living on Social Security alone.

Even those who want to work in old age don't want to have to work. Are we now using the work ethic to cover this great divide?

Our society increasingly values work and the marketplace. We value work as it's defined by a paycheck. But I have a strong feeling that people with creative, autonomous jobs where heavy lifting means dragging an icon across a screen think of work pretty differently than a 66-year-old Java Shop cook whose one big chance was a lottery ticket.

March 30, 2000

C ASCO BAY, MAINE—I set out walking on this late-summer morning like a tourist carrying a guidebook in a foreign land. But my paperback is no Baedeker, no Fodor's, and there are no stained-glass windows, no church spires, no statues on this island.

The worn pages hold the names and colors and images of a thousand wildflowers. I take it with me today to learn my way around this landscape, flower by flower, the way I know my city, street by street.

By birth I am an urban dweller. Nature is my second home. I grew up absorbing the difference between brownstone and brick and concrete. But here I am still a sightseer.

So I have had to learn the difference between a tansy and goldenrod, between the false foxglove and the common primrose. I have had to memorize the names of wildflowers the halting way you memorize a foreign language in middle age, building your vocabulary slowly, claiming and reclaiming each noun, verb, adjective, until you feel at home in its vocabulary.

It's been fifteen summers since I first came here with a tennis racquet and a civilized point of view. Wooed into the landscape by my greed, I went after nature for all I could take: the sweetest berries, the plumpest mussels.

It was years before I discovered where the wild oregano grew and which dandelion leaves to pick and how the mustard seed tasted. More years before I could identify the other inhabitants: the flight pattern of the goldfinch, the rattle of the kingfisher, the elegant posture of the heron.

Now, slowly, I am onto the next course of study. I am coming to know the extravagant variety of wildflowers that complement and compete with each other for space here, that come and go like vacationing mainlanders from one week to the next.

But if I am a late bloomer in this outdoor classroom, I am not the only one. Today, most of us and most of our children have the most un-natural of educations.

The average American child knows a thousand brand names before she is 8 or 9. But how many leaves can she name? A 10-year-old can tell Pepsi from Coke. But can he tell Queen Anne's lace from yarrow?

Teenagers all know a Nike sneaker from a Reebok. But there are few who can name the "weeds" that surround the playground—the blue corn-flower or the lowly plantain.

There was a boy in an ad in my newspaper this morning. He was running freely across a vast, green field under an open sky. But the caption read: "This yard with no fences, brought to you by new Microsoft Office." It seems that his world was bounded by the Windows on a computer.

This is how we live now, most of us, in a built environment, man-made, and paved with commercial messages that run before our eyes like flashcards. Our crops are products and our environment is the marketplace.

We are likely now to visit nature as a zoo, a park, a television show, a video, a software program, a summer vacation. We no longer think of nature as our native country.

I wonder if this isn't the cause of the weakness in our commitment to the environment. In polls, a strong majority of Americans call themselves environmentalists. The core beliefs of environmentalism, we are told, have become as much a part of our value system as the belief in parental responsibility.

Yet all summer, as the new Congress sets out to strip away the protective work of a generation, I have wondered why there wasn't more protest. Why, for all the recycling and hand-wringing, do green issues rarely get to the top of the political layers?

Maybe it is because most of us are armchair environmentalists, city folk watching the spotted owls on television, suburbanites buying an air conditioner against global warming and bottled water against pollution.

Because the environment is something huge out there. It's the environment, not my environment. Because we don't even know the names of our natural neighbors.

In just a few days my island summer schooling will be over. I'll drive down a highway where billboards grab attention from the purple loosestrife growing beneath them. I'll return to an office whose only sign of life is one abused philodendron. It will be hard to remember the lessons I cram for this morning.

But today, visiting among the asters, I try to speak the language of one small piece of land. For one brief moment, nature and I are on a first-name basis.

August 31, 1995

BETTING ON DIVERSITY

T here was a goosebump moment at the convention after all. In the midst of the political ritual and partisan rhetoric, Joe Lieberman stepped up to the moment and said, "Only in America."

He placed his journey on the American path of tolerance. A grandmother who left the bigotry of Europe to be greeted by Christian neighbors, "Good Sabbath, Mrs. Manger." In-laws who were literally rescued by American G.I.s from genocidal Nazis. Time spent in Mississippi registering African-American voters. The senator really didn't need to remind viewers or delegates that he was the first Jewish American on a national ticket. It was enough to say: Only in America.

Forty years ago in Los Angeles, the Democrats who nominated JFK as president overlooked religion. But the Democrats nominating Joe Lieberman as vice president celebrated it.

For one long week, the Democrats touted their own diversity and taunted the Republicans. Rob Reiner mocked Republican diversity as "two guys at the head of the ticket that are from two different oil companies." Democrats included and included and included.

Still, there was a subtle undertone to the congratulations. The Democrats were placing a bet on Lieberman. He described a choice made "with courage and friendship." One commentator after another said that breaking barriers entailed risk. Gore, they said, was both daring and open, as if being open-minded was itself the dare.

In one seminal moment, John Lewis, the civil rights leader, quoted an old Yiddish line used by wary immigrants as a verbal crossing of the fingers. "From your lips to God's ear," he said, "America is ready for Joe Lieberman."

"Ready" is the word that stuck in my mind. Were we "ready" for Joe Lieberman? "Ready" for this first? In 1960, Harry Truman publicly directed this question with an equal lack of subtlety to JFK: "Are you certain you're quite ready for the country or the country is ready for you?"

Ready or not? Why is it that no one ever asks whether we are "ready" for bigotry? It sounds as if there is a tolerance-readiness course that the country has to complete, like reading-readiness, before we can cross any new threshold.

In fact, one of the great chicken-and-egg questions of social change is how fast and far to move. If you push hard, will a backlash send you hurtling? Or will people catch up? If you choose gradual change, will it come more comfortably? Or not at all?

In the world of religion and politics, no one knows precisely what happened in the years between Al Smith's rejection and Jack Kennedy's election. Did time and the war mute the anti-Papism that once ran rampant? Or did JFK turn the tide for those who came next?

Many of us remember that the South was not "ready" to integrate. Until it did. The military wasn't "ready" to accept women. Until it did. Television audiences weren't "ready" to accept homosexuals. Until they did.

When I was a kid in Boston, the marriage of an Irish Catholic to an Italian Catholic was an occasion for family mourning. Not today. I've known parents who would never accept a son-in-law of a different race or a daughter of a different sexual orientation. Now they do.

In these conventions, we saw diversity, ready or not. Were Dick and Lynne Cheney "ready" for a lesbian daughter? I doubt it. Would the McCains' grandparents have adopted a girl from Bangladesh? Would Prescott Bush's country club friends have embraced a nephew who shares Latino roots? Who would have expected Pat Buchanan to choose an African-American woman for his running mate, even one who believes multiculturalism has divided the country.

Now the question is Joe Lieberman. There are Jewish Americans, older ones, who remember when neighbors did not always say, "Good Sabbath, Mrs. Manger." Even young Americans who know how much has changed point to the messages on the Internet where new technology serves old bigotry.

But postwar generations have learned that you cannot wait until people, comfortable with their old narrow beliefs, become ready for change. It's those who step up, speak up, get out of the closet and do not quake at consequences who challenge old ideas with new realities. They change our world.

So the bet is placed. On the platform the "first" said, "We have become the America that so many of our parents dreamed for us." From his mouth to God's ear.

August 20, 2000

t first I dismissed this story as too New York.

Only in New York do limos line up outside preschools that cost $14,400 a year and are harder to get into than Harvard.

Only in New York is it plausible that a $20 million-a-year Wall Street analyst would goose up the rating of a stock so the boss would help get his 2-year-old twins into the right nursery school.

Only in New York would there be a "right" nursery school, for that matter, the 92nd Street Y, a place where Woody Allen's kid was accepted and Madonna's kid was rejected.

But the incriminating e-mail has become a pop-up message on my brain's computer screen. Jack Grubman wrote: "For someone who grew up in a household making $8,000 a year and attended public schools, I do find this process a bit strange, but there are no bounds for what you do for your children."

Strange? Grubman could have bought his kids a nursery school. The desire of the self-made man to turn his twins into the little master and mistress of the Playskool universe has made him the poster father of competitive parenting. But under the scoffing, isn't there something uncomfortably familiar?

There was a time when we used to laugh at folks who lived in Lake Wobegon, where all the children are above average. But don't parents today want their children to be above that "above average"? They want them to go to Leg Up. Leg Up on the other kids.

Trophy children are a rich source of satire. The authors of *The Nanny Diaries* portray an East Side mother telling her preschooler, "Go get into bed and I'll read you one verse from your Shakespeare reader and then it's lights out."

There's a preschool consulting firm in New York actually named Ivy-Wise Kids. But it goes way beyond Manhattan. A recent gathering of college admissions officers, Ivy and (Other)Wise, added "parents" to their list of problems. They swapped stories of mothers and fathers who talk openly about "our application" and "our interview" and threatened to sue when their kids were rejected.

Meanwhile on the school playing fields, there's been an epidemic of parents behaving badly at the kids' sporting events. It's the parents who can't stand to have their kids lose.

One professor noted that New Yorkers have "redefined status distinctions to the pre-K level." But elsewhere we've gone from pre-K to prenatal. It wasn't just New Yorkers who were encouraged to give their offspring a jump start by playing Mozart to the womb.

And while we are on the subject, how long before the Trophy Kid becomes the Designer Baby? We are just learning how to screen and tweak genes. At some point, perhaps the good, caring parent may not only screen for a fatal gene but for a fat gene.

Maybe it's baroque to worry about competitive parenting when we consider the number of neglected kids. Maybe it's foolish to worry about preschool Olympics for elite education when one out of ten 18-to-24-year-olds can't place the United States on a map.

But children aren't trophies. Nor are they proof of our success.

I suspect that we've all felt that protective, competitive itch, watching someone else's 10-month-old walk or someone else's 3-year-old read. A man we know who grew up in the same apartment building as young Leonard Bernstein was nagged by his parents who wondered, "Why can't you play like Lenny?" And none of us is so detached that we can watch our children stumble without feeling it.

Indeed, parenting is a role full of emotions and contradictions. We want what's best for the child. Or do we want our child to be the best? For them or for us? We too may say that there are "no bounds" to what we'll do for the kids. But shouldn't there be boundaries between us and offspring?

It's no wonder that children pick favorites like Pippi Longstocking and Harry Potter off the bookshelves. These are resourceful girls and boys who may miss their parents but revel in freedom.

Eventually, somewhere between womb and college, our own children want both parental approval and independence. They come off the trophy shelf and into their own.

Jack Grubman allegedly gave his boss at Citigroup what he wanted. Citigroup gave a million bucks to the 92nd Street Y to be used for adult performances and lectures. The Y found slots for the Grubman kids in the preschool. It's a New York story.

But whatever else happens to Grubman, this father should be sentenced to take some of the lectures the company paid for. One of them is called: "Raising Children of Integrity."

November 24, 2002

I magine that you have arrived at the emergency room after a horrific car crash. The doctor in charge offers you two pills. One will relieve the inflammation of whiplash. The other will reduce the psychological trauma, muting the nightmarish flashback to a manageable memory.

Would you take one? Would you take both? Is there any difference?

Imagine, for that matter, that a child came to the hospital after being raped or abused. Should she be given a pill if it would prevent the trauma from literally changing the anatomy of her brain and setting her up for a lifetime of vulnerability?

And finally, if your imagination isn't overtaxed already, what about a soldier just back from battle? Should he be treated with medicine that helps dim the effect of the horrors he has experienced?

These are not idle science fictions. Once, we drew a bright line between the pain of the body and the mind, between treatments for physical and mental illness. Now researchers are into the chemistry of emotions, the biology of feelings, the anatomy of psychology.

It appears that memories of shocking events may be like water—an overwhelming flood or a manageable stream. And scientists may be designing chemical faucets.

Just last week, a meeting of traumatic stress specialists heard that a common hypertension drug may help prevent post-traumatic stress disorder. If the human trials pan out, it could, in effect, keep a wrenching experience from being burned too deeply in memory.

There is research as well on treatments designed to interrupt the way a painful event can change the brain. And there is also talk of gene therapies that might make vulnerable people react to emotional injuries like resilient people.

What are we to make of this? The goal is, after all, simple and uncontroversial. Dr. Roger Pitman of Harvard Medical School, who is doing research in this field, says: "I look at it from a medical perspective. We intervene in diseases and disorders to make people more comfortable and to reduce suffering."

Fair enough. A bad memory can be as painful and crippling as a bad back or heart. Post-traumatic stress disorder is not trivialized by those who live with it or treat it. Pitman repeats the words of veterans he has treated: "One said to me, 'If Vietnam was only a memory I would be OK. It's more than a memory. It's happening again.' " If we can heal that, surely we should.

I don't romanticize mental illness. But at the same time, I wonder what will happen if we are able to lighten the load of memory. Would we end up with a drug to make loss "lite," to speed up "closure," to make horror "manageable"? At some point reducing human suffering is editing human experience. For better or for worse.

I remember what happened to Prozac. A drug to alleviate severe depression morphed into what is called a cosmetic pharmacology. It was used to help people feel "better than well," in a phrase made famous by Peter Kramer in *Listening to Prozac*. The class of drugs not only replaced counseling but was routinely prescribed by internists for patients and even by veterinarians for pets.

It's not that hard to envision preventive drugs being offered to those who witnessed a Columbine massacre or the collapse of the World Trade Center. Nor is it hard to imagine preventive drugs offered to parents who have just lost a child. Where do we draw the line on the prescription pad?

Kramer sees benefits in helping those who are truly "overwhelmed and haunted." But he also can see abuse. "Imagine," he says, "a totalitarian, militaristic society giving it to soldiers so they will be immune to the horrors of war." And if the horrors of war or of crime are not so "horrible," wouldn't that change our attitude toward war or crime themselves?

Such worries race ahead of the research. Pitman says succinctly: "We don't want to make people happy automatons. We're not going to eliminate the horrors of war." He says that we won't know where to draw the line—or the dosage—until we know what medicine can do.

But it seems to me that we often find ourselves behind the research curve, playing ethical catch-up with cloning or cosmetic pharmacology after they are on the market and in the doctor's office. Now we are at the outset of treatments that could alter mind and memory and our ideas about humanity.

Today we have to ask the questions first. And so we begin with this one: Isn't human suffering more than a matter of chemistry?

November 14, 2002

CLOE'S FIRST FOURTH

C ASCO BAY, MAINE—It will be her very first parade, her very first Fourth of July. Our granddaughter will be both the newest citizen at the picnic and the newest member of our family.

Cloe, this little girl with shiny black hair and a quiet, curious stare, has come to America and to us. We have embraced her with a loyalty that is all the more tenacious for having not been preordained by biology. We have the sort of attachment that the word "adoption" cannot begin to describe.

Just six weeks ago, Cloe was halfway around the world in an orphanage in China. Six weeks before that, my stepdaughter and her husband got her photograph in the mail. It put a face—her face—on what had been a stack of papers, a mound of red tape, and, of course, a hope.

Psychologists, neurologists, "ologists" of every variety may say it's impossible to bond to a photograph. But we connected to Cloe before she was named Cloe. We connected to her before she had any idea we existed or that there was a world outside the orphanage, outside the province, the country, the continent.

Before the travel papers arrived, we waited anxiously, tracking the reports of SARS, worrying that Beijing would close down the border before our children became parents, before this child of China could become a child of America. But when the moment came to gather Cloe, it seemed as sudden as the wait had seemed interminable.

After all that time, she was just a plane trip away. In a single moment, a year-old child was transferred from one set of hands to another and from one fate to another. The entire arc of her short life was transformed from being abandoned to being treasured.

Now we will take her to watch the parade of homemade floats come down the road and cheer the scramble up the greased pole. We will bring a newcomer to the American birthday party, but she has brought us to the wider world. We have made her an American, and she has made us a part of the global village.

Our Cloe is one of about twenty thousand international adoptions within the last year, one of five thousand girls from China. Over many months, we learned to spot them in the grocery store or the street. We learned to wonder what this wave of girls will make of their experience, of the great economic and political winds that changed the course of their lives.

In China, an ancient culture that still sets a higher value on the head of a boy, has collided with a government policy that pressures families to have only one child. As a result, hundreds of thousands of girls are growing up in orphanages. As a very different result, thousands of girls are growing up in America, more privileged than brothers left behind.

As for Cloe, we know the joy her story brings to our family. But we can only guess at the loss to the woman who left her day-old daughter on fortune's doorstep.

My stepdaughter tells me about the final medical exam Cloe was given on the way out of China. The pediatrician carefully examined the little patient. Then looking evenly at the new parents, she said directly: "You have a very beautiful, healthy daughter. You are very lucky."

What, we still wonder, did this accomplished, modern Chinese woman make of her own country that gives away so many of its daughters? What did she feel about a culture in which this "beautiful healthy daughter" faced the options of either an orphanage or America? For that matter, what did she think of Americans? Does she think we regard the world's children as a product—made in China—to import because we can afford to?

These days I watch our 14-month-old granddaughter race through months of development like a tape on fast forward. She has learned to roll, to sit, to test her legs. She wraps herself in the arms of her parents, where she has discovered a safe harbor. Together, we have all learned about the globalization of love.

America is continually made and remade by newcomers. But this daughter of China has reminded us how small our world is and how vast: a village you can traverse in a day and a place of stunning disconnects and differences, haves and have nots.

Ours was already a global family, brought together with the luck of the draw and the pluck of ancestors who came from places as far away as Italy and England, Russia, and Germany. On this Fourth of July, we add another continent to our heritage and another child to our list of supreme good fortune. Welcome, Cloe, to America.

July 3, 2003

Speed Zone

IF OURS WAS EVER A REPRESSED COUNTRY, IT LONG AGO

TURNED INTO AN EMOTIONAL NUDIST CAMP.

TRUE CONFESSIONS ABOUND. TALK SHOWS REIGN

ON RADIO AND TELEVISION. STRANGERS CHAT INTI-

MATELY ON THE INTERNET. PEOPLE ARE SPILLING THE

BEANS ALL OVER THE NEIGHBORHOOD.

WE USED TO KEEP QUIET ABOUT THE THINGS WE

WERE ASHAMED OF. LATELY WE SEEM TO BE ASHAMED

OF KEEPING QUIET.

—FROM "PRINCE TELL-IT-ALL," JULY 7, 1994

THE MALCONTENT OF A CONTENT PROVIDER

O n one of my very first ventures out of the newsroom and into the green room, a young production assistant handed me a form describing me as "The Talent."

Until that moment, I had always thought that talent had something to do with cellos or tap shoes. So I benignly explained, "I'm not The Talent, I'm The Journalist." At that moment, she looked up and answered cheerily, "Oh, same thing."

This was the same year a close friend left her job at a wire service for a network and cringed when she heard herself defined as "a television personality." We should have realized right then where the news business was headed. But names can never hurt you. Or so we thought.

Fast forward through the era when it became harder to tell the news from the entertainment, the journalist from the talent from the personality. We are now in a brave new media world that just got a little braver and newer when the *Chicago Tribune* bought out the *Los Angeles Times* and created a giant company of eleven newspapers, twenty-two television stations and Internet operations said to attract 3.4 million monthly visitors.

The multi-multimedia universe that ranges from print to pixels has a maw that's widening until the jaw hurts. And in the process, journalists and reporters—those "old media" working-stiff job titles that sound irrevocably stuffy—have gotten another new name. We have become—ta da!—content providers.

The cable stations want "content." The Internet wants "content." Everybody is talking about "content" as if there were a spigot somewhere to fill up the electronic jar.

A recent story in *The New York Times* about a day in the life of a content provider at the Tribune Company describes an employee who hosts a weekend radio show, writes for the newspaper, and announces the winning numbers of the lottery on television. He moves from one to the next with just a touch of powder on the nose.

If the operative word in the multimedia world is synergy, this content provider is the one-armed paperhanger of synergy. His subjects, you will note, straddle the line of news and entertainment—if there is still a line at all.

I am not going into a rant against the steam hammer. We've now learned that some four hundred thousand people would just as soon download Stephen King off the Internet as buy him at the bookstore. The medium is not the message.

As for news, we get it from a cafeteria of choices. And we've already seen a lot of the morphing of media and its working classes. Today there are TV studios in newspaper city rooms. Every news operation has its dot-com. There are journalists, talents, and personalities who reign all over the various cable and Internet clones of NBC News.

Watching a reporter—excuse me, content provider—switch from cable to radio to Internet is not, after all, like watching Pat Buchanan go through the revolving door from presidential candidate to columnist to candidate to talk-show host.

Indeed, the problem isn't with content providing at all. It's the effect on the older, less flashy, less efficient reality of content gathering. You can bet that content providers are going to provide less content in their content.

There is, alas, a limit to the productivity of a c.p. in the real news world. They may be able to talk sports and announce the lottery number with cost-effective speed. But to cover, say, a war, you still have to go overseas, risk your neck, gain the trust of soldiers or civilians, and put it all together in an accurate, fair package.

In politics, the unsynergistic reality is that good reporting takes time. The folks who are rushing from the keyboard to the studio to the standup, from one cable show to another, aren't making that extra call or interview. Those who spend too much time talking about the news in nice little round tables where senators and journalists—excuse me, content providers—call each other by their first names aren't out reporting it.

In my own end of the news business, I am ashamed to admit—it seems so old-fashioned—there really isn't a way to speed up the thought process. You can use all the high-tech equipment imaginable to distribute your thoughts. It's thinking itself that eats up all the hours.

In the end, a journalist is to a content provider as a farmer is to a waiter. They're both in the food biz. But the farmer is the one to count on.

March 19, 2000

RETHINKING THE RAPE SHIELD

I t took me two Google clicks, and there she was—name and photo—under a charming caption identifying her as: the lying bitch.

So it's official. The woman who accused NBA star Kobe Bryant of sexual assault, a Colorado legalism for rape, has roughly the privacy of an exhibit in an online aquarium. Her image is just a surf away.

It wasn't supposed to be like this. Back in the pre-Web 1970s, the media called a rare recess from First Amendment feistiness. They agreed to protect the identity of an accuser on the theory that exposure prevented too many women from going to the law.

Now fast-forward thirty years. The shield offers little more protection in rough weather than a mesh raincoat.

It isn't just the Wild West Web that has penetrated this shield. The supermarket tabloid, the *Globe,* made Bryant's accuser its cover girl with just a black stripe across her eyes. Radio shock jock Tom Leykis made a name for himself by naming her.

Meanwhile, the mainstream print and broadcast media have maintained a kind of technical virginity. They revealed the accuser's hometown and her college. They publicized her failed audition for *American Idol,* a death of a girlfriend, a breakup with a boyfriend, an overdose at school. They quoted friends, current and former, saying either "she wouldn't lie" or she was joking about his private parts at a party. But they haven't—so far—used her name and face.

Now the question is, should we, too, put down the shield? Should we name names?

This is not the first time it's been asked. Thirty years have produced both changes and concerns about protecting identity: Should we protect the accuser but not the accused? Is the shield a cover for the sexist notion that a woman is weak and needs protection? Does it reinforce the idea that rape is indeed something for a woman to be ashamed of?

At times the media seemed to worry more about privacy than the woman did. In 1989, no one used the name of the Central Park jogger. In 2003 she announced it on her book cover. In 1991, after a similar controversy, Patricia Bowman appeared on Court TV in the infamous Palm Beach rape case with a gray blob over her face. After the trial she appeared with Diane Sawyer in prime time.

Now, in the Kobe Bryant case, some strange fellows are sharing a feminist platform bed. Tom Leykis, who regards men as a beleaguered species, claims he actually made a strike against female stereotypes: "It's not any more reason to be ashamed than being (robbed) behind a cash register at Denny's."

Meanwhile, many of my journalist colleagues are wondering out loud whether we have crossed the covered bridge to a postshame society. They are asking whether it's time to identify accusers.

I always assumed that the shield was temporary. And I have always been uneasy with the idea that a falsely accused man could be exposed and a falsely accusing woman protected.

But if rape is the same as a mugging these days, how come no one talks about "consensual mugging"? And before I worry too much about false accusations, how about the false accusations of false accusations? Anybody notice that rape is still a widely underreported crime?

Hard cases make bad law. But celebrity cases make lousy policy. There may be more motive to accuse a superstar. Or more super power to crush an accuser. It is the high-profile cases that fill the Internet.

But if you take the lid off, where do you stop? Do you start naming teens and children who are victims of sexual assault? What if their names are on the Internet? Do we name the everyday victims who would never make the search engines rev up?

Our society hasn't changed as much as our technology. Many offline journalists who ask "isn't it time?" are uncomfortable when the Internet is giving "news" they withhold. I have long thought we should ask accusers if they want their names withheld rather than assuming they do. But I don't think it is time to out every woman, and I don't think we should do it because, as we used to whine to mom, "all the other kids are doing it."

As for now, anyone who thinks we live in a liberated, postshame society ought to go back to the Web. A FreeKobe Web site—motto: "Because We're Running out of Heroes"—has an online store selling pro-Kobe clothes.

Not to worry though. To show their sensitivity, they've taken the thong out of production.

July 31, 2003

I t's not that I held Prince Charles on a pedestal, let alone a throne. Polo is not my sport, and the Windsors are not my kind of folks. The "royals" always remind me of character actors at a Great Britain theme park.

But who would have guessed that the crown prince would abdicate his country's last lingering claim to the stiff upper lip? Now, in a documentary being aired there, here and everywhere, he confesses royal infidelity.

A broadcast journalist asks the Prince of Wales if he tried to be "faithful and honorable" during his marriage. Charles answers, "Yes."

The journalist then asks the prince if he was. "Yes," says the prince, who then pauses and adds, "Until it became irretrievably broken down."

With those little words, Charles leaves behind the old world in which royalty and subjects used words like "faithful and honorable" and enters the new world in which guests and audiences use words like "open and sharing."

So much for British reserve.

Apparently nobody told the prince that he could simply and politely decline the public confessional. Now, instead of giving up the throne, he appears to be giving up his citizenship. He's becoming thoroughly Americanized.

On this side of the Atlantic, we have suffered through two decades of escalating confessions on the part of citizens and leaders alike. If ours was ever a repressed country, it long ago turned into an emotional nudist camp.

True confessions abound. Talk shows reign on radio and television. Strangers chat intimately on the Internet. People are spilling the beans all over the neighborhood.

We used to keep quiet about the things we were ashamed of. Lately we seem to be ashamed of keeping quiet.

Now Prince Charles is dropping his British discretion as if it were a tainted set of genes, while in America some of us are finally questioning why everyone here has become so garrulous. At last, we want to know: Can't anybody shut up?

It's a curious turn of events for Americans. We have a strong right of privacy and an eroding respect for it. We are ferocious in defending our space from government invasion. But we routinely expose it to the elements in the name of openness and self-expression.

Somewhere along the way from Puritanism to Freudianism to Oprahism, we became suspicious of privacy, not to mention secrecy. We regard secrets as if they are all deep, dark things, unhealthy to keep, corrosive until exposed to the light.

We expect that husbands and wives, parents and children, governments and citizens, will keep nothing from each other. We are supposed to treat all relationships as if they are trusting and therapeutic. Anyone claiming privacy is seen as a suspect with something to hide.

The end result is a president who tells us what kind of underwear he wears. An administration that pours out details to the nearest journalist. Estranged husbands and wives—from prince to pauper—who dine out on stories about their ex's. It's a parade of people confessing and expecting understanding from an audience of one or a million.

It all reminds me of a wonderful moment in a Philip Roth novel. One of the characters is so thrilled with his love affair that he wants to share the happy news with his wife. His brother says drily, "She could live without it."

So could America. So could Britain.

In the immediate afterglow of Charles's confession, the majority of the viewers in a British television poll rallied around their next king. Few were surprised. The invasion of Charles and Di's privacy was a cottage industry before they began to turn it into a do-it-yourself operation.

But in the end there's a public need for some privacy and its corollary, dignity. I'm not usually keen on the strong and silent type, but there's something worse than British reserve. It's telling all on the telly.

A final tip from the Colonies. When Jacqueline Kennedy Onassis died, virtually every commentator noted, in an awed voice, her unique characteristic. In an age of compulsive confessors, she kept her peace and cultivated a zone of privacy around a most public life. Onassis neither confirmed nor denied nor explained.

For this, dear Charles, she was considered an American royal.

July 7, 1994

N o one knows exactly why Scott Amedure decided to go courting on the Jenny Jones Show. Why does anyone go on these shows, baring their heart's desires and their life's disappointments to strangers?

"He led a troubled life" says his brother Frank. Last year, some men had beat him and smashed his truck. Once he was missing for two months. But for whatever reason, on March 6, he decided to expose himself as the "secret admirer" of Jonathan Schmitz.

Maybe Amedure thought that the spotlight would provide a warm glow of safety. Maybe the applause of a studio audience, the recognition of viewers, would provide an understanding venue. Maybe he just thought it would be fun.

Jonathan Schmitz apparently went into this event unaware. He went for the kick of it. For the trip to Chicago, for the chance to be on TV, for the harmless joke of being on a show about secret admirers. Why not?

When he saw his friend Donna Riley in the studio he assumed that she was the one. When it turned out to be Amedure, the 24-year-old Schmitz sat politely and said that he was heterosexual and not interested.

In the etiquette of talk shows, the guest is supposed to go along with the joke, to be the life of the surprise party. He doesn't tell them to take the candid camera out of his face. He is a good sport. But three days later, Jonathan Schmitz snapped.

Whether it was homophobia or humiliation, the anxiety of waiting for the show to air or the followup note from Amedure on his door, the Michigan man bought a 12-gauge shotgun and five rounds of ammunition. "I just walked into his house and killed him," he told the 911 operator, "He was after me day and night."

This murder sounds like a perverse subject for another talk show shocker: "Can a Talk Show Be an Accessory to Murder?" Or: "What Happens to the People After the Show Is Over?" But the shock is that it didn't happen sooner.

Back in 1992, Geraldo had a father and daughter on his show talking about their incestuous relationship. Later, the father kept calling up and telling the staff that he was thinking about killing his daughter.

Since then, trash TV has expanded enough to turn the daytime schedule into a waste site of abnormality and amorality. Guests arrive, carrying their ex-husbands and excess baggage, their pathos and problems. Then they are summarily disposed of.

We never know what happened to the 12-year-old star of a Gordon Elliott show entitled, "My Child Is Underaged and Oversexed." Or what happened after the reunion staged by Sally Jessy Raphael between four daughters and the father who deserted them 20 years ago.

For that matter, what happened to the wife and the "other woman" who met on a Ricki Lake show? And does the gay guest in an earlier Ricki Lake show—"Surprise! I Want to Sleep with You"—rest easily these days?

If talk shows were old-time carnivals, the ringmasters would have some understanding of their performers, some obligation to their ongoing sideshow. But in a world of revolving guests, the talk show's "guests" are temps, one-night stands sent back to live their lives as best they can.

Jenny Jones didn't put the shotgun against Scott Amedure's chest. She is a former standup comic, and before this murder she worried about her guests: "What do we do with the feelings that come up?" But every host, producer, booker, knows that when you deal in surprise, shame, embarrassment, you may also get rage. When you push people's emotional buttons, someone will eventually explode.

Last fall, Oprah did a two-part show called "Are Talk Shows Bad?" At the end of it, she swore off trash as if it were a fat gram and watched her ratings slide. Ricki Lake and Jenny Jones climbed within a rung or two. But Oprah knew best.

Talk shows in the 1990s are like quiz shows in the 1950s. The old quiz shows tricked viewers into believing they were witnessing the real thing, brains in action. The new talk shows trick viewers into believing they are watching real emotions in action. They trick guests with the belief that life's problems can be resolved in one public hour.

Jenny Jones never knew Scott Amedure's history or Jonathan Schmitz's breaking point. The TV match made between a "secret admirer" and the unwilling, unsuspecting, object of his affection was as rigged as any quiz show.

It was rigged against real life. Rigged to treat emotions like entertainment. Rigged to deal with the feelings of strangers, casually, between commercials, with an eye on sweeps week. And now with this gruesome murder, we know that the show was also rigged for disaster.

March 16, 1995

I'd like to believe that the crowds yelling "Go, Juice, Go" on the highway overpass and around the Brentwood mansion were just urging him to live. Not to escape.

I'd like to believe that the California man who said "O.J. is still a hero around here," was echoing the American presumption of innocence. Not the belief that O.J. could be a hero and a murderer.

I'd like to believe that all the colleagues and friends who—to a man—found this double-murder charge "unbelievable" meant that as an expression of their shock. Not a permanent judgment on the facts.

I'd rather not believe that O.J.'s fans and friends care more about what may happen to him than about what he may have done.

But I am finding this hard.

On Friday night, the man from the Hall of Fame, the man from Hertz and Hollywood and NFL Live, became a fugitive on the LA freeways. Millions were horrified by the chance that we would witness a superstar suicide live at five or eight or midnight.

In the days that followed, we heard bulletins from jail on his state of dress and state of mind. The man who wore Number 32 in his glory days had been allotted Number 4103970. They'd given him a blue jumpsuit and taken away his shoelaces.

Orenthal James Simpson lost everything but our attention. He alone remained the star of this tragedy. It took the DA to say again and again, "Do not lose sight of the fact that it was Nicole Brown Simpson and Ronald Goldman who are the victims of this case."

The fans and friends watching the public unraveling of a life have shown more than a presumption of O.J.'s innocence. They've shown a passion for his innocence, a wish bordering on denial that some twist would let their hero off the hook. They lost sight of Nicole long ago.

Whatever the outcome of the murder, we know now that O.J. Simpson beat his wife. We know that the violence was, in the words of the police, "an ongoing problem" through marriage and attempts at reconciliation.

The LA deputy city attorney reminded us what Nicole looked like in 1989 when her husband was finally arrested for beating and threatening to kill her: "She had a black eye, a swelling cheek and a bruise to her forehead, scratch marks on her neck."

We know that O.J. bitterly resented police "interference" into "a family matter." And we know that he paid virtually no price—pleading no contest to the charge, finessing court-ordered community service and doing psychiatric consultations by phone between star turns.

Hertz never considered the charge of wife-beating enough of a character flaw to sully his image. Neither did NBC. And, this is the heart of it, neither did his friends.

O.J. Simpson made his living at the center of a nearly all-male culture. His world was made of sports and celebrity, skill and violence, wins and losses, Halls of Fame.

The men who shared his world knew that this hugely strong man had pled no contest to beating a wife. Yet they remain bewildered at the possibility he was violent.

Don Klosterman, a friend and general manager of the Rams, called the murder charge "inconceivable . . . inconsistent. . . . I've never seen him lose his temper." Al Michaels, an ABC sports announcer, said: "None of us has seen a side to O.J. Simpson that would indicate any of this was possible." The list goes on.

Some who knew about the 1989 "incident" talk secretively about O.J.'s side to the story. Others talk about the circumstances—"It happened on New Year's Eve." Some remember Nicole stayed with him two more years.

As the evidence accumulated, some of these men seem appalled by what they didn't see. But how about what they didn't say?

Did anyone utter a word to O.J.? Did anyone say that there is no other side to a story when one side has "a black eye, a swelling cheek"? Did anyone tell the superstar he needed help?

Star quality is blinding. Maybe it was easier to share the belief expressed in his note, "If we had a problem it was because I loved her so much." Easier to nod in sympathy when he bemoaned, "At times I have felt like I was a battered husband or boyfriend."

Four million women are victims of domestic violence every year. As many women are beaten as give birth.

Today the laws and the police are less likely to ignore abuse than they once were. But it will go on until men withdraw their tacit permission and confront each other. It will go on until batterers are banished by their brothers, stripped of any right to the title of hero.

Go, Juice, go? Did anybody ever try to stop him?

June 21, 1994

BOBBITT BABBLING

I t is the story that made strong men cross their legs and strong women giggle about strong men crossing their legs. It was the story that made strong headline-writers give in to their weakness for puns. And more to the point, it was the story that made my husband glance up from the newspaper and say, for the only time in our recorded history, "You could give this a good leaving alone."

Which is, Lord knows, what I intended to do.

One case of male genital mutilation in 200-odd years of American history? You would have thought it was a massacre. After centuries of male fantasies about castrating females, we finally have . . . one—and she becomes the universal symbol of "a shocking new round in the battle of the sexes."

This time I agree with Paul Ebert, who has prosecuted both husband and now wife. "A sleeping man had his penis amputated. It's not a media event. It's a criminal case."

In my book, Lorena and John Bobbitt themselves aren't symbolic of anything. She is a 24-year-old who married Mr. Very Wrong and embezzled from her employer and friend. She left her house on the fateful night with a penis in her hand, but also with $100 and a Nintendo game stolen from the house guest.

John Bobbitt is, in the words of his attorney, "not the most sensitive person" and "not the brightest guy in the world." The former Marine and bar bouncer who was acquitted of marital rape has an old charge of wife-battering on the books. The man who couldn't define "foreplay" on the witness stand may not have differentiated between rape and sex in the bedroom. Nevertheless, at the courtroom in Manassas, Virginia, where Lorena is on trial for "malicious wounding," the vendors are back selling T-shirts that say, "Revenge—How Sweet It Is." The radio station is back giving away Slice soda and wieners. So are the people pronouncing that these two pathetic people are representative of the battle of the sexes.

Well, I don't know why we only call it a battle when women are caught fighting, or fighting back. If John had only abused Lorena, we would have called it violence but not war. Only when the weapon got into her hands did it become a subject for musing on the hostile state of gender relations.

This has happened before. Just a few years ago, with slasher movies filling cineplexes with female blood, one film became the topic for worried gender-watchers: *Thelma and Louise.*

Last year the police blotter was full of abused and murdered wives—an almost unilateral massacre. But one issue seemed to elicit the most copy from our war correspondents: the battered woman's defense.

The Packwood 26, the burning bed, the fatal attraction are all framed as skirmishes. The Supreme Court ruled on sexual harassment by men against women, but it was the possibility of a woman harassing a man that sets the creative juices flowing in Michael Crichton's frontline novel, *Disclosure.*

I know, I know. Female retaliation and female violence are still the unusual stories, the news. When a 5-foot-2-inch, 95-pound manicurist cuts the penis off a 200-pound former Marine, it's news indeed. But when the urban legend arises simultaneously in a dozen cities about the man who wakes up with a red ribbon tied neatly around his penis and a note saying how easy it would be, well, that's battleground fantasy.

Maybe we talk about the war between the sexes now because men, the ones who do most of the labeling, see a dangerous enemy where there was once a victim. If women smile at men who squirm, maybe it's at that recognition of power.

A few years ago, in Olivia Goldsmith's *First Wives Club,* three women plotted retaliation against powerful and abusive ex-husbands. They are not exactly looking for revenge, one said, but for "something more sophisticated . . . like justice."

If Lorena Bobbitt is to convince a jury—or me—that it is OK to take justice in her own hands, she has a tough job ahead. Abuse may mitigate a woman's guilt. It rarely makes her innocent.

But even so, this freakish episode in a single sad marriage doesn't represent some generic new war between men and women. Too many frontline correspondents suggest that as women become more powerful, our relationships with men simply turn into a power struggle. I don't agree.

In the age of inequality, peace between men and women was often the peace of an occupied country. It wasn't peaceful when women were harassed or when marital rape was legal.

The skirmishes in the 1950s were often the bitter sniping of people hiding behind separate roles. One of the reasons to level the field between sexes, to lead lives that were more alike, was so that we could get closer. Many—maybe most—of us have.

And for all the headlines, the grimaces, the smirks, we didn't get here at knife point.

January 13, 1994

ELIAN IN THE MIDDLE

W hat tore it for me was the puppy.

There is Elian Gonzalez, a 6-year-old who watched his mother die, who saw nine other adults drown, who spent two days hanging onto a raft in the sea—and what happens when he gets ashore?

A trip to Disney World, a truckload of toys, a ticket to the circus, television cameras. But nothing was worse than the congressman Lincoln Diaz-Balart bearing a black Labrador puppy.

Here, Elian, your mom's dead, your dad's 90 miles away, your grandparents can't see you—have a puppy.

When Elian Gonzalez first hit the news, I described this as a custody fight between two countries. Well, not anymore. Now it's a political fight with two governments on the same side and the Cuban-American community, with all of its clamor and clout, on the other.

With a rare display of good sense, the Immigration and Naturalization Service ruled that the boy belonged with his father. After a local judge disagreed, Attorney General Janet Reno reaffirmed the INS ruling.

But no one wants to see immigration agents taking a 6-year-old away on the evening news. So the deadline is indefinitely postponed. We still have a puppet to politics—Who taught Elian to raise his fingers in the V for victory sign?—and a puppy.

Not all the politicking is in Little Havana. Ninety miles away, the Cubans held a "March of the Combatant Mothers," which sounds like something out of a 1930s propaganda film.

Castro, on his last legs, is dancing a jig over this story. The old leader, whose own son Fidelito was once caught in an international custody battle, has sent his foreign minister on a ten-day sympathy tour of Europe. Talk about propaganda victories. We gave him this one, because he's right.

On *Meet the Press,* John McCain seemed to enjoy the last nip of Cold War rhetoric. What if the mother had dropped her son over the Berlin Wall before she'd been shot escaping, he asked. Would we still send him back?

Indeed, some share a frozen world view of Havana as Berlin. But in the post-Cold War thaw, it's not clear that one dictatorship is worse than another. Nor is it clear these days whether Cuban refugees come here for political freedom or for economic opportunity.

We have a unique Cuban immigration policy that encourages dare-devil runs to dry land. If indeed, as some of Elian's supporters have said, he would go back to a country without milk or food, how much of that poverty is due to our embargo? And if poverty is the issue, should we separate every poor child from his family, here or abroad?

But I digress from the puppet and the puppy.

Next week, we are told, Congress will be asked to grant this boy citizenship. If, in fact, it merely means that Elian can return as an adult, fine. But if it's a ploy, a means to delay, then indeed Ricardo Alarcon, the head of Cuba's National Assembly, was right in calling this a "kidnapping."

The point is to focus on this child. Does anyone who sees the footage and the photo-ops not wonder what is happening to this boy at night? When, between trips to the circus and to Disney World, he misses his mother, who comes and comforts him?

Perhaps the father can't go to Miami. Juan Miguel Gonzalez told *Nightline,* "I would feel like breaking the neck of all those SOBs." Driven to rage, he is now criticized for anger. He's even, it appears, been threatened with a subpoena if he comes here.

But the grandmothers have volunteered to come. Well, I say, bring them on. Let them enter the house in Miami, privately, quietly. Shut the door. Turn off the camera.

Maybe the paternal grandmother can talk sense into the man in whose house Elian resides. That man is, after all, her brother. Maybe the maternal grandmother can plead the case for being with the only child of her dead only child. Let them talk, argue, talk as family.

Not even the most cynical of politicians would subpoena a grand-mother. Not even the most ardent Castro-hater would be offended if these women carried out the INS order.

Any way you look at it, a child whisked from the sea to Disney World is facing deep, deep trouble. Let these two take the boy away from the spot-light to the place where tears and comfort are permitted.

Elian has lost his mother. He needs his father and his grandparents. Not a puppy.

January 20, 2000

REQUIEM FOR A PRINCESS

I t couldn't have been scripted more horribly. Not even by Hollywood. A Mercedes racing a princess and her lover through the darkened streets of Paris. A gaggle of photographers on motorcycles pursuing their prey like international hounds after the last British fox.

A thunderous crash against one tunnel wall and then another. And finally, the unforgivable flash of a camera as the 36-year-old woman lay dying.

Diana Spencer, so shy a Di that she would take only nonspeaking parts in her school plays, came into the public eye at 19. And what a public eye it was. Insatiable. International. Adoring. Critical. Longing for fantasy. Devouring celebrity.

A billion people attended her wedding to Charles in St. Paul's Cathedral, watching her walk down the aisle from their television perches across the world, smiling as she garbled Prince Charles's name. Now a billion will surely witness her funeral in Westminster Abbey on Saturday.

But in between these covers was a photo album of such vast proportions that she won the uncoveted title of Most Photographed Woman in the World. Starring in the fairy tale and the soap opera, married or divorced, in pain or in love, the "people's princess" became public property, a multimillion-dollar industry. Her every gown and every cause were turned—in the way we do things now—into another commodity for the curiosity shop.

Now in the aftermath of this tragic crash-ending to a life story, Diana's death has become an antimedia media event. "Happy now?" a truck driver yells at reporters in London.

"I always believed that the press would kill her in the end," says her brother from Cape Town. Not even news that the driver was drinking turned the finger of blame.

The word "paparazzi" has become an epithet for a parasitic species of photographer and a synonym for assassin. On television, even reporters and anchors carefully distance themselves—us and them—from the aggressive camera-wielding free agents who sell telephoto lens invasions of privacy. They divide "our" mainstream publications from "those" tabloid papers.

But, of course, it isn't as clear a line as that. Not anymore. Not between the *Sun*, the *Mirror*, and the rest, not between the handful of publishers and the millions of buyers.

In the week before her death, *People* magazine's forty-third cover photo of Diana in seventeen years had blared, "A Guy for Di." The current issue of *The New Yorker* boasts a piece on "Why Prince Charles Loves Camilla."

In the day after her death, as radio and cable hosts begged the audience to "stay with us for more news of this tragedy," it seemed that the celebrity life had merely morphed into the celebrity death. *60 Minutes* turned over its hour to coverage as weighty as dead air. As anchors flew to London, and tabloids rushed to new editions, the line between mourning and exploiting was crossed more often than the Atlantic.

The sorry truth brought to us again in this death is, that the cult of celebrity is not the fringe but the staple of media life, the main course for viewers and readers. Movie stars, sports figures, royalty, even murderers are all collapsed into that amorphous category of the famous. They all become merchandise for the consumer mall.

As a British historian, David Starkey, said without a trace of irony: "She's up there in the heavens somewhere with James Dean, Marilyn Monroe, and Princess Grace, and Jack Kennedy. She's all those rolled into one. She's the biggest thing since Evita."

We know about Diana's "love-hate relationship" with the press. The princess who put her hand over the lens at times also used the media to sell her side of the story. She also tried and often succeeded in using her name brand to sell good works. She wrestled for control of her life, her image, her privacy. But her life was the paparazzi paycheck and our gossip.

It was the world, not just the *Sun* or the *Mirror,* that stalked her every move. It was not just the "ferocious" British press, as Diana fairly described it, but our voracious appetite. How many forgot that Diana was real until she bled?

In the end the saddest picture of all this week was of two motherless sons, William and Harry, sitting on either side of their somber father, no one touching the other, heading for the church service. This picture of Diana's sons was shot, of course, through the window of a moving car.

September 3, 1997

I turn on the news expecting the worst, and I find it. Another girl has been abducted. This time the dateline is Missouri. This time the girl is 6-year-old Casey Williamson. And this time she's been murdered.

Is this the season of fear? The summer of abductions?

On June 5, Elizabeth Smart was taken from her bed in Salt Lake City at gunpoint, reawakening our slumbering terror of the stranger who comes after our children. Since then the names and the details have become all too familiar:

Five-year-old Samantha Runnion was playing Clue outside her Stanton, California, home when she was snatched, sexually assaulted, and murdered. Seven-year-old Erica Pratt was taken from her Philadelphia row house to a basement where she managed, "miraculously," to escape.

On TV we see the anguish of the parents and the anger of the advocates. On one channel, Mark Klaas, whose daughter Polly was abducted in 1993, declares an "epidemic." On another, a cable show host acts like a public health expert warning of a growing outbreak in the community.

And across the country parents seem to describe the same painful symptom: fear. "The world is more unsafe now," says one mother.

"I watch my 2-year-old more closely," says another.

"I won't allow a stranger near my kids," says a father.

Photos of missing children first began to appear on milk cartons in the 1970s. By the mid-1980s, New Jersey began to fingerprint schoolchildren. When Congress declared a National Missing Children's Day, the media spread the alarming statistic that one and a half million children were missing and fifty thousand were abducted every year.

It took time for the facts to catch up with our darkest fantasies. Now we know that the vast majority of the missing are runaways and as many as 90 percent of the abducted are snatched by a parent fighting for custody. We know, too, that as "epidemics" came and went, the number of abductions by strangers hovered between two hundred and three hundred a year. The number of murders by strangers remained around fifty a year.

These were the figures in 1993 when Polly Klaas was murdered. They were the figures in 1994 when Susan Smith drowned her children and blamed it on a stranger. And in all the years before Elizabeth Smart's disappearance started this "new outbreak."

There is no way to exaggerate the pain of parents who have lost a child. No calculator was ever made that could overestimate the sum of their anguish. But it is possible to exaggerate the danger. And so it is worth asking why we are susceptible to this "epidemiology."

David Finkelhor, a University of New Hampshire sociologist who studies crimes against children, says that this is an "archetypal" fear. It touches every parent who has ever lost sight of a toddler in a supermarket or watched a first-grader bicycle off to school or waited—and waited, and waited—for a teenager to come home from the mall.

We may just be programmed to believe that someone from "another tribe" will come and steal our children. The terror of losing a child to strangers is, after all, a staple of old mythology and primal nightmares. Village folklore was full of tales of gypsies and vagrants. Even if there were only five such cases a year, says Finkelhor, it would touch a nerve. "You can't talk people out of that with numbers."

But today our "tribes" feel more fragile and our personal communities less stable. When we tell our children—as we must—to beware of strangers, there are more people who wear that label.

If our immune system is overwhelmed by this "epidemic," it may also be because our children are routinely placed in the hands of strangers—from doctors to teachers to day caregivers. They are placed, as well, in the hands of television producers and Internet Web masters.

As Finkelhor suggests, "All our anxiety about feeling that we don't have control over our children gets symbolically focused on the idea that someone is trying to take them from us."

No, I don't agree with the mother who says "the world is more unsafe now." I remember polio. I remember growing up under the mushroom cloud of the Cold War. This year, terrorism expanded the repertoire of my imagination more than even the horrible tales of child abduction.

But as the images overwhelm the numbers, I notice how we identify and mourn with families we know only through television. Meanwhile, our neighbors become the strangers.

It isn't child abduction that recycles in such overwhelming proportions. It's fear. There is no epidemic of abduction by strangers. But there may be a contagious and chronic case of estrangement.

August 1, 2002

I s this the costume for natives of the global village now, a face mask?

In Hong Kong, a waitress and her customers are photographed wearing the same accessory, looped behind their ears. On sidewalks in that city people are buying masks in basic white or, if they prefer, in a Gucci print or a Burberry plaid. Meanwhile in airports, reluctant travelers on their way to Beijing or Toronto are packing N-95 respirator masks along with their passports.

It's less than two months since the words "severe acute respiratory syndrome" first appeared in the daily newspaper. Now SARS has taken over the news like, well, a virus. We have now clocked 3,900 cases in twenty-five countries, a death toll over 218 and climbing.

Last year's fear was the offspring of international bioterrorism: anthrax or smallpox. This year's fear is the offspring of Mother Nature's terror: a coronavirus never before seen in human beings.

Illnesses have always traveled in the human biological knapsack. The plague spread from one person to another until it killed one of every four Europeans in the 14th century. One out of every hundred people in the world died from the "Spanish Influenza" of 1918, a disease spread in part by soldiers on the move.

Now we are all on fast-forward. In 1955, 51 million people a year traveled by plane. Today 1.6 billion are airborne every year and 530 million cross international borders.

The Great SARS Tour once might have taken months or weeks to spread this far. Now it takes days. A flight attendant becomes the "index case" for 160 infections. A tourist infects seven others in a hotel. A globetrotter here and there brings it home like a biological souvenir.

The world has shrunk to the size of an airplane ticket. And germs don't need a visa. You can have breakfast in Beijing, dinner in London, and end up hospitalized in Toronto. And so, as the Singapore minister of health put it, SARS "gives new meaning to the word globalization."

But before the cough heard 'round the world becomes a symbol of global vulnerability, let it also be said that the way the world has mobilized against this disease is an equal and opposite sign of the value of our connections.

It took centuries to identify the cause of cholera. It took two years to identify the virus that caused AIDS. It took five months to figure out Legionnaires' disease.

But this time under the World Health Organization network, thirteen labs in ten countries put everything else aside.

In a matter of weeks, an international community of scientists identified the coronavirus as the cause. Within a month, labs from Vancouver to Atlanta to Singapore mapped the genome. Soon we may have a diagnostic test for the virus itself. And after that, with luck, a treatment.

If the disease went international with unprecedented speed, so did the response. If oceans no longer can keep people or germs on their own side of the water, neither can they keep researchers apart. Health organizations and scientists also go global.

In describing the race between the bright and dark side of globalization, Julie Gerberding of the CDC wrote in the *New England Journal of Medicine,* "Speed of scientific discovery and speed of communication are hallmarks of the response to SARS." Then, she added, "a very sobering question remains—are we fast enough?"

We don't know the winner yet in this race. We don't know whether this is the beginning or the end of a SARS pandemic. But we can be certain that SARS is not the last—nor the deadliest—virus to hitchhike across the world.

"You always read about the conquest of a disease," says Howard Markel, a historian of medicine at the University of Michigan, "but we don't conquer diseases. We wrestle them to a draw. So what happens in China or Zaire has an effect in Ann Arbor or Vancouver. Globalization has to include the globalization of good public health."

We are in the adolescent stages of this new world, still lurching unevenly and living uncertainly in a time when diseases, like pollution and terrorism, cross the continents. We are discovering that neither biology nor ideology stays put.

In this pandemic, China, which suppressed bad news far too long, may finally learn that it can't play in the global economy without an open and transparent public health system. America, for our part, may remember that we can't meet every global threat alone.

This is a shrinking world in a perpetual rush hour. The way we deal with SARS may predict the way we face the global village—openly or behind a mask.

April 27, 2003

T his is how I spent the week before the war: driving across the Florida landscape, locked in the alternate universe of talk radio.

I tuned in as an act of professional penance, and I'm sorry now that I didn't take my hands off the wheel to make notes. But I took away lasting memories of propaganda, a souvenir list of fact-free opinions delivered by a cast of angry baritones.

Somewhere between Orlando and Tampa, a host spent the morning touting the discovery of an Iraqi drone as the smoking gun in the case against Iraq. Reporters on the scene would describe this drone as a "weed whacker with wings."

There was another host, somewhere between Tampa and Fort Myers, who took antiwar women's groups angrily to task on the grounds that the women of Iraq were bitterly oppressed. He didn't seem to know that Iraq—which surely oppresses both genders—is a secular state where women are more equal than among our friends the Saudis.

On the last lap between Fort Myers and Naples, there was the assertion, repeated again and again, that Saddam was somewhere behind the terrorism of September 11. Never mind that the CIA disagrees.

The only counternote to the drumbeat of war I heard all weekend was from an elderly peace activist who apparently offered himself as a hapless human shield against the host and listeners who attacked him. On this Orlando station, he couldn't get a fact in edgewise.

I am normally protected from talk radio by my day job, but it was no surprise that the hosts were all right wing. That is, by now, a given. Some venture capitalists are trying to start a left-leaning network, but today it's as if one medium has been thoroughly ceded to the right, and in this case prowar, wing.

In my car-bound venture, I kept thinking of the old adage, "Truth is the first casualty of war." But this time, truth became a casualty before the first shot was fired. Truth was wounded in the prewar. Half-truth now limps dangerously to the front line.

In many ways, talk radio seems to have taken up where yellow journalism left off. It bears the trademark disregard for history, casualness about facts, and a penchant for propaganda.

Remember reading about the Spanish-American War in 1898? Publishers like William Randolph Hearst and Joseph Pulitzer built a war constituency and circulation in symbiotic frenzy with headlines like "The Country Thrilled with War Fever." According to legend, William Randolph Hearst sent a telegram to his reporter that said, "You supply the pictures and I'll supply the war."

Today newspapers fret over ethics and hire ombudsmen and run correction boxes. The New York Post may blast the French and Germans with the headline "Axis of Weasel." But most of us have a "one hand" and "the other hand" and often wring them.

The old yellow haze has drifted over to the territory of Rush Limbaugh and Michael Savage, Bill O'Reilly and Sean Hannity. In that territory, the best defense of the right wing media is an offense against the left wing media. Facts are as fungible as the word "infotainment."

March 20, 2003

People Watching

THERE IS SOMETHING IN MY GENERATION THAT LOOKS ON

PERSEVERANCE, ON WORK AS LIFE, WITH ADMIRATION,

ENVY, AND UNEASE. ON THE ONE HAND, WORK—30-YEAR,

GOLD-WATCH WORK—REMINDS US OF THE BAKER IN THE

OLD DUNKIN' DONUTS AD DRAGGING HIMSELF TO THE

KITCHEN: "TIME TO MAKE THE DONUTS." ON THE OTHER

HAND, IT REMINDS US OF A CLAUDE MONET, POISED TO

DO HIS GREATEST ART ONLY AFTER ACQUIRING THE SKILL

AND HANDS OF A 75-YEAR-OLD PAINTER.

—FROM "YOU'RE A GOOD MAN, CHARLIE SCHULZ,"

FEBRUARY 17, 2000

I t was 1970, and I was a twentysomething reporter in a rented car looking for a hill in Bellbrook, Ohio. My editor had sent me out to interview Erma Bombeck, this house-wife-humorist, this anti-Heloise, this funny lady of the home pages.

The fortysomething Bombeck had given me these directions: You head for Ohio and turn left. You take another left at the traffic light. You go down the road until you come to mailbox 3875, only the 7 is missing. Then go to the top of the hill.

A New Englander looking for a hill in Ohio, I passed the RFD mailbox three times before I figured it out, and turned up the five-degree incline to the rambling white farmhouse. There at the top—the top?—was a pond with large ducks and two dogs named Kate and Harry.

These were the first words that Erma Bombeck said to me: "Come in, come in. Harry you stay out there, you've got bad breath. Please don't look at the mess, they're tearing apart the kitchen and there's this brown dust that settles every day all over the house. You must be hungry but the hamburger is absolutely refusing to defrost. Take your coat off."

It was vintage Erma Bombeck, the same in person and in print. She was the mistress of controlled chaos, the head of the house of absurdity. She was a warm and generous woman whose body gave out on Monday—so much sooner than her spirit.

On that distant March day, over bologna sandwiches and Bugles, she talked about mothering and loneliness, about deadline humor and deadly seriousness.

It was the height of the Vietnam War, and some reporter had asked how she was going to observe the day of protest. "I told them I had three weeks of laundry I was going to do." Now she worried, "Am I just sitting here writing a funny column while Rome burns?"

It was the beginning, too, of the women's movement, and she said, "I had a member of the Women's Liberation Movement write to me and say, 'Lady, you are the problem.'"

Erma Bombeck, the problem? I wonder now if that young feminist thought that after the revolution, washing machines would stop eating socks as a gesture of solidarity? Or husbands would stop watching football?

Erma Fiste, the daughter of a teen-age mother, was a reporter in the

1950s when newspaper women were few and far between. Later she would write that as a young mother at home in suburbia with three children, "I hid my dreams in the back of my mind—it was the only safe place in the house. From time to time I would get them out and play with them, not daring to reveal them to anyone else, because they were fragile and might get broken."

She began to work again from home in 1964, just one year after Betty Friedan's book was criticized as the ranting of a neurotic and probably frigid woman. Bombeck's column was pegged—or dismissed—as "house-wife humor." But it was, in its own way, wonderfully, deliciously subversive. When she started, suburban housewives were still pictured vacuuming in high heels in immaculate homes with perfect children. Erma Bombeck cracked open the feminine mystique her own way: with a sidesplitting laugh.

Her crack was a thousand wisecracks. Over the years, she wrote the truth about domestic life in all its madness and frustration, its car pools and appliances. She wrote with the uncanny accuracy of a fellow traveler and a born reporter. She wrote to and about women who were, in the name of her column, "At Wit's End."

This mother never signed on to the mommy wars that pitted women at home against those in the workplace. How could she? She had done it all, and so she wrote for us all. In the late 1970s, she went on the road to sell the Equal Rights Amendment in tandem with the redoubtable Liz Carpenter. "We did the razorback hog call in Arkansas. We sang Baptist hymns in a mobile home cruising through Iowa," she reminisced, "And Liz auctioned off my husband's underwear in Phoenix."

Later, this woman turned her heart and pen to children with cancer. She shared those parts of her life that were not a laugh riot: her experience with infertility, miscarriage, breast cancer, the last fatal deterioration of her kidneys. Whenever "family values" returned with grim seriousness, Erma Bombeck was around to remind us about "Family, The Ties That Bind . . . And Gag."

A lot of columnists write words to end up in the Congressional Record or on the president's desk or at the Pulitzer Committee's door. But Erma Bombeck went us all one better. Her words won her the permanent place of honor in American life: the refrigerator door. Now we are again at wit's end.

April 24, 1996

I)t was an eerie coincidence said some, a fine piece of symmetry said others. Charles M. Schulz died in his sleep just as the last *Peanuts* was loaded onto the last trucks for the last home delivery. His life and his work were completed on the same day, sharing the same national curtain call.

For half a century, until cancer forced retirement, Charles Schulz was the scriptwriter, the producer, and the director for a repertory company of small imaginary characters who never changed, never became trendy, and never grew dated.

He penned more than 18,250 strips that ran seven days a week. He drew them when his hands were strong and his line was sure. He drew them when a tremor made it hard to hold the pen.

Long after his income had topped $30 million a year, he got up every morning, drove to breakfast, then to his studio at One Snoopy Place, worked, went out for lunch and back to work. Only once—under orders—did he take off more than 10 days. Finally, the creator and the comic strip, the life and work, ended together.

His friend Lynn Johnston, creator of *For Better or For Worse*, said the end was "as if he had written it that way." His son Monte said, "I think maybe he decided that his true passion was in the strip and when that was gone, it was over."

In one of the obituaries that talked about Charlie Brown and Linus, Lucy and Snoopy, his biographer said he "spent a lifetime perfecting failure."

After all, as Schulz himself once wrote, "All the loves in the strip are unrequited; all the baseball games are lost; all the test scores are D-minuses; the Great Pumpkin never comes; and the football is always pulled away."

But "Peanuts" wasn't really about failure. It was about perseverance. It was about a hopeful moon-faced boy holding a kite string, day after day, until the rain forced him indoors. It was about his characters' perseverance, and his own. It was about life and work; life as work.

What do we make of a 77-year-old war veteran who had set off for war just days after his mother's death, who described his lifelong anxiety as that of a dog chasing after the family car, never knowing if they would return?

What to make of a man who once asked of his characters, "Good grief, who are all these little people? Must I live with them for the rest of my life?" And stayed with them until the day he died.

In St. Paul, a man who lives in Schulz's childhood home reacted to the news of his death saying, "It's really too bad he couldn't enjoy his retirement." Too bad? Retirement?

Indeed, Schulz once said "Drawing a daily comic strip is not unlike having an English theme hanging over your head every day for the rest of your life." But another time he wrote that he did cartoons for the same reason musicians composed: "They do it because life wouldn't have any meaning for them if they didn't. That's why I draw cartoons. It's my life."

Which was it? A theme paper hanging over his head? The meaning of life? Is it a shame that he didn't retire? Or a blessing that he came to the end, work and life still entwined?

There is something in my generation that looks on perseverance, on work as life, with admiration, envy, and unease. On the one hand, work—30-year, gold-watch work—reminds us of the baker in the old Dunkin' Donuts ad dragging himself to the kitchen: "Time to make the donuts." On the other hand, it reminds us of a Claude Monet, poised to do his greatest art only after acquiring the skill and hands of a 75-year-old painter.

Schulz's World War II generation stuck to their last out of anxiety or grit, luck or guilt. The twentysomething generation skips from one work world to the next, reinventing themselves as swiftly as the Internet.

But my middle generation holds two competing views: One sees the courage to persevere and the other sees the courage to change. One admires those who find the right fit—Monet at 75, if that is not too grandiose a dream—and the other admires those who break out at 50, 60, 70 to reinvent themselves.

Last month, Nebraska's 56-year-old Senator Bob Kerrey wrote himself two letters about his future. One letter explained that he was going back to private life; the other that he was running for reelection. "The first one," he said, "made me smile." Kerrey chose the smile.

Not long from now, the first baby boomer president will face retirement or reinvention, then will come the rest of his generation. How many of us will know or find out what makes us smile?

Not long before his death, Schulz realized, "That little boy is never going to kick the football." In a work and life that ended on the same day, I hope that the cartoon characters made Charles Schulz smile as much he made the rest of us smile.

February 17, 2000

"Did you hear that Kay Graham died?"

The phone calls come in, one after another, in the hours following the announcement. Friends and colleagues calling to let me know and to talk. It's as if there were a death in the family. A maternal death.

In the obituaries that follow, my eyes focus on her date of birth: 1917. Katharine the First, as she was sometimes called for the string of "firsts" that followed her name and gender, was born before women had the right to vote.

That's how short the arc of our history is. That's how remarkable the arc of her history is.

The women's movement of my own generation seems like a cozy plane ride compared to her generation's wagon trail. Whether she chose this pioneer image or not, Kay Graham's life seemed to parallel—sometimes following and sometimes leading—the path of women in the past century.

The woman routinely referred to as "the powerful publisher of *The Washington Post*" was raised in a privileged household "where nothing difficult or personal was discussed." She grew up with all the mixed messages handed to a smart girl.

In her own words, "I adopted the assumption of many of my generation that women were intellectually inferior to men, that we were not capable of governing, leading, managing anything but our homes and our children." She inhaled it through the atmosphere.

When she married Phil Graham, she wrote, "I increasingly saw my role as the tail to his kite, and the more I felt overshadowed, the more it became a reality." When that kite soared and crashed, when a poisonous brew of mental illness led to her husband's infidelity and suicide, she tremulously took over the reins of the family paper.

"Sometimes you don't really decide, you just move forward, and that is what I did," she would write later.

At 46, she was so uncertain of herself that she would practice saying Christmas greetings to her employees in front of a mirror. As a friend told her, she had "been pushed down so far you don't recognize what you can do." But she began to learn. And eventually to teach.

Over the past few years, we have heard much about "the greatest generation." Almost all of it has been about the men—the warriors—of that generation. Have we forgotten how far the women of that generation had to come? Or what they offer us?

A few years ago, when the woman I always thought of as Mrs. Graham was recovering from hip surgery in Boston, my editor Tom Winship invited me to lunch with her and my friend Katherine Fanning, the editor of the *Christian Science Monitor.* At times in this wonderful gossipy lunch, I looked at the two older women with awe.

One, Kay Fanning, had broken out of her life as publisher's wife, "the Grace Kelly of Chicago," to become, through divorce, upheaval, tenacity, and smarts, the first woman president of the American Society of Newspaper Editors. The other, Kay Graham, had traversed the enormous distance from daughter, to wife, to widow, to the powerhouse whose paper virtually brought down a president.

When Kay Fanning died earlier this year, the loss of her wisdom and experience was palpable.

Now we have lost Kay Graham, another link to an era, not so long ago, when women were refused admission to the Gridiron Club and when Washington dinner etiquette still remanded wives to after-dinner ghettos. An era when the publisher of *The Washington Post* broke those codes.

Late in life, Kay Graham's book, aptly named *Personal History,* transformed her in women's eyes from a remote icon to a fellow traveler. Young women who tend to regard their famous elders' lives as seamless twenty-year plans to the pinnacle of success could read, with relief, of her own insecurity, her missteps, even her regrets.

She left a clear-eyed memoir, honest and un-self-pitying, not just an artifact of a greatest generation, but a link to the next. A link to women who do not arrive at midlife fully formed, but who are continually challenged to compose and recompose their lives, looking back as they move forward.

Kay Graham never wanted to be a role model. It must have sounded too static, too good to be true. But she turned vulnerability into courage. That's the role she modeled.

On the memorable night when the momentous decision to print the Pentagon Papers stopped at her desk, she pushed down the fear, took a big gulp, and uttered the motto of her life: "Go ahead, go ahead, go ahead. Let's go."

July 19, 2001

JACKIE WAS A MODEL OF DIGNITY TO THE END

S he went home to die. There would be no strangers coming down her hospital corridor, whispering outside her door. No paparazzi angling to get at her bedside.

The spokesman for the hospital had said, as spokesmen have said so many times before, "Mrs. Onassis and her family have asked that her privacy be respected at this time." The reporters, the curious, the well-wishers were kept at arm's length for one last time.

Jacqueline Bouvier. Jacqueline Kennedy. Jackie O. It was a malignant cancer indeed that killed this most private of public women at 64 years old.

The woman's image was seared into our national photo album half her lifetime ago. She was 34 years old—only 34—on that day when she flew back from Dallas, still dressed in a pink suit stained with the blood of her husband.

In the days that followed, Jacqueline Kennedy become the icon of national mourning. She set a standard for the stoicism we call dignity in the face of death. She did this as she did everything—with courage, in public, under a veil.

Jacqueline Bouvier. The daughter of Black Jack. The 18-year-old who was chosen the Debutante of 1947. The diffident Vassar and George Washington student who bccame the "inquiring camera girl" for the old Washington *Times Herald*. The wife of the young senator from Massachusetts. The first lady.

At times she looked like a deer caught in the Kennedy headlights. She hadn't voted before her marriage, didn't care much for politics, was more attracted to art than policy and liked shopping more than touch football.

We thought we knew her. We thought she belonged to us. She has been on more magazine covers than Madonna. We followed every move, every hairstyle and lifestyle change. We knew her favorite diet dinner— baked potatoes with caviar—and her favorite designers.

But it was a compliment she didn't return, an intrusion she lived with but didn't welcome.

As a single mother, the most famous widow with the most famous children in America, she chose to raise Caroline and John as well and as far from the spotlight as possible.

Once, after Jack died, she said she was reading essayist Thomas

Carlyle, "and he said you should do the duty that lies nearest you. The thing that lies nearest me is the children." She did that duty and had that pleasure.

Years later, when her son, John, made a toast at his sister's engagement, he said: "There were always just the three of us. Now there will be four." And now there will be one less.

America wanted Jacqueline Kennedy to remain frozen in time, circa 1963, circa 34 years old. When she married Aristotle Onassis, the country reacted as if some marauding Visigoth had made off with America's trophy widow. But she did what she wanted.

When she went to work as an editor, she was criticized as a rich woman who had gone slumming at the workplace. But she made her own coffee, Xeroxed her own pages, edited her own books. She made her own life.

The world changed enormously in the years after Jackie was first lady. Gradually the zone of privacy we allow public figures became smaller than a shower stall.

Judith Exner and the girls showed up in Camelot revisions. The president's widow became the extravagant wife of a shipping magnate feuding with her stepchildren. Unauthorized biographers came along slinging their stuff in the name of openness and the right to know . . . the worst.

Now psychobiographies written in psychobabble fill the shelves and turn lives into miniseries. Fame means living long enough to have an actress play you in someone else's script about your life. Jackie Oh.

In the 1990s even politicians are expected to reveal their childhood traumas to talk show hosts. Wives are called upon to do confessional interviews about their inner feelings about everything, including their marriage. Everyday people line up for the chance to discuss dysfunctional families and twelve-step horror stories in the name of "sharing."

But Jackie didn't "share." Jacqueline Bouvier Kennedy Onassis remained the most famous and the most private of women. She didn't comment. She didn't write her memoirs or do interviews about her disappointments.

Call it distance. Call it shyness. Call it reserve, aloofness. Choose your word on the continuum of privacy. May I suggest dignity? At this end of an era, Jacqueline Bouvier Kennedy Onassis did it her way. She died with dignity.

May 22, 1994

FATHER WHO KNEW BEST

What I remember is how he came home from that mysterious place called "the office."

He took off his business jacket and put on his fatherhood sweater. Seamlessly, he stepped back into the family to deliver a bit of wisdom or solve a problem.

Jim Anderson was unafflicted by self-doubt. He never once in all those years turned to his wife in bewilderment, asking "Did I say the right thing?" He never told his children, "I don't know."

When the family sitcom first opened on the radio, it carried a question mark: *Father Knows Best?* But television played the title role straight. From 1954 to 1960, father just knew best. No doubt about it.

Now the star of the show, Robert Young, has died at 91. This decent and troubled man who played Anderson and later Dr. Marcus Welby has joined that pantheon of actors who were not perfect fathers—or doctors—but played them on television.

To the baby boomers, all history begins with television. The Andersons, like the Nelsons and Cleavers, form the collective myth of our origins. Their middle-class subdivisions are our Eden, their nuclear families the cultural baseline against which we judge all other families, especially our own. And all other parents, especially ourselves.

The darker facts of Young's life ran alongside the spine of his made-for-TV story. The man who played Jim Anderson suffered from alcoholism and depression. The layman who played Marcus Welby attempted suicide. The actor who played—week after week—the warm father he never had, admitted that he wore "black terror behind a cheerful face." The TV son in this picket fence paradise described it as "some kind of enchanted forest. It wasn't taking into account the reality of the world."

But such arrows of reality rarely pierce our mythology. They don't shake our visceral belief in the '50s family any more than carbon-dating shakes the belief of creationists.

So, in the obituaries that followed Young's death, he was described over and again as "the perfect father figure." One writer labeled him as "always patient, understanding and sage." Another asked, "Is there anyone who didn't wish they had a dad like Jim Anderson?"

Indeed, Robert Young's death offers up a reminder that it isn't just women who go about our daily lives with Harriet Nelson looking over our shoulders. It isn't just working mothers who compare ourselves and are compared—harshly—to a generation of TV moms.

Fathers too carry some primal memory of the ease with which Jim Anderson, insurance agent, husband, father of Bud, Princess, and Kitten, switched roles at the front door. How he became the father who knew best.

In the real postwar era men and women were going separate ways. Women spent more of their lives isolated in child-rearing suburbs. Men disappeared every morning to work and reappeared every evening to announce: "Honey, I'm home."

All day long, women were the experts on the business of family. But in prime time, fathers were the (benign) authorities, proffering homilies and wisdom, teaching moral lessons, wrapping up dilemmas with half-hour precision.

If women watching these shows wondered how these high-heeled, apron-clad mothers kept their houses so clean, did men wonder how these fathers solved all the family problems? If the girls fed on these images still carry them, so do the boys.

"I'm really struck by the impossible ideal that it set up for men," says Stephanie Coontz who wrote *The Way We Never Were.* "Here is this father who is never angry, never flummoxed, never wrong, never had to negotiate with his wife." The man who never changed a diaper, who was absent from daily hassles, knew. And knew best.

Today, in the literature of mixed-company miscommunication, we are told that women want men to just listen to their problems. But men feel compelled to solve them. A stock character for female comedians is the man who cannot ask directions. But men are not supposed to feel lost.

How many hands-on fathers still carry the burden of fixing everything, of knowing the right way without asking? How many carry the sense that they don't measure up? Up to the Jim Andersons of their fantasy family.

"It's upsetting to go counter to the image," the actor once said. "To play a steadfast happy person when you're not gives you a sense of guilt."

The irony is that Robert Young was no Jim Anderson. Once, late in life, after acknowledging the difficulty of being both himself and our icon, he burst out, "The show is basically entertainment, don't you understand that? What gave you the idea it was supposed to be real?"

Now, at long last, after the death of the father who knew best, we ought to know better.

July 26, 1998

THE SPOCK GENERATION

I t was not a book that parents merely read. We clutched it like a steering wheel. We held on to it like a security blanket through the sleep-deprived terrors of early parenthood.

When the hospital irrationally released the helpless 6-pound infant into our care without demanding to see a parenting degree, a dated driver's license, a passing test score, we had Dr. Spock's index to cling to.

"Newborns: Feelings in the early weeks."

When we were poised at the fearful edge of the first bath, we gripped the spine of this book as tightly as the wobbly head of our newborn and looked it up.

"Bath: In infancy; temperature of; fear of."

When the crying would not stop, when we had changed, fed, hugged, rocked, ignored, run through our entire repertoire and dissolved in panic, we still had Dr. Spock.

"Crying: From air bubble; from fatigue; from indigestion; hard on parents."

Benjamin Spock made house calls day or night. He knew what we were worrying about before we did.

So when he died on Sunday at 94, the obituaries all reported that his book was our bible. At fifty million copies, it was second to the good book.

But our Dr. Spock was no pediatric patriarch. No deliverer of commandments. No unimpeachable authority from on high.

The man who was born at the beginning of the century and died at the end of it bridged the distance from doctor to patient as easily as he did the distance from his 6-foot-4-inch height to his smallest patient.

"Trust yourself," he wrote in the opening line of the book—a line that survived five decades and as many updates, from open adoption to AIDS.

"You know more than you think you do," he told parents who were raw recruits, no more comfortable with newborns than with landing gear on a 747. "Don't take too seriously what all the neighbors say. Don't be over-awed by what the experts say. Don't be afraid to trust your own common sense."

It's hard to realize how uncommon such sense was in 1946. The author had grown up in a strict household in a stern era when parents were told to "harden off" their children like tender new shoots for a harsh, cold world.

Today, when every newborn comes equipped with a pacifier, we forget that experts once advised harsh tactics against thumb-sucking, even strapping the offending thumb away from the needy mouth. A standard guide admonished parents: "Never, never kiss your child. Never hold it on your lap. Never rock its carriage."

The Common Sense Book of Baby and Child Care was delivered as the first baby boomer left the womb. It was grabbed by young mothers and fathers who were far from home geographically and psychologically, in a generation gap less heralded than our own.

Spock told these parents to trust not only themselves but their children. "The children who are best behaved are those who are treated with respect," he said in a phrase that would be continually twisted into some paean to permissiveness.

"Discipline: Based on love; changing theories; firmness."

By the time I looked to him for infant advice, the pediatrician had expanded his practice from the nursery to the world. In 1968, he was tried for antiwar protests. In the 1970s, the old authorities blamed him for raising children out of control—their control.

Spock became an elder of the youth generation, running for president on the People's Platform, fighting against nuclear weapons and for health care. When others criticized a pediatrician playing politics, he answered, "What is the use of physicians like myself trying to help parents to bring up children healthy and happy, to have them killed in such numbers?"

"Idealism: Children's need for."

At some point along the way to his very old age, Benjamin Spock became dismayed by the Spock Kids, disapproving of the baby boomers who settled down in what he saw as an apolitical, self-absorbed materialism. Today the bookshelf that once held Spock alone is filled with Penelope Leach and T. Berry Brazelton.

But it was Benjamin Spock who held our collective hands as we moved from one generation to another. He trusted us, and we returned the compliment. Maybe the final word for this good, struggling man rested with the doctor's own difficult mother. Half a century ago, after reading the book, she said, "Why, Benny, it's really quite sensible."

March 19, 1998

W hat, then, should be her epitaph? What final handle should we choose for the woman who was our adviser in chief? Sensible from Sioux City?

Eppie Lederer died on Saturday, taking Ann Landers with her. The two were, after all, inseparable. For nearly half a century, Lederer/Landers made sense the way other people make cars or computer chips. Sense, however, is a much rarer product, harder to fashion and always in demand.

In her newspaper office, in her apartment, in her bathtub, Lederer answered letters one decade after another until cancer finally did what few editors dared—ended her column.

Ann Landers was as American as a wisecrack and as universal as a broken heart. She was as dated as "doozie" and as timeless as empathy. She was as outspoken as any opponent of the "gun nuts" and as gentle as any judge who ever delivered a verdict of "40 lashes with a wet noodle."

In the end, she wasn't so much a mother confessor as she was a fellow traveler. She was there, offering advice when Stumped in San Diego and Bewildered in Boston were figuring out which values to reassess and which to retain.

Imagine this: Eppie Lederer was born in Sioux City, Iowa, in 1918, two years before women won the right to vote. Imagine Eppie Lederer being unable to make her opinion count.

She was one of twin daughters born to a Russian immigrant, a peddler who eventually made his money in movie theaters. As a woman of her own time, she once had the lining of her fur coat embroidered, "Jules' wife." As a woman of her own making, she competed for her job. She began her career as Ann Landers on October 16, 1955, at the height of the feminine mystique.

From the very beginning, Lederer was conscious of the isolation, uncertainty, and pain that made people put pen to paper, asking for help from a complete stranger. "These people have nobody else to talk to," she once mused. "They write to a name in a newspaper. That's a tragedy."

On the other hand, she acknowledged with trademark breeziness, "I'm free, the price is right, and they can be anonymous. They feel they know me."

Beginning in an era when people still whispered the word "cancer" and didn't "know" any homosexuals, Ann Lander's motto became: "Wake up and smell the coffee." The tiny woman with the brassy voice was the leading indicator and change agent of a world that would come to believe—for better and for excess—in frankness.

"You needed that guy like a giraffe needs a strep throat."

"A father who diapers his daughter until the age of 12 has a geranium in his cranium."

"Masturbation is a normal part of growing up."

Landers/Lederer covered a span from *Father Knows Best* to Ozzie Osbourne. From the love that dares not speak its name to gay marriage. From prudes to penile implants.

The woman who once didn't believe in divorce ended up divorced. The woman who advocated communication and peace was estranged for years from her twin and competitor, Dear Abby.

Through it all this advice columnist had the right stuff: resilience. "How did it happen that something so good didn't last forever?" she wrote of her marriage. "The lady with all the answers does not know the answer to this one." As for her mistakes, "I have learned that each of us is capable of doing something completely irrational and totally out of character at some time during our lives. . . . It simply means we are human."

Today we have a generation of advisers as rigid as Dr. Laura and as judgmental as Judge Judy. Today, TV hosts encourage people to throw off their anonymity to "air their dirty linen" in public. Discouraged in Dayton has become Just Shameless on Jerry Springer.

But in the two-way dialogue of her life with readers, this adviser hewed a careful narrative line of change and tradition. She didn't believe in traditional values as a permanent chain to tie people up in knots. Her values were, rather, a sustaining rope like the ones they string between buildings in her hometown Chicago so that people have something to hold onto when the wind howls.

In the end, the most trusted and enduring value in her life's work was quite simply its humanity. Someone once asked Eppie how she wanted to be remembered. She answered this way: "She did her best. She tried to help. That's good enough."

Eppie Lederer. Ann Landers. She made sense and made it seem common.

June 25, 2002

T here are times when words really do fail us. We don't always have the vocabulary—the nouns, the adjectives, the adverbs—to describe the range of experience properly.

This time it was the verbs that came up as paupers. The simplest verbs in our language—"was" and "is"—were inadequate for the task facing the friends and family of Ronald Reagan, the president now crippled with Alzheimer's.

Speaking in the masterful documentary on PBS, the tenses kept shifting, slipping out of gear. Some said, "He was . . ." Others said, "He is . . ."

At times, the past and present got confused, as if the speaker could not decide whether the Ronald Reagan he knew still existed. In describing Reagan's character as well as his policies, the tense would alternate like an electrical current.

This language became the poignant—no, tragic—background to the memoir of a man who no longer remembers. To the story of a president who can no longer be a source on his own presidency. To the completed history of a man who is still alive.

If these people were tongue-tied, it was because there was/is no correct tense to describe the existence of a person with advanced Alzheimer's. This is a disease that attacks the brain's hard drive like a computer virus, erasing personality byte by byte. It leaves behind a man who is no longer himself. No longer who he was.

This was not the first time I had been struck by such sounds. Two winters ago I was in California when a star-studded celebration was held for Reagan's eighty-fifth birthday. I saw a party arranged for a man who was not there. And was not all there.

As the awkward, even bizarre televised festivities went on, I was struck by how hard it was for the celebrants, for any of us, to come to grips with a disease that alters identity. Had the Ronald Reagan they were toasting really turned 85? Or had he never truly gotten beyond 83, the year he told us he had Alzheimer's? What is the meaning of identity in people who outlive their conscious life?

These are questions that plague those who live in the aura of Alzheimer's. There are about four million Americans with this dementia, among them a mother of a friend and a friend of my mother. Last week, while researchers in Boston talked of a new generation of drugs, another public man, Abe Ribicoff, the former governor and senator from Connecticut, died with the disease.

But Ronald Reagan is the first of our presidents, the first man to engage the entire country in what families of the afflicted describe as the long good-bye.

Today he lives a private and protected life at some point on the sliding scale of the disease. Every time the ex-presidents meet, one is absent. And at every absence there is again the reminder of his presence, not as some Alzheimer's poster boy, but as a shadow: the man who was/is.

As national family members we only wince. It's the family and friends who truly suffer through this disappearing act. These are the people left facing and caring for a stranger in familiar shape.

Today, Patti finds ease in the fact that she reconciled with her father while he still understood. Ron Jr. takes honest if chilly comfort in the fact that they were already prepped in his father's remoteness: "All of us went through some period of our lives when we missed him when he was there." But both let us understand that their father is no longer available.

Dr. Steven DeKosky, director of the Alzheimer's Disease Research Center at the University of Pittsburgh, says that people who deal with Alzheimer's often talk of two selves: the then-self and the now-self. When families and doctors must make decisions about living wills or experimental treatment, they ask what the woman she was would want for the woman she is.

Yet we have only known about this disease for twenty years. As DeKosky says, "We can talk about people who have cancer, strokes, heart attacks, amputations, but this is wholly new. We haven't yet learned how you talk about the loss of self."

Over three years ago, Ronald Reagan wrote the country a brave and fond farewell letter: "I now begin the journey that will lead me into the sunset of my life."

In the long shadows of this sunset, we have inherited the deeply sad obligation to understand what was/is. Reagan's farewell was just the beginning of our long good-bye.

March 1, 1998

LAST DAY IN THE NEIGHBORHOOD

I met Mr. Rogers long after the children in my family had left his neighborhood. Long after they'd crossed the media highway into a much more treacherous and indifferent culture.

One morning in Pittsburgh, I was invited to his TV studio. There was a worn sofa, a chair or two, a pile of puppets. It might have been a humble cul-de-sac in his fanciful TV world.

I felt like a parent squeezing into a kindergarten seat at a parent-teacher conference. And when he told me to call him Fred, I couldn't. To me, he would always be Mr. Rogers.

This was the thing I learned about the man who understood children: He didn't play Mr. Rogers on TV; he was Mr. Rogers. The character was his character. He had the same gentle voice that willed the world to slow down and listen up, to live at child-speed. And he wore civility as lightly and easily as a cardigan sweater.

Before I left, he rustled through a bunch of boxes in search of a Mr. Rogers T-shirt to give me as if I were a young fan—which I was. When we said good-bye, I half expected him to change shoes, put on his sweater, and deliver his closing line, "See you next time."

Now there will be no "next time."

Fred McFeely Rogers died on Thursday. The obits described it as a death in the neighborhood, and so it was. "I have really never considered myself a TV star," Rogers once said, "I always thought I was a neighbor who just came in for a visit." But he came into our homes for one visit and returned for hundreds more.

Born seventy-four years ago, Rogers grew up spending Sunday afternoons with his grandfather on a sprawling Pennsylvania farm. His grandfather used to tell him, "You made this day a special day, just because you were here and you are you. I like you just the way you are." This phrase, this gift, became his inheritance from the old man. And he passed it along to our children.

Roger's television career began half a century ago as an unseen puppeteer. He left broadcasting to study child development, became a Presbyterian minister, and then embarked on a unique ministry. For thirty years, using a blue marking pen on yellow-lined paper, he scripted the songs and scenes of a preschool village. With "speedy delivery" and a trolley to Make-Believe he designed the emotional streets and fanciful front lawns of *Mister Rogers' Neighborhood.*

Mr. Rogers always seemed like a traveler from some other, gentler world. But even in 1964, when he first asked children to be his neighbor, the world had begun to grow out of sync with the pace and needs of childhood.

One of his early programs in 1968 was to help parents explain the death of Robert Kennedy. One of his last programs—out of retirement—was to help explain September 11.

Over the years, in 900 episodes, he created a safe, open place where children mattered. Day by day, he honed a television counterculture, an alternative universe to mainstream media. In new shows and reruns, in one of the longest-running series on television, he offered his vision of a child-friendly village in a child-hostile broadcast world.

Outside of the neighborhood, a Disney World of media moguls gradually defined childhood as a market. Now, small viewers can't tell the Pokémon program from the product. Cartoons are inseparable from commercials. But Mr. Rogers treated his viewers like preschoolers, not consumers. He said, "I want children to know that there is far more to their lives than the latest fad."

Outside of the neighborhood, a cable spectrum of cartoons became populated with "action figures" and driven by violence. But Mr. Rogers's plots revolved around the whole emotional life of children—from the fear of a bathtub drain to the pain of divorce. "It's important," he once said, "for us to give them words for their feelings."

For most of us these days, the media is not a visitor but an intruder. Parents often feel like helpless bystanders, unable to screen the information that beams directly—through and around us—to our children, whether it's a pitch for Big Macs or the image of a plane crashing into a tower. But for thirty years, we had Fred Rogers on our side. Even now, his Web site carries a message on how to explain his death to children.

Mr. Rogers's red cardigan has gone to the Smithsonian. But how do we say good-bye to our neighbor? With one of his favored lines, the sort that garnered so many affectionate parodies? "There's only one person in the whole world like you."

March 21, 2003

Civil & Other Liberties

SOMETIMES, AN OPEN MIND COMES PERILOUSLY CLOSE

TO BEING AN EMPTY MIND. SOMETIMES, TOLERANCE IS A

WAY TO AVOID WRESTLING FOR THE TRUTH. PLURALISM IS

NOT ALWAYS THE ACCEPTANCE OF A RANGE OF HARD-

WON VIEWS, BUT A GIANT SHRUG OF THE SHOULDERS, A

COSMIC "WHATEVER."

—FROM "OPEN OR EMPTY-MINDED?" MARCH 16, 2000

C ould we begin this millennium with a policy that offers kids something more than "zero tolerance"?

Zero tolerance began as a popular promise of punishment for any student who brought the streets into the schools. There would no leniency—that's zip, nada, zero—for violence, drugs, weapons. One strike and you're out. Gradually the name became all too accurate. Zero tolerance for misbehavior evolved into zero tolerance for kids themselves.

We've developed an attitude—and not just in schools where zero tolerance often translates into a quick and dirty way of kicking kids out. We're in a time of a general crackdown—a tough love without the love. Zero is now a symbol of bankruptcy.

In Maryland we just learned again that the much-touted boot camps for young offenders easily turn into abuse camps. The idea that you can straighten kids out by beating them up has been continually discredited without being abandoned.

Next week we'll hear again about two Virginia fifth-graders who allegedly put soap in their teacher's water. The pair weren't given detention, mind you, they were charged with a felony. One plea-bargained this "crime" into a misdemeanor. The other comes up for a hearing on January 10.

We'll also hear from the 18-year-old Floridian who threatened a Columbine High sophomore over the Internet. On January 11, Michael Campbell will be in a Colorado court. A month after his father's death from cancer, the student sent an AOL message saying he was going to "finish what begun" at Columbine. Now he faces five years in prison.

On the same day in Illinois, a court will rule on whether six Decatur students, originally expelled for two years after a stadium brawl, were denied a fair hearing. Jesse Jackson contends that this "zero tolerance" is applied with lopsided mathematics to minorities.

And to complete the picture, in Granite City, Illinois, and in twenty other school districts, grown-ups are putting their millennial hope into fancy new software to "profile" students. They are playing twenty questions to predict which students are likely to become violent.

These are not just random anecdotes; they're dots that connect into a trend. As the stories pile along, says Jim McComb, an opponent of boot camps and director of the Maryland Juvenile Justice Coalition, "you've got to scratch your head and say, 'What's going on here?' "

At the turn of the last century we were building juvenile courts and treating troubled teens as people with a better future. Now we are lowering the age at which children can be tried as adults—in Texas it's fourteen—and throwing away the key. Marcia Lowry, a children's rights lawyer, puts it this way: "I am seeing a lot of willingness to give up on kids at an early stage."

I'm not suggesting that troubled teenagers are misunderstood angels, nor am I dismissing the genuine fear that has spread out from the school shootings. Having ignored a trail of clues left by two suicidal murderers, it's no wonder that nervous Colorado officials take one online threat as if it were the real thing.

Jesse Jackson, for that matter, may not have picked the right boys or the right incident to make his point. But he is right in zeroing in on intolerance.

Whether we're talking about kids who were arrested for putting soap in a teacher's drink, or a girl who died in a boot camp to which she was sentenced for shoplifting, or a teen kicked out of school because he took a troubled friend's knife away and put it in his locker, we aren't paying attention to the individual stories of individual kids. We're punishing them.

The two most searing stories of the past holiday season? One was about the small Memphis boy who went home from school every night to an apartment where his mother's body lay rotting. The boy was so isolated, so afraid he'd end up in foster care that he told no one of her death.

In a second and similar story, a 7-year-old Massachusetts girl who told a teacher that her mother had died, was reportedly scolded, "You shouldn't say things like that." So the girl spent that night alone with the corpse.

I'm not blaming the school or the teacher. But the uneasy truth is that children are often tragically disconnected. The schools don't really know their lives; the communities are clueless.

Paying real attention to the younger generation is labor-intensive. It consists of connections and discipline, expectation and second chances. It's harder to talk with troubled teens than to profile them. But in raising kids, as a parent or as a country, zero tolerance adds up to absolutely nothing.

January 2, 2000

OPEN OR EMPTY-MINDED?

I t's a bit uncomfortable to find myself suddenly questioning the value of tolerance. I've spent an awful lot of time and space defending the rights of others to their beliefs, even when they attack mine. Pluralism is a virtue.

But is there too much of a good thing?

Sometimes, an open mind comes perilously close to being an empty mind. Sometimes, tolerance is a way to avoid wrestling for the truth. Pluralism is not always the acceptance of a range of hard-won views, but a giant shrug of the shoulders, a cosmic "Whatever."

What brings on this dyspeptic thought is a new poll conducted for the People for the American Way on teaching evolution and creationism in the schools. This is not another quick-and-dirty multiple-choice question but a layered, in-depth survey of fifteen hundred Americans done by Dan Yankelovich's firm, DYG Inc.

The good news, for those of us who have rued the fundamentalist attempt at a science class coup, is that the vast majority of Americans—83 percent—believe evolution should be taught in the schools. But a majority of people also think that the story of creation should be taught. What? Whatever?

The poll suggests that this isn't a contradiction as much as a compromise. Americans have, after all, come to believe that God and evolution are not incompatible. As Ralph Neas, the head of People for the American Way, sums it up nicely, "Most Americans believe that God created evolution."

As he analyzes the poll, people have the sense that evolution and creation can coexist in school. Evolution can be taught in science and creation taught in some other part of the curriculum, say history or culture.

Now, this is fine. We're in an era when most of us want to reconcile the split between church and school. We can't teach religion in public schools; but we can and should teach about religion.

Still, I'm afraid there is a darker subtext in the polls. The truth is that most of those surveyed couldn't fully define evolution or creationism.

So maybe they weren't wrestling with two incompatible views of human origins. Maybe it wasn't a struggle at all. Maybe it was: "Creationism . . . evolution . . . whatever."

John Haught, a theologian at Georgetown University and author of *God After Darwin*, compares the survey to what he sees in his classroom.

"Today, there is more tolerance, but the passion for truth doesn't seem to be as strong as it could be."

Haught is no academic absolutist, but he muses, "There is less concern with getting to the 'True' with a capital T. You don't want to step on people's toes. You want to avoid conflict, including meaningful conflict."

No, I am not a fan of those who think they have cornered the market on truth. If you want to know how much trouble these people can cause, read the pope's apology last weekend. The Crusades and the Inquisition were just opening acts.

True-believing troublemakers are still among us. Think about the attempt of the religious right to take over local school boards. Think about the Bible history classes in public schools in Florida that include such "lesson questions" as: "Who, according to Jesus, is the father of the Jews? The devil."

But the passive acceptance of all ideas as more or less equal, the fear of conflict, the acceptance of pluralism as a political default position, don't always get us closer to real and rigorous understanding. Indeed, the postmodern attitude as Yankelovich describes it himself—"Well, you never know, hey"—can lead to what he also has described as "whateverism."

Some of the relativism comes from the skeptical American attitude—certainly in my profession—about everything, including experts.

In medicine, the proper combination of skepticism and pluralism has led the National Institutes of Health to finally explore alternative medicine. But it has also led some to accept chemotherapy or laetrile as either/or cures for cancer.

In history, tolerance and pluralism have led us to seek out different perspectives of events. But they have also led some to accept those "historians" who deny the Holocaust.

As for school, it's one thing to open our children's minds to the variety of cultural stories about human origins. It's quite another to present evolution and creationism as options.

One plus one equals two, not seven. The world is billions of years old, not thousands. And school boards facing a science curriculum still must choose between science and religion, evolution and creationism. "Whatever" is not an option.

March 16, 2000

T his one is dedicated to the late Joseph Heller. After all, the novelist who died on Sunday was the one man who got to the loony heart of military regulations.

Remember the catch in his *Catch-22*? The military rulebook said that anyone who was crazy was prohibited from flying in combat. The catch was that he had to ask to get out. And, of course, any guy who asked to avoid risking his life was sane. So he had to keep flying.

Catch-22 won a place in the modern outlook and language. In the dictionary it is defined as "a condition or consequence that precludes success, a dilemma where the victim cannot win."

But that was just the beginning.

In 1993 the Pentagon, Congress, and the commander in chief came up with a doozie of a new rule called "Don't ask, don't tell." Maybe we should call it Catch-4500. That's the number of homosexuals who've been kicked out under the policy that was supposed to make it easier for them to serve.

Or maybe we should call it Catch-Barry Winchell. That's the name of the 21-year-old Army private who was killed last summer for being gay.

What's the catch this time? Under the 1993 rule, gays can serve as long as they aren't gay. At least not openly. The military "accepts" them as long as it doesn't know they are there. They are gays in a military without any gays.

What does this absurdist view and rule actually mean to homosexuals in uniform? It means staying in the closet. Which is exactly where they lived before this so-called reform.

What does it mean in practice?

It means that gay soldiers like Javier Torres, a former Army private, had to chime in when a superior led the platoon on a five-mile run chanting: "Faggot, faggot down the street/Shoot him, shoot till he retreats."

It means that Barry Winchell remained silent during the gay-baiting and harassment prior to his death. To complain to a superior is tantamount to "telling." To "tell" means dismissal.

And it means that gay soldiers have to pretend or resign. It means "a dilemma where the victim cannot win."

Catch-4500. Catch-Winchell. Remember the line from another Heller book, *Good As Gold*? In that cynical look at government, an aide to the president says earnestly, "Just tell the truth, even if you have to lie."

Well, "Don't ask" was sold as a step forward for the military, the end of witch hunts. "Don't tell" was described as a simple call for "restraint," "discretion," even "privacy." But in truth, it was a policy for lying about something basic: Who you are.

Beatrice Dohrn, the legal director of the gay rights group Lambda, describes it this way: "It says, we have this rule. You can break this rule as long as we don't find out you broke it." It is, she says, "completely contrary to maintaining your dignity."

What the military hostility comes down to is Lieutenant Colonel Robert Maginnis's poncho. On *60 Minutes,* the retired coauthor of this policy described his belief that homosexuals break down the vaunted "unit cohesion," the trust and bonding between soldiers. In Ranger school, he said, "we would, for instance, take this poncho liner, which was something that we would wrap ourselves in when it was cold, so you're sharing body heat."

If he were sharing poncho and body heat with a gay man, said Maginnis, "it definitely would make me uncomfortable."

This is the fear at its most primal level. The irrational fear of being physically close to a homosexual, the panic at possibly being seen as a sex object by another man—these fears define homophobia. It's not the homosexual but homophobia that lurks behind the poncho and the policy.

Over the past week, Hillary Clinton, Al Gore, and Bill Bradley have all admitted that the policy doesn't work. The president has even said it's "out of whack." But the Defense Department has announced that it's taking ninety days to investigate whether "the policy is implemented fairly."

Let me save them ninety days. The order that is keeping gays in the closet or out of the Army is working just the way it was designed. Training won't help, nor will tweaking. It's not the "implementation" that's wrong; it's the policy.

Today's Army has a $268 million ad campaign for new recruits. They're offering a $20,000 bonus for a two-year enlistment. But every day, trained men and women are being kicked out because they can't or won't make their careers in the closet.

The closet. There's the real catch.

December 16, 1999

I t's too bad that we are stuck with the moniker "hate crimes." The label makes it sound as if it were a crime to hate. It has given opponents of hate crime laws a handle for all sorts of clichés: "Every crime is a hate crime." "Nobody commits a love crime."

Today it has become politically correct—in the true meaning of that phrase—to disparage laws that make it worse to commit a crime when the motive is bias. It's become popular to belittle the notion that society has an investment in upping the ante on such acts of bigotry.

Hate crimes are on the docket again because this week the Supreme Court decided to hear the case of Charles C. Apprendi. Five years ago Apprendi, a white pharmacist in Vineland, New Jersey, fired his rifle into the home of the only African-American family in his neighborhood. He told the police he wanted to give the family a message that they didn't belong.

Of course, by the time the trial came around, Apprendi denied that he was motivated by the color of their skin: brown. What set him off, he said, was the color of their door: purple. The judge, however, decided that the crime was racially motivated and so, under the New Jersey law on hate crimes, a five- to ten-year sentence was kicked up to twelve years.

Now Apprendi has come to the Supreme Court demanding that a jury, not a judge, decide his motives.

The New Jersey case is a relatively minor shot at the target of hate crime laws. But Apprendi's lawyers are trying to rein in the law. They are counting on the view that hate is too dicey an emotion, too elusive a motive.

This is what's happening to hate crime legislation: In the 1980s more than forty states passed laws against crimes of bias, crimes committed against someone on the grounds of their religion or race.

Not a single hate crime law has passed since the dragging death of James Byrd Jr. Not a single existing law has been expanded to include homosexuality since the murder of Matthew Shepard. A Senate bill that would have accorded the modest federal hate-crime protection to sexual preference and gender was just rejected by Congress.

A crime is a crime is a crime, we are told. What difference does it make, opponents ask, if you attack a person as an individual or on account of his race, her religion, their sexual preference? What difference does it make if Matthew Shepard was brutally murdered because he was gay or because he was, say, short? What difference does it make if a hate crime penalty is added on to a murder conviction? Two life sentences?

Well, in fact, you cannot add on to a death sentence, and the families of murder victims do feel their pain equally, regardless of the killer's motives. But most hate crimes are not murder and it's absurd—disingenuous—to deny the difference between these and ordinary crimes.

There was, after all, a huge difference between *Kristallnacht*—the night the Nazis rampaged through Jewish homes and businesses—and ordinary vandalism. And there is enormous difference between shooting someone's house because of the color of his door and the color of his skin.

Hate crimes, bias crimes, are disproportionately crimes against people, not property. They are committed, the research tells us, by strangers, by groups, by "thrill seekers." They tend to escalate from a broken window to a broken bone.

But more than that, they are, in Brian Levin's words, "a crime against community and a crime against a pluralistic society." A former police officer who is now a professor at California State University in San Bernardino, Levin has been studying hate crimes for 14 years and has come to believe that crimes motivated by bias "imprint on the rest of society a level of distrust. They're additional poison injected into society."

I don't deny that it can be hard to uncover someone's motive. Not everyone confesses or leaves graffiti on a sidewalk. We cannot read minds or punish people for their bigoted "feelings." But motive often plays a part in punishment and courts often wrestle with this problem of "why."

Today hate crime laws are often criticized as a kind of criminal affirmative action, "special protection" for "special classes of victims." In fact they apply to everyone and have, since the first Supreme Court case upheld a hate crime law when a black man urged a crowd to assault a white passerby, yelling, "There goes a white boy. Go get him."

So, it isn't a crime to hate. But when crime is based on bias or bigotry, when it's as directed as an act of terrorism against an entire group, it carries an extra and public dimension. That's when there—still—ought to be a law.

December 2, 1999

I t is no wonder that we stumble so often when we're forced to decide whether someone is bad or (also) mad. After all, we barely speak the same language.

The medical world talks about mental illness. But the law talks only about legal insanity. The public wonders whether some defendant is mad as a hatter. The judge has to determine only if a defendant is competent enough to stand trial.

This is how it goes now in the case of Theodore Kaczynski, who appears to be both certifiably nuts and legally competent.

Was anyone really surprised Monday when the mathematician-turned-hermit, the accused Unabomber, interrupted the trial before it even began, to read something he had written, something "very important"?

Was anyone truly surprised that he apparently protested in the judge's chambers against being represented by lawyers who want to portray him as mentally unstable?

Ted Kaczynski did what he does best. He disrupted the system. If he is crazy, a former prosecutor told CNN, then he is crazy like a fox. But this man spoke as if Kaczynski could not be both sick and smart, delusional and deliberate—a psychotic fox.

This is at the heart of the trial of a man who worried in his journals that society would see him as "a sickie" rather than a political philosopher. A man who has refused to see a psychiatrist, who has been found "competent" to stand trial according to that low legal standard and so is permitted to direct his own defense.

What does society do about a man who writes with clarity that "The technophiles are taking us all on an utterly reckless ride into the unknown." And then tells his lawyers that he believes satellites control people and place electrodes in their brains. A man who is accused of deliberately planning and building bombs that killed three and maimed twenty-nine. But says he was controlled by an all-powerful organization he couldn't resist.

Is Kaczynski as crazy as Jeffrey Dahmer, who killed and ate his victims? As crazy as John Salvi, who killed two women at abortion clinics that were, he insisted, part of a conspiracy by the Ku Klux Klan, Freemasons, and the Mafia against Catholics? As crazy as Colin Ferguson, who killed six and wounded nineteen rail commuters and said he was charged with ninety-three counts because it was 1993?

All of these men were found to be legally responsible for their actions. Indeed, Ferguson was allowed what Kaczynski may want—to conduct his own defense—even after he asked to put an exorcist on the stand as an expert witness to testify that government agents installed a microchip in his brain.

Ever since John Hinckley shot Ronald Reagan and was sent to a mental hospital, insanity has become a hard defense to muster. As Michael Perlin of NYU Law School says, "There is no question that jurors consistently reject the insanity defense in cases of people who were severely mentally ill and didn't know what they were doing."

It is raised only 1 percent of the time and successful one-quarter percent, and even then, almost always when both sides agree that the defendant is out of his mind. Today, Perlin says, "society wants to try just about everyone."

The law holds people responsible for their actions, while medicine tries to help those who are ill through no fault of their own. These two inexact sciences meet at the juncture where evil confronts illness. In a lock-'em-up era, we have come to believe that insanity is a loophole for evil, not a diagnosis for disease.

David Gelernter, a victim of one of the bombs allegedly sent by Kaczynski, calls the Unabomber an evil coward who deserves to die. But the bizarre part is that to declare him evil and go for the death penalty, we have to accept Kaczynski's own view of reality.

We have to agree that the world he constructed over twenty years in a cabin in Montana is not the delusion of a paranoid schizophrenic, but the rational view of a political ideologue. Sending letter bombs was the rational act of an antitechnology terrorist, not a madman controlled by some omnipotent force.

Not only does Ted Kaczynski insist he is sane, but here is the clincher: The law agrees. Having found him "competent," at least for now, he has won a degree of autonomy and power equal to the time when he forced his manifesto onto the pages of *The New York Times* and *The Washington Post*.

Indeed, as Northeastern University law professor Rose Zoltek-Jick says wonderingly: "He's dragged us down Alice's hole. It's as if he were forcing us to go into a world as crazy as his."

This week in Sacramento, the Mad Hatter is running the show.

January 8, 1998

THE CASE OF THE PREGNANCY POLICE

A while ago, Planned Parenthood ran an ad with a picture of a woman facing two policemen at her door. The caption read: "How would you like the police to investigate your miscarriage?"

Pregnancy police? It must have seemed a bit over-the-top: fund-raising hyperbole for planned paranoia.

But not anymore. Not in Iowa.

Last May a newborn baby boy was found dismembered in a county recycling center. The gruesome story shook the 10,076 citizens of Storm Lake. The police didn't find out if the baby was born alive or even if he was born in the county. They didn't know if the mother who bore him had ever been to a local clinic or to any doctor at all.

Nevertheless, when the investigation reached a dead end, the police went on a fishing expedition—through the lives of the women of Buena Vista County. They subpoenaed the medical records of every woman who had taken a pregnancy test between August and May.

Mind you, the police had already knocked on the door of a 17-year-old Mexican immigrant based on nothing more than a false high school rumor that she'd been pregnant. They swabbed the mouth of the frightened girl to get a DNA sample.

But there wasn't even a rumor to justify these clinic subpoenas. It was what lawyers call a "suspicionless search." It was what others would call a fertility dragnet. With no suspect, every woman who took a pregnancy test became one.

The surprise was that most health care providers turned over records, names, addresses, and phone numbers. Without a peep and without a patient's consent.

Maybe the clinic folks wanted to help. Maybe they didn't know they had a choice. But the pregnancy test results must have made amazing reading to law enforcement officers in a small city where everyone knows everyone else. It must have raised eyebrows when the pregnancy police—excuse me—the patrol cars appeared outside at least a handful of houses.

Sometimes paranoia turns out to be good preparation. The clinic that refused to let the police fish in their pond was Planned Parenthood.

Jill June, the head of Iowa's Planned Parenthood, remembers thinking, "they can't be serious. There wasn't a shred of evidence that this woman was a patient of ours. What would happen if we did give the names? They would go door to door and say, 'You were pregnant in October, where's your baby?' "

Planned Parenthood refused the subpoena on the grounds of patient-doctor privacy. But the prosecutor went on to argue successfully in county court that a pregnancy test wasn't covered by laws protecting the confidentiality because it didn't have to be administered by a doctor or nurse.

Now the Iowa Supreme Court has agreed to hear this case. Planned Parenthood will file its brief September 30. There will be a friend-of-the-court brief filed by the Iowa Civil Liberties Union for a woman whose pregnancy ended in a miscarriage and whose records ended up in the hands of the cops. Anyone with hopes for shoring up the crumbling walls around medical privacy better become a friend of the court.

Privacy and Planned Parenthood? Put those words together and a lot of folks assume the subject is "abortion." But here we get down to the heart of the argument. In Iowa, they will argue about privacy as Justice Brandeis once defined it: the right to be let alone.

Should law enforcement follow a lead? Of course. But if the police have the right to blindly search through the records of every woman who had a pregnancy test in a clinic, they can search through the pharmacy records of every woman who bought a home kit. If they can set out a dragnet for every pregnant woman, why not for every diabetic or epileptic or cancer patient? Why not keep our medical files in the police station?

We protect the doctor-patient relationship because health rests on trust. Today one in every six patients already resists revealing facts to doctors out of privacy fears. Those fears are sure to get much worse under new regulations put out recently by the Bush administration that allow patient information to be shared with others in the huge health care industry—from insurers to pharmacists—without our prior consent.

When news leaked out that the prosecutor had subpoenaed the records, says June, "Women panicked. Our phones rang off the hook. 'What's going on?' 'Don't turn my records over.' "

Now the Iowa Supreme Court will decide whether the pursuit of a crime means that you can treat every patient like a criminal.

September 22, 2002

H e is white, male and middle-aged, and not the sort of man who describes that as his handicap. He will not tell you that he belongs to the last group in America that can be discriminated against without fear.

Indeed, he calls himself a friend of feminists, having been raised that way by his mother, wife and daughter. Nevertheless, there is something bothering him this morning.

The Supreme Court, quickly and unanimously, made it easier for women to prove sexual harassment in the workplace. The law protects women, in Justice Sandra Day O'Connor's words, "before the harassing conduct leads to a nervous breakdown." What this man wants to talk about now is civil rights. Or maybe about civility.

He wants to tell me that during the past year, when things have been tough and he's gone from one job to none to another, he, too, has been— well, victimized is not too strong a word. From time to time, he's been humiliated, demeaned, dehumanized by one or another superior.

In short, he's been harassed. He's been subjected to the sort of environment that, in O'Connor's description, "would reasonably be perceived and is perceived as hostile or abusive." He can match any story told to the Supreme Court by Teresa Harris in this case with one of his own.

But because it wasn't gender-based harassment, or racially based or age-based or disability-based harassment, because it was simply employee-based harassment and individual abuse, there was nothing he could do about it. The boss might have been obnoxious, but it was an equal opportunity obnoxiousness. This middle-aged white man might have been outraged, but it was merely as a human being.

What he asks me is this: Why is it worse to be sexually harassed than personally harassed? Why does the law protect some workers from some abuse and not all workers from all abuse? What about him?

I could give this man the simple legal answer, and I do: The laws were passed to deal with discrimination, not labor relations. The point was to level the playing field, not to raise the quality of life on the shop floor. The courts ask whether men and women, whites and blacks, young and old are being treated equally, not whether they are being treated well.

I could tell this man, and I do, that the laws come from a society that's been forced to pay attention to civil rights. But I cannot tell him why there is less attention paid to civility.

Civil rights and civility. I listen sometimes to the sounds of the workplace. The way the dispatcher talks to the cabdriver, the way the restaurant manager talks to the waiter, the way the foreman talks to the clerk. It isn't always easy on the ear. There is no right to be treated respectfully. No law against being humiliated. There is no equality of politeness between boss and bossed.

Talking to this man, it strikes me that the impatience or even the anger that some men feel at women's complaints of harassment may not be hostility to women's rights. It may be because they are fellow sufferers.

These men do not feel privileged. Indeed, they, too, are "disrespected." Many men see women getting a day in court, but they, too, have their bad bosses at work. They have stories to tell and nobody to listen.

Maybe the impatience is greater now, when men—white and middle-aged, white and young—feel insecure themselves. When unions are weaker and work pressure is greater. And especially when the overall civility index is lower.

Civil rights protect individuals. Civility protects the community. Individuals plead their own case in the courts. Who pleads the case for community?

I always believed that women want change both for themselves and for society. We want equality with men in the world, but we also want to improve that world. Including the world of work.

So today women are attacking an "abusive working environment," a "sexually hostile" workplace. At long last we are making a strong progressive case for civil rights. But as this man reminds me, the rest of the work world waits to be civil-ized.

November 14, 1993

IN THE COMBAT ZONE

I don't know a soul who predicted that the major civil rights fight of the 1990s would be waged over the right to fight. Women in combat? Gays in the military? The last bastion has turned out to be, literally, a bastion.

What an odd venue for this struggle. The armed forces have more restrictions on personal freedom—regardless of race, creed, gender—than any other institution in our society. It is a top-down, follow-orders hierarchy harbored in a democracy. Yet the flag of equality is now staked on this turf.

Surely any savvy movement leader, trying to rally popular support to a cause, could have picked a different fight. For women, family policies would bring out a larger constituency. For gays, AIDS makes a more compelling claim to attention.

Even now, some in these movements find themselves ambivalent or bemused at the military turn of events. They wrestle between a desire to fit into the military, to be accepted as equals, and a desire to distance themselves from it.

Among women, many believe that the movement should not follow men into trenches or cockpits but rather should march for peace. They take pride in the female image of women as peacemongers, not warriors.

Among gays, some would rather work against discrimination in the civilian world. In last week's serious and campy gathering in Washington—part civil rights march and part coming-out party—there was widespread applause for gays in the military. But there was also a smattering of laughter for the mad-hatted supporters of "Gays in the Millinery."

Nevertheless, the Army, Navy, Air Force, and Marines were told last week to drop restrictions against women flying combat missions and serving on most naval vessels. At the same time, Congress held more hearings on gays. This debate goes on.

I suspect that the convergence of the argument around women, gays, and the military is one part historic accident and two parts inevitable. The military is, after all, the last bastion. The cockpit door was one of the last legally closed to women. The barracks door is one of the heaviest still barred to gays who admit to their identity.

But then, the military plays a particular role in our country's psyche. When soldiers risk death or die in a just war, they are accorded a special honor. Even in an era of volunteer armies and career soldiers, fighting for your country means assuming the heaviest of our national burdens.

I suspect we all understand, consciously or not, that no group will be granted true equality without taking on the ultimate equal risk. Indeed, in an era when we are told that everyone wants rights and no one wants responsibilities, this is one time when people are fighting for the right to be responsible.

As for the military command? Officers in the armed forces must feel at times like principals in the public schools. We tell the schools: Teach our children to read but give them breakfast and condoms. Be teachers and also parents, psychologists, police officers. We tell the military: Teach our soldiers to fight but also to get along. Be the best force in the world, and eliminate sexism and homophobia. Be all that we can't be.

We do expect a great deal from the military. We desegregated the Army before we desegregated the South. We had blacks and whites together in barracks before the country was "ready for it." We did it despite warnings that it would wreak havoc on military morale and the military "culture."

The truth is that in America we don't accept the notion that the military is an independent creature. Or that the Army is an entirely separate culture whose job is to protect only our physical borders.

Unlike other countries, we insist that the military is part of and ruled by the larger culture. Time and again, we call on the military not just to defend our land or our "interests" but to defend our values. Among those values we list tolerance, freedom and, of course, equality.

So this battle continues. The most unlikely combat zone for a civil rights struggle is also a most likely zone. Here we are fighting over values. We're fighting about what's worth fighting for.

May 2, 1993

E arlier this summer a young Iraqi went to one of the Islamic courts springing up in the holy city of Najaf to confess to the judge that he'd killed his mother. She'd dishonored the family by committing adultery, he said to the cleric-turned-judge. The son later explained that he'd chosen to make his case to the self-proclaimed Islamic court because it would "rule according to our Shi-ite traditions. This is the true court. This is the ruling of God."

It was a chilling story to Americans wary about the future of Iraq. In the troubled wake of Saddam, we are worrying over the struggle between democracy and theocracy. We are watching it play out in the streets and in the courts.

I never found out how the radical jurists who use the Koran as the law book ruled in this matricide. But I've been thinking of them for the past week as people gathered outside an Alabama courthouse to protect "Roy's Rock." After all, Americans have our own struggles with theocracy and democracy.

The protesters in Montgomery are fans of Chief Justice Roy Moore, who has been dubbed the "Moses of Alabama" though his namesake would have had trouble carrying a 5,280-pound set of tablets down from the mount.

A West Point graduate, a man who herded cattle in Australia and trained as a kickboxer, Moore became known as the "Ten Command-ments Judge" after placing rosewood tablets behind his bench in 1995. He was elected chief justice of the Alabama Supreme Court in 2000 on a plat-form that read, "Still the Ten Commandments Judge."

Was that election a moment of Judeo-Christian democracy? The ma-jority vote for religious justice?

Two years ago, Moore had his huge monument installed in the ro-tunda of the courthouse. But ultimately, a federal judge ruled that it was "nothing less than an obtrusive year-round religious display." When the other eight members of the Supreme Court said it must be removed, Moore refused to obey. Now suspended, he will face a hearing of his own.

The Chief Justice as Chief Protester is an odd role reversal. But then his conservative followers sing "We Shall Overcome" wearing T-shirts with mottos like, "Homosexuality is a sin, Islam is a lie, abortion is murder."

This is not just an Alabama thing. The movement to put the Ten Com-mandments into the public square is more active now than at any time since Cecil B. DeMille gave away four thousand granite tablets as a promotion for the Charlton Heston movie. There have been dozens of protests against the removal of plaques and statues. Some of the same people once found outside abortion clinics have moved on to courthouse lawns.

The Ten Commandments is a crowd-pleasing cause. A huge majority of Americans regard these words as a map for a good life, though an equally large majority has trouble reciting them. In this Disney culture, it's entirely possible more people can name the seven dwarfs—including Doc—than the Ten Commandments.

Americans seem to want the Commandments displayed even if they don't want them all enforced. When was the last time we arrested people at the local mall for dishonoring the Sabbath? When was adultery last a felony?

The Ten Commandments grace the walls of the U.S. Supreme Court building without controversy. Moses stands along with Confucius and Muhammad in a frieze celebrating the history of the law. But Roy's Rock is about as nonsectarian as a sign over a judicial bench reading "What Would Jesus Do?"

Whenever I write about the wall separating church and state, someone dares me to find it in the Bill of Rights. Indeed, the Constitution says the government cannot establish religion and must protect the freedom to practice any religion or, indeed, no religion.

We've had bitter fights over when the state is endorsing religion. Prayer in the schools? Crèches in front of the library? We've had people who believe that government-enforced neutrality is really hostility. Jerry Falwell calls it "religious genocide."

But these days we Americans look at ourselves in the global light of places like Iraq, Iran, Afghanistan. Our breed of democracy does more than let the majority rule. It also protects the minority—the Zoroastrian, Zen Buddhist, Hindu, Atheist, Muslim—and lets us live together.

A protester carrying a 10-foot-tall cross in front of the Alabama courthouse said, "Maybe they can move the monument, but they can't take it out of our hearts." But that, of course, is where it belongs.

Now the monument has been removed. As for the Ten Commandments Judge? Roy Moore has said that religion is above the law, that his monument means more than his job: "To do my duty, I must obey God. . . . I cannot violate my conscience." May he follow his path—and his rock—right out of the courthouse.

August 27, 2003

PORTRAYING FDR–AS HE WAS

These are times when history refuses to stay in its place. Every generation comes to view the past through its own fresh lens. Its vision almost inevitably produces some historic revision—and, of course, a good deal of controversy.

We've seen such historic fights over the Vietnam Memorial and the Smithsonian's Enola Gay exhibit. We've heard arguments over movies about JFK's assassination or Thomas Jefferson's slaveholding.

Now it's FDR's turn.

Next Wednesday the country will mark the fiftieth anniversary of the death of Franklin Delano Roosevelt. At 1:15 P.M. on April 12, 1945, the worn, 63-year-old man who led us through the Great Depression and World War II, suffered a massive cerebral hemorrhage at his Warm Springs, Georgia, retreat and died.

Older Americans who knew him as their president still remember the smile, the jaunty angle of his cigarette holder, the timbre of his voice, the reassuring words: "We have nothing to fear but fear itself." But few of those who mourned him that day knew about the leg braces, the wheelchair, the struggles of a man unable to stand without help.

In an era when a "cripple" could not have been elected to the presidency, in a time when the words "strong" and "disabled," seemed like a contradiction, in a generation when the press colluded to protect a president's privacy, there was a grand deception that kept his paralysis from the public view.

Now we're commemorating his death with a wrestling match about the facts of his physical life, about how the next generation should literally see FDR. About writing and rewriting history.

The terrain for the controversy is the FDR memorial that is finally to be built on the Tidal Basin in Washington. The memorial is designed as a series of open-air rooms peopled with various images of the president. But there is no brace, no cane, no wheelchair, no indication of FDR's physical condition except for a small entry carved into the granite chronology.

To many, especially many in the handicapped community, that seems like a second grand deception, a way to strike his handicap from the public record. Michael Deland, a board member of the National Organization on Disability, believes that "Roosevelt's disability was such an integral part of the man that it needs to be shown—and it's historically inaccurate not to show it."

But others, especially some on the FDR Memorial Commission, regard the pressure to portray his handicap as a kind of post-mortem "outing," an invasion of his privacy. Indeed, grandson David Roosevelt bristles at what he sees as an attempt to turn FDR into "a modern-day poster child, if you will." The commission's executive director, Dorann Gunderson, adds, "Let me say emphatically that FDR would have been very disturbed."

But what do we say when facts collide, when two sides accuse each other of rewriting history? The "fact" is that FDR hid his handicap from the public. The "fact" is that he was handicapped. The view of the public president is different from the view of the private president.

There is not a soul who knows what FDR would say if he returned to a world that treats disability so differently. What would he have wanted? The only memorial he wanted was the block of marble bearing his name in front of the National Archives.

He went to great lengths to disguise his handicap from the public, for political reasons. But sometimes—touring a veterans' hospital or speaking at Howard University—he didn't hide his handicap, for political reasons.

To David Roosevelt, "the fact that he veiled his disability is the overriding reality." But there is another equal reality: FDR did the job while being disabled. A man who couldn't put on his own shoes led us through the Depression. A man who couldn't walk commanded his country through a world war.

No one is suggesting a memorial to The Handicapped President. Our generation is learning that people are more than their handicaps. We're also learning not to hide disabilities. A wheelchair sculpture in one room of the memorial, a hint of braces around his shoes in another—these would not be insults to his memory but artifacts for a visiting and wondering public.

Maybe Anne Roosevelt, a grandchild born after FDR's death, says it as succinctly as possible: "We should portray him as he was, and as he was, he wore braces. As he was, he did things seated. As he was, he looked to his sons for support. This is who he was, and he went on and lived and gave the nation a sense of life and vibrancy that kept all of us going."

FDR left an extraordinary legacy. Half a century later, surely, we can put his history to rest.

April 6, 1995

FROM OUTLAWS TO IN-LAWS

And so we bid farewell to the Texas Taliban as they ride into the legal sunset. The Supreme Court has finally put an end to a long line of theocrats and theojudges who told consenting adults what they could do to whom and with which body parts.

The case began when police burst into a Houston apartment on a false report that two men were fighting. When they found the men making love instead, they arrested, fincd, and jailed the pair.

Thursday, a 6–3 majority ruled that the antisodomy law violated a homosexual's right to privacy. In an eloquent opinion that spoke of dignity and enduring personal bonds, Justice Anthony Kennedy said, "The state cannot demean their existence or control their destiny by making their private sexual conduct a crime. . . . The liberty protected by the Constitution allows homosexual persons the right to make this choice."

The decision was declared a landmark with cheers on one side and outrage on the other. Justice Antonin Scalia, reading his dissent aloud, fumed that "The court . . . has largely signed on to the so-called homosexual agenda."

But for all the hullabaloo, this case feels less like it's breaking new ground than mopping up some old and tired terrain.

Back in 1960, every state in the union had a law against sodomy, whether it was between man and man or man and woman. Today only thirteen states call it a crime and four of them are targeted solely to gays.

As recently as 1986, an earlier Supreme Court shamefully upheld antisodomy laws because, in Chief Justice Warren Burger's words, homosexuality was "morally reprehensible" conduct, and that was reason enough to make it illegal. Justice Byron White added that there was "no connection between family, marriage, or procreation on the one hand and homosexual activity on the other . . ."

But over the last decade, the cutting edge of the gay rights movement has moved toward matters of family and marriage. While gay couples in Texas remained partners in crime, gay couples in Vermont became partners in almost-marriage.

The latest census report lists 600,000 same-sex couples. The "love that dare not speak its name" now announces commitment ceremonies on the pages of the newspaper.

So here we are. The Supreme Court has just declared that homosexuals aren't outlaws. But the New Jersey and Massachusetts courts are getting ready to decide if homosexuals can be husband and husband, wife and wife. Indeed, while our court has just decided gays shouldn't be locked up, a Canadian court has declared they can get hitched up. For Gay Pride weekend, they're planning to keep the Toronto City Hall open for business.

As gay rights lawyer Evan Wolfson put it, "The gay movement has moved from merely seeking to be left alone in our homes to wanting to participate fully in marriage and family under the protection of the law."

In short, and not without irony, a movement that began in search of sexual freedom is now in pursuit of the bonds of matrimony. Those who want to get the government out of relationships now want the government to formalize their relationships.

In Justice Scalia's scathing dissent, he says disapprovingly that the court's argument leaves no justification "for denying the benefits of marriage to homosexual couples." I suspect he's right.

He and others clearly regard the gay rights movement as a threat to marriage, a fear that was behind the Defense of Marriage Act passed in 1996 to limit marriage to heterosexuals. Gays don't want to attack marriage, they want to join it. While many see this as radical, it is, at heart, profoundly socially conservative.

Same-sex couples now come to the courts and to the public eye largely as family members who want to adopt children or share pension benefits. The gay poster children aren't libertines. They're two Michaels who want to register at Crate and Barrel. They're two mommies with one Baby Bjorn.

This conservatism may well have changed public images as well as the courts' attitudes. Today, some 59 percent of college freshmen approve of gay marriage.

The way things are going, homosexuals will win the equal right to enter into those long discussions that heterosexuals have come to know and dread. Where is this relationship going? Is this the person I want to spend my life with? For better or for worse? They're going to enter the wonderful world of prenuptial agreements and nappies—and divorce.

With this court decision, gays are escaping the reach of the Taliban. They are now one step closer to the liberated day when their moms too will be asking, "So, when are you going to get married?"

June 29, 2003

Character & Caricature

TODAY, AMERICANS ARE MORE LIKELY TO BELIEVE THAT EVERYTHING FROM THE POLITICAL TO THE LEGAL IS PERSONAL. EVERY CANDIDATE NOW TALKS ABOUT HIS OR HER BACKGROUND. NO JUDICIAL CONFIRMATION HEARING WOULD BE COMPLETE WITHOUT A LIFE STORY. BUT INDIVIDUALS ARE FAR TOO COMPLEX TO DRAW A PREDICTABLE NARRATIVE LINE FROM BACKGROUND A TO OPINION B. ONE SELF-MADE MAN MAY CONCLUDE THAT WE SHOULD ALL PICK OURSELVES UP BY OUR BOOTSTRAPS WHILE ANOTHER SUBSIDIZES BOOTSTRAPS.

—FROM "THE VIEW FROM SOMEWHERE," JULY 10, 2003

OUT-OF-CHARACTER EXPERIENCES

s a young reporter, I was often sent out to go knocking on doors. When someone in the city had dismembered his dog or his mother, my job was to get reaction from the neighbors.

It was on these assignments that I first encountered the cliché of such stories. A neighbor would open the door a crack and offer up some variation of the same theme about the killer next door: "He was such a quiet boy."

As often as not people would insist that someone who had committed a terrible act had acted out of character. It was as if an incomprehensible scene had been scripted for him by a bad playwright.

Now it seems that people are routinely described as "acting out of character." When Red Sox outfielder Wilfredo Cordero was recently accused of beating, choking and threatening the life of his wife, what did teammate Mo Vaughn say? "This is no indication of his character at all."

This echoed back to the time O.J. Simpson was accused of murder. "O.J. doesn't have the personality to do this," said Frank Gifford. Now Gifford's adulterous behavior is labeled by sympathizers as an aberration.

There is also the new author and ex-con Sol Wachtler. When this chief justice of the New York State Court of Appeals was arrested after stalking his former lover, a colleague insisted that this was not "the person I have known."

And, of course, there are the much honored military men caught in the new sex scandals. Buddies insist: "It wasn't like him."

Out-of-character experiences abound. He was a quiet boy. In a need to see ourselves and one another as predictable and known quantities, we dismiss the "flaws" as inexplicable. And if that doesn't work, we try the other tack. We rummage through the past of a complex life to find a single set of clues that make some misdeed comfortably "in character."

So it is that when Georgia's Mike Bowers, the former attorney general who defended an antigay law before the Supreme Court, confesses to adultery, those who saw him as "Mr. Clean" may be shocked. But those who saw him as a phony say, "Of course."

So it is that Nixon's venal words on tape would have seemed "out of character" to many Americans in 1972. But a quarter-century later, those who heard the Watergate tapes again last week dubbed them as "quintessential Nixon."

In any number of ways we try to avoid facing the possibility that character may be fluid, contradictory, open-ended.

Americans are fascinated by character. But when we talk of character education or character-building in children, it's with the belief that we can set up a permanent ethical core. That belief can be at war with our own evidence.

In an interview in *The Paris Review,* Richard Ford, the author of *Independence Day,* said that when he was growing up, "character seemed to me . . . a rather fixed quotient." But in midlife his own experience of character—his and others—stresses "the incalculable, the obscure, the unpredictable."

"Today I think of characters—actual and literary characters—as being rather unfixed . . . I certainly think we have histories. And based on them we can purport to have characters—invent or allege character, in a sense. And sometimes histories predict what people will do. Though often not."

This view of character suggests the possibilities in all of us. The times we do things we would never do. The fact that what we do cannot be "out of character"—since we have done it.

Bill Bennett, for instance, whose *Book of Virtues* hoes a straight line, sheepishly confesses that in a post-drug czar phase, he snuck cigarettes. Michael Ansara, liberal founder of Citizen Action, admits funneling illegal contributions to a union campaign and "violating the principles that have guided me."

In character? Out of character? The trick that Richard Ford pondered is "how we cope with contingency in ourselves but try still to accept responsibility for our acts."

Forgive me for lumping murderers, wife beaters, and sneaky smokers into one character attack. My point is that character is never completely built. Life goes on presenting us with choices, large and small. This thing we call character is always being reformed by the moral decisions we make.

In the end, we are not just the character actors. We are the authors.

June 22, 1997

L et me see if I have this right. After all, I've gone a few rounds with Mike Tyson, and the brain gets a little addled in these encounters. Fortunately, the only holes in my ears are the ones I put earrings through.

But if I have it right, the outpouring of outrage, the shock on the part of sportswriters and fans, is not because the convicted rapist once assaulted a woman's body in a hotel room but because last Saturday night he assaulted Evander Holyfield's aural organs in a boxing ring.

If I have it right, the postfight crowd that screamed and made obscene gestures at the 31-year-old ex-con for his inappropriate use of teeth never threw water bottles at him for misusing his other body parts. They never attacked him for saying, "I like to hurt women when I make love to them. I like to hear them scream. . . . It gives me pleasure."

If I have it right, moreover, the contrite champ of chomps who admitted that he'd "snapped," who apologized to "the people who expected more from Mike Tyson," and promised to seek help, never expressed the most fleeting remorse, the itsy-bitsiest contrition to Desiree Washington.

Until now, the fact that Tyson is a sex offender who couldn't move onto your street without registering with the police did nothing to undermine his box office attraction. In fact, he was more respected than Oliver McCall, scorned last February because of his refusal to fight.

Now, I admit I have problems with boxing. I don't get it. Never will. Explain to me why it's perfectly OK to beat the brains out of someone but not to bite his ears? Holyfield's lawyer, Jim Thomas, said in high dudgeon, "This is a sport with rules and regulations. It's not street fighting." The idea of boxing as contained violence? Hitting someone without anger? Hurting others by the rules?

How does anyone, especially the Nevada boxing commissioner, get to say, "I'm speechless and stunned"? How does Tyson's probation officer, for gawdsakes, say, "Everyone thought he had a handle on his anger, but maybe we were wrong." A handle on his anger? Was that a left-hook handle or a right?

The gentleman's sport of fisticuffs eludes me and most of those with my chromosomes, not including the two professional woman boxers who were a warm-up act for Tyson and Holyfield. But there is something especially bizarre when this man finally becomes a pariah for breaking the rules in the ring rather than breaking the laws outside the ring.

Let us go back to those magical yesteryears. Not all the way back to adolescence when Tyson's pals remembered him mugging old ladies in the elevator. Not all the way to the days when he said that without boxing, he would have been "in jail or dead. One of those."

Just to the 1992 trial when crowds cheered the champ, and when Desiree Washington was regarded by many as either a woman who asked for it or a racial traitor trying to bring another black man down. If Evander Holyfield were a woman, these folks would have said that Mike was just nibbling her ear fondly and she took it wrong.

Fast forward to the day in 1995 when the Indiana prison doors opened and Tyson was treated as if he'd come out of retirement, not out of jail. To the hero's welcome he received in Harlem that was billed as a "Day of Redemption" though he was redeemed without ever admitting wrong.

Remember the children who danced and sang to the "The Mike Tyson Rap": "True, he's not your mom or your pops, but in some households he's got more props"—meaning respect. The rapist was a role model.

Those of us who hoped the unrepentant fighter would be shunned by fans and such moral forces as Showtime or MGM were drowned out by the sound of the cash register ringing. The ex-con was an even bigger draw.

But now—now—the phones are ringing off the hook in Nevada with folks demanding their money back. Now the Nevada State Athletic Commission has temporarily suspended him. Now the man says he will seek help to "tell me why I did what I did." Now people say, wonderingly, "he turned into a wild man."

Well, don't bite my ear off, but they're a touch late here. Assault a woman and you can still be a contender. Gnaw a tidbit off a man's ear and it's a career-suspending injury.

Desiree Washington knew Tyson a long time ago. Funny, but it wasn't until a piece of Evander Holyfield's cartilage ended up between his teeth that the fans heard the message.

July 3, 1997

T his is the scene that keeps playing in my imagination: the moment when Stephen Fagan turned to 2-year-old Wendy and 5-year-old Rachael and told them, "Your mother is dead."

He must have said it more than once. Much more than once. After all, young children ask questions. How many times over the 18½ years from the day he abducted his daughters to the day he was discovered did he have to answer questions: How did Mommy die? Where is she buried?

How did he comfort these "motherless" children? Did he tell them how he met Barbara Kurth? Did he tell them that he was sad when she died in that "car accident"? How old were they when he turned their mother into a "brilliant doctor" and their bitter divorce into a tragic death?

And did they eventually stop asking questions, reading something into the response of the parent who made their lunch, did their laundry, gave them what the younger sister called his "unfailing devotion"?

These are the details of deception through which I filter the words of the two sturdy young women standing by their father. I think of them when Rachael talks of the man who had "one full-time job, that of raising my sister and me." When Wendy, renamed Lisa, now 21, praises him as the dad who got up at 3:50 A.M to take her to swim practice, and "gave us 100 percent every day."

Rachael, already 5 when her father began weaving his lies, says he taught her to be "honest and true to myself." Lisa says, in words with a special sting, that "He was and is the best mother, father and friend anyone could ask for." He was, they concur, "always there" for them.

What is so haunting in the story is not that Fagan abducted his daughters. That happens 1,000 times a day, literally 354,000 times a year. Not even that Fagan reinvented himself, went to Palm Beach, married one and then another wealthy woman, passed himself off as a lawyer, professor, consultant, CIA agent, White House adviser. Con men are a dime a dozen.

The painful part is that he justifies 18½ years of deception by saying he did it for the sake of the children. And is found innocent by the most important jury of all: his children.

Surely it was a different era in 1979 when Fagan took his kids and ran. Back then, men had trouble getting custody. Women had trouble getting their abducted children back. Officials and the law treated parental kidnapping as a "family matter."

Fagan claims that Barbara Kurth was unfit, a drunk, neglectful. The record shows that the children were precocious, cared for, though she may have suffered from narcolepsy. As for Kurth, the victim of Fagan's imaginary car crash, we know that she was thwarted in the search for her children, that she was hospitalized for depression, that eventually she rebuilt a life, went to college, became a research scientist.

But listening to her daughters, listening to the water-cooler judgments of mother and father, I wonder. Is it conceivable that a kidnapper who turns into Mr. Mom is a good father to be forgiven? Do we expect that little of fathers? Is it conceivable that a victim who eventually gives up the search for her children is a bad mother to be damned? Do we expect that much of mothers?

I don't fault these young women. Not even their disdain for the woman they believe could have and did not find them. They have had only days to up-end their entire life story. They chose the father—How could it be otherwise?—over the stranger. It must be easier to "believe," as Lisa said, "that my father gave up his life for Rachael and I for the sole purpose of protecting us."

Stephen Fagan may believe that as well; the human capacity for self-deception is boundless. But even if we accept Fagan's tale in all its details—and I do not—at some point, this man was not acting for the sake of the children. At some point they were no longer children. At some point—the one hundredth lie? the five thousandth lie?—the father was protecting the fabric of his life and lies.

Sooner or later, surely these young women will begin to wonder and remember. They will remember the small lies. The huge deception. They'll wonder what was taken away in the name of love. But today their verdict feels like bleak injustice.

There is a classic joke about the man who murders his parents and throws himself on the mercy of the court because he is an orphan. Stephen Fagan went one better. He "murdered" Barbara Kurth, and won the praise of his children for carrying the double burdens of a single father. He created a car wreck of life and became a hero for saving the passengers. He was, you see, always there for them.

April 30, 1998

T he story comes cascading out of Washington at electronic speed, accusations and denials, factoids and speculations. A feeding frenzy of reporters, analysts and lawyers is serving up undigested tidbits liberally salted with "allegedlys." The words "affair" and "perjury" and "impeachment" pop up like uninvited guests crashing a White House dinner.

At the same time, my phone line echoes with a mournful reprise from friends, colleagues, and family offering up the most unscientific and honest and dispirited public opinion: "I can't stand this."

It's not clear what the unbearable "this" is. The waft of presidential scandal? The all-sex, all-the-time news that now treats the nation's leader like O.J., the Nanny, the Unabomber? The independent counsel wiring up a woman for sexual gotcha? The destruction of a 24-year-old woman? Of a First Family? The idea that the whole mechanism of government—peace in the Middle East, State of the Union—now takes second place to "perjury" and "peccadilloes"? All of the above?

At this moment the life of a presidency is hanging on a laundry line of "ifs." If it can be proved that Bill Clinton told Monica Lewinsky to perjure herself, it's over. If it can be proved he lied under oath, denying an affair that happened, he's dug a hole that not even the Comeback Kid can pull out of. If it can be believed that he had sex with a 21-year-old intern in the house he shared with his wife, his daughter, and the country, who can stand it, stand for it?

It is being said that this is either the worst scandal or the worst smear in presidential history. My small sample of people who are not Rush Limbaugh listeners and do not laugh at Don Imus find themselves in the unusual and uncomfortable position of actually hoping that a young woman's fantasy life got the best of her.

"I cannot believe that he would do this in the White House down the hall from the Oval Office with an intern. It's too incredible," says a friend, as if she were playing Clue. But she offers enough qualifications to leave behind a trail of her doubts.

On CNN, the political analyst Bill Schneider offers up the "good news" that if it is "just" an affair, Clinton may be saved by the cynicism of the public. Our opinion of politicians cannot be lower. We already expect the worst.

This is how far we have followed Bill Clinton, parsing his personal life as carefully as he perhaps parsed his grammar in responding to questions about whether he "was/is" having an "improper" relationship.

When Gennifer Flowers came out with tales of their affair, the public accepted the candidate's indirect admission that he "had caused pain in his marriage." The operative word was "had."

When Hillary said on television that she was no Tammy Wynette, we understood that marriage can go through a bad patch. And be patched.

When Paula Jones made her accusation, it, too, was old news, dubious news, tainted with conservative politics. In the distasteful and unseemly deposition of the president and Paula Jones, when families had the unenviable task of explaining "distinguishing characteristics" to the children, we were still uncertain about who was harassing whom.

Bill Clinton has skated ahead of the cracking ice of public opinion. His agility, his genuine political gifts, his grab-you-by-the-lapels intensity, have served him well. He ran for reelection as national dad, even as Chelsea's dad. We heard a man who understood what families are going through, how the government can help.

Dick Morris, of all people, once described Clinton as an Achilles without a heel. The heel was never the problem. As a bewildered Katie Couric wondered on television: "If the allegations are true . . . how is it this intelligent, ambitious, politically savvy man can be so foolhardy and such a slave to his libido?"

Make no mistake about it. The deal that Bill Clinton struck with the American people was that the "bimbo eruptions," the "zipper problem," the sexual risk-taking was over.

If . . . If . . . If . . . string them out along the laundry line. But if the president of the United States had an affair with a 21-year-old intern in the White House, it isn't just his wife who's been betrayed.

January 23, 1998

N ot long ago, a friend's 19-year-old son discovered that he was about to become a very unplanned parent. His not-quite-girlfriend was pregnant and determined to remain so.

Suddenly, that grandmother-to-be, a card-carrying, pro-choice feminist for most of her 50 years, was arguing ruefully about her son's right not to be a parent, about the realities of sexual entrapment, about the way her youngest child's life would be unfairly altered by this sexual act.

I was not surprised that her family had trumped her feminism, her love of son trumped her sexual politics. But I did wonder what switch had turned in her own mind. Was it loyalty? Hypocrisy? Or had she just been presented with a more complicated set of facts, a case study so close to home that it challenged and enlarged her older, simpler set of assumptions?

I think of this now during the endless sex scandal that I cannot wish away. The relentless spotlight has now turned on whether and when and why one woman should or should not believe another and another and another.

On TV, the shoe is on the other foot and the smirk on the other cheek. Women who believe Paula and Kathleen but not Anita are calling women who believe Anita but not entirely Paula or unequivocally Kathleen the same names: hypocrites, Clinton groupies in women's rights clothing.

They pull out the old clips and all the stops. See Ann Lewis circa 1991 excusing Anita Hill for following Clarence Thomas to a new job. See Ann Lewis circa 1998 saying that the letters Kathleen Willey wrote Clinton after the encounter are "a contradiction."

The political women who found Clarence Thomas's dirty talk enough to disqualify him from the Supreme Court are being asked about the latest scandals. Now many, like the usually irrepressible Barbara Mikulski, are saying, "I can't have an opinion until the judicial system works." Others swept into office in 1992 on the plank that Republicans "just don't get it" are asked what they think of Kathleen Willey. Carol Moseley-Braun, reluctantly pulled to the microphone, says we have to wait for all the facts.

Is this a change of mind or of the man in the White House? Is it loyalty, hypocrisy, or a sense of this story's complexity?

I am not surprised by this turn of events. Life is easier when politics and sexual politics dovetail, when public and private character adhere.

Nor am I surprised that the attention is on women. The love of a cat fight, the passion for a civil war among the sisterhood, runs deep. We know that Clinton needs female advocates—front women—as much as any company accused of sex discrimination needs a lawyer from the firm of Female Credibility. And we know that such sexual matters really matter to women's lives.

When all is said and done, what many will hold against Clinton is the deep discomfort of supporters who believe that he is at least a sexual mis-conduct-er with a reckless track record—yet feel bound to hold their peace. Women who talk disparagingly of the boss who hits on employees, the professor who leches after students—and yet feel compelled to give the president the benefit of any doubts.

Still, if women in the inner circle, like women in the polls, stay with the man that brought them to the White House, it is not blind loyalty or rank hypocrisy. It is that third choice: complexity.

The complexity that splits the difference between sexual consent and harassment, between a character flaw and an impeachable offense, between Clinton's behavior and Starr's, between what he said and what she said.

It's the complexity that finds Kathleen Willey credible but asks about that book deal. A complexity that is overwhelmed by the preponderance of the allegations but finds a difference between allegations and evidence. It's a complexity that is appalled by lying but can't believe that lying about sex is a crime.

I don't expect that we will ever know exactly what happened or with whom. Nor will we find a permanent line between sexual conduct and misconduct. This whole sorry tale leaves our views of men, women, sex, politics even muddier than before.

As one woman who honked for Anita Hill and clapped for Bob Packwood's exit says now, with morbid humor, "I've lost my virginity in sexual politics." No, not a hypocrite, not even blinded by loyalty. Since the Music Man marched into the White House, she's become the sadder but wiser girl.

March 22, 1998

E t tu, Mr. President?

Let me remind you of the apocryphal story that parents tell each other with a knowing laugh. It's about the mother who has been waiting nervously for "the talk."

Finally her 6-year-old son asks, "Mom, where did I come from?" She takes a deep breath and launches into the story of the birds and the bees, the egg and the sperm.

At the end, she asks her son if he understands. He says, "I guess so, but Bobby says he comes from Nebraska and Jimmy says he comes from Connecticut."

It's a story about sex, about parents and kids, but more than anything else it is about timing and what psychologists like to call "the need to know."

I tell it now because in the tawdry sex scandal that has surrounded the president, we have been both parents and kids. For all the endless jokes, the gossip, the all-Monica-all-the-time news shows, most Americans have wrestled with the question of whether we "need to know" and what we want to know.

This has been a scandal that makes Americans squirm. Parents tell me that what makes them most uncomfortable, even angry, are the questions they are now asked by their children. What is oral sex, Mom? Is oral sex adultery, Dad? Did he do it? Does that mean the president is a bad man?

If we don't want to muster up answers for our kids, it's in part because we don't want to answer for ourselves. The economy is good. Summer vacation looms. We need to fix the schools—pronto—and clean up the health care mess.

In the midst of this, many of us decided, consciously or not, that we'd rather not be told whether the president had sexual relations with an intern in the fancy public housing he calls home. We don't want to be confronted with the president's libido and personal failings. We really don't need to know this.

On Tuesday we saw the best and the worst of the complicated man we elected with our eyes open. In the Capitol Rotunda, he eulogized the two officers who died in the line of duty. Choosing just the right tone, the right lyrics, he sounded like a fine-tuned instrument. This is the president we want to believe in.

But just hours earlier, Monica Lewinsky was granted full immunity with the implication that she would testify—tell all about her and Bill. About sex. About lies. This is the man we don't believe.

Sex scandals have stuck to Clinton's political life like dog droppings on a running shoe. He's mastered the language of ambiguity and deniability. He's given and taken wiggle room.

In turn, we have told pollsters and one another that we picked him to be president, not husband; that there is a line—somewhere—between the political and personal. But like a family, indeed, like his White House staff, we have also preferred not to be presented with the lipstick marks on the cocktail glass.

Kenneth Starr, the relentless private eye of this detective novel, has been intent from the very beginning on catching the president. But Starr's unpopularity comes in part from his role as the "friend" who forces a family confrontation under the banner of truth. That's where we are now.

It seems plausible that Monica will acknowledge a sexual relationship—and do not tell me that oral sex is not sex—but no direct suborning of perjury. We will be left to digest a moral offense, not an impeachable offense.

Clinton may choose to stay in character, to turn Lewinsky's testimony into a he said/she said affair. But if he intends to show character, he must finally and publicly admit what happened. Before the subpoena drags him to the grand jury.

I say this assuming—believing—that there was a relationship of some sort between the president and the intern, despite Clinton's clenched teeth denials last winter. Monica may be, in the words of the tabloids, victim or vixen, but he is the president. And he's running out of that wiggle room.

What Congress would impeach him for what even Henry Hyde called "peccadilloes?" What congressman would hurl the first stone at him for lying about sex? Newt Gingrich?

It's not easy to fess up. Ask any parent who's seen their own image crumble in the disappointed eyes of a child. Ask any wife who's been humiliated in public.

I don't know how the larger, disputative family—the country—would react. But even those of us who wish the scandal had never been revealed cannot wish it away.

There is today, right now, an absolute "need to know."

July 30, 1998

I admit that the words ring awkwardly in my Yankee ears. "Yes, sir" and "no, sir" sound more like the language of a boot camp than a classroom.

But the Louisiana Legislature has just come up with a new language curriculum. Last week, they mandated "yes, ma'ams" and "no sirs" for schoolchildren talking to school employees.

Led by the governor, the politicians decided that you can legislate respect. Or, maybe just obedience.

The Louisiana linguistics order, which will begin in elementary school and graduate to high school, comes at a time when Americans have focused anxious attention on children. There's a kind of generalized crackdown on kids—for the sake of kids.

In the wake of Columbine, some schools have beefed up gun checks while others are testing hair for drugs. In New Jersey, Christie Whitman turned around and decided that a teen can't have an abortion without her parents being told. In Massachusetts, the state Board of Education passed a bill requiring colleges to tell parents if their under-21-year-olds are caught drinking.

Meanwhile, 82 percent of mothers in a *Redbook* survey said it was more important to keep tabs on kids than to respect their privacy. Nearly 42 percent admitted to having read their kids' diaries.

Add to that, a new bill passed by the House Thursday, to allow posting of the Ten Commandments in schools. And the recent rant by Representative Tom DeLay on "spoiled children," "law of the jungle" day-care centers, and schools that "teach the children they are nothing but glorified apes." You can feel the panic rising.

I'm not surprised by all the worrying over kids. They're worth worrying about. The Columbine massacre left parents stunned. A whole school culture was exposed under the tutelage of a principal who didn't know what was going on in the hallways. The bewildered parents of the murderers left the rest of the country wondering whether anyone actually knows what's going on in the mind of a teenager.

Now we seem to have decided that the solution to the terror is to vote in an authoritarian regime. So in Louisiana, the politicians have made respect a law. Yes, sir.

The problem is that it doesn't work that way. Sara Lawrence-Lightfoot, whose new book, *Respect,* wades thoughtfully into this subject, says: "Most people think of respect as obedience, submission to some higher authority that has more status, knowledge, and skills. But respect is not about dutiful compliance to imposed rules from on top.

"Real respect is a much more complex experience of empathy, trust, and connection. It grows in relationship and has to be nourished every day."

Lightfoot grew up as a middle-class Southern African-American using phrases like "yes, ma'am" and "yes, sir." But such words mean what they say only when they reflect the depth of the relationship, not the fear of detention hall.

Nowadays when this Harvard professor of education asks students who the good teachers are and why, she gets back the same response: "He or she respects us." That doesn't mean the teacher is a pushover or a pal. It says that he or she pays the coin of respect: attention.

Remember Columbine? "In that huge school, too many kids were invisible," she says. "The idea isn't to insist that they say 'yes, ma'am' but to create a community in which people feel valued, listened to, worthy."

The response to panic, the reaction to chaos, and the fear of violence is often a retreat to law and order. If we're worried about drugs, get the schools to test. If we can't talk about pregnancy, get the courts on our side. If we don't know what's going on in a teenager's head, grab the diary. If we can't have a civil greeting—make it a law.

But there's a tricky part to raising and teaching children: We have to gradually turn over the reins of authority. We have to renegotiate the relationship of parent and child into two connected, trusting adults. At the end of this long transition, teachers want to turn out caring, responsible—respected—grown-ups.

There is no shortcut in the business of raising the young. Children need more adults in their lives. Not more sirs and madams.

June 24, 1999

TIMOTHY MCVEIGH IS NO ENIGMA

This is how he will die. No matter that his execution has been pushed back, at some point Timothy McVeigh will be strapped to a gurney in front of five handpicked witnesses.

He will die in the middle of the *Today* show in a town flooded with media. He'll die not far from people wearing T-shirts that say "Final Justice" or "Stop the Killing."

He will die unrepentant, unapologetic, unremorseful. And, we are told, he will die an enigma.

These final days are not just a death watch. They are also an enigma watch. We are witnessing a last-ditch attempt to figure out the 33-year-old man who drove a truck loaded with a bomb up to a federal building in Oklahoma City and left the world sadder than he found it.

In one newspaper, a headline asks: "Tim McVeigh was a good kid and a good soldier. So what went wrong?" On ABC, a querulous Barbara Walters describes a man astonishingly "ordinary," "boyish," "disarmingly warm."

One cable analyst asks how this "boy next door" could have blown away children and called them "collateral damage"? Another wonders why this Bronze Star winner destroyed 168 lives and then tagged mourners the "woe-is-me crowd."

The irony behind this enigma watch is that McVeigh has repeatedly said why. He's explained his act of violence in the language of antigovernment militias, in sentiments copped from *The Turner Diaries,* in political slogans rampant among those who identify the American enemy as the American government. He has said in repeated and certain terms: "I did it for the larger good."

Yet in this remarkable hunt for the real reason, many of us simply dismiss political motives as ramblings or rants. We go on rummaging through his biography.

McVeigh talks about Ruby Ridge and we talk about the child of divorce who loved comic-book superheroes. He talks about Waco and we talk about the disappointment of a soldier who failed to become a Green Beret. He talks about government oppression and we talk about the young man who never found romance.

I am thinking of this duality because I have done it myself. I have searched for clues to terrorism in the psyche rather than in the statements. I have dug through a political or religious set of beliefs as if it were merely a cover story for a more telling psychological subtext.

But watching this story, I wonder how many other Americans have forgotten that acts of war or martyrdom or terrorism throughout history were—still are—often motivated by deep beliefs, not dysfunction. By conviction, not depression.

Crusades, car-bombings, suicide attacks, genocide. Religious strife and fascist wars and communist takeovers. Have we forgotten, in our own psychologically obsessed era, the power of ideas?

I say this not to justify McVeigh's action; quite the contrary. It's dangerous when we don't take people at their word. Their political word.

As Timothy McVeigh waits for execution, James Kopp sits in France waiting for extradition. The man who allegedly killed Dr. Barnett Slepian because he performed abortions is dismissed as a head case. But wasn't he a true believer? A good student of ideology?

And then there is Tony Soprano, the godfather of our televised imagination. In the series that has captured a huge audience, he is seen in two worlds, living by the code of the Mafia, analyzed by the code words of the shrink. What better example of how we put a template of psychology over every worldview.

John R. Smith, the court-appointed psychiatrist, says of McVeigh, "I believe he was chronically depressed as a child." He adds, "This whole project was his antidepressant." Well, maybe so.

But the same psychiatrist describes McVeigh as "an idealistic young man." Should we give depression primacy over ideology?

Today most Americans wear their politics lightly. We have a hard time imagining Democrats and Republicans coming to blows over differences in ideology. Politics is, to us, nothing to get excited about.

But what is patriotism, after all, but the willingness to die for your country? Is one man's patriotism another man's psychosis?

Why did he do it? He thinks the bombing made him a hero. I think it made him a monster.

This man is not an enigma. He's a murderer.

May 13, 2001

BOB KERREY'S—AND OUR—LONG JOURNEY BACK

Sometimes I wonder if my generation will go to our graves fighting over Vietnam.

When we start picking up Social Security checks, will we have to form two lines at the office? This one for those who believe we should never have fought in Vietnam. That one for those who believe we should never have lost in Vietnam.

Will we be sitting at dinner in a nursing home when suddenly an argument breaks out: Who was the real traitor, Robert McNamara or Jane Fonda?

Will the child that Bob Kerrey and his new wife are expecting grow into adulthood hearing us bristle and argue over words he or she can barely decode: My Lai, Agent Orange, draft dodgers? Hey, hey, LBJ?

As time goes on, "our war" recycles with less frequency but with equal ferocity. Every time we think we have achieved that mystical/medical word, "healing," something happens to remind us that the scar is a zipper, ready to reveal wounds that still lie close to the surface.

This time it is Thanh Phong, a hamlet in the Mekong Delta, that resonates through our soul and self-doubt. This time Bob Kerrey, a Vietnam vet both heroic and haunted, is questioned.

On the night of February 25, 1969, at least a dozen unarmed civilians were killed. Suddenly, Kerrey is being asked to say what happened more than half a lifetime ago, when the young Navy SEAL led his troops into what he describes as "not a military victory" but "a tragedy." Was it a firefight or a massacre? An act of war or a war crime?

His own version is searing enough.

"The thing I remember, and will remember until the day I die, is walking into a village and finding, I don't know, fourteen or so, I don't even know what the number was, women and children who were dead," he has said.

He describes his emotion as far more than guilt: "It's the shame. You can never, can never get away from it." But one member of his commando team, Gerhard Klann, describes more than shame:

He describes deliberate murder.

The New York Times and *60 Minutes II,* in raising this story from the dead, reported the conflicting memories of old soldiers. We do not know if Kerrey and other members of the team strain their own memories through the mesh of what they can bear to believe. On the other hand, we don't know if the most horrific memory is the most accurate.

Kerrey the lieutenant was 25 and terrified in the dark night of a free-fire zone. But to believe his story is not just to believe his men but to believe in the chaos of war, and in the moral chaos of this war. And that is not hard.

The former senator from Nebraska lost more than a part of his leg in Vietnam. Like so many others, he lost the boy he had been; he lost the gung-ho warrior who wanted to take Hanoi with "a knife in my teeth."

Kerrey carried the demons and moral seriousness of his Vietnam experience throughout his political career. They strengthened his ambition and burdened his ambivalence. But wearing his Medal of Honor lightly and his conscience darkly, he drew respect from both sides of this dividing line.

But I remember 1991 when Bob Kerrey offered up a lonely vote against the Gulf War. When he came out into the Senate hallway, he told reporters: "I hope you understand what we've done here today. This is not just some play on the geopolitical chessboard. We are sending boys and girls off to risk their lives and to kill people in the name of our country. You make sure that the American people understand that."

Today we look back admiringly and wistfully at "The Greatest Generation." We forget that their war produced the acronym SNAFU—situation normal, all fouled up—and their war had its Dresden bombing, its combat chaos, murdered innocents, its memories and silences.

But World War II was unequivocally just. And that is the difference.

Now we have again unzipped the war wounds of Kerrey's generation. In the days since this story broke, old doves are talking again about how we lost our innocence in Vietnam. Old hawks are talking about how we lost our nerve.

But as Senator John Kerry, a Vietnam vet himself, explains, "We did not find Hitler among the enemy; we did not see Roosevelt among those we had been sent to protect." He says, "The faults of Vietnam were those of the war, not the warriors."

Yet once again, the morality of the war lands back in the lap of the warrior. And a generation still finds peace elusive.

May 2, 2001

American Taliban at 20, he's already had an assortment of monikers. Doodoo@hooked.net. Suleymanal-Lindh. Abdul Hamid. But the label that he'll carry for the rest of his life is this one: American Taliban.

An American Taliban? Is that the ultimate oxymoron? The handle for a brainwashed cultist? A latter-day Benedict Arnold? The clash of two cultures personified in one man?

John Walker Lindh was born in 1981, named after a Beatle, John Lennon, and a chief justice, John Marshall. He was the middle child of a middle-class California family. But one morning in late November, he emerged from the flooded dungeon of the Qala Jangi prison and into the spotlight.

Face filthy, hair matted, body emaciated, speaking in tones oddly accented in Arabic, he uttered phrases incomprehensible to his country: "Yes, I supported the attack on September 11." Bragging or confessing that he was a member of Al Qaeda, that he'd met Osama bin Laden, he presented the country with a question. How did it happen? How did he go from Marin to Taliban?

In odd interviews his stunned father, Frank Lindh, sounded like the bewildered parents of the Columbine killers. He described his son as making a "bad decision," being "in the wrong place at the wrong time." He said he'd like to give his son "a little kick in the butt for not telling us what he was up to," as if the man-child had come in late from a date.

But he also said honestly and painfully, "I can't connect the dots between where John was and where John is."

Others are by no means as reticent to connect those dots into their own black-and-white portrait. We now hear that the culprit is cultural liberalism, permissiveness to the point of no return. The problem is Marin County, that much lampooned suburb of San Francisco, tolerant to a fare-thee-well.

One conservative social critic, Shelby Steele, declared that "a certain cultural liberalism cleared the way for this strange odyssey of true belief. . . . Walker came out of a self-hating stream of American life." A *Wall Street Journal* writer described Marin County as the "Mecca of moral muddling," saying that "John Walker was raised in an atmosphere so swamped with tolerance it's small wonder he began to drown."

Lord knows, Marin County is an easy place to parody. Those who live there do it all the time. It's easy to point to the Lindh parents, now divorced, who believed that their children could pick and choose any path from a spiritual smorgasbord. "It is good for a child to find a passion," said his mother, who didn't hear the alarm bell when he started down the wrong path.

And for all we know, the boy who surfed the net for information and identity, who went from hip-hop to the Koran, needed more guidance and less freedom. Indeed, maybe the unstructured school led him to grasp at what Robert Jay Lifton calls "totalism," an all-or-nothing belief system.

But let us remember that Marin County sent one son to the Taliban, not an international brigade. The Lindhs lost one child to this cult, this religious sect, this enemy, not all three children.

There is something odd in this glib profiling. Before the emergence of John Lindh from the cave, the Taliban were described as the end product of religious absolutism. Suicide bombers were held up as proof of the danger of a rigid, authoritarian education whose aim was to close minds. Their Islam was the one true faith that justified destroying Buddhas and skyscrapers alike. In contrast, America boasted of its open-mindedness. Our children are taught to think for themselves.

Now what are we saying? That authoritarianism breeds an Afghan Taliban and liberalism breeds an American Taliban? That we can blame rigid schools and patriarchal parents for terrorists but blame open schools and liberal parents for traitors?

I belong to the hands-on, engaged, worry-wart school of parenting. I cannot imagine giving my 17-year-old a blessing, let alone a check, to study Islam in Yemen. If my 19-year-old child called for more money, as John did, I'd use it for airfare. But I think it's possible to be open-minded without being air-headed, to impart values without force-feeding them. And I don't think we can glibly connect the dots that end with John Lindh in Afghanistan any more than they ended with Timothy McVeigh in Oklahoma City.

The path from Marin to Afghanistan is not a paved highway full of pilgrims but a sorry and solitary journey. Tolerance does not a Taliban make.

December 13, 2001

As someone who makes a living telling people what she thinks, I am aware that opinion-mongering is a dicey business. Even the dictionary offers this slippery definition: "a belief or conclusion held with confidence but not substantiated by positive knowledge or proof."

Of course, it is a problem if you are discussing cilantro or the Red Sox. It's more unsettling when you're talking about the law.

So when the Supreme Court ended with a bang, it left some queasiness behind. In the affirmative action case especially, there's been a good deal of conversation about the gap between Sandra Day O'Connor and Clarence Thomas.

These two justices are arguably the "affirmative action babies" of this court—the first woman and the second African-American. Each lived through an era when race or gender worked against them, and each was picked for the court at a moment when race or gender worked for them. But they ended up with opposing opinions.

The woman who graduated from Stanford Law School a half-century ago and was offered a job only as a legal secretary wrote that affirmative action is good for the country. The African-American who graduated from Yale Law School and went on to success as a black conservative argued that it is bad for the "beneficiaries."

Observing this difference, Harvard law professor Laurence Tribe muses, "Justice O'Connor drew the lesson that even though she may have received a rare boost by virtue of being a woman, the opportunity to prove oneself is wide open and no stigma needs to result." But Justice Thomas? "It seems as though from Yale Law School to the present he has lived under some kind of doubt about who he is and why he is there, and assumes that doubt is an inevitable consequence."

Not all, or even most, judicial opinions conjure up a judge's experience. But this odd couple left many asking: How much are they, or any of us, the products of our past? Is biography destiny? Or do we reshape our own biographies?

This is not just the kind of question about nature and nurture and free will you missed in Philosophy 101 or in Sunday school. For a long time, many believed that the best opinions on every subject were the products of a detached intellect. They believed justices should—and could—check their biographies at the courthouse door. They could adopt what philosopher Thomas Nagel described as the "view from nowhere."

Today, Americans are more likely to believe that everything from the political to the legal is personal. Every candidate now talks about his or her background. No judicial confirmation hearing would be complete without a life story. Indeed, part of the belief in diversity itself—on the bench or on the campus—comes from a belief in the importance of biography. We assume that in order to understand where leaders will take us, we have to know where they are coming from.

But individuals are far too complex to draw a predictable narrative line from background A to opinion B. One self-made man may conclude that we should all pick ourselves up by our bootstraps while another subsidizes bootstraps.

On the Supreme Court itself, Clarence Thomas and Antonin Scalia have little history in common, but they are joined at the head. Scalia and Anthony Kennedy, both born in 1936, both Roman Catholics, both Harvard Law School grads appointed by Ronald Reagan, couldn't have been further apart on the gay rights case. And Sandra O'Connor and Ruth Ginsburg, two brainy women of a certain generation, often take the same side on discrimination, but the Arizonan and the New Yorker part company on many issues from west and east.

Yet even in this complex context, Thomas is a paradox. He disparages the use of race and then uses it. He described a good judge as being like a stripped-down runner—someone who leaves personal history out of his rulings. Yet he oozed biography in an opinion describing affirmative action as "a cruel farce" under which "all are tarred as undeserving."

It's hard to unravel our own biographies and beliefs. We need a good dose of self-knowledge, an ability to acknowledge experiences and reflect on their impact. Indeed, it's the one way we can be enlightened by the view from somewhere, not blinded by it.

In the end, Justice Thomas, the man who wants to overturn his own past, seems trapped in it. Justice O'Connor has accepted the past and moved on. He's still uncomfortable in his seat. She has made the robe her own—and made affirmative action our own.

But then, of course, that's just my opinion.

July 10, 2003

THURMOND'S PAST IS OUR PRESENT

There's a certain justice in the fact that Trent Lott got into this passel of trouble by attending a birthday party. Not just anybody's birthday, mind you, but Strom Thurmond's one hundredth celebration.

Before Lott lauded the old Dixiecrat as the "Man Who Should Have Been President," he was all set to lead the Senate. More astonishingly, Thurmond was about to roll out of the public spotlight with no more controversial epitaph than the last words he uttered on the Senate floor: "That's all."

Now they're both tripped up on, of all things, history.

The senator from Mississippi wasn't the only one who praised the departing centenarian. The president saluted Thurmond's "patriotism, courage, and lifetime dedication to South Carolina." Senator Orrin Hatch described him as a "great" man who had "done great things in his life."

Most of the senators called him a "living legend," as if longevity was legendary. Just a few were as discreet as Chris Dodd, who said, "He's not just a witness to the entire twentieth century, he was a full participant." This diplomatic phrase reminded me of my father's response when forced to compliment an infant: "Now there's a baby."

Today Lott is getting appropriately skewered for praising the segregationist who would have saved the country from "all these problems." But Thurmond himself passed 100 in a haze of nostalgia as if he'd never done anything more controversial in public life than stand on his head and marry a beauty queen.

We don't mention the Strom Thurmond who defended Jim Crow. The Thurmond who called civil rights advocates communists. Or the presidential candidate who said, "There are not enough troops in the Army to force Southern people to admit the Negroes into our theaters, swimming pools, and homes."

Lott said he was "trying to honor the man, not the policies"—as if you could separate the two. Can you separate the Dixiecrat from segregation? Can you honor Thurmond's endurance, his bladder-defying twenty-four-hour filibuster in 1957—the longest on Senate record—without mentioning that he was filibustering against civil rights legislation?

Is it politeness or ageism that defangs the past and renders an elder harmless? A 100-year-old man gets a pass on the first two-thirds of his life?

Maybe if he lives long enough, any man who fought progress can become a "living legend" in the same way that the former groper in the elevator becomes merely a "ladies man." Did any of those C-SPAN watchers hear the joke made by a former staffer at the party? "I see so many people here today whose life Strom Thurmond has touched—and some he even squeezed." How adorable.

Lindsey Graham, who will occupy Thurmond's seat, says, "It's not fair to freeze this man in time." Eventually, Thurmond hired the first black aide in a Southern senator's office. Eventually, he voted for Martin Luther King Day. Eventually, he chose to keep his seat rather than his old ways.

But it's also not fair to edit a biography. When you clean up history, you discredit the struggle for change. You make it read as if change were inevitable. Strom Jr. said of his father, "He has a résumé that reads like a snapshot of the 20th century." That includes some appalling images.

"In some ways Trent Lott has done us a favor," says Ferrel Guillory, who teaches Southern politics at the University of North Carolina; "He forced us back into confronting history."

We have trouble with that these days. In just the last weeks, we've seen the return of Henry Kissinger, Elliott Abrams, and John Poindexter. Anybody remember Vietnam, Iran-contra?

Indeed, when history breaks through, it's like an unwelcome stranger. In the Supreme Court the other day, Clarence Thomas's baritone cut through the silence. Did a law against a burning cross violate the First Amendment? A burning cross, he said, is "unlike any symbol in our society. . . . It was intended to cause fear and terrorize a population." Anybody remember?

Near the end of his life, the segregationist George Wallace went around seeking forgiveness, even redemption. "I am not a bad man," he would say to himself and anyone who would listen. The closest Thurmond came to repentance was saying, "times have changed." Is this what they call an unapologetic conservative?

Now Lott, with a growing paper trail weighing down his political future, is expressing sorrow for "a poor choice of words" and regrets "to anyone who was offended." But Thurmond was on the wrong side of history, and so is his fan.

Maybe Lott should memorize the lesson of that other man from Mississippi, William Faulkner: "The past is never dead. It's not even past."

December 15, 2002

A fter all these years, I have finally come up with the definition of a liberal wimp. It's someone who feels sorry for Rush Limbaugh.

Here is a man who has kept 20 million dittoheads on a closed loop of right-wing rhetoric for three hours a day, five days a week, for 15 years. Here is a man for whom the word *bombastic* was invented.

Imagine what he would say about some "feminazi" caught popping 30 illegal pills a day. Imagine how forgiving he would be to an "environmental wacko" scoring OxyContin while tree-hugging. Or any liberal who had to be outed by the *National Enquirer* before he took "full responsibility for my problem."

This is a man who created so many petards over the years, it's hard to know which one to hoist him on. How about the title of his book: *See, I Told You So.* Or how about one of his many tirades against druggies: "The answer is to go out and find the ones who are getting away with it, convict them and send them up the river, too." It's Rush, after all, who complained, "We're becoming too tolerant, folks."

But every time I rev up a rant, I imagine the demigod of dittoheads skulking around a Denny's parking lot to get his fix. I imagine the man waiting, surely, for his housekeeper/drug dealer to drop a dime. I imagine a lonesome, 275-pound guy who apparently never even told his wife when he went into rehab and relapsed twice. A man so hooked he may have sacrificed his hearing to his little blues.

And I, gulp, feel sorry for him.

This is the curse of liberal wimpathy. Conservatives talk of right and wrong. Liberals talk of strengths and weaknesses. The right thinks of drug abuse in particular as a moral failing; the left thinks of it as a medical illness. When one of ours goes bad, they jump on him like a churchyard dog. When one of theirs goes bad, we tend to . . . understand.

With a few exceptions, conservatives have shown some fancy footwork in defending Rush. Former Bush speechwriter David Frum said, "I don't think any less of him for having ordinary frailties." Gary Bauer, president of American Values, made a moral distinction between getting addicted in order to get high and getting addicted to kill pain. Rich Lowry, editor of *The National Review,* defended him to Don Imus because Rush never claimed to be a victim. And a dittohead caller on his show said, "We all make mistakes."

Meanwhile, opponents, like this wimpette, who would generally like to put a sock in his mouth, are restrained to the point of gentility. Even Al Franken, who wrote *Rush Limbaugh Is a Big Fat Idiot*, said, "I don't wish that [drug addiction] on anyone." Joe Conason, author of *Big Lies*, said, "It's hard not to feel sorry for anyone whose suffering causes them to hustle narcotics." And Howie Kurtz, the media voice of a favorite Rush target, *The Washington Post*, wrote, "I suspect most people, even those who can't stand the guy, will see a man struggling with his personal demons and be careful about condemning him for his weakness."

Does being a member of the righteous right mean never having to say you're sorry? The closest Rush came to an apology is saying, "Well, I am no role model," for going into rehab. But his fans give him a prayerful pass.

His opponents, however, are members of a left that has always been touchy (and feely) about value judgments. The worst charge that a liberal launches at the personal misbehavior of a Bill Bennett or Rush Limbaugh is one of "hypocrisy!" Gasp. Last time I looked, hypocrisy wasn't even on the waiting list for additions to the Ten Commandments.

Limbaugh once described himself as an "epitome of morality, of virtue, a man you could totally trust with your wife, your daughter, and even your son in a Motel 6 overnight." We have yet to see whether the police agree. But in the court of public opinion, the talk master and voice of the angry white man, who once had his bags carried into the White House by George Bush the First, is being treated with the sort of tolerance and forgiveness that he disparages.

So call me a wimp. When bad things happen to bad people, I have trouble going for the jugular. Wimpathy by another name is plain ol' empathy. And, willy-nilly, Rush gets a slice of mine.

In his statement, Limbaugh asked us to pray for him. Well, I'll pass. But I will hope that while big Rush is in rehab, he learns to walk a corridor in somebody else's shoes.

October 16, 2003

Family Matters

I SHOULD KNOW BY NOW THAT THE CHANGES OF ONE

GENERATION PRODUCE THE CHOICES AND CONFLICTS

FOR THE NEXT. WE ARE WALKING ON GOLDA MEIR'S

BONES, AND OUR DAUGHTERS ARE WALKING ON OURS.

WE MADE A NEW PLACE; TO OUR DAUGHTERS IT'S THE

OLD PLACE. AND IT NEEDS SOME FIXING UP.

—FROM "WALKING ON OUR MOTHER'S BONES,"

JANUARY 10, 2003

I am up to my elbows in Thanksgiving prep when the phone rings. There are macadamia nuts to the right of me, pecans to the left. Flour and eggs are wrestling in my mixing bowl.

I reach for the phone, cradling it between my ear and my shoulder and hear the voice of a television producer. She wants to know whether I might be available to comment on the decline and fall of the American family. A story for the season.

As I stand there, covered in batter, she rattles off the horrific list of stories that make her case. The South Carolina mother who drowned her children. The nineteen toddlers found in a squalid Chicago apartment without food or clothes. The Pittsburgh couple who took off for two weeks without warning, abandoning three kids to teenage babysitters.

I listen to this familiar litany with an equally familiar sense of gloom, and then I decline. I'm sorry, but this afternoon, I promised to visit my mother. Tomorrow, the cousins are coming from California. The next day is our wedding anniversary. Tuesday, the young adults we call "the kids" are arriving. And there is a crisis in the care of an aged aunt.

I hang up the phone, wiping pastry dough from my hair and savoring the irony that flavored this exchange. The irony of being too busy with family to comment on its breakdown.

Folding in the last ingredients of my much-too-elaborate recipe, the annual proof of Stewart's (as in Martha) Disease, I wonder how many of us live with this duality. We are convinced that the great amorphous, generic American family is falling apart. At the same time we are occupied with family maintenance.

All year, I have heard a steady drumbeat of despair about "family values." The overwhelming majority of Americans agree—98 percent in one recent poll—that other people are not living up to their commitments. Yet in the same poll only 18 percent believe they're irresponsible themselves.

Everywhere I go, when people talk about what they value, the topic is their family. The coin of the conversational exchange between friends and even strangers is the state of their parents, their children, their spouses.

In our daily lives, we work at and for family. At four o'clock in the morning, when we worry, it's about our family.

Today, we have higher demands on ourselves as the parents of growing children and longer demands as the children of aging parents. But every morsel of evidence of success—did you read that eight out of ten high school juniors and seniors list parents as the people they trust?—comes lost in a survey of family woes.

What do we make of this duality? I wish the producer had asked me that. Some of it comes perversely from the very struggle to do a good job. The harder most of us try, the angrier we are at those who don't and at the price society pays.

But we are also reeling from something akin to negative advertising about the American family. The horror stories that make the front page, because they are so extraordinary, have slowly begun to be accepted as ordinary.

The radio talk shows, the Limbaughs and Liddys, provide an endless stream of antigovernment messages. But the Jenny Joneses and Montel Williamses, the Sally Jessy Raphaels and Geraldos present an unbroken stream of pathological families.

On any day, we can channel surf across this electronic byway from murderous mothers to husband-stealing sisters to proud mothers of teenage strippers. If Norman Rockwell's Thanksgiving family were on the air, grandpa would be a child molester, grandma a recovering drug abuser and the kids would bear sexually transmitted diseases. The abnormal is the norm.

I'm hardly a Pollyanna about family life. I know about the stress of the sandwich generation, trying to be all things to all bosses, parents, children, spouses.

I know that every family has troubles. At some time or other, in some light or other, we all look dysfunctional. But the fact is that most of us are functioning. And loving.

Somewhere along the way Americans have lost a sense of proportion. We've come to believe that I'm OK, but you're not, and that thing called The American Family is most certainly not.

This Thanksgiving Day has always been been more about family than food. It's the time when Americans travel through airports, highways, ZIP codes, in order to squeeze around the family table and discover how many adults can sit on a piano bench.

Standing in my kitchen, covered in homebaked proof of my holiday excess, I wonder if those of us who are connected by bonds of DNA, marriage, affection and above all else, commitment, can forget for a while that we're supposed to be falling apart.

November 24, 1994

MEET YOUR CHILDREN

S ome time ago, my friends adopted a baby and set about the business of getting to know him.

I watched this process from a distance of many miles and from a perspective of many parenting years. I saw them become familiar with their son, and become family in the slow way that other people become friends.

The boy had come from another continent at the age of six months. He traveled here out of his own brief history on their passport, and they seemed to regard him from the very beginning as both their baby and his own person. They paid studious attention to this new subject of their affection—not just to their affection.

The boy woke up slowly in the morning, happy with some time alone. Then, on some internal cue, he started a small lament that would, if untended, turn into a loud, raucous cry of need. He had a greed for breakfast, a taste for apricots, a temperament that was cheerful and careful.

Over the months, I saw them taking cues from this little boy. People who were, in their own lives, curious and impatient were, in their son's life, curious and patient.

The father was a man who had, in youth, jumped onto racing bikes and out of planes. The boy approached a new tricycle as if he had to memorize the driver's manual before he stepped on the pedals.

The mother was a woman who tore apart the pieces of a broken toaster and reassembled them—usually—from memory. The son was one of those children who studied his toys before he played with them.

They noted these differences with amusement rather than surprise. And let the boy set his own pace.

The point—or at least the point to me—was that their parenting had come without a full genetic set of assumptions. This son was no more different from his parents than many biological children. But the parents were different.

They didn't assume that their own strengths and weaknesses had traveled along the DNA to their offspring. They didn't assume that he had inherited his mother's nearsightedness or musical talent, his father's straight teeth or short attention span or mathphobia.

They didn't look for proof that he was just like them, or just like Aunt Emily, or just like Grandpa Bill.

So they set out to know him as himself. And in the process let him be himself.

I have been a parent for over two decades. A biological mother, a birth mother, a child-raising mother, an adult child's mother . . . the works. And it seems to me that my friends started out in the parenting business one step ahead of the rest of us.

Those of us who give our genes as well as our love to children set out to reproduce . . . ourselves. We deliver unconscious expectations in the birthing room. We think we know them. Because they are ours.

During their early years, we often assume that they will be as much like us in interests, in habits, in mind-sets, in hopes, dreams, whatever, as they are in biology.

The absolute cliché of parenting is surprise. It's the tennis coach surprised to find that his son prefers to read. The down-to-earth parents surprised at the fanciful inner life of the child.

Parents say, "I don't know where she gets it from." We say—if only to ourselves—that nobody in our family ever played rugby or the cello. Our people were always quick at languages or mechanics.

Only later, sometimes much later, are we forced to get to know our children as they are, to stop assuming and start listening or watching. In adolescence they begin to insist, noisily, sometimes angrily, on their own identities. In their 20s we stop, finally, raising them and start, finally, listening to them. Or else we lose them.

What I have learned from my friends and from their son is that our children may be our own, but we can't claim ownership. What I have learned is that sooner, in their case, or later, in mine, we must learn to share children. We share them with the world. But most particularly, we learn to share them with themselves.

August 29, 1993

A CHILD ROBBED OF HER CHILDHOOD

She was barely old enough to fly alone . . . as a passenger. The Jessica Dubroff who shines out from all the videotape looks like one of those precocious children, the unaccompanied minors, who sometimes sit next to you on a plane.

With a baseball cap boasting "Women Fly," she was the child who gets the kiddie meals, the flight attendant's attention. The kid who always wants the window seat.

This was what this 7-year-old liked best about flying—looking out the window. "It's a joy for me to be up in the air," she said, and you could feel it. What she wanted to do on this trip was see the Statue of Liberty. Kid stuff.

What she also wanted, or what her dad wanted, or what she came to want—choose one of the above—was, of course, to break the record, to become the youngest pilot to cross the country in the glare of the spotlight.

So on Wednesday morning, this 4-foot-2 child in a pint-sized leather flight jacket strapped herself into a booster seat, put her feet on the extenders used to reach the pedals and set off to play pilot.

The stories that morning treated her like a midget Amelia Earhart. A girl with a dream. Her quest was framed by the camera like some cute, brave stunt. As one reporter put it, "It was a neat story about a neat kid." Quite the little gal.

Even then, many of us—parents who cannot put our kids in a car without worrying—wondered about the madness of this mission. But we shook our heads and went about our business. Until, that is, Thursday morning when the adventure and the lives of this girl, her father, and her instructor crashed near an airport in Cheyenne, Wyoming.

I will not be glib over their graves. But spare me the explanations of how safe flying is—even a child can do it—with a double set of controls. Maybe adult judgment about the weather is to blame for the crash, not a child's ability. It may have been nothing more than an accident.

But should a 7-year-old who cannot drive a car be allowed to fly a plane? Of course not. Should a 7-year-old, however bright, however eager, be allowed to set off on an eight-day endurance contest to break a record? Of course not.

To me, the story of Jessica Dubroff is not just about the tragic end of one child's life. It offers some chilling footnotes on the end of childhood.

With all due respect for the dead, I cannot get over the words of Jessica's late father: "This is just another experience that Jess has selected for herself."

With all due understanding for the grieving, I keep hearing the words of Jessica's mother: "I don't want this to mean that you hold your children down, you don't give them freedom and choice. And God, that's what her beauty was. She got to choose."

What do such words of choice and independence mean when you are talking about a 7-year-old?

This is an odd time in our history. We seem to be caught between protecting our children and pressuring them to grow up.

Jessica herself was shielded from the risks of watching television and the uncertainties of public education. But she was allowed to fly a plane. If her divorced parents prided themselves on anything, it was their children's joyful spirit. But was Jessica as vulnerable as any child to a parent's pride in her performance?

Today, Americans lobby for V-chips but praise precocity. We want 17-year-olds to wait for sex but 12-year-olds to go for the gold. We applaud when children are prosecuted as adults but cheer when they perform like adults.

When we tell our children to act their age, we are not telling them to act like children.

In sports, the stars are getting younger and younger. The 16-year-old gymnast has become the 13-year-old. Women's tennis has become girl's tennis. Children are encouraged to be the first, or at least the youngest.

In 1993, an 11-year-old became the youngest pilot to cross the country. In 1994, the record went to a 9-year-old. In 1995, the pilot was 8. Jessica was 7 when she died trying. With a network camera in the cockpit and adults cheering her on.

In the eighteenth century, children were dressed and treated like short adults. The line between childhood and adulthood barely existed. Now at the end of the twentieth century, on the ground and in the air, the line is blurred again.

A family friend said of Jessica, "She was 7—going on 20." He meant that as a compliment. But, in fact, this child was 7, going on 8. And she will never see 20.

April 14, 1996

OVERWORK OVERWHELMS

I t's dusk now when I leave the office. The day is turning up its hem like a new fall skirt.

I see the kids in my neighborhood scurrying to comply with parents' orders that they be home before dark. Orders that the parents cannot always obey themselves.

On my way home these days, I think of my own childhood, of the fathers coming home on the same commuter trains, walking up the same streets at the same hour each day. Today it is the children who greet their parents.

My father was home by six. I suppose some modern company, proud of its high-pressure productivity, would describe his schedule as "mommy hours." But in the 1950s most of the fathers worked "mommy hours." In the 1950s, most of them earned "family wages."

Not so in the 1990s.

It's not a news bulletin that we have evolved to a two-worker economy. If ever a final chapter was written on the Ozzie and Harriet era, it was Harriet Nelson's death this week.

Nor is it news that "the family wage" is now the combined salary of two parents who may be working two shifts, or three jobs. In the endless reruns of the old sitcom, the surprise is not just that Harriet is home, but that Ozzie is home.

In some reverse of labor history, the working class of today—upper, middle, lower working class, which is to say nearly everyone—works longer hours than most of our parents. We seem to be evolving into two classes, the underemployed and the overemployed—those who are desperate for work and those who are desperate for time. Especially family time.

When the autoworkers struck at the GM plant in Flint, Michigan, last week, the tired middle-aged men and women carrying picket signs talked of 66-hour workweeks, of mandatory overtime, of missed Little Leagues and birthday parties, of lives that weren't lived. The overtime had once been gravy. Now they were drowning in gravy. What good is more money, they said in a dozen different voices, if you don't have time?

In some ways, they told the story that echoes across the country. In manufacturing jobs, the average workweek is now some 41 hours, higher than at any time since World War II. That average includes a substantial portion of workers for whom eight and ten hours of overtime have become routine.

In the white-collar world the average workweek is now just under 44 hours. Among executives it's 46.5 hours. Among male executives, it's 48.2 hours. In every workplace that's been downsized and sped up, in every office where workers are doing three jobs for the price of two, in every office where the CEO brags that "productivity" is up, the workload is going up and up.

Employers have learned that it's cheaper to pay fewer people more money than to hire more people and pay benefits. Workers have learned that those who say "no" may be the next to go.

Not long ago the president wondered out loud, how come the economy is doing better and we don't feel better: "Why aren't we happier?" There's no big secret.

As economist Juliet Schor, who authored *The Overworked American,* says, Americans feel a decline in their economic quality of life. Scratch the surface of that discontent and you find that "the time issue is very central to how they feel about what they are doing."

"In every poll," she says, "we see a larger fraction of people saying they want more time off the job." In a Gallup Poll, a third of the work force said they would choose shorter hours in exchange for a 20 percent pay cut. If it were offered.

Instead, in this peculiar economic recovery, many find the work hours growing longer. As that happens, what Schor calls "the culture of resistance" is growing stronger. Especially among the struggling descendants of Ozzie and Harriet.

Just last month, a USAir flight attendant with a husband at work, a babysitter going out the door and a 6-year-old in bed with chicken pox was ordered to take a late overtime flight away from home. For arguing with the scheduler she was fired.

Now in Flint, Mich., a modest victory has been won by workers who struck for less money and more life. GM has tentatively agreed to hire more permanent workers.

At last the message of the resistance movement is echoing from one workplace to the next. In the new, lean, mean economy of the 90s, the currency in shortest supply and greatest demand, is the one called time.

October 6, 1994

STRANGERS AND DANGERS
ON A SUMMER DAY

CASCO BAY, MAINE—I pass the children every day now as they walk and bike down the island roads by themselves. They are off on their own errands or adventures.

The parents who come here from the mainland have finally shed their anxieties like three-piece suits. Sometimes it takes days for city folks to let a 4-year-old out of their grasp and an 8-year-old out of their sight. It takes days for parents to feel safe and for children to be set free.

Gradually the summer adults ratchet down the level of warnings they routinely deliver to their children. They go from "beware of strangers" to "watch out for poison ivy." Gradually the children, unleashed, grow sturdy with independence. And trust.

Just this morning, a small girl I don't know stopped me on my walk to point out an injured swallowtail. We talked for a minute about the fragility of a butterfly's wings and then went our separate ways.

It was a passing event but one that might never have happened on a city street. In cities, suburbs, even small towns, children are now carefully taught to be afraid of people they don't know. Their wariness is worn like a shield. A stranger becomes reluctant to penetrate that defense.

Far south of here, in Union, South Carolina, Susan Smith has gone on trial for drowning her two small children. As the cameras return to that little town, I remember how this saga began. Not as a horror story of two children buckled into their death seats by their mother, but as a classic, mythic tale of the stranger.

Susan Smith came to national fame as a distraught mother, a self-described victim of carjacking and kidnapping. When it all unraveled and she was taken to court for arraignment, many people lined the streets shouting epithets at her. One woman said it all: "We believed you!" It was strikingly easy to play upon the fear of the stranger.

Far west of here, in Petaluma, California, another murder trial has begun this week. This defendant is indeed the stranger, a man named Richard Allen Davis, who confessed to abducting 12-year-old Polly Klaas at knifepoint from a slumber party while her sister and mother slept nearby.

Nearly two years later, another Petaluma mother of kids 11 and 13 says, "I'm still very leery when my kids go out. I won't let them go out by themselves. I say, 'Remember Polly Klaas.' "

In vastly different ways, these two horrifying trials are evidence of what has become a national obsession with the fear of strangers. As fact and fantasy, they are evidence of our terror about the abduction of our children.

It was only a decade ago that missing children became as common on milk cartons as nutritional labels. It wasn't until then that we began to fingerprint and toothprint children. But by 1991 a study in *Clinical Pediatrics* showed that parents had more frequent worries about abduction than about anything else, even car accidents. That was before Polly Klaas' death.

In fact there are two hundred to three hundred kidnappings a year by non-family members out of sixty-three million American children. The missing children on the milk cartons have most likely been taken by a noncustodial parent.

However bone-chilling the idea of stranger-danger, more children are murdered by parents than kidnapped by strangers. Susan Smith is more the norm than Richard Allen Davis.

Yet every magazine has had its cover stories on stranger-danger. Every television show its scare segments. Every school its lessons. In every home, parents wrestle with their terrors and with how to warn their children away from the unfamiliar.

I'm not surprised that we have become so protective of children. It isn't just the broadcasting of such tales. We live in a time when neighborhoods and families are less stable. As our children spend more time out of our care, we worry more. As we know fewer people in our communities, there are, by definition, more outsiders.

But at some point in time, we must also begin to acknowledge the risks of protectiveness. Risks that come when children are taught to be afraid. Risks that come to a diverse society when kids grow up suspicious of "others."

Without even knowing it and with the best of intentions, we can stunt our children with our deep longing to keep them safe.

Somewhere along the torturous way, somewhere between the reality of Richard Allen Davis and fantasy of Susan Smith, the freedom to ride a bicycle and the independence to walk up the road by yourself is becoming a sometime, summertime thing. These days, even the ease of talking with a grown-up about butterflies can, and maybe has, become as rare as a July day on an island road.

July 13, 1995

N ow the Bible is turned on its head: The sins of the sons are visited upon the fathers.

In the days since the Littleton massacre, the country's eyes have turned to the families of Dylan Klebold and Eric Harris. We've racked up the evidence—a handwritten diary, a sawed-off shotgun on the dresser, bomb makings in the garage—and asked: Where were the parents?

The angry sheriff said, "Parents should be accountable for their kids' actions." The governor said, "Charges will and should be filed." The attorney general talked about criminal liability. The president advanced a gun control package that would make parents outlaws if their children commit crimes.

At last the advocates of parental responsibility laws seem to have found their poster parents. The Most Wanted parents now are the Klebolds and the Harrises—parents whose unfathomable grief is laced with the arsenic of unending "whys."

How reassuring it is to point a finger at Wayne and Kathy Harris, Thomas and Susan Klebold, as proof that we would have known—wouldn't we? How easy to cast them as stunningly, aberrantly "irresponsible" rather than listen to the minister who buried Dylan: "He was their son—but they don't know the kid who did this."

But how do we judge the "crime" of irresponsibility?

In the last few years waves of laws have been passed to hold parents legally culpable for the actions of their children. These laws were born, understandably, in despair about parents who willfully excuse themselves from the work they give birth to.

Since then, a Michigan couple was fined for failing to supervise their drug-using, church-robbing, one-boy crime wave. A Florida mother was sentenced to probation because three of her five children refused to go to school. In Illinois, the parents of a 13-year-old sued the parents of a 17-year-old who murdered their daughter. In Louisiana and California, parents can go to jail if their kids fall in with gangs. Thousands have been fined, sued, or sentenced to counseling or jail.

But the truth is that in many cases it is not at all clear whether the parents were ineffectual or evil, gave up control, or had it wrested away by their teenagers. Some didn't try, but others, like the jailed mother of the truants, said, "You know, you can try like hell and fail."

In the wake of this shooting, how many parents have breached the forbidden threshold to their teenagers' rooms, searching the drawers, the closets, opening the diaries, checking the computer "bookmarks" and "favorites." Suspicion is the order of the post-Littleton day, and distrust has been revalidated as the responsible act.

But is there anyone who doesn't know the line that we walk as parents of teenagers? How can you screw up raising a teenager? Let me count the ways. By being too authoritarian, too lax, too intrusive, too removed, by treating them like children, by assuming they're adults, by trusting them, by mistrusting them.

Getting into a teenager's mind is like spelunking down a cave without a miner's light. It's a wonder more of us don't get lost.

The Klebolds and the Harrises were not Fagin-like adults who set up their sons in the business of murder. We hold them responsible rather for what they did not know and did not do. For the diary, the Web sites, the trench coats, the arsenal. Where were the parents?

But as the days go on we get another view that seems more complicated than criminal. A judge remembers that when the boys were in trouble the two dads came to court, set up curfews, took control. A Little League coach describes the Harrises this way, "Eric's parents are what we could call dream parents." A pastor portrays the Klebolds as "hardworking, very intelligent."

As for warning signs, put these beside the trench coat. In the last weeks of their lives, Eric was trying to enlist in the Marines and Dylan had gone with his father to place a deposit on a college room. As Thomas Klebold told his pastor, "I thought I was ready to let him go—he was a finished product."

I remember my own fury at other parents who put my daughter at risk by their laxity. I also remember what my parents knew of my inner life at 17—absolutely nothing.

Parental responsibility, neighbor responsibility, school responsibility, peer responsibility? Do we criminalize parents as if they were the sole owners of an 18-year-old?

Before we prosecute parents for the sins of their children, I have a question. Tell me what punishment the law can administer that's greater than a life sentence of pain for families who will forever ask themselves "Why?"

May 2, 1999

OF JEWELS AND LAWS

S ooner or later it always comes down to earrings.

At some point in the debate, a legislator, politician, or moralist who has never previously shown the slightest interest in the public policy on body piercing will utter the same rhetorical battle cry:

"If a teenager can't get her ears pierced without parental consent, why should she be able to get an abortion?"

Frankly, the analogy still escapes me. We are, after all, talking about the realities of reproduction, not jewelry.

Teenagers can have sex (alas) without parental notification. Teenagers can continue a pregnancy, receive prenatal care, and indeed deliver a baby without having our names on the hospital permission slip. They can even give the baby up for adoption without our say-so.

Nevertheless, about half the states have passed laws that say there is one thing a teenage girl can't do without the notification or consent of a parent or judge: She can't end her pregnancy.

And now Congress is poised to top that with another little gem.

When they return next week, the House is expected to vote on a bill that would make it a crime to accompany a minor across state lines for an abortion if the requirements of her home state aren't met. A sister, aunt, grandmother, or friend who drives a pregnant teenager from a state with parental consent laws to a state without such laws would be a criminal.

This bill is euphemistically called the Child Custody Protection Act, as if strangers all over America were abducting pregnant girls from their homes. It's wrapped in slogans about family and child-parent communication.

Indeed, with all the pro-life pressure and pro-family dressing, says Harvard law professor Larry Tribe, "it is hard to get people to pause, peel back the label and say this is not about protecting parental custody of children at all, but singling out abortion for unique burdens."

How unique? For one thing, the law casually turns the federal system into a pretzel. It says that an American citizen must obey the laws of her home state even when she goes over the state line. That's akin to making it illegal to cross the border in order to drink, gamble, or shop on Sunday. Under the federal system, states are expected to have different laws. Citizens are allowed to vote with their feet.

Today, Iowa has a different idea about how you protect a pregnant minor than neighboring Illinois, and Massachusetts has a different idea than New Hampshire. But under this bill, a citizen of Massachusetts who goes to New Hampshire is still subject to Massachusetts's rules. As Tribe says, "It's not quite imprisoning you within your home state, but it comes pretty close."

One can only imagine the checkpoints for enforcing these laws at the state borders. As Gloria Feldt of Planned Parenthood says, "What are they going to do next? Dogs and searchlights?"

More bizarre is the fact that this law wouldn't make it illegal for the girl herself to cross state lines to get an abortion without involving parents. It would make it illegal for the person—sister, aunt, friend—assisting her.

The most desperate of pregnant teenagers, the very ones who won't talk to their parents, or hassle through the judicial bypass process, will be the ones forced to go it all alone.

Now let me say that I won my merit badge in raising a teenager. I wholly understand the gut fear that something is going on in our child's life and we're out of the loop. I understand the fury that someone else could take our daughter through a crisis without our knowledge.

But I also know that most teenage girls—more than 75 percent of those under 16—have talked to a parent before seeking an abortion. I know some can't or think they can't—and that a third of those who don't notify parents have been victims of family violence. These figures stay the same in states with and without consent laws.

Despite all the ear-piercing rhetoric, this is the bottom line: You can't write a law forcing parent-child communication. That requires a very different set of family skills. It has little to do with earrings. And a lot to do with listening.

July 9, 1998

THE ANSWER IS LOVE, NOT SCIENCE

T he irony is that it all began as a plea for child support. Paula Johnson took her ex-boyfriend Carlton Conley to court in search of more money for 3-year-old Callie Marie.

The judge in turn ordered a paternity test. That's how deep the relationship between biology and family law goes. For the most part, the law says: No blood, no money. No DNA, no obligation.

The paternity test proved that Carlton wasn't the biological father. But more startling was a maternity test proving that Paula wasn't the biological mother.

That's how we came to know that Callie and another little girl named Rebecca were sent home from the hospital in the arms of each other's birth mother.

All week the headlines have read "Switched at Birth," as if this family affair were a Gilbert and Sullivan comedy. Which it is not. It's been labeled routinely as "every parent's nightmare." Which it also is not. Every parent's nightmare is the July 4 car wreck that killed Kevin Chittum and Whitney Rogers before they knew their Rebecca was born to Paula.

As reporters descended on two Virginia towns, we heard all sorts of commentators talking casually about "the wrong child" or "the wrong parents." We heard townsfolk saying how "sad" it is that two women were each "raising a child who wasn't hers."

It took a distraught Paula Johnson to set the emotional record straight when she told a packed news conference the truth about "this mistake." Sounding precisely like a distraught mother, she said of Callie: "I love her wholeheartedly, with all my heart. There isn't anything I wouldn't do for her."

It's not a surprise that the tale of the two babies has grabbed our attention. It swirls around a primal question: What exactly makes a child "ours"? The DNA we contribute or the time and love? The womb or the sweat equity?

Today nature again seems to be trumping nurture. We have developed a passion for the genetic basis of everything. We have parents seeking any high-tech method possible to have "their own" children. We have adult adoptees routinely searching for birth parents.

By and large, the law also weighs in on the side of biology. Yet we know that there is a larger duality. We know it from the experience of adoptive parents and from our own gut.

We can see this duality in Paula Johnson's love for Callie. And her curiosity about Rebecca: "She looks just like me." We can see Rebecca's grandparents' devotion. And their hope against hope that the 3-year-old now being tested has their genes.

Few of us can imagine "swapping"—like shoes—the child we raised and loved for the child we bore and do not know. And few of us can imagine forgetting the other child's existence.

Any court case—and I do not mean the inevitable lawsuit against the hospital—would raise questions hard enough to stump a jury of Solomons.

Who has first dibs on an orphaned Rebecca? The biological mother or unbiological grandparents? If Rebecca belongs with her birth mother, what about Callie? Is she better off with the woman who raised her? And what of the biological father? Does Carlton have rights or obligations to either of these "daughters"? Does it matter that he has been accused of battering Paula?

For that matter, what happens to the younger "sister" and older "brothers" of these girls? How on earth, finally, do we assess the best interests of these children?

With such a list, the one hope for Rebecca and Callie is for the adults to follow their original instincts. To stay as far from family court and custody fights as possible.

These were already, to put it mildly, nontraditional families. Neither set of parents married. The Johnson children have more than one father; there are two pairs of grandparents now raising Rebecca.

The choice is between the worst of two worlds and the better of two worlds. Either both families and both daughters will be torn, wrenched apart physically or emotionally, or a new family will be stitched carefully, extended uneasily, created and recreated one step and one visit at a time.

What makes a child "ours"? Sometimes it's genes. But it's always caring. Who do the girls "belong to"? The whole family—if they can make it work.

August 9, 1998

TAKING DAD'S CAR KEYS AWAY

"Well, I'm off. Wish me luck," says my fellow traveler as he rolls his carry-on bag down the aisle and out of the plane. "I'll come back with the car keys or on them," he adds with an Odyssean touch as he disappears into the terminal.

We have flown together up the fogbound East Coast to the town that this man grew up in and that his parents still call home. Sometime between the long-delayed liftoff and landing, he described the classical task set before him this weekend: to convince, to urge or, if necessary, to order his 83-year-old father to give up his place in the driver's seat.

This is what has happened over the past year. His father's lingering pride has come into conflict with his failing eyesight. One car accident escalated into the next until finally he drove over the curb and into a neighbor's trash barrels. Next time, the family worries, it could be a neighbor's child.

The task of key removal has fallen to this eldest son, a 56-year-old manager, by birth order and default. His mother had said, "I can't talk to him about it." His brother had demurred, "He listens to you best." And so the manager bought a ticket and took on a job that looms as an unexpected and unwelcome filial chore.

What was on this son's mind as we circled over Providence en route to the last roundup of the old man's Taurus? The middle-aged son was remembering the time, forty years ago, when this dad taught him how to drive.

They headed for an empty supermarket parking lot. The father handed over the keys, the sweaty-palmed son grabbed the shift. The father patiently taught him to drive, stop, start, park, clutch in and out. The older man gave the younger his wheels.

It was a rite of passage to independence that this son repeated with his own sons—with a car that had automatic drive and a teacher with less patience. Now it has come to this, he said uneasily, a much less welcome rite of return passage.

As we part company it occurs to me that my fellow traveler has not embarked on this route alone. The manager is part of a much less-recognized sandwich generation: the triple-decker generation. The middle-aged children of elderly parents, the 50- and 60-something children of 80- and 90-something parents.

These days, I meet more and more people who are the filling between adult children and aged parents. Their emptying and empty nests are bursting—surprisingly—with worries about parents.

I hear friends with fledgling grandchildren focused on their own fading parents. I hear them saying, we have raised our children and now we are—what is the right word?—lowering our mothers and fathers.

Our country is growing older by the decade. Many of our parents have outlived their own parents by a decade or two. If the baby boomers are unprepared for Social Security they will be even less prepared for providing this emotional support.

There is no Dr. Spock for the middle-aged and young-old children of elderly parents. There is nothing that sets out what to expect dealing with the stages of 70s, 80s, 90s. There are no Terrible (Seventy-) Twos.

We don't even have a language for that process by which we try to take care of aging parents, to watch out for them and yet respect their independence. We have few ways of thinking about whether it is our right and when it is our responsibility to ease them out of the driver's seat.

In raising children, we are told, the pendulum swings between permissiveness and authoritarianism. Between exercising too much or too little control. But what about relating to our elders? How do we avoid being overbearing or neglectful? When does our respect for their autonomy leave them in the lurch? When does caretaking take away their own power? The gears do not mesh easily.

Add to that the fact that the triple-decker generation is now in the penumbra of its own old age. We are now caring for our elders while looking around a corner of two or three decades at what we too would want. And what we will do.

For my fellow traveler the car keys are a real problem, but also a symbol. With luck, his father will give him another driver's lesson, and show him how to navigate this twist in the road with grace and good sense—as a passenger.

But for the moment, I cannot help wondering why the parents who gave us those wheels never taught us how hard it is to put our family roles into reverse.

May 31, 1998

T oward the end of this marriage-in-everything-but-name, this wedding-in-every-sense-except-the-legal, the rabbi lay two wrapped glasses on the lawn. One was for my cousin Adam. The other for his partner, Rodrick.

The rabbi told the friends and family on that meadow that the custom of breaking the glass had many origins, but one seemed to fit this occasion. Once, people believed that there were demons in the world out to thwart the chance for human happiness and to harm the couple. So the couple broke the glass to scare them away.

No, there were no demons in our late summer gathering, unless you count the mosquitoes. But we understood the rabbi's analogy when he offered his blessing. May the breaking of this glass, he said, protect Adam and Rodrick from "contemporary demons who seek to denigrate their love and deny the sanctity of their relationship."

So when they shattered the glasses with a matched set of determined footsteps, there was a spontaneous cheer of "mazel tov," good luck.

Adam and Rodrick had invited us to celebrate their commitment. It is the word *celebrate* that graced their invitation. We were not invited to tolerate their commitment. We were not invited to accept it. We were invited to celebrate it.

There were some people who had come a long way to be there, and I do not mean just geographically. Together, we witnessed this pair standing under the canopy made of one's grandmother's lace tablecloth, drinking the wine out of another's great-grandfather's cup. We were there to toast two people who had found each other and pledged to each other.

But I am writing about this family event, with their blessings, because of those demons.

Much is written these days about gay rights and gay marriage, about advances and backlash. Just north of here, in Vermont, the state has approved civil unions. In Canada, gay marriage may soon be the law of the land. In Massachusetts, we are waiting for a high court ruling on whether the state can still deny what many families, friends, rabbis, and ministers now celebrate.

In the meantime, a conservative movement has made opposition to gay marriage its centerpiece of recruiting and fund-raising. One group has declared Oct. 12 Marriage Promotion Week. There's pressure for a constitutional amendment to prevent same-sex marriage. And on some pulpit or dais, a religious or political figure is preaching again that God created Adam and Eve, not Adam and Steve. He doesn't know Adam and Rodrick.

Their ceremony was not a political statement. A lawyer and a college fund-raiser, both in their 30s, they are not a gay poster couple. Adam and Rodrick—forgive me, guys—would not make the Fab Five in *Queer Eye for the Straight Guy*. Adam would have worn a T-shirt and jeans to this event, if anyone had let him get away with it. The closest he's ever been to offering home-decorating advice is the day he emptied an impoverished client's apartment of a ton of newspapers so the man wouldn't get evicted.

Still, when I am told by Focus on the Family that gay marriage would be "a devastating and potentially fatal blow to the traditional family," I think about my cousin and the warm, funny Southerner he has brought into our lives.

What exactly is so "devastating" about the couple who bring an annual excess of mixed olives and good cheer to Thanksgiving? How on earth could their commitment—or marriage—for better or for worse, be a "fatal blow" to my own marriage? For that matter, how could their desire to adopt and raise children undermine their cousins' families? My daughter, stepdaughter, and nieces, all deep in parenting, only hope that the next generation of cousins will grow up together the way they did.

In the middle of the evening, during dancing far too reckless for any middle-aged back, I realized again that what seems to me so rich about America—this great, open, changing, diverse society—is what frightens and sometimes angers others. They see an assault on family values. We see family. Our family. Our values.

My Uncle Mike, who has been married to my Aunt Charlotte for 62 years, carries an image from his days as a World War II bombardier. In aerial navigation, no matter how lost you are, once you spot the North Star you're safe and can find your way home. If you are lucky in love and life, he says, you find your North Star, your lodestar, your home in times of trouble, the fixed person in your universe.

That's what we want for our children. It's what we want whether they are Adam and Eve or Adam and Rodrick.

October 5, 2003

I f you ever find out who came up with the old saying about motherhood and apple pie, let me at 'em. Apple pie may be the bland and generic American dessert but the idea that the mother 'hood is a placid suburb of agreement that thrives on a diet of platitudes doesn't fit my vision of the modern landscape.

We may wake up Sunday with breakfast in bed and a bouquet in the vase, but this Mother's Day truce won't last as long as the flowers. Childbearing-and-raising has become a fractious territory. We've argued so intently about biology and economy that motherhood has become, well, the mother of all controversies.

Consider what's going on now at either end of the financial and fertile scale. On one end, we are worried about poor and young mothers having children. On the other, we are worried about well-to-do and older mothers not having children.

Over the past generation the weight of the culture has turned the tide of teenage motherhood. There is universal agreement that the young and the hormonal need to postpone childbearing.

We know that young women get financially and even emotionally derailed by maternity. We repeatedly warn teenagers that they need to get their own futures together before they take on another future.

Meanwhile back on the *Time* magazine/*60 Minutes*/op-ed front, we are in the midst of another round of anxiety-producing statistics about whether uppity women end up alone. Or at least without children.

Sylvia Hewlett's book, *Creating a Life,* which dovetails with some new fertility research, has focused the national eye on high-end women who follow the plan to make the most of themselves and then find they can't make babies. Her survey of 1,168 professional women found that 42 percent of 40-year-old executives in corporate America are childless. Not because they've made a choice, she says, but because of what one woman calls "creeping nonchoice."

Well, I have been around surveys too long not to be a skeptic. So I wonder if we are dealing with chickens or eggs. Half-full cups or half-empty.

The women she surveyed may be childless because they're successful or successful because they are childless. For that matter, 28 percent of college graduates among the first generation of uppity women, circa 1920, had no children between the ages of 35 and 44. That number is down to 20 percent. And if half the women making $100,000 today are childless, is that progress or regress?

As for "choices" and "creeping nonchoices," I'm not sure how you tell the difference. I'm not even sure that Hewlett is a reliable guide. After all, Hewlett went through three years of fertility treatments to have her fourth biological child at 51.

Mind you, the recent debunking of hype on fertility treatments is long overdue. But in the furor of the timing-crunch of biological and professional clocks, we've been left with lingering and dual social messages.

Kids: If you can't afford them, don't have them. But if you wait to afford them, will you still be able to have them?

Kids: Don't have them until you finish school, find a good job, find a good husband, and maybe even find yourself. Don't wait too long and do too well or you'll end up on the cover of *Time* mournfully cradling a Palm Pilot and a briefcase.

Is this a Mother's Day greeting? I'm all in favor of planned parenthood, but the window of opportunity barely lets in enough air to get a Lamaze breath.

Hewlett's heartfelt advice to young women in this timing-crunch was enough to make many of us laugh down memory lane. She tells them, "Figure out what you want your life to look like at 45" and "be as strategic about your private life as you are about your professional life."

I don't think I knew what I wanted my life to be at 45 until I was 47. I had a job at 22, a daughter at 27, a divorce at 30, a second marriage at 40. You call that a strategy?

In fairness, this economist is also a strong advocate of making the workplace friendlier to mothers. But I keep noticing that when push comes to shove, we expect individual women to figure it all out on their own.

This Mother's Day, society's stretch marks are showing. If we can't overhaul the biological time frame—where is evolution when you need it?—surely we have to change the economic clock. Instead, we keep trying to manipulate maternity to fit the economic plan.

Want a portrait for the perfect Mother of the Day? Not too young, not too old, just right. She sounds a lot like Goldilocks. Wasn't that a fairy tale?

May 12, 2002

T here is a moment in Allison Pearson's adrenaline rush of a novel that stopped me cold. Kate Reddy, the 35-year-old heroine of *I Don't Know How She Does It,* is comparing her life as (over)working mom in the macho world of London money movers to that of a first-generation immigrant in a new world.

"You know it's probably not going to get that much better in your own lifetime," she muses to herself, "but just the fact that you occupy the space, the fact that they had to put a Tampax dispenser in the toilet—all that makes it easier for the women who come after you." Then she says: "We are the foundation stones. The females who come after us will scarcely give us a second thought, but they will walk on our bones."

Wait a minute, I thought as I folded down the edge of the page: That was our line. That's what my generation of working mothers said to ourselves when we first got our toes or high heels into the doors that were closed. Sure it's hard for us, but if we hang in there, it'll be easier for our daughters.

We mumbled this mantra as we changed the suit jacket our babies had just spit up on. We murmured it as we called the boss to say that we had appendicitis or a root canal or had been trampled by buffalo—anything except the truth: that the babysitter didn't show up.

We thought we were the first generation of immigrants heading for operating rooms and executive suites, and the next generation would walk on our bones or in our footsteps. Now the woman sitting at the desk behind the door we opened is saying the same thing.

I am thinking of generational change today not only because I am old enough to be Kate Reddy's mother but because the baton, or the rattle, is being passed in my own family. My daughter is about to become a mother.

Just to write that sentence down still seems to me joyful and incredible, though we have had eight months to get used to it. In a matter of weeks—I knock on everything these days—we will both graduate to new titles and emotions: mother and grandmother.

Many things fill my expectant grandmother's brain, from names of boys to the names of products—what is a Baby Bjorn?—but there is room left for wondering. What has her generation inherited from mine along with the genes?

When I entered the new motherland there wasn't another pregnant woman at the office. There was no maternity leave. There was not a single child-care center in my town or a single after-school program. Every question to a new working mother—"who takes care of your children?"—came with an edge or a hammer of disapproval.

Forgive me if this sounds as if we walked four miles in the snow to school. Kate Reddy said that the next women will hardly give her a second thought. We didn't want credit as much as we wanted change.

Now our daughters consider themselves pioneers. And I guess they are. Doing it all is the norm in their motherland. Today, everyone's workload is ratcheted up. Today, a lawyer discovers that the forty-hour work week is now "mommy hours," not partner hours. Today a woman, under welfare reform, discovers that a poor mother's place is in the work force.

Last year, two mothers, both firsts in the White House portrait—Karen Hughes and Mary Matalin—stepped off the trail they blazed for a less-frantic side path. Just the other day I heard of a corporate mom with a shiny promotion telling her own mom, "I thought I won the brass ring, but it's the bit between my teeth." To these immigrants the terrain seems fresh, unplowed, rugged.

When I had a shower for my daughter, friends brought pieces of advice like gifts of the Magi. I came across a quote from Golda Meir. She was prime minister of Israel in 1969 when my daughter was an infant, and she remembered: "At work, you think of the children you have left at home. At home you think of the work you've left unfinished."

Didn't this "immigrant" think it would be easier for my generation, too? Well, it was. And it wasn't.

I should know by now that the changes of one generation in this long movement produce the choices and conflicts for the next. We are walking on Golda Meir's bones, and our daughters are walking on ours. We made a new place; to our daughters it's the old place. And it needs some fixing up.

So every generation enters the motherland as an immigrant. Grandmother to mother, mother to daughter, we bequeath to them a passport and a blessing. They will find their own way.

January 10, 2003

At Large

ON SEPTEMBER 11, 2001, WE WERE SIMULTANEOUSLY, COLLECTIVELY, THUNDEROUSLY, UNITED. FIREMEN AND FINANCIERS SHARED THE SAME CALAMITY. CRANKY AND CONTENTIOUS NEW YORKERS WHO COULD GROUSE ABOUT LUKEWARM COFFEE TOOK CARE OF EACH OTHER AND OF STRANGERS. FOR THE MOMENT WE HAVE CHECKED OUR SINGLE SELVES AT THE DOOR, AND BE-COME ONE COMMUNITY WITH A PROFOUND RECOGNITION OF COMMUNITY. BUT HOW DO WE HOLD ON TO THE REAL-IZATION THAT WE ARE IN THIS—THIS COUNTRY—TOGETHER?

—FROM "ALL IN IT TOGETHER," SEPTEMBER 23, 2001

Z ohra Rasekh spreads her snapshots before me as if she were a tourist and these were pictures she'd taken of the colorful natives. "This is a doctor," she tells me, "and this is a teacher."

I nod, although it is hard to tell one of these women from another. They are covered from head to toe under a heavy black burqa, looking at the world out of a rectangle of thick netting.

It wasn't always like this. Forty percent of Afghan doctors were once women; more than half the teachers were women. But in 1996 the Taliban took over, and in one day with one stroke they flipped the switch off.

Under the guise of Islamic law they declared a state of gender apartheid. Women can no longer hold jobs. They can no longer go out in public without a burqa and a male relative. They can no longer go to school. A bare ankle or wrist is cause for a public beating. The teacher in the photograph became a beggar.

So earlier this year, Rasekh, a young Afghan-born public health researcher for Physicians for Human Rights, traveled to the refugee camps in Pakistan and then into Afghanistan to talk to women. She went with her questionnaire and her daring, to document what it's like for half the population living under virtual house arrest. For two clandestine months she took first-time, firsthand testimony to document the state of women's health when male doctors are not allowed to treat women, and women are not allowed to be doctors.

On December 10 we will celebrate—if celebrate is the right word—the fiftieth anniversary of the Universal Declaration of Human Rights. The cornerstone document of human rights was forged under Eleanor Roosevelt's guiding hand in 1948. Back then the world was painfully aware of how quickly an entire population—the Jews of Europe—could be reduced from citizen to murder victim. It was aware of what happens when other nations just watch.

Today we also know how easy it is to roll back rights in places such as Yugoslavia, where assimilation disintegrated into ethnic cleansing. But in no other place has the reel reversed itself so brutally for women. Forbidden to work or learn, with only one primitive hospital allotted for their sex, Kabul makes Margaret Atwood's darkest fantasy of *The Handmaid's Tale* look like a feminist utopia. It is this bleakness that has made groups like Physicians for Human Rights and the Feminist Majority take on the world's compassion fatigue.

The statistics that Rasekh brought home about the consequences for women's health seem coolly academic: Of the 160 women from all walks of life she surveyed, 71 percent had experienced a decline in their physical health, 87 percent a decrease in access to a doctor, and 97 percent exhibited major depression. One-fifth considered suicide.

These figures and the stories behind them debunk the myth that women are content, or at least safe, under the Taliban. Safe? Tell that to the educated woman, an amputee, beaten and jailed because she stepped on the bus through the front door reserved for men, not the back door relegated to women. Content? Tell it to the woman whose daughter died because she couldn't afford a burqa to leave home in search of medical care.

Tell it, for that matter, to Rasekh. One day on her rounds, a Taliban carrying a stick with a metal end pointed at her exposed wrist, called her a "shameless woman" and chased her until she jumped a wide ditch and escaped.

It is not just women who are suffering human rights violations under the Taliban. Men are also punished for breaking the rules of the Islamic absolutists down to the smallest detail of the length of their beards.

Nevertheless, many foreign policy-makers have closed their eyes to Afghanistan, writing it off as an international basket case or declaring that at least there is peace under the Taliban. Even in the United Nations, some have declared that the "cultural" matters of burqa and gender inequality will take a long time to change.

But if we have learned anything in fifty years, it's the difference between "culture" and politics, between peace and the eerie quiet of hopelessness and oppression.

Today, Rasekh still has one memory that overwhelms the snapshots and statistics. "Day after day for two months I didn't hear a woman happy," she says softly. "I didn't hear a woman talk about her hair or if she wanted to get married. Day after day, I didn't hear a woman laugh."

Fifty years after the world declared human rights for all, the silence of these women is almost as searing as the silence of the world.

December 6, 1998

THE FIRST INTERNET WAR

There are times in my life as a frequent flier when I glance at the plane phone with a dark, imaginative eye. What would I do if this plane were in trouble, I wonder. Would I call home? Would I reach out to make a final contact?

I remember the image of the doomed climber on Mount Everest talking by radio-telephone link to his pregnant wife as he died. He was without hope, on an icy mountain in Nepal. She was helpless, in a cozy home in New Zealand.

These are not ordinary events or everyday fantasies. But it seems to me that all the new tools of communication tease us with the possibility that we can reach out, especially in a crisis, over vast distances and deep gulfs of experience. We can make a human connection.

Now this expanding technology is changing our experience of that deepest human crisis—war—and feeding another illusion. We are knee-deep in what has been dubbed "the first Internet war."

The Vietnam War was the first TV war. Historians tell us that the images beamed into our living rooms made us rebel. Maybe so, or maybe that's when we learned that you could get up from the sofa during a battle and get a Coke.

The Gulf War was a first war, too, the first live war broadcast in CNN time, in "You Are There" color. It too brought war home . . . or let us be comfortable voyeurs to a live fireworks show over Baghdad.

Now the conflict in Kosovo is a chat room war, an e-mail war, a Web site war, a war in which anyone with a PC and a phone line can quite literally become a correspondent. A war in which anyone with a netserver can log on to the war zone.

It's the human-to-human connections that make this war correspondence unique. An ethnic Albanian e-mails his story to whom it may concern: "When darkness comes I will have to leave my home again and find some place to hide." A Macedonian writes into the ether about the refugees in her house, especially the little boy who puts some of every meal in a plastic bag to save for his missing father.

On the Albanian border, a Serbian monk sets up a Web site. In Belgrade, an architect laments the destruction of buildings created by a follower of Le Corbusier.

A physicist educated in the United States writes long urgent e-mails insisting, "We are all so similar deep down." And a high school boy in California holds on to the messages from an Albanian high school girl in Kosovo about fear and music, about life under siege and "the luckiness I feel for just being alive."

The only people not logging on to the world, it seems, are the desperate refugees in camps and fields.

But there is a true disconnect, an odd duality in the notion of an Internet war. After all, the Internet gives us the impression that we live in a world that is growing smaller by the day, higher tech by the week. The war in the Balkans tells us about a world in which people are splintered by hatred as ancient as tribes.

The Internet makes us believe that we can be in touch all the time. War teaches us about the devastating breakdown of ties, the bleak refusal to understand.

Those people who live online may think of themselves as Netizens, citizens of the world. But the warmongers talk of "ethnic cleansing." The Internet breeds a population at home in cyberspace; the war creates hordes of homeless refugees.

And even as the Internet watchers take pride in erasing time zones, they remain as disconnected from the brutal reality of war victims as a wife in New Zealand was disconnected from a husband on Mount Everest.

Albert Einstein once said that the atom bomb "has changed everything save our modes of thinking, and thus we drift toward unparalleled catastrophe." The Internet has changed much about the way we can communicate. Yet, in this most recent drift toward catastrophe, it does little to change the old modes of thinking, the ancient habit of hating. So we log on and log off this war at will. Meanwhile, a video artist about to escape Belgrade writes in her e-mail diary: "And the news is really bad. . . . If there will be no more electricity, I'll continue sending messages through the clouds. Someone may catch it."

April 8, 1999

AFTER THE "GOTCHAS"

For the past week, I've been carrying around an ad from *The New Yorker:* "Fact: Almost Everything You Learn Today Will Be Obsolete in 12 Months."

The cheery ad is, of course, a statement about the high-tech economy. The state-of-the-art software you are struggling to conquer today won't be worth its space on your hard drive next spring.

But as the presidential race lurches to Election Day, it reminds me of the obsolescence of the high-political campaign. Everything we are learning today will be—OK, may be—obsolete in twelve months. Or one month.

This year we've had the luxury, and I do mean luxury, of a trivial political pursuit. In the midst of peace and prosperity, there are actually days when the loudest debate is about whether anyone is picking up the phone for the pollsters.

Some of the trivia of the political information age comes courtesy of a dangerously bored media.

In the week between debates, they let us know that Bush wore cufflinks and Gore did not. We discovered that Al's shirt collars were narrower than George's.

After endless and vaguely patronizing analyses of the women's vote, we even got equal opportunity insults to the men's vote. Why do men like Bush more than Gore, you wonder? *The New York Times* cites the California car quiz: If George were a car, he'd be a Maserati, while Al would be a Volvo. Press save.

Of course, cars and fashion are planned to be out of style in a season. But even investigative journalists this year are grinding their teeth on political snack foods: Gore did not go down to Texas with the head of FEMA, the Federal Emergency Management Agency, to tour the fires. He just held a press conference there. Gotcha!

Bush could not have read *The Very Hungry Caterpillar* when he was a child. It wasn't written until he was in his 20s. Gotcha back!

But trivia is not the only reason this campaign may be obsolete as soon as it's over. For all our obsession with the speed of change, we have forgotten how vulnerable we are to it. We have forgotten how what goes up—the economy—can come down. We have forgotten that peace is fragile and the world is a dangerous place.

Sometimes when I listen to the wrangling over a projected surplus—

$25 trillion? $4.5 trillion? $350 billion?—I suspect that Americans from baby boomers to the echo generation have been lucky or spoiled. We've had no war on our soil. It's become easy to believe that our own entrepreneurial cleverness keeps the economy afloat and the stock market aloft.

In political life anyone who wonders aloud whether these are our good old days will be declared guilty of scare tactics or that great American sin: pessimism. And in a season when David Letterman jokes move polls and a sober Ralph Nader does *Saturday Night Live,* there is still a politically incorrect idea: Maybe it's time to take politics seriously.

I venture this thought because the world—a place that has barely made a cameo campaign appearance—has begun to intrude. In one week a revolution in Serbia turns out Milosevic and turns in Vojislav Kostunica, a man whose name I could neither recognize nor spell in September. In the same week, the peace process in the Middle East disintegrates and old animosities break out, threatening an unholy war in the Holy Land.

These are stark reminders that we don't just choose a president for the good times. Indeed, the good times can take care of themselves. We elect a president for troubled times. We pick the man who will be waked up in the middle of the night with decisions to make.

In the trivial campaign, Gore has been dubbed the class know-it-all and Bush the class clown. A laugh on both their houses.

In a campaign of factoids, Gore the Volvo is mocked for reciting the names of the countries that once formed Yugoslavia. Bush the Maserati is mocked for flubbing Milosevic.

But in a serious campaign, when tough questions rise through the surface of cynicism, there is a big difference between a man who sometimes seems too big for his britches and a man who is clearly too small for the job.

George W. has an ad of his own running in a dozen states. In that ad, he faces the camera in an open shirt saying, "I trust you." That's a fine slogan for the good times, for an economy on a roll and a world without crisis. But in hard times the question that matters is, Whom do we trust?

Fact: Almost everything else we learn will be obsolete.

October 12, 2000

T uesday morning our world changed. I say it that simply because there is no need for melodrama in our mourning. The facts will do.

On September 11, four planes took off in synchronized suicide.

Two left the airport that I know as well as my own neighborhood and slammed into twin towers proud enough to challenge the Manhattan sky and ordinary enough for tens of thousands of people to call it "the office."

A third dived into the defenseless center of our national defense.

A fourth, headed God knows where, made a big crater in Pennsylvania.

On television, all day and night, the videotape from lower Manhattan replayed in an endless loop. We watched the tape like survivors obsessively retelling the same story. We watched the plane crash again and again. Watched the towers melt and collapse. Watched as if eventually, if we witnessed it often enough, stared at it long enough, we would believe our own eyes.

But twenty-four hours later, even a construction worker from a nearby building who had witnessed the attacks, who had counted forty-three people choosing air over fire as they jumped from the towers, could only say, "It was like the worst movie I'd ever seen."

What a lens from which to view this horror story, as if movies were our only, innocent, frame of reference. Have most Americans only faced deep national fear as a special effect?

All summer, the news that filled the airwaves seemed at times like a trivial pursuit. The TV and newsmagazines made sharks our number one enemy. The cable shows covered Gary Condit like a blanket.

Stories on "air rage" chronicled the anger of passengers at planes that were . . . late. And even the news of repeated suicide bombings in Israel had become, I am ashamed to say, numbingly ordinary.

Some evenings, I turned the TV news on, heard the headlines and turned it off declaring scornfully, "No news tonight." Yet I knew always, deep down, what a luxury it is to live with "no news." What a profound and spendthrift luxury to feel removed, even immune, from the world. To feel safe.

In the midst of this attack, Americans had to reach back sixty years into our grab bag of metaphors to find a Day of Infamy. After all, since then generations of Americans have lived, in many ways, a charmed life.

Some of us have held onto that charm tightly, anxiously, ever since we were taught to duck and cover in the schoolroom. We felt our luck shaken at those times when Kennedy stood off Khruschev over Cuba, when hostages were taken in Iran, when a government building was brought down in Oklahoma City.

But we've only known war offshore. We've only known intellectually the ease with which a cosmopolitan city like Sarajevo can be reduced to rubble. The ease with which cities like Jerusalem and Belfast can become war zones.

We pushed aside the sense of our vulnerability—not to a nation-enemy with a missile, but to a handful of men armed with plastic knives and hatred.

Now terror has become our reality show. A so-called World Trade Center has become another vulnerable local bazaar. "Survivor" is no longer entertainment. And we recoil when Palestinians on the West Bank celebrate the toppling of American towers as it if were—to them—only a movie.

Today, we search for souls left in the rubble of these buildings. We search as intently for the trail that led onto those planes and for the villains who didn't die in the wreckage of their own making.

At the same time, our own connections grow as we search the lists of victims. Our luck has changed. We call ourselves lucky now if there is one degree of separation between us and the neighbor hijacked on American Airlines 11. We call our life charmed now if a cousin had not gotten to the office yet. Blessed now to learn that a friend's brother-in-law got down the 45 flights.

The television reporters refer to the site of the World Trade Center as Ground Zero. I would not tempt the fates that way. We need no more metaphors.

But our world has changed. Terrorism they call it, as if it were a philosophy or a political party. The point of terrorism, said more than one political leader, is the terror.

Mission accomplished.

September 13, 2001

H e apologized as if it were a breach of etiquette or a case of bad timing.

With the country united in mourning before the fallen towers, the preacher spattered his words across the devastated landscape. In a moment of crisis, the evangelist linked theological arms with the enemy.

Before a television congregation, Jerry Falwell offered up his credo: "I really believe that the pagans and the abortionists and the feminists and the gays and the lesbians who are actively trying to make that an alternative lifestyle, the ACLU, People for the American Way—all of them who have tried to secularize America—I point the finger in their face and say, 'You helped this happen.' "

His henchman, Pat Robertson, seconded the motion, "Well, I totally concur."

Their Rolodex of villains had made, they said, God Almighty remove his curtain of protection. Remove it, presumably, from the thousands of Americans drinking their morning coffee in the twin towers and turning on their computers in the Pentagon.

What better spokesman for the Taliban? Our fundamentalists agree with theirs. God is on their side. America's sins are to blame.

What better allies for the men who call America the Great Satan? After all, the religious zealots who took over Afghanistan may not know the ACLU, but their first acts were against tolerance, against secularism, and, most zealously of all, against the idea that any woman could determine her own life.

But I forget: Falwell has apologized. He now calls these words "insensitive," "uncalled for," "unnecessary." He calls them everything but wrong.

On a Web posting on September 17, he says, "I sincerely regret that comments I made . . . were taken out of their context."

He says, "I should have mentioned the national sins without mentioning the organizations and persons by name."

He says his mistake was making these remarks "on television where a secular media and audience were also listening."

Falwell apologizes in the way that politicians apologize. He regrets it "if"—yes, if—"my statements seemed harsh and ill-timed." And we are to accept his apology.

What a week has followed this vast national tragedy. We've seen the best and the worst of religion.

We've seen bigots, propelled by religious illiteracy, attack a Sikh mistaken for a Muslim and make some Americans afraid to go out on the street. But we've also seen, in far greater numbers, an instinctive and deliberate reaching out in gatherings as multicultural as the list of victims.

In this scheme of things, one preacher is a reminder of our own fault lines. One man talking about the judgment of God is a warning about how we will stand. Together or apart.

"There are people in each religion who hold their beliefs in a tight-fisted way as if it were the only thing that could be true," says Diana Eck, who has written about the explosion of religious diversity in "A New Religious America." "There are also people in each religious tradition who hold their beliefs in an open-handed way, an invitational way, making their faith part of a complex and multireligious world."

In all the talk of clashing civilizations, do we understand that the basic clash is between fanaticism and tolerance, the open and closed fist? This line cuts across borders and nationalities and through the heart of virtually every religion—Islam, Christianity, Judaism, Hinduism, Buddhism.

"Every one of these religious traditions is a battleground now with a fringe of fanaticism and xenophobia," says theologian Harvey Cox, who teaches comparative fundamentalism at Harvard Divinity School.

"Every religion has its social justice vision, its ecumenical wing, the wing in which religion inspires compassion and concern for the weak. And then there is the other wing, the poisonous and rancid side of religion, especially when it mixes with nationalism."

We need no more proof about the world we live in—a world that is global and tribal, ecumenical and xenophobic, religious and secular. We too live among people who believe that God is on their side and among people who do not believe that God takes sides. We live among people who believe that God removed his protection from the man who got to work on time, but not the man who was late. And among people who will never swallow that.

The preacher and terrorist both claim that we must agree with their religious or political views—or be damned. So now we know who the dividers are.

But of course, I forgot again. Rev. Falwell apologized, didn't he?

September 20, 2001

ALL IN IT TOGETHER

as it only weeks ago that the Army was recruiting young Americans to become an "Army of One"? Was it so recently that they were enticing 20-year-olds to come march . . . to the beat of a different drummer?

I don't mock these recruiters for putting out this ad on *Friends* and *Buffy the Vampire Slayer.* "Army of One" was the hip slogan for the era. It was the not-so-clarion call to arms asking a nation of individualists to think about what their country could do for them.

We knew long before the terrorist attacks that the old tension between two sets of American values—the values of individualism and the values of community—had gotten out of whack.

For more than a decade, I've heard a refrain of regret about the breakdown of community. Our national motto may be E Pluribus Unum—out of many, one—but sometimes it seemed that the only thing Americans collectively agreed upon was our right to be free of community.

The World War II generation and the Sixties generation each in its own way rued the loss of connections. Some 80 percent of Americans told pollsters two years ago that there should be more emphasis on community.

Yet we went on, in Robert Putnam's resonant phrase, "bowling alone."

Then on September 11, 2001, we were simultaneously, collectively, thunderously, united. Firemen and financiers shared the same calamity. Cranky and contentious New Yorkers who can grouse about lukewarm coffee took care of each other and of strangers.

Midwesterners who long regarded the city as if it were a foreign capital know that we are all New Yorkers now. Washington-bashers have discovered that the hole in the Pentagon was a hole in the heartland.

"Maybe we bowl alone," reflects Alan Wolfe, the author of *One Nation, After All,* "but when we survive, we survive together."

In his speech to the nation on Thursday night, President Bush said "the entire world has seen for itself the state of our union, and it is strong." Across the country it seems that every Jiffy Lube carries the same special on the billboard: God Bless America. People draw together in religious and public squares. They overwhelm blood donor lines and sign checks and share the same question: "What can I do?"

For the moment we have checked our single self at the door, and become one community with a profound recognition of commonality. But how do we hold on to the realization that we are in this—this country—together?

Putnam, who wrote *Bowling Alone,* recognizes the signs. "After any major tragedy, flood or fire or earthquake there is a similar upsurge of community." But we don't know, he adds, "whether next February, we'll look back on this as Princess Di's death or as Pearl Harbor." We don't know whether the sense of commonality will surge and disappear, or whether this moment marks a sea change.

For years, we've heard the government described as a wastrel and as a thief. Many politicians have run against the government they would run. Now we see the government in the troops and the firefighters and the Social Security checks going out to widows and children. Will we remember?

We also ignored the frayed connections between the financial wizards at the top of our economic tower and the folks below them. When the New York Stock Exchange reopened, the bell was rung by a rescue worker. Can those ties hold?

Will we remember that the airline employees losing their jobs today are collateral damage? Will the stunning divide between CEO and worker also seem unpatriotic when they are equal targets? Can we see the children of other towns, races, classes the way enemies see them—as equally American?

A renewed sense of community can be a sustaining force or it can dissipate.

"For Pearl Harbor it wasn't the images that transformed the patterns of society and culture," says Putnam. "It was practices, not images." It was, he says, the practices of people in their daily lives—the victory gardens and war bond drives and neighborhood folks checking in on one another as well as military service—that changed the civic lives of a generation. Now we have to find ways to practice what we preach.

In his powerful speech, the president said, "Americans are asking, 'what is expected of us?' " Calm, patience, confidence, he said, and "I ask you to live your lives and hug your children." It will take more than that for those on the home front.

I find no silver lining in this cloud that hangs over us. But for the moment no one has suggested that New York pick itself up by its own bootstraps. For the moment Americans are reconnected through shared vulnerability and loss and citizenship.

For the first time in a long while, we are an army of many more than one.

September 23, 2001

RELIGION HEALS AND DIVIDES

I don't know if I can tell this story without being misunderstood—either by Muslims who are fearful or by bigots who are hateful. But let me try.

The other night I went to a meeting of educators, 30 or more, who had come to comfort one another and to think together about teaching students in the aftermath of September 11. A Muslim who lives nearby spoke soberly about his sorrows and worries, about the distorted images of Islam.

When it was over, a young teacher came up to this man, reaching out to shake his hand in gratitude. But he looked at her and said, "My religion doesn't allow me to shake a woman's hand."

Now I know as well as anyone that Islam comes in every shade, from feminist to fundamentalist. I know that it could have been a man from another religious tradition, an ultra-Orthodox Jew, for example, refusing to touch a woman. I know moreover that every custom is not an insult and that the stricture against touching a member of the opposite sex is explained away by some as modesty, not sexism.

Nevertheless, it felt as if this young teacher had her extended hand slapped. I was shaken by this disconnection, a refusal so at odds with the spirit of the gathering.

I left that evening grappling with a hard reality at the heart of this multicultural country. We have the absolute guarantee of freedom of religion—even for religions that do not share core civic values.

In the past weeks, we've talked more about religion than ever in my memory. Americans have sought and found comfort in cathedrals and synagogues and mosques. We've also found confusion and dismay in the hard reality that religious fanaticism—an ancient evil—has reached our own shores.

On the morning after this encounter, I opened my newspaper. A letter to the editor under a headline "Let us pray" was one sarcastic sentence long: "Is it OK to pray in the schools now?"

On Page 2, around the news about terrorism, there was word that the Supreme Court is going to hear a case about school vouchers. The justices are going to decide whether Ohio—and by extension, any state—can give money to parents who want to send their children to private schools, which are almost all religious schools.

Over the past decade, many Americans have come to think of parochial schools of various faiths as nothing more than orderly, uniformed and often high-standard alternatives to decaying public schools, especially in the cities.

The operative phrase is "school choice." The favorite notion is that parochial schools provide "competition" for the "monopoly" of public schools.

But now we are back to basics, as they like to say in school. And the basic here is not funding or "choice," but the old constitutional bedrock: separation of church and state.

The generation that wrestled over the creation of this country knew all about religious diversity and national unity. These founders established the freedom of religion, the freedom of any American to worship as he or she wishes. On the other hand, they established a set of civil values that make us Americans.

We wrestle with this duality. People can believe that the world was created in seven days. They can believe their own race is supreme, that gays are sinners, that men are tainted by the touch of a menstruating woman. They can believe that their religion offers the only way to heaven, and every nonbeliever is damned to hell.

A church has the absolute right to uphold its own beliefs and teach them to children. Without that, it would have no center. But are Americans of different religions to fund those teachings?

Proponents of "school choice" have used the language of discrimination to claim that the government is biased against religion. In a Supreme Court ruling over a year ago, Justice Clarence Thomas wrote that rules excluding religious schools from government programs were "born of bigotry."

But we are getting a refresher course in the power of religion to divide as well as heal. We are being reminded that secular is not a dirty word. Our shared civic values need shoring up—as do the public schools, the places where children are molded into citizens.

There are old questions being asked these days. How does a country respect multiculturalism and uphold a shared set of civic beliefs? Should we be tolerant, even of intolerance? Is this a strength of democracy or a weakness?

In these arguments, the commitment to a separation of church and state is not a cliché. It's a core and constitutional value. We have to shake on it.

September 30, 2001

F rom time to time, you see one cross the screen.

A spectral heap of humanity covered head to toe.

You've been told that there is a woman under the burqa, but there is no way to know. There is, after all, no public face on the women of Afghanistan. Nor is there any public voice. Laughing out loud is illegal. Singing is a crime.

From the very beginning, when the Taliban victory was welcomed by some as a promise of stability, this was the prime target of their campaign against unbelievers, against modern life, and against the "West." The fundamental enemy of their fundamentalism took the female form.

The victims of their harshest internal terrorism were women, forbidden to work, banned from school, beaten for an exposed ankle, stoned for a lark. The female half of the population was placed under virtual house arrest, or if you prefer, slavery.

Now we see the Islamic fundamentalist attitudes toward women in new forms. In the will that one terrorist left behind ordering that "women are to be neither present at the funeral nor appear themselves sometime later at my grave." In the promise that "martyrs" in this jihad will secure a place in heaven—with seventy-two virgins to serve them.

Is "misogyny" too weak a word? Does "patriarchy"—sprinkled so liberally in Western feminism—pale beside the real thing?

For well over a century, arguments about tradition and change have taken place over women's bodies and women's rights. It has happened in Afghanistan ever since the 1920s, when the reformist Afghan King Amanullah called upon the queen to remove her veil before a meeting of tribal elders, helping unite a rebellion against him. It has happened there since the 1980s when educated Afghan women were demonized as Soviet stooges.

But it's not just Afghanistan and not just Islam that have seen women as the symbol of life spinning out of control. Lynn Freedman, a public health professor at Columbia University, talks about a "family resemblance" between fundamentalisms. All of them.

If fundamentalism, she says, "can be seen as, in part, a reaction to a sense of dislocation and a sense that their own culture is under siege, often women become the symbol of that. Women out of control are a symbol of their own situation out of control."

Indeed, in every text and every tradition, from Baptist to Buddhist, we can pick and choose references to support women's equality or to prove their inferiority. "It's a misconception that fundamentalism is going back to some agreed-upon pristine tradition," says Freedman. Pick and choose we do.

Every religion—Islam included—has its own long history of women activists. At the same time, fundamentalist Christians designate the male as head of household and fundamentalist Jews restrict women to one side at the Wailing Wall. Says human rights activist Charlotte Bunch, "each of the fundamentalisms has a way of wanting women to stay subordinate."

Right now there is, of course, nothing to rival the regime or the repression in Afghanistan. An Afghan women's rights group operating out of Pakistan puts it best on its Web site, www.rawa.org: "Thank you for visiting the homepage of the most oppressed women in the world." It is a sorry but accurate distinction.

So today, in what we call "the homeland," America is finally staking out women's rights as part of the moral high ground in the struggle against terrorism. But internationally, I am afraid, we still tiptoe around the subject of subjugation.

In the first shaky weeks of this war, we are making friends with the enemy of our enemy. This Northern Alliance may allow its women to go to school and to shop in public and to ride in the back of a truck if they have permission. But need it be said that these men are to the Taliban as the benign slaveholder is to the vicious slaveholder?

From the day that terrorist planes hit their targets and Americans asked why, the president answered: They hate freedom. He has said more than once that we are in a struggle for freedom.

Now, catching a glimpse of the dehumanized shapes crossing the TV screen we know that freedom includes the women who form a mute and invisible backdrop to their own history.

October 11, 2001

ON EVIL

I t's more than six weeks since September 11, and I'm still trying to figure out why my skin crawls when I hear the word "evil" sprinkled into the rhetoric of war. Why is it that I recoil when enemies are labeled evildoers?

After all, I believe in evil. I don't think that every criminal or terrorist is just an unevolved adult in need of a hug. I don't agree that there are no truly evil people anymore than I believe that there are no truly bad dogs. I have met a few pit bulls in my time.

More to the point, if there was ever a "pure play" in evildoers, the pilots who flew planes full of innocents into buildings full of unaware workers fill the bill.

Why then do I also recoil when I hear someone talking about terrorism as the product of our foreign policy? Why do I get jumpy when someone describes the attacks as "blowback" or points to Al Qaeda as chickens coming home to roost?

After all, I have no doubt that we've made some terrible blunders. We've supported repressive regimes, favored oil over democracy, winked at Middle Eastern "friends" whose schools taught jihad against America.

More to the point, if there was ever a candidate for blowback, it was our policy that supported Afghan "freedom fighters" against Soviets and then ditched the people like a one-night stand.

The truth is that I find myself homeless, a foreigner in the neighborhood of people who talk about evildoers and in the neighborhood of people who talk about blowback.

On the one hand, it seems to me that the language of evil describes a conflict that is permanent and a condition that is immutable. The word doesn't allow for the shifting sands that end up with the photograph of George Bush and Vladimir Putin and Jiang Zemin—president of the United States and heirs to the Evil Empires—now allies in Chinese silk jackets. It doesn't allow for Iran striking deals with the Great American Satan.

The language of evil evokes, as Princeton's Elaine Pagels suggests, the apocalyptic view of God and Satan contending for the world. "That's not just a cosmological picture, not just a religious picture," she says, "it describes a social world divided between God's people and Satan's people." In such a view, surely "God's people" are justified in doing anything to "Satan's people." And while Osama bin Laden may be willing to believe that, I am not.

On the other hand, it seems to me that the language of blowback, pinning the blame on the donkey of American foreign policy, implies that we made this happen. If somehow we had only walked a mile in their shoes, aided Afghanistan, gotten to "yes" with fundamentalists, bin Laden would have been our best buddy.

This view comfortably ignores the fervor of religion. It forgets that the pilots flying those planes were apparently not dispossessed young men but middle-class fanatics. It discounts the fact that many Muslims who chant hatred of America on the streets aren't trying just to establish a Palestinian state but to eliminate an Israeli state. And what kind of American foreign policy would please the fundamentalist view of women's rights?

Standing like many Americans, at the heart of this debate, while a cacophony of voices swirls around and inside me, I long for a simple argument, a simple solution. But I resist and resent the simplified arguments and the simplistic solutions.

We are right now in the middle of a crash course on terrorism, watching foreign policy being improvised on a dangerous stage. I think many Americans feel how deeply, frustratingly complex this new world is.

We understand that the people who were attacked by planes and possibly anthrax were innocents, but our government's policies in the Middle East were not always innocent. We understand that we have no choice but to win. And no choice but to win populations over.

At this moment, Americans are open, confused, paying attention. Sooner or later, we will each create a narrative, a story line to explain what we now call loosely "the events of September 11." I am less afraid of the current confusion than the coming certainties of evil or blowback.

We need to learn how to contain an abiding and unresolved internal dialogue in our heads not unlike the double message raining down in Afghanistan of bombs and, yes, food packages, for all the absurdity of the peanut butter. This is an argument that simultaneously confronts enemies while it puts forth our own moral values.

These arguments today twist and turn like a double helix, at once divided and connected, separate and in concert. But the double helix of today's hard conversations will become the DNA of America's engagement in the world for the rest of our lives.

October 25, 2001

T he flags are still draped from the houses on the block. They went up in September in quick succession, like sports fans in a stadium performing the wave. They've stayed there, day and night, huge flags somewhat the worse for the weather, covering the sides of the tall houses for more than three months.

But now a neighbor who has hung one asks me sheepishly, "how will I know when it's OK to take it in?"

His is not a case of fading patriotism, just a question. When, he is asking, do we return to whatever normal is? When do the alarm bells recede into white noise? Is it disrespectful to wonder when life goes back or forward to some semblance of ordinariness?

On September 11, we said, everything changed. Safety was shattered. Irony was dead. Materialism was trivial. Comedy was an inappropriate affect.

On the first day of that post-September 11 era, with fresh, horrific images, everything felt like a matter of life and death. We made resolutions under the influence of our emotions—to live intensely, to care, to remember.

Now we face the new year. September 11 suddenly becomes something that happened last year in a country that has too often trivialized the past as "sooo last year."

We get up in the morning waiting to see if the other shoe—a black high-top stuffed with explosives perhaps—has dropped. We check to see if they've caught bin Laden. We watch the rescue workers still pulling bodies out of the wreckage. We watch widows and children achingly struggle through the holidays.

But questions tiptoe over the threshold of the new year that feel as delicate as my neighbor's query about the flag. When does Afghanistan go on Page 3? When is it OK to again "lose it" in traffic? When is it permitted to worry again about . . . your weight? How do we hold on and move on?

January, we are told, is named for Janus, the Roman god with two faces looking in opposite directions. One toward the past, the other toward the future. That feels about right for January of 2002. We stand here with two minds, struggling with remembrance and resilience.

Last night, watching a year-end review, I asked myself: How often will they replay the plane crashing into that tower? If they stop, will it dim our memory of terror?

It is remarkable how much Americans have adjusted to a changed reality. When the president instructed us to be vigilant and go about our lives, we asked each other: How? What yoga position do you practice for that twist?

Yet, driving into a downtown parking lot these days, I automatically pop my trunk and take out my ID to show the guard. Going to the plane—two hours early—I take off my shoes without a second thought.

Does resilience, the return to some set point of normalcy, come with the price tag of muted remembrance? What is the alternative? When will we stop commemorating the 11th of every month? February 11? March 11? Will it feel disloyal?

As one year turns into another with Janus guarding the gate, we are experiencing what all mourners go through, although I do not in any way equate our shock, our loss of security—even innocence—with the loss of friend and family. Those who suggest that we all share the families' pain remind me of earnest young couples who insist "we are pregnant." Only one goes through labor.

But after every traumatic loss, there is the fear of being paralyzed with grief. And the fear that recovery requires forgetting. There is relief when an hour and then a day and then a week goes by without the sharp stab of memory. And there is guilt.

The mantra of twentieth-century history was "Never Again." I never knew if that meant we should live every minute with our dukes up, expecting the worst of history to repeat itself. Do we recover from history only to be shocked again?

Soon it will snow again, and maybe then my neighbor will bring the flag in and fold it away for the next holiday. At some point, September 11 will find its rightful place on the calendar beside December 7 and November 22.

On New Year's Day by tradition, we make resolutions. Resolution itself is a word with dual meaning. One points to the past, resolving old problems. The other plans for the future.

Past and future. Remembrance and resilience. The complexity of dealing with loss and life split the god Janus in two. But we move on, carrying memory in our most human knapsack.

December 30, 2001

WHEN SUICIDE BECOMES A WEAPON

hen did the term suicide bomber enter the daily vocabulary of war? When did human weapons become a normal entry in the military arsenal? Hand grenades . . . Rifles . . . Suicide bombers?

We are no longer shocked by young Palestinians who strap explosives to their bodies, turning themselves into cheap and mobile killing machines. We are no longer surprised by the willingness to die in the act of murder. Or to murder in the act of dying.

There have been six suicide bombings in six days. Probably more by the time you read this. A 22-year-old destroyed himself along with twenty-four Israelis at a Passover celebration. An 18-year-old killed herself and two others, including one her own age, in a supermarket. A 23-year-old blew himself up in an ecumenical murder of Jews and Arabs at the Matza cafe.

Suicide bombers have become so common that a reporter describes a 10-year-old Israeli girl mimicking the morning news anchor: "It's 8 A.M., and there's been another suicide attack." A 4-year-old defines the word ambulance as the car that picks up dead children after a suicide bomb.

Of all the horrific news from that dead end known as the Middle East—and there is horror to spare—nothing has so colored this cycle of violence than the ordnance of walking weapons whom the Israelis call terrorists and the Palestinians call martyrs.

We are witnessing a parade of young people who finally figured out what they want to be when they grow up: dead. And we are witnessing a culture that cheers and glorifies this ghoulish march.

I know something about suicide. I know shattered families left to pick the emotional nails and screws out of their skin years after the event shattered their lives. I know families who still ask themselves why and how and what if. So I understand the words of the grief-stricken Arab father of one suicide bomber, the 18-year-old Ayat Akhras: "I taught my children to love others. We hope for life."

But I do not understand the words that come so much more often from Palestinians, words that describe suicide as good and brave. I don't understand the mother of another bomber saying: "I was very happy when I heard. To be a martyr, that's something." Or the father of a young man who set off a bomb on a crowded commuter bus boasting, "My son will go to heaven." Or an older brother saying, "We're proud."

If suicide attacks are the weapon of terrorist choice, it's because they shake the foundation of belief that at least we share a desire for life with our enemies. But in this conflict, a Hamas leader famously countered that belief by scornfully saying that Jews "love life more than any other people, and they prefer not to die."

Many of the human weapons detonated in cafes and markets are described simply as "desperate." Indeed, there is plenty of reason for despair among young Palestinians. But in the attention to the psyche of the suicide bomber, we have focused too little on the community of adults encouraging what one Middle Eastern columnist called, "a popular sport, a grand aspiration of thousands of young Palestinian boys and girls."

These adults begin with the recruiters who carefully transform the desperation into devastation by promoting and outfitting, planning and praising suicide as the solution. They include adults who announce suicide bombings in the newspapers as if they were weddings. And elders who hang posters in the Ramallah hospital of bombers as heroes.

The fans include religious leaders who twist the Islamic proscription against suicide by describing self-destruction as martyrdom that paves the way to heaven. They even depend on families to praise their children's bravery publicly, to express pride in their "accomplishment," and in the process condemn more parents to mourning.

In the Middle East, it's said by everyone that the Israelis want security and the Palestinians want land. Two bitter old men, Sharon and Arafat, who could make a deal are locked in a death struggle that may take their people with them. I have no more respect for one than the other.

Moreover, others have lauded suicides as war heroes. Kamikazes in Japan, Tamil Tigers in Sri Lanka. And virtually every tribe has sent its young out to risk their lives.

Nevertheless, any culture that takes pride in having the next generation as a ready supply of cheap weapons has already lost its future. Any leader who cultivates or condones suicide as its war plan has lost all moral standing. What do we say about societies that practice human sacrifice?

"It's 8 A.M., and there's been another suicide attack." Suicide is not a defense weapon but a delusion added to the ordinary ordnance of this conflict. That in itself is cause for mourning.

April 4, 2002

A plane flies low across the city as I walk to work this sky-blue September morning. I look up as I always do now. It has become automatic since Flight 11 and Flight 175 left my airport on their suicidal, homicidal mission.

I follow the plane as it disappears briefly behind a skyscraper and reemerges . . . safely. Then I continue on my way.

This pause in my daily routine is no symptom of post-traumatic stress. It's hardly more than a wince. It is my mind's homage to what has changed the most since the twin towers fell and the Pentagon was breached, and dust came to dust on Pennsylvania soil: the imagination.

On the day when the planes turned into missiles, a construction worker who counted forty-three people leaping from the building—making their final choice of air over fire—told a reporter: "It was like the worst movie I ever saw." Stunned Americans who witnessed this event on TV used the same words: "It looked like a movie."

It was as if, before September 11, we'd only known terror as a script. Only known disaster as a special effect. Only seen it on the big and little screen.

Indeed, in the days that followed Americans watched a plane crashing into a tower on an endless TV loop. We watched and watched to prove to ourselves that this reality programming was, in fact, real.

Now we approach the first anniversary of a disaster. And what looked like a movie has become a movie . . . and a TV program and a book and a magazine and a newspaper and even a T-shirt.

There are endless hours of TV scheduled on every place but the Food Network. There are nearly 150 books on sale by poets and photographers, by serious historians and self-helpers offering *Seven Steps to Get a Grip in Uncertain Times* and *Chicken Soup for the Soul of America*.

On the talk shows, hosts are jockeying for the best "gets" of the most articulate survivors. Every newspaper will paper this paper anniversary. And every pollster will publicize the public pulse.

Is "overkill" too unseemly a word to use in this case? Only the irreverent *Onion* has dared to parody this anniversary lineup, mocking a producer promising, "Fox News Channel will be right there with a shoulder to cry on."

The truth is that we would fault a magazine that put Julia Roberts on this week's cover. We would trash a TV station that declared that everything was "normal" by filling the 9/11 air with the next *American Idol.* We would accuse an editor of the crime of forgetting.

But there are times when the storytellers, the narrators, the directors, and producers who package "real life" into products, squeeze even the most searing event dry of its authenticity. Tragedy is transformed into entertainment and Americans into an audience.

This is no screed against exploitation. Not all producers and publishers are deliberately treating the first anniversary of September 11 as if it were Princess Di's fifth or Elvis Presley's twenty-fifth. If you are looking for pure exploitation, the all-time winner was the entrepreneur who tried to put a trademark on September 11, 2001, just hours after the attack.

But we are witnessing how our culture deals and deals and deals with a genuine national tragedy.

"Let's roll," the ordinary phrase from an extraordinary man, becomes a T-shirt and a book title and a football cry. How long before it becomes a cliché?

Ready or not, a firefighter is turned into a hero. How does this survivor find his own reality?

A 12-year-old who lost her father becomes the "9/11 kid," a media "celebrity." What happens when a real mourner plays one on TV?

By sheer repetition, the genuine article begins to tarnish already. Rudy Giuliani's true leadership turns into his shtick. And the survivors from Cantor Fitzgerald, people who suffered a stunning loss, now share their pain in a company ad.

I know that it's impossible—and unbearable—to retain the first shock of any disaster. But when "healing" and "closure" are marketed, when anger and sadness are produced, I cannot be the only one who rejects the packaging of my own experience. I cannot be the only one who feels manipulated into caring . . . about what I truly care about.

Today anniversary introspection has become an industry and 9/11 is running 24/7. We have no idea whether September 11 was the worst day in the war on terrorism or merely the first. We don't know if our new imagination will stretch to Iraq or if we will look back on this anniversary as the (relatively) good old days.

It's hard to find an emotion that hasn't been scripted. But real anniversaries happen in small personal moments. Today a plane flies low over the city. A plane to keep an eye on.

September 8, 2002

IRAQ: HOW DID WE GET HERE?

T his is how we start the day now. We wake up, eat breakfast, and watch the dogs of war being taken out for their early morning walk.

On one channel, a Pentagon spokesman is tallying up nearly 300,000 soldiers ready for battle. On another, an administration source drops another number into the air—3,000 bombs in the first days. On a third, a general talks about a "shock and awe" strategy.

And then many of us go about our business, wondering how we got from there to here.

There? There was September 11, 2001. There was a time we were collectively stunned by the realization that we had enemies, religious fanatics, who did indeed hate America more than they loved life.

There was when the French brought flowers to the American embassy in Paris and *Le Monde* ran a headline that read: "We are all Americans now."

There was when America was united behind the terrible necessity and moral clarity of bombing the Taliban out of their government seats and Al Qaeda out of their caves.

But here? Here we are on the cusp of a preventive, preemptive war against Saddam Hussein, not Osama bin Laden—against a secular dictator, not a religious fanatic.

Here the French, the Germans, the Chinese, and most of the world worry about our arrogance, not our vulnerability. Here the British public is evenly divided in one poll about who is the greater threat to peace—Saddam Hussein or George Bush—and the Turks equate a stand against America with a stand for democracy.

Here our own country is not only isolated but divided with a protest movement that is by no means limited to those who "always" blame America.

There to where? James Carville, in his own irreverent style, asks, "How do you lose a PR war with Saddam Hussein?" How do you lose in the court of world opinion against a certifiable despot who makes human rights violations his hobby?

This run-up to war has looked all too much like a PR battle, a matter of spin control. Last summer, Andrew Card said the White House was waiting until Labor Day to kick off the plan to confront Iraq. "From a marketing point of view," he said, "You don't introduce new products in August."

Since then, the White House has tried different tag lines and pitches on their product. They've made grander claims for Iraq's nuclear threat than they could back up. They've made stronger links to Al Qaeda and 9/11 than the CIA did. They've tried to sell their own idea of multilateralism—getting other countries to use our brand. They've even used their superstar, Colin Powell, going back and back to the well of his credibility.

But it's conviction that fueled the trip from there to here. "You've probably learned by now, I don't believe there's many shades of gray in this war," said President Bush a year ago. "You're either with us or against us. You're either evil or you're good. This great nation stands on the side of good."

The president's deep conviction, on display at his sober press conference Thursday night, is that anything "good people" do must, by circular definition, be good. His conviction of Saddam Hussein's treachery put regime change at the very top of his ethical checklist. But what happens when the belief in a good war comes up against the idea of a just war? When good is not necessarily wise or right?

Iraq falls into Bush's least favorite color: gray. None of the scenarios except the rosiest ones pit simple good against simple evil. We are stuck with choices between relative good and lesser evil. Between containment and war. Delay and invasion.

The pressure from the UN pressured in turn by the United States has made the dictator, stalling for time, disarm one missile after another. It's working. Why put aside a multilateral strategy of pressure for a unilateral strategy of "shock and awe"?

Preventive war, said Bismarck, is like committing suicide out of the fear of death. He knew about the unintended consequences of war. About the dogs of war.

Back in the 60s, Vietnam protesters said we should declare victory and leave. We can't do that with Iraq. We can acknowledge our success and stay this course. After all, if the president fears we don't have the patience for another season of pressured peace, would we ever get the patience for war itself and its uncertain, lengthy aftermath?

Many worried that a war in Iraq would upend old alliances, create chaos in the Middle East and unleash more anti-American sentiment in the world. Well, that mission has already been accomplished. And here we are.

March 9, 2003

W hen this war is over, I will remember a soldier from Rochester, New York, standing at a new playground built by a contingent of American soldiers in Umm Qasr. The man, carrying a picture of his 2-year-old taped inside his helmet, watched the Iraqi kids playing and said: "It kills me to see a little kid without shoes. It kills me."

This was the same day a coalition tank turned its guns on a Baghdad hotel full of journalists, killing two. The same day a B-1's bombs struck a residential neighborhood in hopes of busting Saddam's bunker.

War often strikes these jarring notes. But this one has more than any other in my memory. The war in Iraq is cast, after all, as destruction for liberation. The mission, as the government defines it, is to destroy the enemy and befriend the people.

This is the mission we have dropped into the laps of the military. Soldiers are now expected to be both efficient warriors and humanitarian aid workers. They march a fine line between the use and abuse of power. They are expected to kill and yet to be "killed" by the sight of kids without shoes.

My sense of how emotionally complex this task is has colored my view of the war, and also of the military scandal that has occupied so much home-front attention. Over the past months, as we went to war in Iraq, a sexual abuse scandal unfolded at the Air Force Academy that is only now bringing a new leadership team to that campus.

For the most part, the alleged rape and assault of dozens, perhaps hundreds, of cadets over the years has been cast in civilian terms as a tale of predatory men and victimized women. But it may be more important to think of it as a crisis in the culture that goes to the heart of the modern military mission: the need to train leaders in the tricky, heady, dangerous, controlled exercise of power.

We know something about the women who were chosen for the Air Force Academy from the top of their high school classes. Most of them were, as one rape victim described herself, "excited about proving myself as a woman in a man's world." If these young female cadets—16 percent of the student body—were nontraditional women, we know from studies that the other 84 percent tended to be more traditional than men their age.

The world they cohabited is one where the welcoming sign read, "Bring me men." This is also a world designed to teach the next generation of military leaders how to command and control others. To give and take orders.

In the culture at Colorado Springs, upper classmen command and freshmen obey. "If they say jump, you say how high," says one woman who became a victim. But in the hierarchy of sex and rank, something went terribly awry. Most of the sexual assaults, the rapes, were committed by male upperclassmen against female freshmen or what are called "four degrees." One woman, out ranked, followed orders and says she walked down a path to the site of her own rape.

In a pattern that defines the abuse of power, sexual assault became a form of hazing that strong young women were supposed to "take." Christine Hansen, director of the Miles Foundation, a military victim support group, says assault became, "a rite of passage." One upperclass female cadet is said to have told a new cadet: "If you want a chance to stay here, if you want to graduate, you don't tell. You just deal with it."

Many of the strong young women who came to Colorado Springs to be empowered ended up feeling powerless. Some "took" it. Some complained to an administration that as often as not turned on them. More than one woman was given a "hit" or infraction for "sexual activity" after reporting rape. Not one of the accused rapists was convicted. Nearly all graduated into leadership.

It's bad enough that our own cadets were treated like our worst fantasies of female POWs. But what is equally disastrous was the message about power and control imparted to this elite corps.

Today the sign—"Bring me men"—is down. There is an "Agenda for change," including the dubious clustering of women's rooms together. But the issue is not segregation; it's the integration of values.

Humanitarian warfare may be an oxymoron. But in Iraq, where soldiers bomb buildings and build playgrounds, Americans are expected to make war on enemies and friends of the people. It's a delicate dance of restrained power, controlled violence. They are expected to learn the difference between the use and the abuse of power. That military lesson still begins at home.

April 10, 2003

IRAQ: THE AFTERMATH

I know the defining image of victory over Iraq will forever be the flight-suited president landing on the deck of the Abraham Lincoln. Nevertheless, I have been carrying around a far less telegenic postscript to the conflict.

What haunts me is an offhand remark of a congressional aide in a *New Yorker* piece about missing weapons of mass destruction. The man said that he didn't think their absence would "sway US public opinion much." After all, he said, "Everyone loves to be on the winning side."

I can't let go of this, because I'm afraid he's right. I don't think the question is whether we'll find such weapons, or how many or how lethal. The question is whether it matters.

This week a new CBS/New York Times poll showed that almost two-thirds of Americans know we haven't yet turned up a cache of biological or chemical weapons. Nearly half believe the White House overestimated their existence and two-thirds of those believe the administration did so deliberately.

But here's the kicker: The majority of Americans believe that even if we never find the tons of lethal stuff we were told existed, it's OK. The war will have been worth it. It doesn't matter why we dunnit as long we wunnit.

Is it the pleasure at seeing Saddam toppled, which I share? Is it the unearthing of mass graves? Or is it that everyone loves to be on the winning side?

To raise questions about the original justification for invading Iraq is, I am well aware, to be as welcome as the skunk at the victory party. To hold people to their word is like being a grammarian trying to edit hip-hop lyrics.

But what did we say our reason for war was again? Wasn't it the Iraqi threat?

In October, Condoleezza Rice warned, "We don't want the smoking gun to be a mushroom cloud." In January, the president's State of the Union address talked about tons of munitions, thousands of liters of anthrax and botulinum toxin. In April, Ari Fleischer described weapons of mass destruction: "That is what this war was about."

Well, the imminent nuclear alarm was something of a scam. And now, the US search team is getting ready to leave Iraq without having found a smoking gun or solid evidence of WMDs.

We're told alternately that they were destroyed or deterred or hidden or smuggled to Syria. That may be so. But for the moment it's hard to find what we were preventing or pre-empting in this preventive, preemptive war.

And while we are on the subject of slippage, in his speech at sea, the president made yet another connection between the Twin Towers and the regime change: "The battle of Iraq is one victory in a war on terror that began on September the 11th, 2001."

Where was the reminder that there is still, no matter how many times it's said and no matter how many people believe it, no verified link between the hijackers and the Iraqis?

Everyone wants to be on the winning side. To hold the winner to some standard of truth has come to seem quixotic. It's as impolite as remembering that Al Gore won the popular vote. It's as quirky as demanding footnotes on myths.

I am by no means sorry to see the end—presumably—of Saddam. But does success mean never questioning how you were conned into conflict?

We have become tolerant, even appreciative, of spin skill. We've been conditioned by a compassionate conservative who wants Clear Skies legislation and to Leave No Child Behind while enacting a tax cut for the rich that will be "helping American families." When this White House issued updated excuses for the flight-suit photo-op, most criticism went to its critics. But when is the spin so fast that it melts into lies?

I'm not much for ranting, but I have a lifetime habit of journalism. The newspaper, they say, is the first draft of history. They also say that the winners get to write history. There's inevitably a conflict between the reporter and the mythmaker.

For the past week, my profession has been in an uproar over Jayson Blair, the young *New York Times* staffer who fabricated stories out of plagiarism, imagination, and lies. The fury comes from those of us who spend long nights on the phone with editors, fact-checking and second-sourcing, and sometimes sweating out corrections.

But what is the price to be paid by the politicians who cut and paste the truth? Who is there to demand a correction for the sales pitch for war?

The president landed safely at sea and his approval ratings float in untroubled waters. Everybody loves to be on the winning side.

May 18, 2003

aybe it's best that Jessica Lynch doesn't remember what happened. The doctors say she doesn't recall the ambush and capture, the April days that transformed the private first class into a first-class war hero.

So Private Lynch, at least, had no part in the making of the Legend of Private Lynch. When the nonstop coverage began, she was a survivor being carried on a stretcher in and out of planes and hospitals. When producers "took meetings" for TV specials and docudramas, she was having her bones meticulously pinned back together.

When the big names of television tried to woo her with lockets and books and deals, when they tried to "get" her as if she were a charm for their bracelet, they didn't know that the star of the story couldn't actually tell the story.

There is something terrible about the alchemy that tries to turn a human into a symbol. In this case, the alchemists took a young soldier from the hollows of Palestine, West Virginia, to the hollow world of myth-making. And now we are discovering the fool's gold.

Two *Washington Post* headlines bookmark the story of Jessica Lynch. The first was on April 3: "She Was Fighting to the Death." The second was on June 17: "A Broken Body, a Broken Story, Pieced Together."

In the first rough draft of history, a 19-year-old supply clerk had fought fiercely, emptying her gun. She was riddled with bullet and knife wounds. As a prisoner of war, she was abused and finally rescued in a daring night raid. It became the defining story of the war.

In the revised draft of history emerging in bits and pieces, chaos as well as courage, fear as well as bravery play a role. It was a Humvee accident that shattered her bones. She was never shot or stabbed. Her M-16 jammed and was never fired. If she was abused by her captors, they were gone when the rescue team arrived.

The original tale was, in the words of one *Los Angeles Times* reporter, "the first feel-good story of the war." But what felt good in April is now prickly to the touch.

In June, everything about this war seems to be up for revision—from the way it began, with declarations of weapons of mass destruction, to the way it hasn't ended. So Jessica Lynch has now become a redefining story of the war, with skeptics asking whether the Pentagon spun the media or the media hyped the story.

But weren't we all embedded—in the creation and adulation of a new war hero?

I confess that I was wary from the get-go of this story. I carry in my head the voice of my first city editor: "If the story is too good to be true, make some more calls." The team of *Post* reporters who wisely and carefully revisited the story still call it "irresistible and cinematic." But there was something cartoonlike about Jessica, warrior and prisoner of war.

The mythological Lynch was both Rambette and Damsel in Distress.

For a military wrestling with women in its ranks, she was the woman fighting ferociously—"She did not want to be taken alive"—and the slight, blond teenager who needed to be rescued.

For the media she was a human interest story in the world of tanks. She was news—the woman in combat fatigues—and the crossover star who might attract women viewers the way Annika Sorenstam brought them to a PGA tournament.

Whatever the conspiracy theorists say, this dog didn't need to be wagged. Just tweaked a little. As one military public affairs officer told the *Post*, he knew the video of Private Lynch's rescue "would be the hottest thing of the day. There was not an intent to talk it down or embellish it because we didn't need to. It was an awesome story."

The not-so-secret is that media and military and citizens live in a world where war only interrupts our regular programming. We are expected to digest simple story lines about both the reasons for conflict and its heroism. It's also a world in which a Jessica Lynch is fit into an empty slot between a Laci Peterson and a Martha Stewart.

But to turn a human into a symbol, you have to take away the humanity. In the pursuit of fool's gold, you burn away the metal. By making Jessica into a cartoon hero, we may have missed the bravery of the young soldier now recovering in Walter Reed Army Medical Center.

Pfc. Jessica Lynch didn't empty an M-16 into the enemy. But she has learned how to take a hundred steps with a walker, one step at a time. That's heroism enough for one lifetime.

June 22, 2003

SEPTEMBER 11 SPIN

T here are dates that simply won't stay put. They leap off the calendar like a headline in the agate type of time. December 7, 1941, is like that. So is November 22, 1963. And of course, September 11, 2001.

It's two years since we counted planes—one, two, three, four—as they crashed into one tower and then another, and then the Pentagon and the Pennsylvania soil. Two years since we stopped in our daily tracks, gasps replacing the ordinary hum of a back-to-school morning, shock trumping every other emotion except horror. And fear.

This morning, watching a 767 cross the city skyline, I remember my own raw, first impression tapped out within hours of this catastrophe: The world had changed. Our sense of safety evaporated; our vulnerability ratcheted up to new levels. Terror had become the new reality show. We knew we had enemies who did indeed hate America more than they loved life.

Of course, everything did not change. Eventually, we used up the duct tape, put away the gas masks, and ate the emergency supply of granola bars. But we retained that muscle memory of the world as a dangerous place in which we are high-risk patients.

Last year, on the first anniversary, when 9/11 ran 24/7, I thought the media had turned a disaster into an industry. I worried that our emotions had been marketed into movies and books and T-shirts. Now, on the second anniversary, I am watching politicians take September 11 out for a spin.

The day, with its emotional scars and lessons, is being manipulated, handcuffed to the "war on terrorism." Nearly every battle, every action, every foreign policy, every call to follow the leader, is justified—no, sanctified—in the name of September 11.

Sunday night, we saw a sober president admitting that the scenario of swift victory in Iraq was far too rosy. This was no flight deck photo op.

The "Mission Accomplished" speech of May has become the "Mission Prolonged" speech of September—with an $87 billion price tag.

But repeatedly, deliberately, the president connected the dots between September 11 and the war in Iraq. Since "those deadly attacks on our country," he said, "we have carried the fight to the enemy." "For America," he said, "there will be no going back to the era before September 11—to false comfort in a dangerous world." And finally, he told Americans that we are fighting the enemy today, "so that we do not meet him again on our own streets in our own cities."

The trouble is that the dots he connected are cartoon bubbles drawn by the White House and its speechmakers.

Nevertheless, Americans have followed them. A *Washington Post* poll recently showed that 69 percent still believe it's likely or very likely Saddam Hussein was involved in September 11.

The emotional link—bad guys do bad things, Saddam is bad, 9/11 is bad—has become a successful political link. Fifteen of 19 hijackers were suicidal Saudis, all were members of Al Qaeda. There was no connection.

Osama and Saddam, the religious fanatic and secular despot, are brethren only in brutality.

Nevertheless, the Taliban and the Ba'ath Party are portrayed as allies in terrorism. The war in Afghanistan and the war in Iraq are conflated into a war on "terror."

Did you read the story about a young Florida woman who was determined to sew a quilt for the family of every American soldier who died in the Iraq war? As the death toll rose to over 300, she remained committed to her kindness and to the war. "We have to stay there as long as it takes and take care of it once and for all," she explained. "No one wants another September 11."

When does the small, repeated exploitation of this belief become the big lie? What do we make of a patriotism of fear?

In my Cold War childhood, "godless communism" was the unifying all-purpose enemy that justified everything from an overkill arsenal of nuclear weapons to a host of unsavory allies. September 11 not only ended the end of the Cold War, it ushered in a new all-purpose enemy: terrorism.

So this is how we commemorate September 11, 2003. The preemptive, preventive war with Iraq has not made us safer. North Korea and Iran lurk in the nuclear imagination. Patriotism is calibrated by a willingness to follow the dots of propaganda.

On the calendar a sacred space has become a sacrilege. The White House has sent September 11 spinning.

September 11, 2003

Three Steps Forward

PRETTY SOON WE'LL NEED A LABELING LAW. IT'S

HARDER TO TELL THE DIFFERENCE BETWEEN THIRD-

WAVE FEMINISM, LIPSTICK FEMINISM, POST-FEMINISM

AND PRE-FEMINISM. OR RETRO-FEMALE-ISM.

–FROM "BLONDE AMBITION," JULY 20, 2003

S naps to the little girl leaving *Legally Blonde 2* three steps behind me. There I was trying to figure out what happened to the original fizz when she said to her mom: "Don't you think she was dumber in this movie?"

YESSS. And a middle-schooler shall lead us.

As a blonde by nature and nurture, I kind of liked the first Reese Witherspoon comedy about the sorority shopaholic dumped by a preppy boyfriend who told her, "If I'm going to be a senator by the time I'm 30, I need to marry a Jackie not a Marilyn."

She went on to challenge the dumb stereotype, to ace Harvard Law School, and free her client while remaining true to her roots in every sense of the word. Despite her mom's warning that law school was for ugly girls, she found her blonde ambition. Girls who just wanna have fun can make Law Review. It's possible to do hair and torts.

But the sequel is a retreat-quel. The dumbing back down of Elle Woods. She goes to Washington to make the world safer for dogs who are being used to test cosmetics, saying, "I taught Bruiser (her dog) how to shop online, I think I can handle Congress." She's supposed to be Mr. Smith, but she ends up Ditsy Chick.

I know this movie is aimed at a generation that may not remember that the pink suit and pillbox hat Elle wears is—ouch—a knock-off of the outfit Jackie wore to Dallas. At least one reviewer called this "a feel-good empowerment flick" for young women. Witherspoon herself has been dubbed a post-feminist icon. And in a Liz Smith interview she said, "The film is about female potential in the future and that's what's really exciting to me." But this future looks an awful lot like the past.

Does life imitate art? Or movie stars? The current Miss America, Erika Harold, starts Harvard Law School in the fall. On the other hand, two Harvard graduates, Laurie Gray and Nancy Redd, will be vying for Miss America this September as Miss Rhode Island and Miss Virginia. "This is what third-wave feminism is all about," says Redd. "Be a career woman, be a stay-at-home mom, be Miss America."

Pretty soon we'll need a labeling law. It's harder to tell the difference between third-wave feminism, lipstick feminism, post-feminism, and pre-feminism. Or retro-female-ism.

Is someone who remembers when the Miss America pageant was picketed supposed to applaud Miss Harvard America? Is someone with mixed feelings about Anatomically Incorrect Barbie supposed to applaud *Legally Blonde 2* Barbie—yes, there is one—as a training toy of empowerment?

Mothers, grab your daughters. Even the folks marketing itsy-bitsy, teeny-weeny Speedo bikinis to teens now declare that "wearing bikinis is an issue of empowerment." And if that weren't enough, there's a television ad for underwear with a (role) model who calls herself Susan B. Anthony.

Drew Barrymore throws *Charlie's Angels* into the same third wave. She wanted the angels to be "their feminine selves," she says, and also do "what men do in action films." All the while being directed by an invisible male boss.

You can sell anything with a progressive hue—which is both the success and failure of feminism. It's a new Hollywood message that women can be dolled up and successful. Or the old message that you're only successful if you're a doll.

Does this make you nostalgic for the good old role model in Katharine Hepburn movies? Beware. Hollywood billed the trouser-clad Hepburn as "more modern than tomorrow." After her death, virtually every obit described her as the independent, strong-willed screen star.

We remember her as the *Woman of the Year* and forget how her character capitulated, desperately making breakfast to win back her man. For that matter, we prefer to remember *Pat and Mike* rather than the real relationship between Spencer and Hepburn. Did Kate actually say, "One builds one's own jail"?

Now, generally speaking, I follow Elle Woods's motto: "Never underestimate a woman with a French manicure and a Harvard Law School degree." But Hollywood has gone directly from pre-feminism to post-feminism without trying the real thing. We've gone from Hollywood babes to lawyers with liposuction.

Instead of becoming "free to be you and me" (check your mom's record collection), the next generation is told they're free to don Jimmy Choo stilettos in the halls of Congress and on the runways of Atlantic City.

Here we are on the steps of the Capitol. And still pretty in pink. The good news is that somewhere little girls are wondering, "Don't you think she's dumber?"

July 20, 2003

THE ABORTION ART GALLERY

I n the drawings all you see of the woman is a womb.

The black-and-white sketches that have become truly graphic art for the debate over late-term abortions don't show the shock on Vikki Stella's face when a routine pregnancy became "Oh, my God."

They don't show Tammy Watts' expression when the doctor reading her ultrasound said quietly, "There is something I did not expect to see."

Nor do they show Coreen Costello's pain when she discovered that there was something horribly wrong with the child she was expecting and that the amniotic fluid puddled in her uterus could rupture at any time.

The woman, her family and her humanity have been cropped out of the illustrations shown on the Senate floor as if they were irrelevant.

As for the fetus in this prolife portfolio, the perfect, Gerber-baby outline of a fetus in the birth canal? It doesn't look much like the one in Viki Wilson's sonogram, with two-thirds of her brain lodged in a separate sack, looking "as if she had two heads." Nor does it look like the Watts' fetus, which had no eyes, six fingers and six toes and a mass of bowel and bladder outside of her stomach.

Would full-color, real-life illustrations be too graphic for legislators? Would it have been too sensational to show torn cervixes on television, fetuses for whom the decision wasn't life or death, but what kind of death? Or are they too vivid a portrait of the real tragedies that force families and doctors into painful decisions.

Over the past months, we have watched the phrase "partial-birth abortion" forced into the political language by sheer repetition. It's been used over and again to mislabel a rarely used medical technique called "intact dilation and evacuation."

A bill to criminalize this procedure—described with inflammatory inaccuracy as the scissor-stabbing murder of a conscious baby—sailed through the House. It barely lost momentum in the Senate and was temporarily detoured last Wednesday to the Judiciary Committee.

But when the hearings begin on Friday, the chamber will once again be turned into an antiabortion art gallery.

What is clever about this new visual tack of the antiabortion leaders is that any late-term abortion is gruesome. What is malicious about this attack is that it's aimed at families that wanted babies, at women whose pregnancies went terribly awry.

A reckless Maureen Malloy of the National Right to Life Committee described "healthy women carrying healthy babies." An overheated Bob Smith, the Republican senator from New Hampshire, waxing on about the trip through the birth canal, called the doctor "an executioner."

They talked as if women carried their pregnancies for 36 weeks and then decided, "oops, I changed my mind." As if doctors performed such treatments "on demand."

If you only saw these drawings on the board you would not know that state laws already restrict late-term abortions except for the life or health of the woman. Nor would you know that this procedure is sometimes the best of the rotten options—the one that may best enable a woman to have another baby. You wouldn't even know that anesthesia ends the life of such a fetus before it comes down the birth canal.

But this artwork is just the most recent rendering of the antiabortion strategy. For years they have targeted doctors, the "weak link" of abortion rights, through harassment, death threats, violence. Now they are threatening them with jail.

For the first time Congress has been asked to outlaw a medical procedure. If it works, right-to-life advocates hope to eliminate abortion, one procedure and one prosecution at a time.

Under the current bill, doctors who don't practice the congressionally approved protocol risk two years in prison. Even if the Senate amends the law to permit this technique to save the life of a woman, it would not be allowed to "merely" save her health. What would that mean? A legislated ruptured uterus? A "mere" hemorrhage? Who would decide?

Senator Barbara Boxer, a mother and grandmother, spoke to her colleagues last week and asked these senators to, yes, think about "babies." She asked them to think of their own babies, growing and grown daughters, whose futures could be at risk.

Now the hearing room is set to become a "drawing room." Stark, black-and-white renderings of womb and fetus will carry all the easy appeal of propaganda into the Judiciary Committee.

But life doesn't always imitate art. And in this real world, only the women whose pregnancies turned into "Oh, my God" can paint the whole picture.

November 12, 1995

FLORIDA FETUS FIGHT

I t's too bad that she can't understand irony. What else would a 22-year-old make of the state of Florida's sudden interest in her? What else would she make of Florida's belated desire to stand guard over her body?

J.D.S., as she is known, was abandoned into the arms of the state before she was 3. When she turned 18 without in any way becoming an adult, the state failed to provide a guardian. When she was 22, the care-givers in the state-licensed group home failed to protect her from rape.

Only when the victim was five months pregnant did the entire system, including the governor, suddenly take notice.

But J.D.S., who weighs only 88 pounds and suffers from seizures, autism, and cerebral palsy, is mentally retarded to the age of an infant. So she can't understand irony. Indeed, she can't speak. She can't say who raped her. She can't evaluate the risks of pregnancy.

And she most certainly cannot understand how her body was trans-formed into a symbol, a linguistics test, by opponents of abortion.

One thing is universally agreed upon. This pregnant rape victim needs someone else to oversee medical care, to make decisions about her health, the health of the fetus, even to collect DNA evidence for the crime.

When the state originally asked for a guardian, there was no talk about an abortion. Nevertheless, the governor, first brother Jeb Bush, per-sonally intervened to ask that that a second and separate guardian be ap-pointed for the fetus.

Now, maybe if you were Jeb Bush, you too would prefer to have the focus on a fetus. Florida's Department of Children and Families, where J.D.S. languished, is a service so scandal-ridden that it "lost" hundreds of children in the system, including a Miami girl missing for 15 months be-fore department officials knew she was gone.

But this was also a preemptive strike, a political prolife ploy to give the "unborn" the same legal status as the "born." Governor Bush's move is part of a well-calibrated attempt to legally define a fetus as an "unborn child" and define a fertilized egg as a "person."

As an ally and antiabortion activist, Brian Fahling of the American Family Association said approvingly, "Something has to be said, finally, about who occupies the womb." Well, something is being said. And not just in Florida.

We're witnessing a linguistic coup through laws and regulations designed to separate the woman from her womb and, of course, from her right to decide.

Last year, the other Bush administration, run by brother George, began allowing states to extend health care coverage directly to the "unborn child." The regulations talk about enrolling fetuses in the State Children's Health Insurance Program, as if pregnant women were just minivans delivering them to the doctor.

This year, the Unborn Victims of Violence Act is back before the Congress, renamed for the horrendous murder of Laci Peterson, eight months pregnant with the son she planned to call Conner. Well, there's not a soul who doesn't recoil from the special horror of violence against a pregnant woman. Many states have feticide laws that coexist with abortion laws. Others have laws, like "Jenny's Law" in Connecticut, that add huge penalties for an assault on a woman that results in the loss of her pregnancy.

But the sponsors of the act have deliberately chosen a way to challenge law and language. This bill would create a new class of federal crimes dealing with an assault on an "unborn child"—fetus or fertilized egg—as a separate "person."

Language is not trivial. In 1989, the Florida Supreme Court ruled that fetuses can't have guardians because they aren't legally people. This is the precedent that Jeb Bush is challenging.

If an "unborn child" carries the same legal weight as the woman, so much for abortion rights. If someone can be convicted of murdering an "unborn child," how long before a doctor can be so accused, or a woman? If there are two guardians arguing over health—one for the rape victim, one for the fetus—who wins? Can every fetus have a guardian?

In a final irony, the state that failed this profoundly disabled woman in so many ways has failed her again. A judge postponed the decision to appoint any guardian at all until June 2, past the point of pregnancy that may effectively preclude any abortion option.

J.D.S. suddenly, briefly, cynically, became the center of attention. Not as a woman, but as womb. We know little about her health, less about her fetus's health. She was lost in a battle of words, a fight over language as biased as the label "prolife." She now returns to her normal status: neglect.

May 25, 2003

F irst of all, imagine a place women greet one another at the market with open arms, loving smiles, and a cheerful exchange of ritual compliments:

"You look wonderful! You've put on weight!"

Does that sound like dialogue from Fat Fantasyland? Or a skit from fat-is-a-feminist-issue satire? Well, this Western fantasy was a South Pacific fact of life. In Fiji, before 1995, big was beautiful and bigger was more beautiful—and people really did flatter one another with exclamations about weight gain.

In this island paradise, food was not only love, it was a cultural imperative. Eating and overeating were rites of mutual hospitality. Everyone worried about losing weight—but not the way we do. "Going thin" was considered to be a sign of some social problem, a worrisome indication the person wasn't getting enough to eat.

The Fijians were, to be sure, a bit obsessed with food; they prescribed herbs to stimulate the appetite. They were a reverse image of our culture. And that turns out to be the point.

Something happened in 1995. A Western mirror was shoved into the face of the Fijians. Television came to the island. Suddenly, the girls of rural coastal villages were watching the girls of *Melrose Place* and *Beverly Hills 90210,* not to mention *Seinfeld* and *ER.*

Within 38 months, the number of teenagers at risk for eating disorders more than doubled to 29 percent. The number of high school girls who vomited for weight control went up five times to 15 percent. Worse yet, 74 percent of the Fiji teens in the study said they felt "too big or fat" at least some of the time and 62 percent said they had dieted in the past month.

This before-and-after television portrait of a body image takeover was drawn by Anne Becker, an anthropologist and psychiatrist who directs research at the Harvard Eating Disorders Center. She presented her research at the American Psychiatric Association last week with all the usual caveats. No, you cannot prove a direct causal link between television and eating disorders. Heather Locklear doesn't cause anorexia. Nor does Tori Spelling cause bulimia.

Fiji is not just a Fat Paradise Lost. It's an economy in transition from subsistence agriculture to tourism and its entry into the global economy has threatened many old values.

Nevertheless, you don't get a much better lab experiment than this. In just 38 months, and with only one channel, a television-free culture that defined a fat person as robust has become a television culture that sees robust as, well, repulsive.

All that and these islanders didn't even get *Ally McBeal*.

"Going thin" is no longer a social disease but the perceived requirement for getting a good job, nice clothes, and fancy cars. As Becker says carefully, "The acute and constant bombardment of certain images in the media are apparently quite influential in how teens experience their bodies."

Speaking of Fiji teenagers in a way that sounds all-too familiar, she adds, "We have a set of vulnerable teens consuming television. There's a huge disparity between what they see on television and what they look like themselves—that goes not only to clothing, hairstyles, and skin color, but size of bodies."

In short, the sum of Western culture, the big success story of our entertainment industry, is our ability to export insecurity: We can make any woman anywhere feel perfectly rotten about her shape. At this rate, we owe the islanders at least one year of the ample lawyer Camryn Manheim in *The Practice* for free.

I'm not surprised by research showing that eating disorders are a cultural byproduct. We've watched the female image shrink down to Calista Flockhart at the same time we've seen eating problems grow. But Hollywood hasn't been exactly eager to acknowledge the connection between image and illness.

Over the past few weeks since the Columbine High massacre, we've broken through some denial about violence as a teaching tool. It's pretty clear that boys are literally learning how to hate and harm others.

Maybe we ought to worry a little more about what girls learn: To hate and harm themselves.

May 27, 1999

I shouldn't be doing this. Listening to angry voices on talk radio—sopranos and altos this time—isn't a good way to sustain my belief in even the skim milk of human kindness.

Today a 19-year-old British au pair named Louise Woodward stands accused in a Cambridge courtroom of shaking and slamming an 8-month-old baby to death. The boy's parents, Deborah and Sunil Eappen, have described in wrenching detail what it was like to say goodbye to their son before he was removed from life support.

But over the airwaves, a caller says angrily, "I think she's guilty of manslaughter." And the "she" is the baby's mother.

Another woman finds this working mother guilty merely of neglect, not manslaughter. "The kid comes first," she says. "Bottom line. End of story."

Finally someone suggests (Can this be what the caller meant? Does this level of malevolence exist in the world?) that the Eappens got what they deserved: "Apparently the parents didn't want a kid. And now they don't have a kid." A dead baby is proper punishment—an eye for an eye—for a mother not at home.

As a battle-weary correspondent from the front lines of the mommy wars, I shouldn't be surprised. I know how the battle lines are drawn. Exactly half the mothers of infants are in the work force and half are at home. Many on both sides have hunkered down defensively in their trenches.

But this "nanny case" is not being broadcast gavel-to-gavel across the country as just another murder. It's a Court TV warning, a cautionary tale, a horror story about what can happen when you leave your child in someone else's care.

How long ago was it that the scary tales were about sexual abuse in day-care centers? Now it's death at home with the nanny. Maybe that fits the times when skirmishes in the mommy wars can sound so much like class warfare.

What is the subtext of this case about a two-career couple who hired a British teenager to care for their two sons? Deborah and Sunil Eappen are invariably described as "doctors" with all that implies, and I do not mean caring for others. "Doctor" in this story is rather a synonym for status and wealth.

It is the MD that riles the callers. One swears she would be more sympathetic to a waitress. They have targeted this mother as a driven professional, an uppity "career woman" who didn't "have to" work.

The fact that the Eappens don't fit the stereotype is irrelevant. Fresh out of training and deep in debt, Deborah chose what her peers would call a medical mommy track. An ophthalmologist who worked three days a week, she described her life as a "juggling act" structured for balance.

But even this woman didn't fit between the narrow lines of Good Mother that gets our cultural seal of approval.

Consider, if you will, two coexisting and conflicting images of the Good Mother today. On one side of the tracks, the maternal role model of the moment is the high-powered professional woman, like PepsiCo chief executive Brenda Barnes, who chucks it all to be with the kids. On the other side, the role model of the moment is the welfare mother who leaves her children for the work force.

There is no child care good enough to justify the working mother staying in the corner office. There is no child care poor enough to justify the welfare mother staying at home.

The class bias and uppity woman bias in this double vision of motherhood goes without saying, although it goes without saying in both directions. Doctors and welfare recipients, mothers and, oh yes, fathers are part of the majority of Americans stuck in the work and family muddle.

Married or single, today or tomorrow, middle or working class, we search desperately and individually for "good enough" child care and flexible enough jobs while our antennae pick up the hostile messages of society and the nightmares of Court TV.

On this cultural split screen, a nanny trial in Cambridge competed Thursday with a White House child-care conference in Washington that offered depressing details of inadequate care and the desultory "hope" expressed by Hillary Clinton that it would "create some grass-roots, bottom-up concern."

What of this concern? Stephanie Coontz, a family historian and author of *The Way We Really Are,* asks, "How much longer will we pretend that individual women will be able to cobble together these personal solutions to a major social problem while we continue to slap them across the face every time they fail?"

Deborah and Sunil Eappen have lost their son. Surely they are too numb to feel the slap across the face. But what a different country this would be if angry, blaming voices mellowed into a chorus that understood: "There but for the grace of God go I."

October 26, 1997

THE END OF MOTHERHOOD
AS WE KNEW IT

I n the rush to overhaul welfare, we must have missed the eulogy hidden in all the rhetoric. After all, this policy-making isn't just about ending welfare as we know it. It marks the end of a long cultural debate about motherhood as we knew it.

Democrats and Republicans, Senate and House, left and right, are wrangling over the details. But they have already arrived at a consensus as radical as it is unacknowledged. It's a consensus that says: A mother's place is in the work force.

The Democrats called their plan "Work First." They labeled the Republicans' plan "Home Alone." But no one in this rancorous session argued that poor mothers should be at home with their children. Rather, they were arguing about child care funds, about whether anyone would be with those children.

To consider how profound a shift this is, just look back to the origins of welfare. Over half a century ago, the program was deliberately set up to enable widows to care for their children. It purposely discouraged them from going to work. People assumed that children should be with their mothers and that it was pound-foolish to pay others to care for these young. Mothers knew best.

Fast forward to the 1950s when the cultural pressures were overwhelmingly in favor of full-time motherhood. Fast forward to the late 1960s when the women's movement first broke through those domestic boundaries. Even then, feminists self-consciously, deliberately, insisted that they were in favor of choice: a woman's choice to stay home or go to work.

Fast forward again, at dizzying speed, through the 1970s and 1980s when a tidal wave of mothers went to work, not to exercise their choice, but because they had no choice. They entered a work world that remains to this day resolutely hostile to family life.

In a world of working mothers, we have arrived at the point where there is virtually no public support for AFDC. Indeed, the women struggling hardest at the lowest-paying jobs are often the most angry at paying taxes for others to stay home. This anger is the real "mommy war" in America.

The ideal of motherhood—the images and the emotions wrapped up in the age-old portrait of mother and child—makes this a tender subject, too tender to be dismissed in public corridors. It's never explicitly said that children are not better off with their mothers.

Indeed, in the welfare debate, it is remarkable how rarely the word "mother" is heard unless it is preceded by the phrase "teenage" or "unwed." The preferred phrase is "people on welfare" and occasionally "able-bodied recipients"—as if AFDC had suddenly become an equal opportunity program.

"People," said Newt Gingrich, "ought to have to do something for any resources they get if they are able-bodied under the age of retirement."

"I want a comprehensive welfare bill," said Phil Gramm, "that asks the people riding in the wagon to get out of the wagon and help the rest of us pull." So much for the old button that read "Every mother is a working mother." These "people" are not doing "something"; they are burdensome passengers in the wagon.

The message about what constitutes good motherhood circa 1995 is clear. This summer, Massachusetts Governor Bill Weld, waxing poetic about welfare reform, talked about the proud look in a child's eyes when his mother went off to her first job. Was that child 15 or 2? Does it still matter? So too, Bill Clinton, who initiated the movement to "end welfare as we know it," talks regularly about "parental responsibility." But "parental responsibility" for a poor mother now includes a job.

We continue to praise middle-class women who leave the work force for child-raising. No leaders worth their reelection would demean these women or preach that they are somehow "irresponsible." But we insist that poor women leave their children for work.

Rather than acknowledging any conflict in these messages, we divide the two groups of unemployed mothers—not by class or by fate or by a husband's paycheck—into moral categories. The one virtuous, the other promiscuous, lazy, maybe neglectful. We would rather not know how many of today's AFDC mothers were yesterday's married mothers.

There's no doubt that we need to reform welfare. And I see no way out of this mess except through work.

But as a working mother nearly all my life I know how hard it is. I know how laughable the supports are that this Congress proposes as part of the package to overhaul the lives of families on welfare. And as someone who has watched the vast transformation in American society, I see the old ideas of motherhood finally crashing to the ground with hardly a wince.

We have come through a great change of mind about mothering. And yet we still haven't answered the question asked at the onset: "Who will take care of the children?"

September 17, 1995

THE REALLY MEAN GIRLS

You have to hand it to Ally McBeal. In with the zeitgeist, out with the zeitgeist—and without ever gaining an ounce.

Oooh, was that mean? Well, never mind. Meanness is the point.

In the final episode of the series, everybody's favorite neurotic was driven out of town by a pack of 10-year-old girls. Ally gave up her job, her friends, her apartment to rescue her daughter Maddie—product of a college egg donation—who was being tormented by classmates otherwise known as the RMGs: the really mean girls.

Does this final twist of the plot sound like something lifted from the latest media mania? It should. For the past several months, mean girls have been everywhere. On best-seller lists, on talk shows, in magazines. We've been inundated with anxiety about Alpha females, queen bees, girl bullies, and RMGs on a rampage of "relational aggression."

Three years ago, right after the Columbine killings, everyone seemed to be worried about the schoolboy culture. Now suddenly everyone seems to be in a panic about the schoolgirl culture.

The fact that girls can be mean to one another has been designated "news." The power of girls to harm one another has been dourly and duly described as "on the increase." Ted Koppel even put this revelation on *Nightline*, proclaiming, "I am just fascinated by this."

Frankly, I doubt that this is news to any woman past fourth grade. Margaret Atwood described this girl world first and best in her novel, *Cat's Eye*. When Patricia O'Brien and I went to write about women's friendships in *I Know Just What You Mean*, we saw that "cliques are to girls as bullies are to boys." It's out there.

But maybe there's a new, or at least revisionist, subtext to this bad-girl news. See, girls aren't all empathic, they're also vicious. See, girls aren't victims, they're perpetrators. See, girls don't lose their voice at adolescence; it just turns to whisper campaigns. See, it isn't just boys who are aggressive; so are girls. Girls just do it with words instead of their fists.

Bingo. Boys and girls are the same. They may be awful, but they're equally awful. Case closed.

I think it's useful to hold the adolescent culture up to the adult light. But it's also useful to keep a little perspective.

When Rachel Simmons, author of *Odd Girl Out*, told Oprah that being shunned was "meaner" than getting hit, I wanted a time out. Wasn't Columbine worse than a cruel instant message?

More to the point, this isn't a contest. Sexism, if I remember Women's Studies 101, doesn't only affect women. Both genders are pushed into narrow, constricting roles. And bullies, of the male or female persuasion, are the gender police.

Marie Wilson, president of the Ms. Foundation, notes that girls turn on one another just as the boy-girl thing clicks in. They look at the world and find that their mothers and other women aren't really in charge. If they can't have power upward, she says ruefully, "they control downward." She adds, "It's the way boys are masculinized and the way girls are feminized that turns some of them into bullies."

Think of it as "informal initiation rites," says psychologist Carol Gilligan, who's done seminal work on girls. In her new book, *The Birth of Pleasure*, an elegant and powerful narrative that runs through mythology, memoir, and literature, Gilligan observes that boys begin this initiation as young as 5. "The cultural force driving this initiation surfaces in the often brutal teasing and shaming of boys who resist or do not fit cultural codes of masculinity."

At adolescence, she adds, girls "experience a similar initiation into womanhood . . . manifest in the often vicious games of inclusion and exclusion." Gilligan has compared adolescent girls to "sheepdogs." When one moves out of the pack, they herd her back in line. Girls are forced to "toe" the line, especially in sexual behavior and appearance.

But why, she asks skeptically, has the old-girl culture come into the spotlight now? It's good to talk about what once felt shameful. But there's no proof that the old-girl culture is stronger today.

The "mean girls" media mania, says Gilligan, "gives it a feeling of inevitability. I don't think it is inevitable."

As parents, we also have initiation rites when our children recycle our own experiences. It's only inevitable if we decide boys will be boys and girls will be girls. They will be unless we step in and create new ways for them to feel strong and safe.

Ally McBeal's law firm always did seem like a bad high school. Now she ends her run by giving up to the RMGs. Too bad for her—and for her daughter—that she didn't stand and fight.

May 26, 2002

HILLARY 1: THE CANDIDATE'S WIFE

Chicago—Just about 15 minutes after Hillary Rodham Clinton left the podium, I came up with Reason 339 of Why I'm Glad My Husband Isn't Running for President. It was when CBS began interviewing her date for the high school senior prom. Spare Me!

There was this stiff, this blast from the past, offering up serious thoughts on Hillary, and how good it had been to get to know her better than he had in the school hallways. At least he hadn't taken Elizabeth Dole to the junior prom or we would have endless comparisons about their dancing styles.

It's been that kind of a week. Up to and including the long-awaited speech of a lifetime, we have been subject to endless speculations on Hillabeth. (Or is it Elizary?) This is yet another reminder of the bad old high school days when girls were pitted against each other for the title of "Most Popular." Two women whose resumes bear impressive similarities are contestants for "best wife."

In one of these television debates on Hillabeth, I made the mistake of saying that the whole spectator sport, the longing for a first ladies' debate or a mud-wrestling event, made me want to throw up on my shoes. (Sorry, mom.)

But it was everywhere. In the polls that gave out their "approval rating." In the magazine covers that had them jousting. Even in the Illinois delegation that had a sign saying "Anything Elizabeth can do . . . Hillary can do better."

Well, in fact Hillary's star turn was not better than Elizabeth Dole's. Nor was it worse. It was different.

Elizabeth Dole narrated the TV show "This is Your Life, Bob Dole." Hillary Clinton gave a serious speech, making the connections between private life and public issues, the family and the village.

The lasting image of Mrs. Dole's night was the candidate's wife walking the convention floor. The lasting image of Mrs. Clinton's night was of a beaming 17-year-old watching her mother. And it was the rousing, the unrelenting cheers of a crowd out to deafen the jeers of the Hillary-haters.

I was on the convention floor in 1984, the night that Geraldine Ferraro was nominated vice president. The hall erupted with cheers and goose bumps. The applause that greeted Hillary Clinton was equally deafening. But this time it was defiant. This is nothing if not a Hillary support group.

The best applause line in Chicago this week, the one sure-fire cheer-getter at every event and in half a dozen speeches, is a defense of Hillary Rodham Clinton and her "village." The Democratic faithful are absolutely and rightly convinced that the first lady has been subject to four years of unrelenting attacks on everything from Whitewater to "seances" with Eleanor Roosevelt.

Remember Hillary's reference to the child-saving gorilla? If Hillary were Binti and carried a child carefully to a door, 35 percent of the population would wonder what she was up to. Trying to start a government rescue program?

For many, Dole's jibe at her and the deliberate mis-description of her village as "collective" was the last straw. Women who wake up in the morning with a deadline at work, a husband out of town, and a child with the measles, don't think of the village as a Commie plot.

But in the end, even the most fervent Hillary fans acknowledge that this is a no-win competition.

At the heart of the Hillabeth debate are two remarkable women being judged and compared as wives. First wives, to be sure, but wives. They matter in this race because of what they do "for" or "to" their husbands' chances of success. What they "say" about their husbands.

It's one thing to be "graded" for yourself. Another as his wife. It's one thing to rise or fall on your own, speak for yourself. It's quite another when everything you do reflects or backfires on your husband.

This is an era when a whole lot of American couples are trying to figure out how to have separate roles and be partners, how to be individuals and a couple. It's women who are most conscious of the juggling act between being independent and "wifely."

For now, Hillabeth has found the glass ceiling for independent wives. It's located in the West Wing of the White House. Come to think of it, that's Reason 340 of Why I'm Glad My Husband Isn't Running for President.

August 29, 1996

I s it possible that Hillary Rodham Clinton is, after all, Tammy Wynette?

Has it come this far from the Super Bowl Sunday six years ago when Gennifer Flowers, not Monica Lewinsky, was the lady of the hour? The night an unknown candidate's wife told *60 Minutes,* "You know, I'm not sitting here—some little woman standing by my man like Tammy Wynette."

If she was not Tammy Wynette, neither was she Lee Hart, staring like a deer into the headlights of humiliation. There was the sense among those of her generation—including women who do not take wandering husbands lightly—that Hillary wouldn't be hanging around if Bill were still fooling around.

Now she is back from the minor leagues of the East Wing, the photo-ops of first ladyhood, back as the most important person on Bill Clinton's defense team. Once again they are full partners. Buy one, get two.

Today the country parses Bill's every sentence for flaws. But it dissects Hillary's every expression for puffiness around the eyes, misery around the mouth.

We listen for clues on the *Today* show as she defends her husband and talks about right-wing conspiracies. We check for cracks at a Harlem school where the subject is values. We watch her at the State of the Union address.

What did it mean when the first lady told Matt Lauer that she could remain calm because "I've just been through it all before"? Was there some subliminal message when she echoed the schoolchildren's value lessons, saying, "Boy that's a big word—responsibility—isn't it?"

Americans have discovered in Bill Clinton an awesome capacity to compartmentalize and carry on. But the president has nothing on the first lady. If, as anthropologists tell us, humans react to danger with two instincts—fight or flight—this wife has chosen to fight.

In battle gear, Hillary Rodham Clinton seems much less Bill Clinton's "little woman" than his lawyer. But his survival, his presidency may depend—again—on his wife.

The drama being played out in Washington is about a president—and a husband. The public opinion polls present a complicated picture of job approval and character approval. These attitudes come down to what a young mother in Atlanta told me: "If he committed perjury, that's our problem; if he had sex, that's their problem."

Indeed, if Kenneth Starr with his ruthless vacuum cleaner cannot find a lethal dust ball and if, on the other hand, there is no clean bill of health, we may end up torn between presidential behavior and marital misbehavior.

If that happens, the public will take its cue from the leading lady.

"We've been married for 22 years," Hillary told Lauer, "and I have learned a long time ago that the only people who count in any marriage are the two that are in it."

In the past years we've had all too much experience with public and private infidelities. We know women—and men—who use their strength to get out of a marriage and those who use it to hold the marriage together. We know marriages that survive by courage. Or by the lack of it.

For the most part, we remain outsiders to the mystery of other people's marriages. But there is an unforgivable sin these days in the public mind. It's not breaking a commandment, it's causing pain in a relationship; it's not how a political man is seen in the eyes of God, but what we see in the eyes of his wife. We may be more tolerant of sex these days, but we are less tolerant of abuse.

One thing Hillary Clinton refuses to be is a victim. Another thing she refuses to be is weak. If she accepts it, we will accept it.

I do not believe that Bill and Hillary have "an agreement" in place of a marriage. This couple has defended each other at every turn; this family has circled the wagons against outsiders.

I will leave it to the kitchen-table marriage analysts to wonder when a wife is defender or enabler, when one woman's forgiveness is another man's permission slip. When you protect your marriage and when you pack your bags.

But this is Hillary, not Tammy. A wife dressed in armor, not black-and-blue marks.

We are watching a lawyer with a client, a wife at her job, a public show of strength. Monica Lewinsky may yet prove to be a "stalker" with a fertile imagination. But if we are asked to pass judgment on a man who handles his public job but not his private life, Hillary will be his last, best shield.

In the world of presidential sex and politics, everything hangs on the woman who hangs tough.

January 29, 1998

HILLARY 3: THE CANDIDATE

S urely, this was the right moment for transition. The torch was passed on the first night, not just from Bill to Al but from Hillary the political wife to Hillary the political candidate.

On the podium, Barbara Mikulski welcomed Hillary Rodham Clinton into the sisterhood of senators. For the last time, she performed a prime-time duet as Bill's wife and her own woman. Maybe it would be easier now to run than to juggle.

Watching this, I remembered the convention eight years ago when I sat at a rally of women being introduced to Hillary. A New Yorker in my row yelled above the crowd, "Isn't she great!" And then followed her cheer with a wistful aside, "I wish she were running for the Senate."

That was the Year of the Woman but most decidedly not the Year of the Wife. In 1992, women who liked Hillary wished, however quietly, that she was running on her own two feet. Women who didn't like Hillary wished she would shut up.

Late one night at the '92 convention, she acknowledged the difficulty of being seen as both independent and wifely. "I thought I understood how to walk through that minefield of defining myself and striking a balance between my own needs and family needs that we all struggle with all the time," she said then. She was "surprised," even "bewildered" by the national furor over her role. After all, she said, "We are all trying to work this out."

That year, Hillary took the slings and arrows that might otherwise have been aimed at the Boxers and Feinsteins. For the first time it was easier for a woman to be a candidate than the candidate's wife.

Eight years have passed. Bill may have been Houdini, but Hillary was caught in all the double binds. Tammy Wynette or Lady Macbeth? First lady or co-president? Victim or enabler? Candidate or carpetbagger?

Now, she told the country, she's moving on. "Bill and I are closing one chapter of our lives and opening another." She is stepping up to her own political career, while he is stepping down from his post. But the page may still turn on the plot of her marriage. Can voters, women in particular, see her outside, around, over, behind, through the story of her marriage?

In a rash of LA interviews, Hillary told one TV anchor after another that the people fighting her actually oppose her positions on abortion or health care or children. Indeed, at the Republican convention the button that escaped the "niceness" censors read "Stop Hillary Now," and in right-wing fund-raising, Hillary has replaced Ted Kennedy as liberal scarecrow.

But even among women who thought of her as a role model and share her agenda, the marriage matters. In one poll after another, white women choose the other guy—Giuliani or Lazio or whomever—by 5 to 9 points. The question that trips her up is not whether she is in favor of prescription drugs and a patient's bill of rights but "Why did she stay with the guy?"

Suburban moms who should be her core don't "get" Hillary because they don't "get" her post-Monica marriage. They can't figure out how she functions because her marriage seems dysfunctional. And more to the point, they have trouble voting for someone they don't "get."

Is there a double standard at work here? Sure, but not the old one. We have special expectations of women in life and in politics. We expect women to see life whole, and in return we judge their whole lives. The political is more—perhaps, too?—personal for women as candidates and voters.

This is the first time since 1972 that I've attended a convention as a civilian in front of a screen instead of a journalist behind the scene. I watch Peter Jennings interview Hillary as wife and politician. As a pol, he asks how she feels about young women who "resent you because you didn't leave your husband." As a wife, he asks, how will Bill handle his exit from power while she's running for the Senate: "What if he needs you?" No, she hasn't cut through the double bind.

But Bill Clinton has a split in his psyche of Grand Canyon proportions. Nearly two-thirds of Americans disapprove of him as a person and approve of him as a president. A flawed husband, a good leader? Do we allow this distinction for men, but not for women? For husbands, but not for wives? For Bill, but not for Hillary?

In a TV news story about public attitudes toward Bill, one woman offered up a pretty fair sound bite: "I wouldn't want to be married to the guy, but I'd vote for him." Why is it so much harder to say, "I wouldn't want to be married to the guy, but I'd vote for her"?

August 17, 2000

EW YORK—What a portrait for the history books. Up on the podium of a jammed Grand Hyatt ballroom, the president of the United States is holding his daughter's hand and fighting off tears.

The portrait of a political spouse, he's standing silent, smiling, while the victorious candidate is running down her thank-yous.

"I know I wouldn't be here without my family," she says, and then comes the list: "I want to thank my mother and my brothers, and I want to thank my husband and my daughter." Tonight the president is just a "husband."

Hillary has won, big time. After years as a performer in a high-wire balancing act, standing behind her man and on her own two feet, she's made the double-digit leap from first lady to senator, from the East Wing to the Capitol, from political wife to politician.

She's made a transition unprecedented even for a generation of women composing and recomposing their lives without a plan or even a road map. It's her turn.

Eight years ago, in a ballroom on the other side of this town, I watched Hillary speak to and for a line of women running for the Senate in the so-called Year of the Woman. A New Yorker standing beside me cheered her on and then sighed, "Gee, I wish she were running for the Senate."

Right from the start, folks who admired this political wife wished she were speaking for herself. And right from the start, folks who hated Hillary wished she'd shut up.

A polarizing figure? Even in the two-for-the-price-of-one days, before health care, before Monica, she was—as she has said with unabating wonder—"a Rorschach test" for the messy, complicated changes in women's lives and ambitions.

Since then, she's been a lightning rod for the right wing, a sure-fire target for half-a-dozen books, a magnet for fund-raising. When Rick Lazio went looking for dollars, he wrote smugly: "It won't take me six pages to convince you to send me an urgently needed contribution. . . . It will only take six words: I'm running against Hillary Rodham Clinton."

Now she's standing exuberantly before a crowd saying, "You came out and said that issues and ideals matter." But the truth is that in this race, the issues were all Hillary. It was Hillary, her motives, and her marriage that mattered most. When she was running against Rudy Giuliani and when she was running against Rick Lazio, it was really Hillary vs. Hillary.

From the outset, when I thought she was nuts to run, New Yorkers didn't know whether the first lady was running to get out of the White House or get into it. They argued about whether the Senate race was therapy for a humiliated wife who didn't want to be seen as a victim or a celebrity cakewalk for an ambitious outsider.

But gradually New York cynicism became grudging respect and then just plain respect. It wasn't always a pretty race. Nor was it always high-minded. The debates hinged on "moments" when the moderator asked Hillary why she stayed with Bill and when Lazio came on the attack. The last weeks were small-minded, nasty squabbles in the state's ethnic turf wars.

In the end, though, she won this election, as Charles Schumer, the other senator from New York says, "the old-fashioned way; she earned it." Hillary earned credits in Intensive New York. She became a New Yorker one handshake at a time. She became a New Yorker by getting knocked down and picking herself up.

By October she seemed as comfortable in her skin as she was in her black pantsuit. She found her own voice the way she finally found her haircut.

The candidate even won over her toughest critics, the women who couldn't figure her out because they couldn't figure out her marriage. As Ann Lewis, a Democratic veteran who worked this campaign, says: "It was 16 months of 16-hour days. Women began to see her as someone who worked hard to meet her responsibilities. That was the key that opened up the door so she could have a conversation with women voters."

Now, back on the podium this election night Hillary is rattling off statistics. The campaign started, she says, on a sunny July morning and "62 counties, 16 months, three debates, two opponents, and six black pantsuits later . . . here we are."

Hillary Rodham Clinton has been called a lot of names from "rhymes with witch" to carpetbagger. Now she's called senator. The man standing behind her is leaving office; she's entering. This first lady gets a second act.

November 9, 2000

I n the past few weeks, as I leafed through some newspaper columns that Eleanor Roosevelt wrote during World War II, I found myself charmed by one in which the First Lady exhorted American housewives to save cooking fat.

Cooking fat? Who knew? It appears that used cooking fat contained glycerin, and glycerin was used in gunpowder. So Mrs. Roosevelt made her patriotic pitch. "I have heard many a woman ask how she could do her bit," she wrote. "Here's one very important way and don't let's forget it."

I know this ode to cooking fat warrants only a footnote in the legacy of the woman who spent World War II as the eyes, ears, and legs of a president. Mrs. Roosevelt went to Buckingham Palace during the Blitz. She visited hospitals full of wounded soldiers. She kept the faith of civil rights during wartime. But she was also aware of the home front, right down to the kitchen.

I'm thinking about the greatest woman of the greatest generation as I watch our own first lady during these opening days of a very different war.

Before September 11, Laura Bush—librarian, teacher, wife, mother— had staked out familiar ground for her tenure. The woman who once said, "I've always done what really traditional women do, and I've been very, very satisfied," expected to be involved with books and schoolchildren.

If anything, a public worn out by the Clintons was relieved by the traditional Bush marriage. If anything, a public that had loved and hated Hillary let Laura go her own way. One poll showed that 64 percent of Americans liked her even though they didn't feel they knew her.

Then terrorists attacked. Laura Bush found herself catapulted into a most public role. She was at memorials and school sites, on *Oprah* and *60 Minutes*. Her demeanor was composed but genuinely stricken and just right.

A magazine dubbed her "comforter in chief" and the moniker stuck. One article after another talked about how Laura Bush's role as first lady had changed forever.

As the weeks wore on, I began to fear a retreat. Most days, the Reuters wire service datebook entry for the first lady read: "No public events are scheduled." Then on Thursday, she chose to speak at the National Press Club on life since September 11. Composed and engaging, fighting off a cough, the first lady came with pages of warm anecdotes and appreciations. She talked about patriotism and kindness, the prewar "self-indulgence" and the wartime "goodness throughout the land." She was simple and straightforward. "I get a sense of a new America," she said. "We're a different country than we were . . . we're sadder and less innocent."

The better she was, the more I waited expectantly for some hint that Mrs. Bush was ready to enlarge upon her post as comforter in chief. Ready to take on some work more tangible than uplifter in chief.

Is this likely? The first wife lives at the calming center of her husband's life. She sprinkles her speeches with the word "calm" as a mantra. She has a strong personal inclination to privacy.

Nevertheless, the world has changed. As Kati Marton, who has written about presidential marriages in *Hidden Power,* says, "we have been rudely reminded that as much as we would like to detach from the world, we can't."

Today, many Americans are questioning the meaning of what they do, trying to reassess what's important. I suspect this is as true inside the East Wing of the White House as outside.

Mrs. Bush told about a friend who had always felt sorry for her life in the eye of the media storm. After September 11 the friend felt a pang of jealousy. "She realized and reminded me that I have a large opportunity to reach out to a large audience and help them." But in what way?

We don't save used fat to win the war on terrorism, but we are looking for the 21st century equivalent of a victory garden. We are searching for concrete ways average citizens can practice patriotism in our daily lives.

On Thursday night, her husband called for a deeper civic engagement and volunteerism in America. I cannot imagine a temperament better suited to help hone and lead that search than the first lady's. I can't imagine a time better suited for Mrs. Bush to go beyond her comforting and comfort zone to the place we now call the home front.

Mrs. Bush was asked if she saw her first lady role more as Eleanor and Hillary or Bess and Mamie. She answers forthrightly, "I view my role as first lady as Laura Bush." Hear, hear.

But nearly every first lady has confronted a moment of national crisis that brings change. Not all of them take on a powerful and public responsibility. The ones who do go down in history as the great first ladies.

November 11, 2001

THE SILICONE STORY

T o get to the heart of the silicone story, you have to go back to the very beginning.

Back to postwar Japan, where young women trying to attract American soldiers had industrial-strength transformer coolant injected directly into their breasts.

Back to Las Vegas, where 10,000 women, waitresses and showgirls investing in a topless career, had liquid silicone pumped into their bodies as an invisible, internal "falsie."

A feminist conspiracy theorist couldn't have written a better story of original silicone sin. It's replete with dark morals about sexual beauty and sexual business, self-sacrifice and self-improvement, women disfigured in pursuit of a better figure.

When the terrible effects of liquid silicone became known, the gel was packaged before it was installed, and the market expanded. During the 1970s and the 1980s—the sexual revolution to the Reagan revolution—1 million women added silicone to their measurements.

These were not mostly women in the sex market. They were women in the self-improvement market. They were not mostly women who had lost breasts to cancer. They were women who wanted their breasts "augmented," their body images "enhanced."

During these years, the American Society of Plastic and Reconstructive Surgery pushed the procedure as a cure for the small breasts they described as "deformities" that were "really a disease." The silicone marketeers, for their part, sold the product before the studies on animals were completed.

In this cultural context, it's no wonder that a bitter controversy around silicone implants raged for a decade before Dow Corning's latest agreement on Wednesday to a $3.2 billion settlement to resolve the claims of 170,000 women who believe that silicone made them sick.

Anyone appalled at the pressure to slice and dice female bodies until they conform to some Barbie shape would find vindication in the idea that implants were a danger foisted on women by greedy corporations. Indeed, everything about the silicone story would lead a garden variety feminist to believe in a villain. Everything that is, but the scientific facts.

The agreement deliberately does not resolve what is most important about the silicone cases: how much, if any, harm came from the silicone implants.

One lawyer for the plaintiffs said simply, "There comes a time when you have to agree to disagree and get the job done." The lawyers for Dow Corning—which no longer makes implants—seemed more focused on ending the dispute and getting the company out of bankruptcy than finding the truth.

It seemed that both sides were rushing to settle before the long-awaited conclusions of a court-appointed science panel were finally released. If this tentative agreement is approved by enough of the women, the legal case will be closed.

But as Dr. Marcia Angell, who has written a book on the implant cases called *Science on Trial,* says, "Justice without truth seems like a pretty shaky proposition."

We have proof enough of the painful and unsightly localized effects of ruptured implants. That's not at stake. The bulk of the suits, however, are based on deep convictions and claims that silicone caused devastating systemic problems—lupus, rheumatoid arthritis, chronic fatigue.

But the problem is that in recent years, 15 well-designed studies have concluded that breast implants have either no effect at all on those diseases or one that is too tiny to be found.

At the moment, science and the law, the lab and the courtroom have come to a split-the-difference financial settlement. But what happens when sexual politics conflicts with scientific fact? As Angell says: "Even if you reach a conclusion for the most noble of reasons, it's not good to have it utterly divorced from facts. It wreaks havoc with your thinking."

Today, if anything, there is more push for surgical self-improvement. Cosmetic surgery is sold as if it were a new blush-on. Face lifts are the female Viagra.

Many of us hold two views about such surgery. We understand the self-esteem that comes with a new look. We also know about the world that makes women feel bad about their bodies and then offers a surgical solution for the disease it's created.

Implants are made of saline these days. But the healthy women who still choose to enlarge their breasts are driven by the same old "marketing" pressures as the women in postwar Japan. This is what we've learned from the silicone story. It's not science at fault. It's the cultural facts we have to face.

July 12, 1998

W hen they write the history of hormone therapy, you can bet that they'll begin with Robert Wilson.

In the 1960s, Dr. Wilson promoted estrogen as the older woman's salvation—and I mean that literally. *Feminine Forever,* his blockbuster book on menopause as an illness and estrogen as the cure, begins with a husband's complaint about "the change" in his wife.

"Doc," the man said, "they tell me you can fix women when they get old and crabby." His complaint? "She's driving me nuts. She won't fix meals. . . . She picks on me all the time." Then came the clincher. The husband reached into his pocket and laid a gun on the doctor's table: "If you don't cure her, I'll kill her."

Dr. Wilson finished this tale by musing, "I have often been haunted by the thought that except for the tiny stream of estrogen . . . this woman might have died a violent death at the hands of her own husband."

Does this sound like a scene from *The Vagina Monologues?* The doctor's book and speeches that put hormones on the map and in the medicine cabinet were, according to his son, funded by Wyeth, the company that made the drug.

But Wilson's saga of hormone "salvation" is just the opening tale in this history lesson. In the 1980s, a compelling ad showed a middle-aged woman anxiously observing an elder with a dowager's hump. The choice was humps or hormones.

In the 1990s, another ad promoted hormone replacement therapy as the one beauty treatment to take to a desert island. In this century, Lauren Hutton and Patti LaBelle model their medicated menopause.

But now we may have read the final page of the hormone history book—or at least its denouement. It comes in a letter to the women who took a combination of estrogen and progestin as participants in the massive Women's Health Initiative study: "Stop taking your study pills." Hormone replacement therapy does more harm than good.

This is not just another in the dueling studies that have driven us more "nuts" than the husband in Dr. Wilson's fantasy. For a decade we've had a raging hormonal debate over heart disease and breast cancer, osteoporosis and uterine cancer.

But this is the gold standard of research, comparing placebos and hormone replacements among 16,000 women over an average of 5.2 years. The women who had not had hysterectomies and took the combination therapy faced risks that outweighed benefits. They experienced small but real increases in breast cancer, heart attacks, strokes, and blood clots that outbalanced decreases in colorectal cancer and hip fractures. The National Institutes of Health called an early halt because the verdict was in: Stop.

What, then, is the history lesson for the 6 million women on hormone replacements? Is hormone therapy a drug company conspiracy? Were doctors duped and patients conned?

It's not that simple by a long shot. Hormone replacement therapy is no fen-phen, the deadly diet drug combination. Hot flashes aren't fantasies, and hormones offer relief to symptoms. The smorgasbord of observational studies did indeed seem to promise protection against heart disease.

But it's also fair to ask whether the millions of prescriptions that put healthy women on a drug for life were, as Cynthia Pearson says, "a triumph of marketing over science."

As head of the National Women's Health Network, Pearson has every reason to say I told you so. When the drug was promoted for everything from A to Z, from Alzheimer's to Zest, the Women's Health Network kept demanding proof. When Wyeth wanted to promote hormone replacement therapy as a way to prevent heart disease, these advocates joined the women in Congress lobbying for a random, controlled study.

Now 6 million alarmed women—surely even Patti LaBelle—are asking what's next. Cold turkey, hot flashes? Will some use hormone replacements for short-term symptoms? Will others decide that the individual risks are minimal and keep taking pills?

Somewhere a drug company or an advertising agency also is asking what's next. Will they now market hormones, like Femhrt, as a "cosmeceutical," an antiwrinkle pill? Will they produce and promote a lower-dose, different hormone that isn't the "bad" one? Noting the power of marketing to doctors and patients, Jacques Rossouw, director of the Women's Health Network Study, says, "We hope that truth will win out over advertising."

We have come far since Dr. Wilson declared that "all post-menopausal women are castrates." This generation of middle-aged women invented "post-menopausal zest" and wears buttons boasting: "These aren't hot flashes, they're power surges."

But most of us, I suspect, are still vulnerable to fears of aging, to hopes and hype for health. What we can take from this stunning chapter of history is that other side effect of age: experience. And with it a healthy dose of skepticism.

July 11, 2002

I can't imagine what Virginia Woolf would have made of the Oscars, though surely she would have turned up her pointed nose at the proboscis worn by Nicole Kidman in the role that won her an Academy Award.

But wouldn't Woolf have loved the irony: a Hollywood version of a novel based on her novel has ushered in her own revival. *The Hours* has returned *Mrs. Dalloway* to the best-seller list about 78 years after Woolf sent that London woman out to buy flowers for her party.

It was a pleasure to reread this novel as a woman of Clarissa Dalloway's age rather than a college student. But after putting aside both Clarissa and Nicole, I dove back in time for the Virginia Woolf I most admired— the tough-minded essayist and feminist. I picked up "Three Guineas" again, that elegant, layered argument that she penned as the war clouds gathered over Europe.

Woolf's 1938 essay was prompted by a letter from a man looking for money and support for his society, as well as an answer to the question: "How, in your opinion, are we to prevent war?" On her desk were two other letters asking her to help a women's college fund and a woman's employment fund. Skillfully, she braided three responses into a treatise on women, equality, and war.

Woolf raised questions that not only echo back through generations but forward to our own time. Especially our own war time. How do women change society if they don't have equal status and power? If they win equal status do they still want to change society?

Woolf declined to join the man's group. "For by doing so," she wrote, "we should merge our identity in yours; follow and repeat and score still deeper the old worn ruts in which society, like a gramophone whose needle has stuck grinding out with intolerable unanimity, 'Three hundred millions spent upon arms.' "

She promoted instead an Outsiders Society based on ways in which women were different. "The Society of Outsiders," she explained, "has the same ends as your society—freedom, equality, peace; but that it seeks to achieve them by the means that a different sex, a different tradition, a different education and the different values which result from those differences have placed within our reach."

How much easier it was to think of women as outsiders in 1938. What would she say now in this war on Iraq? Women as different? Now about 15 percent of the troops at war are females. Now Shoshawna Johnson is a prisoner of war shown on TV. Now our national security adviser, Condoleezza Rice, is a member of the inner circle who believes that the way to prevent war is preventive war.

At the same time, women have been leaders in the antiwar protests from Code Pink to the Lysistrata Project. And in the run-up to the war there was a recurring gender gap of more than 10 points between men and women.

Insiders? Outsiders? One foot in, another foot out? Women were less supportive of preemptive war, more likely to believe there will be casualties, less likely to want to go it alone. Before the war broke out, said pollster Anna Greenberg, "American women looked like Europe."

In 1925, the very year Woolf published *Mrs. Dalloway,* an American rear admiral disparaged women's "seemingly insatiable desire to interfere in matters they do not understand." He went on to say, "war they understand least and from it they instinctively recoil. . . . Women now have the vote and they outnumber the men. . . . In spite of themselves, we must protect the ladies!"

Now "the ladies" in the military protect themselves and our country side by side with men. Yet on the home front there is still a sustained and measurable difference.

I am impatient with the idea that women are genetically programmed to be more nurturing or peaceful. We share with men an equally strong desire for personal and national security—evidenced after September 11—but the polls suggest that women have a measurably different definition of security and a real reluctance to act unilaterally.

This reminds me of the question Susan Sontag asks in her new book, "Is there an antidote to the perennial seductiveness of war? And is this a question a woman is more likely to pose than a man?" She answers in tentative parentheses: ("Probably yes.")

Over the past three decades of change, female outsiders have come inside—to the military, to the government. Yet Virginia Woolf's wonderings linger:

As we break down the double standard, do women rally to the old single standard which was male? Or can we help create a new one? And if the differences between men's and women's lives disappear, will it make a difference?

March 27, 2003

Tech Trail

IT SEEMS THAT WE NOW USE MORE TIME AND ENERGY ON

THE TECHNOLOGY THAT WAS SUPPOSED TO SAVE US TIME

AND ENERGY. AND EVERY DAY WE GET MORE TOOLS TO

DO THINGS THAT WE DON'T REALLY WANT TO DO BUT

FEEL DUMB FOR NOT LEARNING TO DO. ANYBODY WANT

TO PROGRAM THAT?

—FROM "ME AND MY PALM," MAY 27, 2001

I didn't make it in time for the delivery. It was just one of those things. A traffic jam on the Internet. Creep and beep. Stall and crawl. Everybody trying to get to the same Web site at the same time.

When I was finally admitted to the birthing room at www.ahn.com in the Arnold Palmer Hospital in Orlando, Florida, Elizabeth had already given birth to the 7 pound 8 ounce baby boy with the full head of black hair. And everyone, save Baby Sean, was cheerfully congratulating themselves for an Internet birth well done. The Sean Show had begun.

Well, bless Sean's heart. He will go down in history as the first child officially born online to an international, logged-in audience. Bless the cameraman's angle; they won't be showing Sean's trip through the birth canal at his junior high graduation.

But doesn't anyone around here have the itsy-bitsiest sense that something in life, like conception or birth, ought to be kept out of the public chat rooms?

I have no idea if the medical Web meisters who dreamed up The Sean Show have seen *The Truman Show,* that magical metaphor-a-minute movie about celebrity and privacy. But the similarities are kind of creepy.

In *Truman,* Jim Carrey plays an unwitting TV star raised on a set dubbed Seahaven, apparently modeled after the Disney-planned community of Celebration. In "Sean," the innocent Internet kid was born in a hospital named after a golf champion in Disney World's hometown.

But if Truman symbolizes the heroic desire to escape the camera, to rebel into privacy, Sean's family story shows the lure of the fishbowl.

There are, I suppose, two sides to the celebrity story. On the one hand, our post-Diana world is full of antipaparazzi sentiment. The public sympathy goes to stars like Woody Harrelson who try to protect their kids from a roving camera eye. The empathy goes to Jim Carrey when he says, "I've brought family pictures to Fotomat and had them end up in newspapers."

On the other hand, we have guests lining up for Jerry Springer and subjects volunteering for "reality programming." We have Jennifer Ringley putting her entire life online at JenniCam.

In between we have Monica Lewinsky's protectors both protesting the paparazzi and posting her for *Vanity Fair.* We have Mom Elizabeth dilating for the user-friendly world but withholding her last name from the newspaper.

In the movie, there is an ironic moment when the producer who secretly broadcasts Truman's every move is welcomed on a talk show with the comment, "We know how jealously you guard your privacy." In reality, we don't guard privacy jealously enough.

I remember the old days when *Candid Camera* made people a touch squeamish and when the PBS series on the Loud family made us voyeurs. Now the town of Roslyn Heights, New York, installs 35 hidden surveillance cameras that feed live pictures of anyone moving on the streets onto the Internet.

Of course, there were 5,000 cameras lurking around Seahaven waiting for Truman. Yet we are led to believe that a worldwide audience tuned in because Truman was so "real." They were longing—we are longing—for authenticity.

There is something perverse in the invasion of the privacy snatchers. As private space shrinks, the public's hunger for authenticity grows. As the hunger grows, the deeper we invade private life to find something real, and the shallower it gets.

The truth of Truman or true life is that broadcasting changes reality into reality programming. The truly authentic moments are the private ones. Only out of the klieg lights are we freely, unself-consciously ourselves. When too many pieces of our lives are shared, when too many people we've never met know all about us, we lose the sense of wholeness.

I don't think Sean will have his own Web site. After Elizabeth gave birth live and online, the narrator told the parents, "You've shared a miracle with the whole world." But there are times when a miracle shared is a miracle diminished. There is no such thing as Internet intimacy.

Let me remind you what Jim Carrey said in one of the many interviews before the release of his star turn. When asked to talk about his marriage to Lauren Holly, he said: "Beep, access denied. Beep, access denied."

Now, there's a handy bit of software for the times.

June 21, 1998

REACH OUT AND MISS SOMEONE

We are at lunch when my friend leans over the table to share his latest encounter with telephone technology.

It all began with a voice-mail message, which wasn't in itself so startling. But my friend was at his desk when the phone didn't ring. A colleague, it seems, had learned how to dial directly into voice mail—avoiding the middleman, or middle ear, entirely.

Was my friend, a man who parses moral dilemmas for a living, insulted that this caller didn't want to speak to the real, live, and available him? Was either of us aghast at some new techno-wrinkle of rudeness? Appalled by the state of the art of message dropping?

No, we were delighted, curious, envious. How on earth did he do that?

I am old enough to remember black rotary phones, the model-T of this technology. I remember when the telephone was a beloved instrument of conversation. Furthermore, I was raised to believe in courtesy as one of the cardinal virtues.

But we are in the middle of a communications revolution that feels increasingly like guerrilla warfare. Everywhere you turn in this revolution, machines are pointed at you. Today, anyone near a phone can end up feeling like the target of snipers.

Half a dozen years ago when I read that Martha Stewart had something like six or seven voice-mail numbers, I was bug-eyed in astonishment. Now I have three voice mails, three e-mails, three fax machines all collecting messages in assorted buildings that are nowhere nearly as well decorated as Martha's—but you get the point.

To understand how the world has changed, think back to the warm and fuzzy telephone ads that once encouraged us to reach out and touch someone. Compare that to my favorite telephone ad of this season. It features Paul Revere in his full midnight ride regalia trying to reach John Adams, who is, of course, screening his calls: "John, John, this is Paul. Pick up. It's important."

In this revolutionary atmosphere, it isn't a new communications weapon that is lusted over by patriots seeking their personal freedom. It's an anticommunications weapon.

We want technology that enhances our ability to not talk to people. We want a personal Star Wars defense system to screen and shoot down, avert and disarm the incoming missives. We long for the ability to be out of touch.

This has created a whole new etiquette called "etiquette be damned." The dirty little secret of corporate America is the number of people for whom phone tag is actually dodge ball. All over the various midtowns of our country, there are people waiting to return calls until they are pretty sure the other person is at lunch. Who hasn't picked up a phone to have a startled caller exhale: "Oh, I just wanted to leave a message"?

Of course, the invasion of the dinner snatchers has created an additional wrinkle. People who know the words to "Solidarity Forever" and are generally sympathetic to the plight of the new working class now greet marketing callers by snarling, "Why don't you give me your home number, since you have mine?"

This is now leading to a high-tech arms race, a kind of mutually assured destruction. First you pay to put a phone in your house/office/car. Now you can also pay to keep the calls out.

Just last month, Ameritech announced a service to let customers reject the sort of unwanted telephone calls that come from telemarketers. "Customers are screaming for this," said the CEO.

We are also "screaming" for what I would call, in oxymoronic fashion, one-way conversations. The linguistic types call this asynchronous talk. In that sense the phone is becoming more and more like e-mail. One person leaves a message for the other who leaves a message—look ma, no hands. It's like playing virtual tennis.

But such is the reality of modern life. All the advances have ratcheted up the number of "exchanges" we're expected to make until our own circuits are overloaded. Efficiency trumps courtesy. We don't just talk, we use the phone as a drop-off center.

Remember Alexander Graham Bell's first words over the newfangled phone? "Mr. Watson, come here, I want you." What would he say today? "Watson old boy, when you get a minute, have your voice mail call my voice mail."

October 11, 1998

BRAIN HOUSEKEEPING

I t is a scene for which the word "fuggedaboutit" was created. A woman is crossing the room in my direction, and I am entering a state of social panic.

A mere half-hour ago we had an engaging, friendly, and lengthy conversation. Now here comes the pop quiz. I have to introduce her to my husband. By name.

My mind scans the alphabet madly. A, her name is Alice? No, Allison? B, her name is Betsy? How about Cathy?

I am having what we usually call—with a touch of insouciance—"a senior moment." Only it isn't a moment. Somewhere between bifocals and Medicare, the moments have linked together into minutes. The short-term memory has deteriorated into a mass of fuggedaboutits. D, her name is Debra?

But now a reassuring—I think—theory suggests I am not suffering from Rotting Brain Syndrome or Mid-Life Losing It Disease. I have merely run out of storage space.

This theory comes from H. Lee Swanson of the University of California, Riverside. Swanson studied working memory in 778 persons from ages 6 to 76, testing their ability to remember—with cues, cues, and more cues—such things as the name and number of the supermarket at "8651 Elm Street."

It isn't "cognitive skills" that present a problem for the over-45 crowd, he suggests in the journal *Developmental Psychology*, it's the "capacity limitations." In short, it isn't that my brainpower is weak but that my mailbox is full. It's not a lack of gray matter but of RAM.

Alas, I cannot yet buy more brain RAM. So the good news is tempered by the problem at hand: G, her name is Grace?

But these computer-brain analogies have encouraged me to design an entirely new software for the memory problem. May I introduce Brain Housekeeping 99?

What the aging baby boom generation needs is a way to clean out the mental storage shelves and thus make room for new inventory. This is a program to empty the mental hard drive of everything that is defunct, useless, self-destructive, irrevelant, or just plain annoying.

Feature One: With this new software, you can download everything you are no longer using—I mean, "utilizing"—to a disk.

Consider my own brain, for example, currently cluttered with camp songs, circa 1958, leaving no room for string theory or Alan Greenspan's reasoning. Using BH 99, I can transfer Camp Woodlands' green team songs onto a disk in the rare event that I ever need them again for a camp reunion.

I can store them along with the entire score of my college production of *Guys and Dolls*—don't ask—and the Prologue to *The Canterbury Tales* which I now use only to impress students in Olde English.

Feature Two: This software also offers a recycle bin for the brain's desktop. What better place for the child-raising theories that litter my frontal lobe long after the infant has graduated college? Permissiveness, potty training, and phonics—get thee to a bin! Make room for the human genome project.

The recycle bin can also, of course, store last year's advice on such things as hormones and breast cancer. Or you can lock in an override feature—a true space saver—and automatically replace last year's research with this year's research. Which is good until next year.

Feature Three: Let's not underestimate the most popular function of BH 99: the delete button. Haven't we all wished to wipe something out of the memory bank permanently? Seventh grade for example. With this new program, junior high can be history. And how about the first six months after a divorce? Trust me, you won't miss them.

Feature Four: For an additional price, this software allows the user the option of permanently expunging those images that clog up the memory bank against our will: sitcoms, Budweiser ads, George Stephanopoulos, etc. It can not only delete all memory of the Monica Lewinsky scandal—which has used up all the megabytes reserved for understanding Social Security reform—but includes an antivirus program that blocks the entrance of any new gossip. T, her name is Tina Brown?

With BH 99 you too can remove Latin—except for the Roman numerals—to make room for Spanish. You can delete the 1963 map of Africa—Tanganyika! Rhodesia!—to make way for Tanzania! Zimbabwe! You can even delete the name of the 16-year-old who done you wrong in return for remembering: Z, her name is Zelda?

Brain Housekeeping 99 will no doubt be ripped off by some poorly dressed, sleep-deprived, IPO-fantasizing Gen-Xer in Silicon Valley. But you read it here first. Remember that. If you can.

August 5, 1999

I have decided that my Palm Pilot deserves a better home. It needs a family able to encourage its true potential. A parent who understands its basic talent. A boss who will help it push the envelope of its artificial intelligence.

I have come to this unhappy thought after having the electronic creature in my custody for five months. During this cohabitation, I have discovered that my Palm was endowed by its creator with certain inalienable rights to do e-mail, check stocks, book travel arrangements, and browse the Web.

But I have merely used it as a Rolodex and a datebook. I have done nothing to allow it to grow, change, or strut its stuff. Only rarely have I even taken it out for a hot sync or a rendezvous to beam with its pals. Left to my own devices, this device has grown to be a slacker. In my hands, this Palm is an underachiever.

I know this because every time it emerges from my pocketbook, some other Palm Piloteer eagerly shows me some "neat," "cool," "awesome" function. Which of course I cannot replicate. I'm afraid to tell them that I haven't yet figured out how to write a question mark.

So I have come reluctantly to the conclusion that my Palm is a high-functioning offspring in a dysfunctional family. It's OK/I'm Not OK.

Frankly, I never used to feel guilty about disappointing inanimate objects. I had enough people to worry about. But ever since the Palm arrived, I have had the creepy feeling that I'm not living up to the expectations of any of my technology.

It used to be just the VCR that found me inadequate. It could program, I could not. Now I have a cell phone that can do everything . . . but not with me. I have a television set that has a screen within a screen . . . or so I'm told. I even have the ability to download digital audio books to my PDA, MP3 player . . . if I had any idea what those initials meant.

Indeed it seems to me that more of us are living in a world created by the sort of techies who have never needed a "Dummies" book. A recent *Wall Street Journal* article warned us of the onslaught of more such gizmos, from a refrigerator that doubles as a videophone to a sewing machine that uses a Nintendo Game Boy to sew 150 different stitches.

There's even software that one man programmed to announce, "I'm not fat, I'm pleasingly plump" when his wife stepped on the scale.

Well, I'm not a technophobe, I don't write with a quill pen and I believe a certain amount of technological adeptness will keep my brain cells alive. In fact, I (under) use a handful of software programs every day, though lately I have felt that Lotus Notes is also wondering when I will rise to its level.

If I am living over my technological head, it is in part because I resist spending an enormous amount of time forming relationships with technology that I know from experience is likely to leave me. Let me put it this way: If you learned French, you can always speak French. If, however, you learned DOS, you can only speak to a docent at a computer museum.

Our electronic companions tend to become obsolete as soon as we've become comfortable. The VCR you can't operate becomes the DVD you can't operate. Palm V is removed from the throne by Palm VI and on and on.

I have no idea how much time and energy American businesses now spend endlessly "upgrading" technology. But I am pretty sure that too many of us are puffing up the anaerobic learning curve just for the exercise.

Let me put it this way: In the same amount of time, I can either learn the inner workings of my Palm Pilot or of the human genome. In the same amount of time, Americans can figure out their new software or their new tax package. We can learn to download something to read or we can read.

It seems that we now use more time and energy on the technology that was supposed to save us time and energy. And every day we get more tools to do things that we don't really want to do but feel dumb for not learning to do. Anybody want to program that?

As for my guilty relationship with my own electronic underachiever, I am reminded of the words my husband once directed at our dog: "Sam, you deserve more attention than I'm willing to give you."

Yes, I will keep my Palm in hand, underemployed as a telephone and date book. We will go on living together, but I fear we will never be in hot sync.

May 27, 2001

BACK TO CIVILIZATION?

CASCO BAY, MAINE—It's time to leave. The light has changed, filling the cove with the clarity of a thousand autumn watts. The blackberries that fell abundantly into my hands just two weeks ago now cower in secret September spots.

The bags that I will carry onto the boat are packed full of props for my other life. A laptop fills one. City costumes and makeup—proof that we are only acting on the urban stage—fill another.

For my last few minutes, I retreat to the porch, coffee cup in hand, feet in their railtop groove. This has been my post, my observation tower this vacation. I am at home on this porch, neither indoors nor outdoors, neither domestic nor wild. It's been a borderland that I claim as my own. But now it has new meaning.

Over these languid weeks, away from the multi-tasking demands of workaday life, I have embraced the country dwellers' conceit. For days on end, I pride myself on living off the land, eating what nature had to offer: the mussels from the rocks, the striped bass from the cove, the tomatoes from the garden, the lobsters from my neighbor's traps.

But this morning, in transition myself, the line between natural and artificial, between civilized and uncivilized, between what is touched and untouched by human hands, seems much less certain.

Over the porch railing, I see our fingerprints across the land. Yesterday, we cut back the sumac to make more room for raspberries to grow. We hacked away space for the "wild" rhubarb that we recovered from some old farmer's patch.

The lobsters that our neighbor "catches" are, in fact, "ranched" across the bay, an oceanic range covered with thousands of pots whose bait feeds and raises the next generation. The striped bass we catch are kept or released, according to human regulations.

Indeed, the clams we eat are licensed, the tomatoes we plant are hybrids, and in what has to be an oxymoronic moment, we cultivate a wild-flower garden.

The truth is that our own species is in charge of evolution now. In the Darwinian struggle for the survival of the fittest, we are the big players, choosing roses over bittersweet, eggplant over crabgrass. We now decide what is fit—for us.

This summer, nature seemed to dominate the discourse. The future of the wilderness in Alaska and the future of stem cells in medicine engaged our attention in some natural duet.

The House of Representatives voted to violate the Arctic National Wildlife Refuge for oil. The president, home to the heartland in an air-conditioned truck, interrupted his vacation to address the nation on the biology of human nature.

These issues come before us again this fall—and again. We set the path now for everything from the fate of vast wilderness acres to the microscopic stem cell.

In *The Botany of Desire*, the engaging book that decorated my porch reading this vacation, Michael Pollan writes: "All of nature is in the process of being domesticated, of coming or finding itself under the (somewhat leaky) roof of civilization. Indeed even the wild now depends on civilization for its survival."

The young bald eagle that soared over the cove this summer doesn't know that its survival was threatened and saved by our interest. The embryonic stem cell that became a blood-making cell under the auspices of biologists at the University of Wisconsin has no consciousness to wonder why.

But Pollan is right. Humans now live uneasily, sometimes unwillingly, with the knowledge of our own role. We are as in control as the traffic signals that I will return to.

I will carry memories with me down the turnpike to the city. This year my 2-year-old great-nephew arrived from Paris knowing the word for every truck in two languages, but needing to learn that he could eat from a bush. An old friend with half a century of politics behind him had never seen asparagus growing. Nature doesn't come naturally.

Soon the boat will leave, so I desert my post, collect the half-ripe tomatoes I cannot bear to leave behind and stash a handful of yellow periwinkle shells in my pocket where I can use them as winter worrybeads.

"Well, back to civilization," I sigh to my husband as I get up, and he answers, "Is this un-civilized?"

In the country or the city, here or there, we live now in the borderland. The world has become our porch. Now we must become its keepers.

September 6, 2001

I arrive at my office, uncap my coffee, unwrap my bagel, open my e-mail, and face the first searing public policy question of the day: "Do you want to watch teens make their first porn video?"

Ah, yes, Good Morning, Spam. Good Morning, Spamerica.

This charming greeting is followed by a medical offer of a guaranteed deal to "lose 12 pounds in 48 hours!" That is followed by other golden opportunities for (1) a "preapproved auto loan for up to $23,990"; (2) a nutritional supplement known as "horny goat weed"; (3) a cure for snoring; (4) a sure-fire stock pick; (5) a plea for "Uregent (sic) Help" for a Nigerian in political asylum; and (6) a "Valentine Must: Viagra Orders Made Easy."

By the time I get to the last shiny deal—"Would you like to earn money while you sleep?"—I have deleted as many of my own expletives as e-mails. Somewhere between the "hot girls and wild horses" there is, I am sure, a correspondent. But as I dump the junk, I remember how spam supposedly got its nickname—from the famous Monty Python skit in which a poor couple's attempt to place their restaurant order is drowned out by a chorus of Vikings chanting "SPAM, SPAM, SPAM."

My spam, your spam, everyone's spam is nothing if not a growth industry. On average, 11 percent of all e-mails now are spam. The average e-mail user got 1,470 unsolicited commercial messages last year. At this rate we can expect as many as 3,800 apiece by 2005.

If you are above average—a dubious distinction in this case—and have a feeling that the volume has greatly increased since September 11 and snail-mail anthrax, you're right. And this is not just because of the creep who sent his pitch out just hours after the terrorist attacks, "No terrorist here! Join our porn site!"

As Internet guru Esther Dyson says, "The magic of e-mail is that you can e-mail almost anyone. The tragedy is that almost anyone can e-mail you." Spam is now clogging the national e-mail box the way its namesake clogs the arteries.

What's a victim to do? "Meet Singles Just Like You"? "Save up to 70 Percent on Your Life Insurance"? This month the Federal Trade Commission announced a proposal to help rid us of our most frequent dining companions, the telemarketers, with a national "do not call" list. But there's no plan for a "do not e-mail" list.

Part of the problem with getting a lock on spam is that we have more cyber addresses than phone numbers. Moreover, the Internet is unregulated and worldwide. Ban spam here and it will arrive via Mexico, Taiwan, or Minsk. Many spammers have already moved offshore.

In the name of self-defense, Internet service providers have filters. Some are as effective as containing water in your hands while others are as quirky as the AOL filter that bumped out Harvard's early acceptance letters. Meanwhile the most effective filter operations, notably Brightmail, are waging a 24/7 guerrilla war with ever-evolving spammers.

But the only thing as annoying as a spam attack is paying for self-defense. As Tom Geller, the executive director of the SpamCom Foundation, says, "I don't feel I should have to do any filtering. I don't want to pay for it. It's my computer. I shouldn't have to."

There are, not surprisingly, a host of schemes for fighting spam. My whimsical favorite is Esther Dyson's proposal to make any unwanted e-mailer pay for your attention. She fantasizes charging anywhere from a few cents for a small advertiser to $100 for an old boyfriend. But this plan is not, to put it mildly, ready for operation.

There are also about 18 states with anti-spam laws. In California this month, an appeals court upheld one law that makes spammers identify ads in the header rather than saying "Hi Sweetie" or "I checked this out!" And a Washington state citizen with the license plate NERDPOWR recently won four cases against misleading spammers.

Similar laws are wandering around Congress, and the FTC has at least and at last said it will go after the real spam con artists. ("Please Help Buddhist Monasteries in Tibet!") But the real trick, says John Mozena of the Coalition Against Unsolicited Commercial E-mail, is to give companies and Internet servers the right to post a no-trespassing sign.

Spam costs the spammer almost nothing. It costs the rest us time, money, and irritation. My fantasy is to locate the spammers and subject them to endless telemarketing calls.

Ah, yes, I know. Somewhere in my delete file there is an honest and humble businessman. But if he's the one who offered me "Penis enhancement . . . real science . . . new pills," he'd better check his customer base.

February 10, 2002

LIFE BEFORE THE CAMERAS

From time to time, my husband and I ask each other a humbling question about the human condition: How would you like to see your 10 worst moments on videotape?

This is the fate that befell Madelyne Toogood last month when she was captured on a security camera in a department store parking lot. The mother was taped slapping around her 4-year-old daughter as they got into their SUV.

Toogood got to see this moment—which we sincerely hope was one of her 10 worst—again and again and again. The police saw it. The entire nation saw it. On October 7, the Indiana court where she will be tried for a felony charge of battery will also see it.

Toogood's tape has become the Rodney King tape of child abuse. A debate ensued about parenting and "spanking," about the line between discipline and abuse. The mother's only defense after seeing her self-portrait was to swear, "I'm not a monster." That too was debated.

In fact, the public air was full of heated opinions and judgments about everything . . . except the videotape itself. No one seemed too concerned about the image or its trail from Kohl's to CNN.

We have gotten so used to the idea of a security camera peering at us out of every ATM and parking lot, every airport and school, every department store and public square, that we no longer question it. When the booty of a department store's private eye is open to the public eye, we don't flinch. We just watch.

Indeed, the only story alarming enough to raise privacy hackles these days came from Washington state, where two men were arrested for taking pictures up women's skirts. But these men were acquitted of voyeurism by the state Supreme Court because the pictures were taken in public places where, the justices ruled, people don't have a "reasonable expectation of privacy."

It seems that the old expectation of privacy in public has become unreasonable. There are now video cameras in the remote part of a national forest for the stated purpose of catching people growing marijuana. There are at least 2,397 surveillance cameras on the streets of Manhattan.

We've become a nation of surveillance with remarkably little discussion. Few of us are asking the questions offered by David Sobel of the Electronic Privacy Information Center: "What becomes of any tapes created by such systems, who has access to them, and how might they be used?" Nor are we asking what it means for a nanny or a student or a shopper to be on permanent candid camera.

It sounds old-fashioned to fuss about being watched. The philosopher Jeremy Bentham once described the perfect prison as a "panopticon" where prisoners were under complete surveillance and yet could not see the watcher. But that was in the 18th century.

In *1984*, the inevitable textbook of Big Brotherhood, George Orwell wrote: "There was of course no way of knowing whether you were being watched at any given moment. . . . You had to live—did live, from habit that became instinct—in the assumption that every sound you made was overheard, and, except in darkness, every movement scrutinized." But he wrote that in 1949.

Today people audition to go on *Big Brother 3*. A woman gives birth on the Web. Since Jennifer Ringley "jennicammed" her way to fame, many others have chosen to live in the public eye, 24/7.

If the threshold of privacy has been lowered, the threshold of anxiety has been heightened. So we accept scrutiny as the price of security.

In this process, we don't always recognize when the camera has become the voyeur. Ads for Web cams pop up over the Internet featuring shadowy images of couples in bed. William Staples, sociologist and author of *Everyday Surveillance,* notes that "the sell is security but the hook is voyeurism." Meanwhile, one security camera picks up Madelyne Toogood in a "moment." But another may tape a couple necking in the car or a customer tripping over her feet. Next thing you know your image is out there on the Internet, says Staples.

Frankly, I am comforted by a security camera in a parking garage late at night. And I know that videotapes are useful for police investigations— after the crime. But if security is overrated, intrusion may be underrated.

The Toogood reality show ended with a mother in court and a child in foster care and a second debate about whether this did more harm than good. Surely we should spend some of the same energy debating the collective life of the videocammed American? How many little brothers add up to a big one?

Look up there. Is that a security guard watching? Or is it a Peeping Tom?

October 6, 2002

AN OLD-FASHIONED UPGRADE

I am afraid we have to recruit the Greatest Generation for one last mission. I know, I know. They overcame the depression, won the war, raised the baby boomers, and deserve to rest on their laurels.

But once more into the breach. This time the technological breach. They are needed as a National Guard against creeping complication. They need to be enlisted in defense of simplicity.

My call comes after a long visit with my mother and her TV set. Once upon a time, all she needed to watch TV was an on-off switch. Now she has to coordinate three buttons on two remotes. Worse yet, this TV may well be on its last legs.

I would happily replace it except that new TVs come fully equipped with the options from hell. Watching television now requires the training and skill of a pilot at the controls of an Airbus 300.

We call this progress. We just assume that every younger generation will have to help the elder function in the world of increasing "functions."

One month I help my mother program her new phone—don't ask. The next month my son-in-law spends so much time walking me through new software that he answers the phone, "Microsoft Help Line!" Meanwhile, somewhere out there, a 12-year-old is ready to tell the thirtysomethings that using the USB to hook up the external CD burner is as easy as "plugging in a toaster."

The problem is that the manufacturers keep marketing to those 12-year-olds.

In the past year, seduced by the user-friendly advertising, we bought a digital camera that will, I am sure, send wonderful pictures over the Internet. My sister replaced a stove with a convection oven so complex it comes with classes. Not in cooking.

It has come to the point where the average American of average age needs tech support just to run the living room. Every "upgrade" now downgrades the quality of life. The more functions, the more dysfunctional.

We have hit the tipping point where many of us break out in hives at the thought of buying new "stuff." At the current rate of creeping complication, the economy may grind to a halt at DSL speed.

This is where the elder generation comes into play. Or rather, back to work. Which would you rather buy? A new product so simple that "even a

12-year-old can use it"? Or a product so simple that his grandmother can use it?

It's time to draft a random sample of the greatest generation to form a national consumer screening board, a kind of technological FDA. Nothing would be allowed onto the market until and unless it passes through their hands and wins the seal of approval of the greatest generation.

This is not a plea to lower standards, nor is it patronizing. The greatest generation has ATM-ed out of one century and is e-mailing into the next. At the same time they are the canaries in the mine of frustration.

We have learned that every time we simplify life to make it work for our elders we make it work for the rest of us. Build ramps for wheelchairs and we use them for strollers. The little town of Dunedin, Florida, for example, is becoming "elder-ready" by giving pedestrians 15 seconds more to cross the street, shelters for bus stops, and street signs with big letters. Sounds good to me.

Our new board will indeed set a high standard—of simplicity. No ad will be able to claim a product "user-friendly" without making friends of these users. To get the Greatest Generation Seal of Approval, any "improved" technology will have to pass at least three tests:

Test One: This product must perform the central task—TV watching, music listening, cooking, driving, photo-taking, etc.—as easily as the equipment it replaces.

Test Two: Seven out of 10 panel members must be able to read and understand the instructions—no longer than one page (in large type)—without having it translated from the original Geek.

Test three: Nine out of 10 panel members must be able use this product without calling their grandchildren.

Techies will tell you that this is just a phase we're in. Those with young thumbs and nimble brains will grow up and old in a more gadget-friendly frame of mind. But if history is any guide, they'll also be phased out.

Instead of forcing consumers to fit the equipment, make the equipment fit the consumer. This is not dumbing down; this is simplifying up. And do we ever have the right generation for the right job.

Mom, Dad, Grandma, Grandpa: Uncle Sam Wants You.

May 9, 2002

Trail Mix

FOR EVERY SELF-DECEPTION THERE IS A MOMENT WHEN

REALITY BITES—OR PERHAPS, SIPS. FOR ME IT WAS IN THE

WELCOMING LETTER FROM THE QUIET, YOGA-INSPIRED,

SPIRITUAL WEEKEND RETREAT TO WHICH I HAD SENT MY

DEPOSIT. AS THE DAY APPROACHED I REALIZED I WASN'T

THINKING ABOUT WITHDRAWAL FROM THE WORLD BUT

FROM CAFFEINE. I WASN'T CONTEMPLATING NIRVANA

AND KARMA BUT SUMATRA AND FRENCH ROAST.

—FROM "CAFFEINE WARRIOR," FEBRUARY 18, 2001

DON'T FRET, MES AMIS, ABOUT LE HOT DOG

T here I am, nibbling my *croissant* and sipping my *cafe au lait* at the *Au Bon Pain* when the terrible news flashes before my American eyes.

The French are convinced that we are making a bid for the hostile takeover of their language. So they are trying to put up trade barriers against imported English words.

The protectionists of Paris seem to be suffering from what is known among the young and hip in their land as *le stress*. They do not like the fact that cars in France are equipped with *le air bags* or that their monetary system is suffering *le cash flow*. They are alarmed that their people are flying in *le jumbo jets* and reading *le best sellers*.

It's not really English that has created this *cause celebre*. It's the pushy dialect known as American. We are the ones who have the French eating *le popcorn* and watching *le talk show* or listening to *le hit parade*.

So the National Assembly is going to vote this spring on a law that would prevent our words from taking up permanent residence in the official French language. Government and business communications, radio and TV broadcasts, would be forbidden from using an immigrant word where a native equivalent exists or can be concocted.

Well, pardon my French, but as we say in America, it's *déjà vu* all over again.

The linguistic trade policy of the French government has been hostile to Americanisms ever since a book was published called *Parlez-Vous Franglais?* That was 30 years ago, when the French had just begun to do *le shopping* at *le supermarket*.

In the early '80s, the High Commission for the French Language described Anglo-Saxons as cultural imperialists trying to rule France by words rather than weapons. These commissioners drew a linguistic Maginot line around the French border. It collapsed faster than you could say *le microchip*.

But now they are at it again and more seriously.

Frankly—frankness is important when speaking to the French—I always thought the Japanese were the protectionists. After all, the French had invented *laissez-faire* economics. Or at least the name.

It turns out, however, that while the Japanese care about what they make, the French care about what they say. What the auto is to Japan, the *bon mots* are to France. The Japanese care about economics, the French care about culture.

My guess is that the French intellectuals who have reignited this trade war aren't really angry that their lives may be saved by *le air bag*. They are appalled at the cultural takeover by the likes of Arnold Schwarzenneger and EuroDisney.

Here is the country that gave us *ballet* and what did we give them in return? *Le disque-jockey*. They gave us *haute couture* and we give them *le jeans*. They gave us a *gourmet* cuisine and we gave them *le fast food*.

The people who exported the very word *elite* to the States have imported a mass culture that's enough to make a *quiche* curdle and a *soufflé* collapse.

It's insulting that the White House is replacing a French chef with a homegrown cook. (*Le Cook?*) The more ignominious fact is that the French people are actually eating *le hot dog*. But before the trade war becomes a *fait accompli*, may I remind the French that during a long and glorious era of free trade among languages, words have traveled both ways across the Atlantic.

When we had only underwear, you gave us *lingerie*. When we had mere flowers, you put them in a *bouquet*. When we had toilet water, you created *perfume*.

You gave our apple pie its *a la mode*. You gave our soup its *du jour*. You helped us know the *chic* from the *gauche*. You let us turn a mundane meeting into a *rendezvous*.

If you ban *Franglais*, I'm afraid we'll have to ban *Englench*. And while we may screw up from time to time, surely you don't want to commit such a terrible *faux pas*.

So let us remember that France has always been among the *avant garde*. In this world of instant communication and word proliferation, language barriers are simply *passé*.

March 31, 1994

I t is breakfast time and I am staring a bagel in the face. This is not your father's bagel. This is not the bagel your fore-bears ate in New York. This is The Bagel That Ate New York.

How did I hold my tongue about the saga of the Incred-ible Expanding Bagel? I was too focused on the multicultural, ecumenical takeover of this ethnic item. For over a year, I have been grumbling at the chocolate chip bagel, the jalapeno bagel, the honey-wheat-cheddar-cheese-blueberry bagel, concoctions that would make my ancestors roll over in their graves. But, then, they were thin enough to do so.

The breakfast before me however is a bagel on growth hormones. It has heft and girth. It doesn't weigh in at the government certified 2 ounces accorded its species, but rather at 5 ounces. In fact, it has added relatively more to its diameter than I have added to mine (but enough about that!).

Forgive me for this antibagel rant. (Have you seen a muffin this morn-ing? Sure, you have. You just thought it was a cake.) But it occurs to me now that my rotund breakfast—thank God for the hole in the middle—is not the only food that has been growing before my very eyes.

In the food world, less is now measurably more. At the movies, the small popcorn box of my childhood has tripled into the large bag they now label small. The 6-ounce bottle of Coca-Cola, circa 1916, has grown up to be a 12-ounce Coke. The 1-ounce Hershey bar now comes out of the vending machine 50 percent heavier.

Anyone who eats out—and a third of all American meals are now out of the house—can tell you that the appetizer is now the size of an old entree. At McDonald's, the small order of french fries is the size of the original large. At my favorite coffee shop they have eliminated small and medium al-together so that the dialogue with the server sounds like a comedy routine:

"I'd like a small latte, please."

"One tall coming up."

"No, a small."

"Tall is small."

"Tall is small?"

"Yes, medium is grande!"

What is going on here? We don't have to be entirely paranoid to won-der if we're being fattened up for the cardiovascular kill. If food is a growth industry, we're already in plus-sizes.

Before the era of the Incredibly Expanding Food, one in four Americans was overweight. Now it's one in three. (Hello, you muffin, you.) About 44 million of us say we want to lose weight.

Lisa Young, a nutritionist at New York University who has been roaming the streets of Manhattan with a small food scale for her research says that our perceptions are changing in, um, proportion to portions. Remember when mom said, your eyes are bigger than your stomach? Well, even our eyes are growing bigger.

Young had a class of students bring in what they thought was a "medium" potato, a medium apple, a medium muffin and, yes, a medium bagel. Their "medium" dwarfed the USDA definition of medium.

The bigger-is-better theory of marketing isn't all that complicated. It's about selling more food. If you give more you can charge more. Most of the cost of a soft drink is in the label and bottle. By now Americans are convinced of the value of the "giant economy size." So convinced that research shows we buy "two for $1" even when one is 50 cents.

NYU's Marion Nestle offers up the underlying secret, "We greatly overproduce food. The American food supply provides an average of 3,800 calories for every man, woman and child on a daily basis." But most of us don't need much more than 2,000 calories. You do the math.

The doggy bag is now a staple of restaurant dining. But when we buy giant economy-size, we do actually eat giant economy-size. Last year an Illinois researcher had parents go home with videos, popcorn, and M&Ms. The folks who got the one-pound bag of candy ate 112 M&Ms, the folks with the two-pound bag ate 156 M&Ms. They all ate half the popcorn whether it was the huge "medium" or the gargantuan "jumbo."

So my giant bagel is a value on the same scale as buying a larger dress because you get more yardage for the buck. The only difference is that at this rate, the larger dress will fit.

No, I won't join the folks who think we should have a higher tax on junk food, though perhaps a graduated food tax would be appropriate with a sliding scale from super-colossal to merely tall. I will hold that thought until the magical moment my bagel reaches dinner plate proportions.

Alas, that won't happen soon since the size of the plate itself is also increasing. The 10-inch plate is becoming a 12-inch plate.

Need I say more? The last word this morning belongs to Miss Piggy who once admonished us all: "Never eat more than you can lift." Ah yes, that's what this bagel is for: weight lifting.

February 28, 1999

H ot Damn. I should have saved the dress my mom wore to the wedding. But who knew?

For years, my mother maintained one wry claim to fame. She was the only woman who changed for the wedding of Jack and Jackie in the restroom of a gas station just north of Newport, Rhode Island. Put that on the record.

My folks were on the low end of the guest list. They sat on the Boston side of the aisle. We lived in an apartment, not a Newport "cottage." Tacky as it sounds, my mom even wore the dress with the princess waist and the bolero jacket again. And again.

In fact, the last time that family hand-me-down made a public appearance was in a school play when my daughter played Anita in "West Side Story."

But in one of those fits of cleaning to which Jacqueline Kennedy Onassis was clearly never subject, I gave it away to Goodwill.

Who would have dreamed that someday a stranger would bid $42,500 for her tape measure? If someone paid $18,000 for a salt and pepper shaker that Jackie might never have touched, how about a dress that certifiably danced at the wedding?

Oh me of little foresight!

The Jackie O auction, the Camelot yard sale, had jaws dropping all over America. And not just the one on the man who paid half a million dollars for a cigar box.

Never mind the big stuff, the desk and the diamonds. Somebody actually paid $11,500 for an inscribed copy of Norman Mailer's *Harlot's Ghost*—a novel remaindered down in the dollar bin of my local bookstore. Somebody paid $9,200 for a few wicker baskets that look as if they came with a crocus plant from the local florist.

This was the stuff that the kids didn't want. The stuff that the Kennedy Library didn't want. It was what one wag labeled Jackie's Junque, with due apologies to Mr. Onassis's 40-carat ring.

I kept expecting to see some chipped cups come up for sale, or some spoons that had been eaten by the disposal. I kept wondering who paid $11,500 for the selected speeches of Chiang Kai-shek. Ah, those hours of reading pleasure.

As for Jack's golf clubs? I'll put my money in Big Bertha's.

(Note to the person who bought the $300 gold and black enamel lighter for $48,500. This is God's way of telling you that you have too much money.)

The auction with its jewelry flotsam and human jetsam reminded me of the scene from *Zorba the Greek* where the neighbors came into the house of a dead woman and stripped it bare. Only this was what it looks like when the "neighbors" are rich and the town is Sotheby's.

If the whole thing did begin to seem a little creepy, well maybe it's because Jackie's stuff went up for sale the same day a judge in Wisconsin ruled that serial killer Jeffrey Dahmer's property would also be auctioned. Though not at Sotheby's.

In a world where cannibals and former first ladies are both dubbed celebrities, who knows what's valuable anymore? Maybe Dahmer's drill bits and sledge hammer will fetch more than the $42,550 paid for Jackie's childhood book of French conjugations.

But the 70,000-odd folks who phoned and faxed these bids seemed to want some very material connection with a fanciful moment in time. Or with a fantasy family. It wasn't the "simulated" pearls or the "distressed" furniture that made the prices skyrocket, but the airbrushed memories.

The kids' things, the rocking chair and high chair, were the ghostliest of sale items. How odd for a grown-up John Kennedy to see how nostalgic people are for John-John. Is it any wonder that Caroline has written a book about privacy?

And Jackie? A lot of her neighbors and admirers said that Jackie O would have hated to see the scene at Sotheby's. At least one woman harrumphed: "She's spinning and kicking in her grave."

But I don't buy it. Jackie might have been laughing, but she wasn't spinning when a 9-inch statue of a white mouse on a corncob brought in $11,000 for John, Caroline, and the IRS.

If there was one thing Jackie cared about, worried about, worked for, it was her children. She was a good mom. And—ask Sotheby's—she was one helluva provider.

As for me, what do I tell my daughter about grandma's dress? Sorry, babe, I threw away a fortune.

April 28, 1996

T he ceremonies are over, but I would like to suggest one last way to commemorate the golden anniversary of the defeat of the Nazis. How about a moratorium on the current abuse of terms like storm trooper, swastika, holocaust, Gestapo, Hitler? How about putting the language of the Third Reich into mothballs?

The further we are removed from the defeat of the Nazis, the more this vocabulary seems to be taking over our own. It's become part of the casual, ubiquitous, inflammatory speech Americans use to turn one another into monsters. Which, if I recall correctly, was a tactic favored by Goebbels himself.

Just in the past month, the NRA attacked federal agents as "jack-booted government thugs" who wear "Nazi bucket helmets and black storm trooper uniforms." In the ratcheting up of the rhetorical wars, it wasn't enough for the NRA to complain that the agents had overstepped their bounds; they had to call them Nazis.

Twice more in recent days, congressmen have compared environmentalist agencies with Hitler's troops. On May 16, Pennsylvania's Bud Shuster talked about EPA officials as an "environmental Gestapo." Before that, Missouri's Bill Emerson warned about the establishment of an "eco-Gestapo force."

On the other side of the aisle, Senator John Kerry recently suggested that a proposed new kind of tax audit, on "lifestyles," would produce an "IRS Gestapo-like entity." And Democrats John Lewis and Charles Rangel compared silence in the face of the new conservative agenda to silence in the early days of the Third Reich. They didn't just disagree with conservatives; they Nazified them.

Then there are the perennial entries on the Hitler log. Antiabortion groups talk about the abortion holocaust—comparing the fetuses to Jews and the doctors to Mengele. Rush Limbaugh likes to sprinkle the term "femi-Nazis" across the airwaves—turning an oxymoron into a laugh.

Much of the time, the hurling of "Nazi" names is just plain dumb. As dumb as the behavior of punk groups, who think they can illustrate their devotion to anarchism with symbols of fascism. Singers like Sid Vicious, groups like the Dead Boys, once sported swastikas without realizing that in Hitler's time and place they would have been rounded up as enemies of the Reich.

As for pinning the Nazi label on the supporters of abortion rights, the propagandists surely know that Hitler was a hard-line opponent of abortion. (Did that make him prolife?) In *Mein Kampf* he wrote, "We must also do away with the conception that the treatment of the body is the affair of every individual." A woman's body wasn't hers; it belonged to the state.

Femi-Nazi? Call sisterhood powerful or pushy if you like. But tell the dittoheads that feminists were a prime target of the Nazis. The Fuehrer vowed to return Germany's uppity women to "children, cooking, church." And he set about doing it.

Even when Nazi-speak is not historically dumb, it's rhetorically dumb. The Hitlerian language has become an indiscriminate shorthand for every petty tyranny.

In this vocabulary, every two-bit boss becomes a "little Hitler." Every domineering high school principal is accused of running a "concentration camp." Every overbearing piece of behavior becomes a "Gestapo" tactic. And every political disagreement becomes a fight against evil.

Crying Hitler in our time is like crying wolf. The charge immediately escalates the argument, adding verbal fuel to fires of any dimension, however minor. But eventually, yelling Nazi at environmentalists and Gestapo at federal agents diminishes the emotional power of these words should we need them.

In time these epithets even downgrade the horror of the Third Reich and the immensity of the Second World War. They cheapen history and insult memory, especially the memory of the survivors.

It's one reason George Bush was so quick to take offense at the NRA's Nazi-isms. As a veteran of World War II, he still knows a Nazi when he sees one and knows the difference between the Gestapo and a federal agent.

Exactly 50 years ago this spring, his generation liberated the concentration camps. Americans learned then, with a fresh sense of horror, about the crematoriums, about man's inhumanity, about the trains that ran on time to the gas chambers.

This was Nazism. This was the Gestapo. This was the Holocaust. This was Hitler. If you please, save the real words for the real thing.

June 4, 1995

FORWARD THINKING

I first got involved in integrating golf last summer, as a member of a small feminist subcommittee at a quirky nine-hole course in Maine. We quietly and subversively liberated a ladies' tee with a sign renaming it the forward tee.

This was not done, I hasten to add, because the women on the committee longed to play from the Men's Tee. It was a subtle boon to older island men who could no longer make it over the gully from the greater distance and who also wouldn't lay a club on anything labeled Ladies. In short, it was a ploy to make the game unisexually easier.

This is what distinguishes me from Annika Sorenstam: I think golf is waaaay too hard already. Of course, what also distinguishes me from Annika is about 90 yards on our best drives. But let's not go there.

It's the search for a challenge that brought this champion of the Ladies Professional Golf Association (the Forward PGA?) to the Colonial Country Club in Fort Worth, Texas. She is the first woman to play in the PGA since the redoubtable Babe Didrikson Zaharias in 1945.

Annika has won 49 LPGA tournaments, 11 in the last year, and once turned in a score of 59. With that wipe-out record, no one surely would deny her the chance to test herself against the PGA. Well, actually Vijay Singh would, but the Fijian pro bowed out of the tournament after wishing her ill. And pro Fred Funk sounded like Fred Flintstone when he grumbled, "she'll be taking a spot from somebody who's trying to earn a living."

Anyway, what's intriguing is not the remarks of men whose handicaps are higher off the fairway than on. What's notable is that Annika did not get the attention of the world until she was picked to play with the boys.

Before that, she was arguably the least-known best athlete around.

She earned $2,863,904 last year, which isn't exactly peanuts, but it was 41 cents for every dollar Tiger earned. That's worse than the average working woman's 76 cents to the male dollar.

Now, she's had gigs on *60 Minutes* and Jay Leno. *Sports Illustrated* said she had the best head in the game, and hundreds of reporters went to record her every shot.

There is something a wee bit familiar about all this. It's not just an echo of the Billie Jean King match with Bobby Riggs. (Fortunately this was not cast as another Battle of the Sexes.) But women do get more attention—criticism and respect, money and status—when they compete with men on male terrain.

We know this is still true in the work world. But it seems true as well in professional sports. A lightweight boxer doesn't have to "move up" to the heavyweights to get the same status, but in many sports women are still dubbed second class as long as they are separate class.

This puts us in something of a pickle. We're watching a generation of remarkable women athletes. The list of "first" and "only" and "breakthrough" women grows longer. Today's female stars, like the buff Annika, would wallop yesterday's male superstars.

There's no reason why women can't compete on the same turf in sports such as horse racing or stock car racing when, as Donna Lopiano, the head of the Women's Sports Foundation, quips, "the athlete is the horse or the car." We have as well a growing list of sports such as mixed doubles in tennis that are constructed for coed teams.

But in sports where strength matters, including golf, what happens if the exceptions such as Annika move "up"? Does the No. 1 woman become the No. 28 man? Does she leave a void in the LPGA? Does that help or harm women's sports?

I've wondered about that from time to time as I've watched school sports. I have cheered the new girl on the boy's team. "You go, girl." We applaud the individual athlete. At the same time, I'd rather the entire girls' team moved up a notch in skills and status. "You go, team."

Marcia Greenberger, a Title IX advocate who shares some ambivalence, says about school sports, "Separate hasn't yet become equal. But if we didn't have separate, we'd be even further from equality."

Ultimately, Lopiano suspects, we'll have three categories of professional sports: his, hers, and theirs. The real fun of sports, she adds, is competition between equals. It's more fun seeing Serena against Venus than against Andre Agassi.

So, Annika—you go, girl. Playing the PGA is probably a one-shot thing and a publicity shot thing. But all in all, it would be better to find the competition growing and the spotlight glowing on the women's own turf.

That's my idea of a forward tee.

May 22, 2003

MENO-POSITIVE

Damn, what did I do with that T-shirt? The one that says "These aren't hot flashes, they're power surges." Where is it now that I've finally found just the right occasion?

Ever since the baby boomers started hitting 50, the cutting edge of this ever vigilant, ever youthful generation has been trying to get us all to think positively about the pause.

A fleet of pop (or rather, mom) psychologists has emerged to remind us that the reproductive finale doesn't mean the productive end. A choir of gender spinmeisters (or rather, spinmistresses) insists that midlife begins when fertility ends.

This is a marketeer's dream. There are 37 million postmenopausal women in America already. In another dozen years there'll be 50 million. It's no wonder that there are workshops offered on how to embrace the inner crone, videos on sex in the postovum era, and power T-shirts.

Frankly, though, it's been a tough sell. With hormones to the right of us and trophy wives to the left, the basic messages about the value of postmenopausal women are still enough to give anyone night sweats. We may have postmenopausal pregnancy poster gals. But the culture is still haunted by witches and the ancient specters of genetically useless old hens.

Too many of us facing "the change" were raised on anthropologists of the Lionel Tiger stripe and evolutionists of the survivalist school who have never figured out whether there is a biological purpose to postovum living.

Female humans are the only primates that survive long beyond their last pregnancy. Some assumed that older women were an evolutionary accident. Fifty- and sixty- and seventy-something women were dismissed as modern medicine's little luxuries, creatures who are irrelevant to survival of the species. Nature's leftovers.

I doubt that many of us stayed up at night worrying about our role in evolution. I never put all my eggs in the biological basket. Nevertheless, I'm downright aglow at the recent piece of anthropological revisionism.

I feel a power surge coming on.

A group of anthropologists studying the Hadza hunter-gatherers of northern Tanzania reports in *Current Anthropology* that postmenopausal women are the serious breadwinners in that community. They work longer and harder hours out in the bushes. They bring home the berries. And the tubers.

The children provided for by these senior women, their grandmothers and great aunts, are the children most likely to survive. When the nursing mothers are attuned to the youngest, it's the senior women who make sure the older kids are fed well.

Anthropologist Kristen Hawkes of the University of Utah uses this to put forward a Grandmother Hypothesis. She goes so far as to suggest that post-menopausal zest may account for the runaway success of our kind of primates.

In the great Darwinian scheme of things, it isn't just the number of offspring but their fitness that spells survival. Here Grandma makes the best provider.

I know no Hadzas, though I'm delighted that the gatherers are getting their due along with the hunters. When I took anthropology, it sounded like the men went out for the woolly mammoth bacon while the women waited at home with little blueberry garnishes.

Frankly, most of the grandmothers I know do their gathering at Baby Gap. And the fiftysomething women who have reentered the workplace to support their families make the Hadzas' pace of tuber-gathering look leisurely.

Still, it's good for the modern woman's soul to contemplate a new image of their senior foremothers. If the Hadza are any indication, ancestral sisterhood was powerful. Older women were programmed into the big picture.

We were meant to be older and wiser. When childbearing ends, gear up to the job of making life better for the whole clan.

Meno is just the pause that refreshes.

October 5, 1997

I t's not that I've been in denial, as they say in rehab. Denial is not my strong suit. For years I acknowledged my addiction with a blithe one-line toast: "ah, coffee, the last drug of my generation."

Technically, of course, it isn't the last drug. Or even the last legal drug. But alcohol has been limited to nonpregnant, nondriving people in non-liver-and-life-destroying quantities. Smoking isn't banned but banished to doorways where a community of folks look like they're having much too much fun.

Coffee, on the other hand, is culturally approved, universally accepted, socially enabled, and financially promoted. There's a fix on every corner.

Still, I comforted myself with the notion that I wasn't a coffee junkie. Junkies drink the sludge at the bottom of the day-old pot hanging around the office. I am a coffee gourmet.

I own at least six caffeine delivery systems from a Melitta to an espresso machine. Like an alcoholic who only consumes vintage Bordeaux, I choose beans of a certain provenance. I drink politically correct, organic, bird-friendly, shade-grown coffee cultivated by small farmers who get their fair-trading share of the profits. Seriously.

Besides, I only drink about two cups. Every single day. First thing in the morning. Immediately. Or else.

But for every self-deception there is a moment when reality bites—or, perhaps, sips. For me it was in the welcoming letter from the quiet, yoga-inspired, spiritual weekend retreat to which I had already sent my deposit.

The brochure reminded retreaters that we were heading to an environment that was: drug free, of course; nonsmoking, praise the Lord; vegetarian, no problem; alcohol free, fine; and caffeine-free—AARRRGH!

Those two little hyphenated words struck terror in the heart of someone eager for a weekend of yoga classes, downward facing dog positions, and silent breakfasts. I could do without words, but without coffee??? A postscript said they would dole out tea bags like methadone to anyone who asked at the front desk, but it wouldn't be served in the dining room, aka the dining chapel.

As the day approached I realized that I wasn't thinking about withdrawal from the world but from caffeine. I wasn't contemplating nirvana and karma but sumatra and French roast.

So it is that a woman who doesn't even cheat at golf arrived at a spiritual retreat smuggling a small but humiliating amount of ground coffee, a one-cup coffee maker, and a travelling mug. So it is that Saturday morning found me away from everything worldly except for the need to find hot water for my illegal stash. NOW!

One secret cup of coffee later, one furtive tooth-brushing and room-airing later, I was fine, alert, anxiety-free, and ready to face my first piece of personal enlightenment. No caffeine, no karma.

I don't mean to equate caffeine with cocaine or to suggest a plot for *Traffic II* tracing little black beans from the heart of Costa Rica to a blissful shop in Seattle. But my correspondence from the decaffeinated front line may give joe-heads a way to look at the questions that rarely get aired in the drug wars.

What makes one drug OK and another forbidden? Is the problem in the substance, in its abuse, or in its illegality? Is the war waged in the name of morality, public health, behavior, or fighting crime? Have we ever figured out a rational way to explain and triage which drugs should be banned for which reasons?

Sitting furtively with my contraband, I ruminated on whether addiction itself is considered the moral problem. A question of highs and withdrawals? If so, coffee drinkers of America, caffeine 'r' us. And while I would never steal or sell my first born to support my habit, I had already become a fugitive.

Of course, coffee itself is a treatment for asthma, which I don't have, but never mind. But we haven't triaged the drugs that are deadly to life, work, family, or brain tissues from the drugs that are only a problem if you don't have them.

Today I write this, happily, under the influence of a drug. My breathing stayed yogic, my breakfast stayed silent, and I was able to meditate on something other than drug policy.

But next time, I plan to go clean. That is, as long as I can bring one little bitty chocolate bar.

February 18, 2001

Gender & Other Gaps

WE LIVE IN AN ERA OF GREAT ATTENTION TO SMALL

DIFFERENCES. SCIENTISTS FOCUS THEIR RESEARCH

ON MALE AND FEMALE BRAINS. POP BOOKS TELL US

THAT WOMEN ARE FROM VENUS AND MEN ARE FROM

MARS, THAT WOMEN RUN WITH WOLVES AND MEN WITH

ROBERT BLY.

—FROM "ONE-SIZE-FITS-ALL EDUCATION," MAY 26, 1994

T he whole scene takes no more than 30 seconds.

A six-pack of teenage boys in sneakers and shorts, with baseball caps turned front and back, hanging out on a steamy summer night.

Two girls—14 or 15, no older—in halters and shorts, walk down the street, their sandals slapping the concrete.

The boys check them out, who's hot, who's not. They close ranks, narrow the sidewalk, so the girls must pass single file.

It's then that I see the girls' antennae go up, notice the way they speed-read the scene, the boys, and the single file between play and danger. The taller girl strikes a pose as a good sport but not a willing player. The smaller takes on a role neither offended nor interested.

The boys stare; the girls smile slightly but make no eye contact. The oldest and boldest of the pack pretends to untie one girl's halter top as she goes by. The girlfriends reach the corner and break into nervous giggles.

Thirty seconds and the boys, like sidewalk hall monitors, have let them pass. It's over.

For once, I don't take this scene for granted. I'm struck tonight by how carefully, precisely, the girls read these boys. How they calibrate both the danger and their own reaction.

How much time and energy went into acquiring these street smarts? Where did they learn? Did their parents teach them to be sexually literate? For their own safety?

Safe sex—no, safe sexuality—is on my mind. In the weeks since I wrote about the Central Park assaults on some 50 women in broad daylight, my mail has been filled with people, many sharing my dismay. But in the mix, there were questions: Didn't I see how some women were playing along? Didn't I see what some women were wearing?

One man described women on the infamous videotapes who would "giggle and laugh as the guys doused them with water. Only when they felt things were getting 'out of hand' did they complain. . . . They got exactly what was coming to them."

Another man wrote about female "exhibitionists" who send the "wrong message" to men: "It's akin to dangling a pork chop over a pack of starving wolves."

A woman wrote of "skin" fashions, of women with expressions that said "Hi, sailor, want to have some fun? All sailors want to have fun."

And still another reader forwarded a newspaper column on the Central Park assaults by Stanley Crouch that detoured onto "scantily clad young women" and told approvingly of a father admonishing his teenage daughter, "You are not leaving this house looking like a prostitute."

I won't revisit the argument that safety can be found in a dress code. If that were true, rape would have been much rarer among our crinoline-covered foremothers. Such a belief leads backward to the sad, distorted thought of a Bangladeshi woman. Brutally disfigured by acid, she proclaimed herself a convert to purdah: "If I had been kept under the veil, Rakim (her assailant) would not have seen me or been able to talk to me."

But I am struck by the difficulty our daughters still have being safe and sexual. They are supposed to calibrate the continuum from horseplay to harassment to assault. The culture expects them to be sexy but not "pork chops," to attract men and beware of them. And to maneuver carefully through this terrain, single file.

Remember the sexual assaults at Atlanta's Freaknik celebration, the rapes at Woodstock? Some women were labeled "fair game." In Central Park, "good sports" who laughed as their T-shirts were sprayed with water were less credible "victims" when those T-shirts were torn off.

Boys—and men—are also subject to double messages. They're surrounded by R-rated images of playgirls who just wanna have fun, and lectured on sexual harassment. They know girls who want to be seen but not stared at.

But girls are the more endangered of our species. So even those who want our daughters to be comfortable in their own skins, to feel powerful in their own bodies, and to be sexually at ease, end up teaching them to be wary.

Girls learn to read boys. They learn that they have to maneuver—single file—to be safe. They learn who owns the street and the park. These lessons of sexual danger sometimes linger even in relationships with men they love.

There are times when I'm convinced we've updated the book on men and women. But until we teach our sons their own set of reading lessons, this piece of the story will remain the same.

July 16, 2000

S o we part company. Again.

Just a couple of weeks ago, I took some small comfort from the fact that this sex scandal had not opened up a gender gap. Since then, I've been reminded in no uncertain terms that it's opened up the intra-gender gap. Again.

Women who once came from different ends of the political spectrum to skewer Gary Hart have now retreated to opposite sides over the fate of Bill Clinton.

A phalanx of women's rights leaders to the left. A coterie from the ranks of the Independent Women's Forum to the right. The religious right and the secular left. Talk show volleys and polling thunders. Again.

When the Gary Hart affair broke, an odd coalition of puritans and feminists censured him. Holding hands around the good ship Monkey Business, they looked as if they were made for each other. But under that thin veneer of agreement, one was concerned with relationships and the other with commandments. Now that they have split, it's clear that this was never a marriage of the minds.

I am not surprised by either the earlier alliance or the current breakup of this pan-female agreement. It's hardly the first time.

Way back in the suffrage movement, we had all sorts of women marching shoulder to shoulder in favor of the vote. But when you looked closer, they were marching on different grounds. Some staked the moral claim to the vote on women's equality and others on women's purity.

The conservative women in the Temperance movement were persuaded that it was all right, indeed godly, to get out of the house and work for suffrage—because abolition was a goal and Demon Rum an enemy. The more liberal suffragists led the charge—civil rights were the goal and inequality was the enemy.

When the women's movement re-emerged a generation ago, sexual politics raged most furiously around sex itself. As one veteran remembers the conundrum of consciousness-raising groups, "One week we were saying, 'Smash monogamy,' and the next week we were saying, 'Wait a minute, that's what the men want.' " One week the focus was on sexual liberation for women, the next week on protection for women.

Sisterhood repeatedly splintered over sex. Consider the odd bedfellows against pornography. Radical feminists and reactionary religious groups have testified together in favor of banning porn. But they don't even define it the same way.

The antiporn feminists, such as law professor Catharine MacKinnon, define pornography as sex discrimination. But the moral majoritarians define it as sin.

One group fights porn as sex-ploitation that is wrong because it keeps women in their (lower) place. The other group fights porn as evil. One would X-rate those movies, videos and whatever, that maintain a power imbalance. The other would mandate fig leaves.

It's not hard to imagine a gentle video between two sensually consenting and equal adults that would pass muster with the power-conscious left and drive the prudish right nuts.

As for sexual harassment? After Clarence Thomas and Paula Jones, after the Army, the Navy, and a handful of Supreme Court decisions, we must know how allegiances break down. One side worries about the harassment and the other about the sex. One side worries about an abuse of power going on in the corner office or the factory floor. The other worries about hanky-panky.

Of course things are not always quite that clear. At times we all get involved in exhausting searches for the line between sex and exploitation, private behavior and public disqualification.

But in the case of Monica and Bill, the folks who hitch up their politics against sexual abuse, split up over consensual adultery. Both the unhappy campers at NOW and the smirking stalwarts at the Concerned Women for America are standing by their—well, their principles.

One other thing remains consistent in this ramble through history. In one way or another, the country still looks to women to be the arbiters of sexual behavior. And we're expected to sing in a single voice of sisterhood.

But any time I hear sexual harmony in soprano, a little tuning fork dating way, way back tells me: This ain't never gonna last.

And so, here we go again.

October 4, 1998

Arceli Keh wasn't doing this for the *Guinness Book of World Records*. As the World's Oldest Mom said after her identity was uncovered: "I wasn't trying to make history. I just wanted a baby."

Nevertheless, when the post-menopausal, pre-Medicare birth announcement first blasted across front pages all over the world, the California woman was regarded as a freak of nature. Or unnature.

Strong men gasped at the vision of senior-set maternity. Strong women broke into a Lamaze pant at the idea of spending their golden years lactating.

But pretty soon, the story of this sixtysomething mom was transformed into a case study of the double standard. From all parts of the country, a few men and a whole lot of women began to ask some variation of the same question: "Hey, if Tony Randall can be lauded and cigared for having a baby at 77, what's wrong with Arceli Keh giving birth at 63?"

In short, and with apologies to Jonathan Swift, what's sauce for the gander has now become high-tech sauce for the goose. What's sauce for 77-year-old Tony Randall, 78-year-old Anthony Quinn, 65-year-old Yasser Arafat, 64-year-old Clint Eastwood, and their younger mates is sauce for Arceli Keh and her 60-year-old husband. Gender equality through biotechnology!

Well, I bow to no one in my desire to merge the double standard. There is indeed a whole lot of sexism and ageism in the notion that her wrinkles—but not his—disqualify her. Arceli got to be treated as a sexually viable woman the old-fashioned way: She lied about her age.

I can even dredge up some good news about senior maternity. Medicare could pay the obstetrician. You could stay home and raise the tyke on Social Security and a pension. And to be fair, a whole lot of grandmas are acting moms.

But there is something wacky in this pseudo-equality. Pregnancy never was equal-opportunity employment. It's more—how shall I say this?—labor-intensive for women than men. We put in the sweat equity.

As for child-raising, since time immemorial, men have left their genes behind for women to raise even when they went off to war. Under my single standard, I would rally men who think of fatherhood as a commitment to raising a child, not producing an heir.

But Keh's experience is not quite the blow for equality that some believe. After all, to become pregnant after menopause you still need a younger woman's egg. Arceli is the gestational mother, the birth mother, the nurturing mother, but not the genetic mother.

What we have here, Guinness notwithstanding, is a kind of do-it-yourself surrogacy. This wife went into a high-risk pregnancy—diabetes was one side effect—to carry the offspring of her husband's sperm and another woman's egg to fruition.

Is it too far-fetched to wonder what traditional cultural pressures about gender carried over into the late-life quest to bear a (his) child? And while we are asking questions, would the egg donor approve of an elder donee? Does it matter?

I know that the biological clock is lamented as proof that life isn't fair, that men have more options than women. They can start later, or start over, with a second wife or a third trophy. Women have to figure it all out earlier.

But I have always thought of menopause as the built-in female advantage. Because, guess what? There is a biological clock. It is ticking. It's the life cycle.

"Our age doesn't matter," Mrs. Keh told a British tabloid, *The Express*. "We feel young at heart and love our child." But age counts. It counts the years.

When Cynthia Keh leaves for college, Arceli will be—hopefully—82. Yes, I know, when Julia Randall leaves for college, Tony will be—very, very hopefully—95. Young parents can also die or deteriorate. But we are talking odds.

There's no reason to cheer the biotechnology that allows the goose to do what nature neglected to prevent the gander from doing.

I don't see how we can legally ban elder women from getting eggs. But we can insist that human eggs be allocated as wisely by doctors and donors as livers or kidneys.

Not that long ago, women depended on Mother Nature to help make their decisions. Now we, too, have to depend on that much less reliable biological tool: the human brain.

May 1, 1997

THE FIRST CAMPAIGN
FOR FIRST GENTLEMAN

T he woman is sitting at the beauty parlor scanning the pages of *Esquire* when he pops up. Bob Dole, World War II veteran, presidential candidate, Senate leader and svelte spokesman on impotence—no, erectile dysfunction—is staring out at her. Again.

Surrounding his photo is the word "Courage." Beside him is the admonition that other men go see their doctor. In the lower right hand corner is a small logo for Pfizer, maker of Viagra.

This woman is a certified believer in male openness and sharing and touching and feeling. She prefers Bob Dole to the Pfizer ads of an older couple twirling on the dance floor as if you could swallow Viagra and turn into Fred Astaire.

So she is about to declare "good for him" clear across the sound of hair dryers when suddenly out of nowhere, Alter Ego hisses into her ear: "Good Lord, he's got to stop this before his wife announces for president!"

The woman swirls around in the chair and prissily asks Alter Ego: "What on earth do you mean?"

"Oh come on," Alter answers. "Here we have the first woman with an actual chance to become president, and all we'll be able to think of is her sex life. If he doesn't quit this, she'll be a sex object!"

"A sex object?" the woman blurts out.

"You know what I mean. They'll look at her and think Viagra. She'll be giving a speech late one night and somebody will wonder if he's back at the hotel wasting a $10 pill."

The woman huffs: "You have a dirty mind!"

"I have a dirty mind?" demurs Alter Ego. "Where have you been the last year? Do you actually think that the American people still want to know about the sex life of a couple who might inhabit the White House?"

Woman and Alter Ego testily debate sexual politics for another minute or two.

Who would have guessed that the man from Kansas, a bit of a dour puss, would have violated the male code of silence and talked about ED? Good for him.

Who would have guessed that the woman from North Carolina, a bit of a control freak, would have agreed to make their private life so public. What is she thinking of?

Gradually, it occurs to both Woman and Alter Ego, as the hair on their head(s) is being snipped, that the political power couple must have a method in this libido madness. These two pols would never have done Pfizer without a focus group.

After all, how many times had Bob promised to be supportive? How carefully did they keep him from her campaign video? How dutifully did he promise to be First Gentleman? Just this week, Dole told a reporter: "It's been a one-way street until now. Mostly the men get support from the women. But the men should support the women."

Finally the woman turns to Alter Ego and snaps: "Maybe this isn't a pitch for Viagra. Maybe this is a pitch for role reversal. Maybe this is Bob Dole preparing for the part of First Gentleman."

"Oh puleeze," says Alter Ego.

"No, really. Long before Betty Ford became a clinic, she spoke up for addiction. Nancy Reagan became a poster woman for breast cancer. Barbara Bush did Graves' disease. First Lady-nominee Kitty Dukakis wrote a book announcing her mood and alcohol problems. And how many people prefer Hillary as a survivor of adultery rather than as a health care guru? We like spouses with flaws and problems."

"Yeah," sneers Alter Ego, "but Hillary Clinton suffered in silence."

"Never mind," the woman insists. "These days the president does policy. The First Lady does emotions. He's the executive. She's the healer. Elizabeth's running for president; Bob has to run for healer."

She goes on: "Remember when they ran the first of these ads? What did Elizabeth say? 'It's a great drug.' That's policy. Remember what he said? 'My view is that it's up to the men now, just as the women took charge of their lives with the leadership of Mrs. Ford and others.' That's healing."

Slowly, as they get up from the chair, there is a meeting of the minds between the woman and her Alter Ego. The first campaign for First Gentleman has begun, and Elizabeth and Bob want to be that couple dancing on the White House ballroom floor under a Pfizer logo.

"OK, OK," concedes Alter Ego grumpily. "But couldn't he just have had cataracts?"

April 1, 1999

H ave you noticed a certain rise in attack ads this year? Not a numerical rise, mind you. What you might call a tonal rise.

The political voices broadcast in ads across the nation have been ratcheted up as much as an octave on the scale. Assaults that used to be launched by baritones are now set off by sopranos.

Follow this musical "trip-tik" across the sound waves of the political season.

You're driving along Route 66 when a narrator warns about a moral crisis: "The problem isn't in your house. The problem is in the White House, Bill Clinton's White House."

You're slumped in front of the TV set when a voice intones, "Bill Clinton said he'd lead the war on drugs and change America. All he did was change his mind."

You're deep in Colorado or in the suburbs of New Jersey when the voice-over on television castigates a Senate candidate for opposing a flag-burning amendment: "Some things are wrong—and they've always been wrong."

Or maybe you're in Massachusetts when you make TV eye contact with a mother accusing a Senate candidate of being soft on criminals: "Maybe John Kerry wants to give them another chance, but I just want to get them off the street."

This may be standard traveling music in the world of negative campaign advertising. But this year's recruits in attack ads are increasingly women. The latest weapon is a nicely tuned set of female pipes.

The notion that a female's place is in an attack ad is not entirely new. The most famous such ad is the one that scared voters away from Barry Goldwater in 1964. It was a little girl counting daisy petals before the nuclear countdown.

If there are more women today, it may be a perverse sort of progress. Some of us remember when advertisers used only male voices, explaining that only men had the authority. As a consultant once explained to political scientist June Speakman of Roger Williams University, "The voice of God is a male's voice."

Women still rarely sound almighty in political ads. They still take minor roles. One of the lingering curiosities is that female voices are almost never used in ads for female candidates.

But when you hear them, they're probably on the attack. With the exception of Liddy Dole, who stars in a terribly polite ad reassuring Americans that she is going to vote for her husband, we're talking about ads in which a woman throws the first punch. Recently, the Clinton campaign has used three women narrators all going negative. Four of six Dole ads with female voice-overs returned the offense.

The sneaky part is that women's voices are being used to "soften" the attack as they mount it. This is a year in which voters get negative about negatives. It's as if the consultants all sat around asking: How do we reconcile the voter's longing for civility with the old-fashioned success of negative ads? Eureka! Let's give it the woman's touch.

As Kathleen Hall Jamieson at the University of Pennsylvania puts it more delicately, "The perception among consultants is that a female voice softens the attack and makes it more acceptable."

The job opportunities for women in attack ads remind me of the growth market for women lawyers to defend sleazy defendants. Remember the lawyer for the Menendez brothers? For Mike Tyson?

Today, the head of the NRA is a woman, busily softening the handgun image. And sometimes it seems that every industry with troubles hires a spokeswoman. Check the Tobacco Institute.

Once rejected for their "femaleness," they are now often hired for their alleged "femaleness": that warm, nurturing, softening something or other. Any day now I expect to see women defending Serbian leader Radovan Karadzic.

Consultant Bob Shrum says, "Voters are pretty smart and will catch on to it." But in the interim he admits, "I hate to create the sense that if you are using a woman's voice it must be something sinister." That would be the ultimate irony. Baritones and tenors singing Mr. Nice Guy for an audience that wants civility. Sopranos and altos doing the nasty doo-wop.

This may just be a stop on the way to some rough sound of equality. But today the stereotypes survive. We have women cast as Venus doing Mars without getting any closer to playing God.

In 1996, the attack ads are striking a note that is distinctly falsetto.

October 18, 1996

ONE-SIZE-FITS-ALL EDUCATION

 T-shirt on campus compares the Citadel's cadets to the spotted owls. It calls them both "endangered species." A button worn in the visitors gallery of the courtroom makes its own point. It reads: "Save the Males."

Once upon a time the Citadel epitomized every image in its name. The military college in South Carolina was a fortress, a stronghold, a fortified place, a bulwark. Most of the men who marched across its parade grounds never had a military career, but they joined the highest ranks of the state establishment.

And now they are feeling threatened.

The Citadel—along with the Virginia Military Institute—is literally the last bastion of the all-male public military colleges. It's a bastion under siege by a young woman named Shannon Faulkner, who wants to join the cadet corps and thinks she has the Constitution on her side.

In the past weeks a curious spectacle has unfolded in the Charleston, South Carolina, court. A spectacle of the Citadel's men defining themselves as victims of change. A spectacle of lawyers for a traditional college using—or abusing—feminist arguments to defend their all-male turf. A spectacle of men waving the flag of institutional diversity to justify denying access to women.

Forty years ago, the Supreme Court ruled in *Brown v. Board of Education* that racial segregation in the public schools was unconstitutional. Now the Citadel is arguing for separate but equal public colleges for men and women.

There is no attempt to deny that the Citadel discriminates against women or against Shannon Faulkner, who was accepted on her record and then denied on account of her sex. Instead, the Citadel's lawyer challenged the premise of admitting women: "The case is not just about the Citadel or just about Shannon Faulkner or just about higher education. It's about a unisex world view of the law of the land."

He used the word "unisex"—rather than coed or egalitarian—deliberately. The Citadel is hanging its hopes on the belief that we have somehow gone "beyond" the notion that men and women are the same and should have the same education.

Indeed, today we live in an era of great attention to small differences. Scientists focus their research on male and female brains. Pop books tell us that women are from Venus and men are from Mars, that women run with wolves and men with Robert Bly.

Many women, too, have come to regard the promise of unisex institutions the way they regard unisex sizing in a catalog. It's as if we have been offered the chance to try to fit our own female shapes into the existing male molds.

Women's colleges now argue that women do much better in all-female institutions. They argue that the cutting edge of feminist change is sharpened in these encouraging environments.

But if colleges like Wellesley and Smith are the female avant garde, all-male colleges like VMI and the Citadel form the rear guard. On the Citadel campus, testified one witness and graduate, the word "woman" is used in a derogatory way "every day, every minute, every hour." And yet the lawyers use the arguments of the Wellesleys and the Smiths to defend the Citadel. They perversely use the arguments of change agents to defend the resistance.

VMI has done that as well. A judge recently allowed the college to remain male as long as the state provided a separate but equal program for women at nearby Mary Baldwin College.

"If VMI marches to the beat of a drum," he wrote, "then Mary Baldwin marches to the melody of a fife, and when the march is over both will arrive at the same destination." But how does he know that they are headed in the same direction?

More to the point, the constitutional point, what about the young woman who wants to march to the beat of the drum? Can she be excluded because there is a fife corps in the neighborhood? These are questions the Justice Department will ask in the appeal.

The Citadel, however, hasn't even drawn up a parallel program for women. They are pleading for institutional "diversity" in the "unisex" educational environment. They are hanging their case on the all-male school's status as an endangered species.

But if the Citadel wants to stay all-male, it can do so without calling upon some educational protection agency. Women's colleges are private. The Citadel can save the males by rejecting public money. Despite the appeal to gender and difference, the issue hasn't changed much since the first cases against discrimination. Taxpayer money is going to an institution that prohibits any chance of access to Shannon Faulkner or half the population of South Carolina.

I don't remember anyone rallying to save the last school that segregated African-Americans in the name of racist diversity. The endangered species here is not men. It's discrimination against women. And I won't be sad to see that wiped out.

May 26, 1994

A KINDER, GENTLER PATRIARCHY

I t came to him as a cardiovascular epiphany. Bill McCartney, former football coach and founder of the Promise Keepers, was jogging on the Washington Mall when he felt his heart "yanked toward heaven."

This spiritual aerobic high led him to call for a gathering of men to "Stand in the Gap." Not The Gap store. Not the gender gap. The biblical gap recorded in Ezekiel when God went looking for a few good men to save a country.

So it is that half a million men are expected to arrive in the nation's capital this weekend for a Saturday of male bonding and male bashing. They will be uttering an all-male mea culpa for the abuse and neglect of families and children. If the pattern of such rallies holds, these men will be sharing their feelings and taking responsibility.

This gathering of what is arguably the largest men's movement in the country sounds at some levels like the fondest feminist fantasy. Hundreds of thousands of men collectively eschewing adultery and pornography, violence and abandonment. Men pledging publicly to keep their promises to their wives, to change diapers and bring flowers and offer respect.

Yet many of the women excluded from this mall male event call the leaders of this assembly the enemy. Indeed, the National Organization for Women has put together the darkest analysis of their goals and gone so far as to declare a policy of "No Surrender" in what they define as a battle of the sexes.

This is the duality that has tracked the Promise Keepers since the movement began drawing followers to religious rallies in the comfortable male venue of sports stadiums. A mixture of old-time muscular Christianity and New Age sensibility, the group has raised hopes and hackles in almost equal proportion.

On the one hand, the Promise Keepers appeal to men alienated from each other and their families, men uncertain about what masculinity means anymore, men in search of spiritual healing. On the other hand, the organization is deeply connected to the Christian right, profoundly hostile to homosexuals, opposed to abortion and "liberal women's groups" as well as "atheists and Satanists."

On the one hand, it promises women husbands who will, in McCartney's words, "take responsibility for their actions, who are faithful to their families, who keep their word, even when it's difficult or costly." On the other hand, it assumes a trade-off: wifely submission to a kinder, gentler patriarch.

I don't believe that the Promise Keepers are Women's Enemy No. 1. Or even No. 10. During their peak years, the rallies offered more than 2 million men a safe place to atone, to acknowledge what was missing in their lives, even to change.

But at the same time, the Promise Keepers point a way out of the current conflict of roles and identities which is a way back.

The leaders speak to an old familiar view of authority in our culture. This is a view that says power is granted in return for protecting the weak and vulnerable. It's a view that says, in turn, the weak and vulnerable (must?) follow that leader, accede to that authority, in order to be protected.

This was the deal once struck between kings and subjects, men and women. It does not acknowledge that, sooner or later, every protection can become a protection racket. It prefers the clear lines of authority to the muddle of egalitarian democracy.

In many ways, the Promise Keepers' message echoes the words of the secular fatherhood movement. McCartney blames "a decline in responsible manhood" for the problems of children who grow up without fathers, for crimes of assault and rape.

But what he means by a responsible man is a take-charge kind of guy. Women, in this scheme of things, are left with the choice of a dangerous man, no man, or a sole head of household.

McCartney, trying to reassure women especially of his good intentions, has compared a country of shattered families to a losing football team. "In the game of football," he wrote, "if your team is getting trounced, you'd better have a serious talk with the men at halftime and identify the problems."

You don't have to be a sports analyst to find the flaw in this game plan. In the world of Promise Keepers, men are the only players. In the locker room, they identify the problems and call the shots.

On the field, whether it's the Washington Mall or the family back yard, a woman's designated place is on the cheerleading squad.

October 2, 1997

I know that educated women have always made some people nervous.

In 1873, when less than 15 percent of the college students were female, Harvard's Edward Clarke explained scientifically how expanding a woman's brain would make her uterus shrink.

In 1889, when women still made up less than 20 percent of the college students, the eminent scientist R.R. Coleman warned college women, "You are on the brink of destruction. . . . Beware!! Science pronounces that the woman who studies is lost."

Now it's 2002. The fall semester opens with reports that 57 percent of bachelor's degrees will go to women. And—surprise—it's being heralded as a national crisis.

Throughout the summer, there were dire headlines asking, "Where are the guys?" Christina Hoff Sommers, author of *The War Against Boys,* was everywhere saying that "we have thrown the gender switch" and "girls have been getting strong and stronger and boys weaker in almost all the ways that count academically."

Meanwhile, college presidents overseeing a female, um, dominated campus are working on what they do not call affirmative action plans for men. And the Business Roundtable, an organization of CEOs of the nation's top corporations, is funding a study to figure out what's happening to—dare I say?—their heirs apparent.

It seems that everyone in higher education is majoring in the same subject: the gender gap. The pop quiz has three questions: Are women winning? Are men losing? Is good news for the goose bad news for the gander?

Before you answer, a few facts. There are about 8.3 million women and 6.4 million men in college. The gap is the latest phase in a gradual trend that began after the Vietnam War, when men had a strong incentive to stay in school—college or combat. In the last two decades the number of men with bachelor's degrees has risen, but the number of women has increased much faster.

Jacqueline King at the American Council on Education calls this "more of a success story for women than failure for men." Of course, "success" also has its limits. The gender gap reverses by the time you get to doctorates and goes into full-tilt retreat down the tenure track.

But even when we are counting bachelor's degrees, gender is just the sexy part of the statistics. The real educational gap has a lot more to do with race and class.

For openers, there is no gap between traditional-age white male and female students. The real differences appear among minorities. In fact, most of the overall gap is due to a huge increase in the number of minority women. Among African-Americans, two women get degrees for every man.

As for income, we know that low-income students of every ethnic group are less likely to go to college. But it turns out that more low-income women than men still find their way onto a campus.

This has a lot to do with the job market, says King. An undecided low-income male may look around and see a job that looks decent by an 18-year-old's standard, she says. But a woman "can't get a job in the traditional female worlds of health care or office work without some postsecondary school." Indeed, the good/bad news is that a woman still needs a college degree to match the income of a man with a high school diploma.

I don't want to minimize a real problem. We should worry about young people left behind in an economy that is increasingly dependent on education. And it's worth asking why low-income and minority men are less successful academically than other populations.

But if there's a crisis, it's not a man vs. woman thing. As Jacqueline Woods, head of the American Association of University Women, puts it, "They're saying that women are replacing men and isn't this alarming. Those people are playing a zero-sum game, and I refuse to play."

You don't need a bachelor's degree to pick up a subtext in the crisis reporting: Somehow or other, women are upsetting the natural order of things. Even, or especially, the marital order. As Thomas Mortenson at the Pell Institute told one reporter, "There's 170,000 more bachelor's degrees awarded to women than men. That's 170,000 women that will not be able to find a college-educated man to marry."

Hmmm. Was anyone alarmed when there weren't enough educated women for the bachelors with bachelor's degrees? College women hear this: "You are on the brink of destruction. . . . Beware!!" Get the degree and you face a shrinking population of marriageable men.

Let's see now, is that better or worse than a shrinking uterus?

September 1, 2002

L et us begin with the Corporate Titan standing at the annual banquet, thanking his "Wife and Partner Without Whom" he would never have been elevated to the financial stratosphere.

Now, fast-forward and check in on Mr. T a year later. This time he's at the lawyer's office insisting that his wife was not the helium in his rise to the top but the old ball and chain.

What a difference a year makes. What a difference a divorce makes. One year, a homemaker wife is the coauthor of a success story. The next year, she is a corporate welfare recipient.

It's not just that we rewrite the story of our own marriage when it goes kaput. We rewrite the idea of marriage itself.

This is the issue in the latest and most celebrated case of the rich and now famous Lorna and Gary Wendt. This couple's marriage began 30-odd years ago with high hopes and $2,500. It ended last week in a Connecticut courtroom with bitter recriminations and the division of over $100 million.

Gary Wendt became a top executive of General Electric, putting in 80- to 90-hour weeks at the office. Lorna earned her PhT—Putting Hubby Through—at Harvard Business School and then took care of kids and home.

When all was said and done, including the marriage, Gary thought Lorna should be "generously rewarded" with somewhere around $10 million, all she would ever "need." Lorna thought she was "entitled" to $50 million—half—and that "need" had nothing to do with it.

Now admittedly it's hard to think clearly while breathing the thin air of those very rarefied numbers. In the end, the judge awarded her an estimated $20 million. In corporate boardrooms they worried whether a spouse was entitled to future earnings. And the judge awarded her some. But in the public annals it became known as the "what is a wife worth" case.

Here is the short, she-said-he-said story:

She said: "My end of the partnership was to take care of the family, the household, the caretaking so he could go out and take care of his end of the partnership, which was having the job."

He said: "Do you think having somebody clean the house when you go out and play tennis . . . is hard work? Tell me please."

She said: "Marriage is a partnership, and I should be entitled to 50 percent. I gave 31 years of my life. . . . I worked hard, and I was very loyal."

He said: "I worked hard. She didn't."

Now, as far as I know, sweat equity is not written into the marriage vows. It is intriguing how this case of the unbelievably rich focused both parties and the public on what she did or didn't do to deserve the marital millions. Nobody questioned what he did to deserve corporate millions.

There is no maximum wage in this country for corporate executives. But in many states there appears to be a maximum wage, a ceiling for their former wives.

In Connecticut, where the Wendts lived, the court has to give an ex-wife an equitable, but not equal, share. In practice "equitable" has a ceiling, loosely described as "enough is enough." But here is where a divorce says a lot about marriage.

Marriage these days is described in polite company and therapy as a 50-50 proposition. But when push comes to shove comes to split, it may be rescripted as an 80-20 proposition. The equal relationship based on love is suddenly recast as an economic relationship based on pay slips.

We can literally see two value systems collide. Those of marriage and the market. Love and money.

After all, we go to work as individuals but live as couples. We get one name on the paycheck, but we think of marriage as exempt from the marketplace. We acknowledge conflicts between our two points of view only in notoriously skimpy prenuptial agreements—or in divorce court. That's when we see how people really feel about "our money" versus "my money."

There is no way to assess what a wife—or husband, by the way—is worth in sweat equity. We marry for richer or poorer, and may work harder for poorer. But if there's no floor on our partnership, why should there be a ceiling? The real question is whether we mean what we say about marriage as a partnership.

I suppose I am an incurable romantic, worrying about the effects of divorce agreements on marriage. But the Wendts have taught us about the legal limits of romance.

This is the aftermath of their corporate breakup: Lorna is starting a Foundation for Equality in Marriage. Gary is planning to marry again. She has set up a Web site. He plans to sign a prenuptial agreement. Ah, love. . . .

December 11, 1997

Bio & Other Ethics

OF LATE, IT SEEMS THAT OUR FASCINATION WITH THE BIO-

LOGICAL BASIS OF EVERYTHING HAS LED TO A BELIEF

THAT DNA IS DESTINY. IN A PERVERSE WAY, DOLLY MAY

FORCE US TO REMEMBER THAT PEOPLE ARE NOT JUST

CONCEIVED; WE ARE RAISED.

–FROM "HELLO, DOLLY–AND MOLLY AND POLLY AND LOLLY

AND FOLLY," FEBRUARY 27, 1997

I suppose that those of us who have been in this struggle a while can be forgiven for taking a little pleasure at the civil war erupting among our opponents. Suddenly, politicians who call themselves "prolife" are fighting over who deserves to wear that uniform.

Orrin Hatch, an antiabortion stalwart, is now saying defensively that "people who are prolife are also prolife for existing life." Our point exactly. Isn't this why prochoice folks resent the coopting of the term "prolife"?

But smugness won't do. We are witnessing what happens to every thoughtful person who wades into the moral terrain of reproductive technology.

This time the firm line drawn by the prolife forces—life begins at conception—begins to soften. The simple battle cry—a fertilized egg is a human being—begins to develop a counterpoint. The solid ground under the absolutists is beginning to shake.

This civil strife is over embryonic stem cells. These cells, harvested from five-day-old fertilized eggs, may offer the best hope—better than adult stem cells—for curing some pretty awful diseases, from Alzheimer's to Parkinson's to juvenile diabetes. So the Bush administration must decide whether the government will fund research that uses stem cells from fertility clinic embryos.

The argument over using the "leftovers" of couples who have given such permission has divided old antiabortion allies. On the one hand, senators like Strom Thurmond and Connie Mack and Gordon Smith have come to agree with Hatch that stem cell research is "the most prolife position" because of the possibility of saving lives. On the other hand, Republican House leaders like Dick Armey and Tom DeLay and J.C. Watts warned Bush: "It's not prolife to rely on an industry of death even if the intention is to find cures for diseases."

The president, stalling for time, searching for an elusive compromise, has said he will decide "in a while." But which will it be? Using the stem cells for potentially life-saving research? Or letting the embryos remain in some fertility clinic locker to be frozen or destroyed?

To condemn stem cell research as an "industry of death," you must begin by opposing in-vitro fertilization. The Catholic Church, consistent if nothing else, opposes the creation as well as the destruction of a fertilized egg outside of the womb.

But most Americans regard in-vitro fertilization—IVF—as a blessing for many couples and see fertility clinics as places where life begins. So, as bioethicist Bonnie Steinbock says, the political wrangling must leave these people scratching their heads.

"You mean," she says, imagining their conversations, "creating surplus embryos is fine, discarding embryos is fine, keeping them in the freezer in perpetuity is fine, the only thing that is not fine is using them for medical research?"

Steinbock, a professor of philosophy at the University at Albany, part of the State University of New York, says many who are normally prolife cannot reconcile discarding or freezing eggs as more respectful of life than using them to find a cure. Those who may not identify with a desperately pregnant woman in search of an abortion find themselves siding with a desperately sick person in search of a cure.

In some ways, the endless abortion argument has driven all other discussion over reproduction to the extremes. At one end, the fertilized egg is talked about as little more than tissue. On the other end, it is given the full moral stature of a human being.

Those who favor abortion rights have been challenged by the grim choices of late-term abortions. Until now, though, as Thomas Murray of the Hastings Center says, "The prolife movement has been able to dodge a problem within their ranks for many years: the moral status of the very early embryo, prior to implantation, perhaps not even within a woman's body."

Now, in this civil war over "life," they face a parallel divide. "Most people," says Murray, "do not view either birth control as murder or IVF then freezing as equivalent to placing your 5-year-old in the deep freeze."

If there is one thing that comes out of this political skirmish, it's the understanding that an embryo created in a dish is not a thing and not a person. We cannot use embryos for frivolous purposes. "We don't make earrings out of them, we don't use them in high school labs," says Steinbock. But we can, with seriousness and respect, use them for medical research that will, one hopes, save lives.

Yes, being "prolife" also means being "prolife for existing life." Those who now call themselves prolife and pro-stem cell research have had to give up the simple and simplistic idea that a fertilized egg is a full and equal human life. Welcome. There's plenty of room under the banner that reads: It's more complicated than that.

July 8, 2001

I n the beginning, there was Dr. God. We brought our bodies to his medical altar with a certain amount of fear, a lot of awe and some hope of salvation. Dr. God told us what to do and we did it, praying all the while that he—almost always he—would save us from experiencing the afterlife before our time.

We lost this medical Eden for the same reason we lost the biblical one: knowledge. We came to know what doctors didn't know. We became more informed and more skeptical. We even learned to get a second opinion. This is not something that you do with God.

In due time, Dr. God became Your Partner in Health Care. Dr. Partner laid out the information, offered up the options with their assorted risks and benefits. In this collaborative effort over our bodies, we learned to read the fine print and keep up on the research.

Now Dr. God is terminal. Dr. Partner has become the norm. But Dr. Partner is rapidly turning into another Health Care Provider.

This change in the title doesn't just signal another demotion from the heavenly heights. It hints at a real shift in the relationships.

Dr. Provider is now cast as a purveyor, a kind of grocer to the human body. Dr. Provider doesn't have patients but consumers. And consumers are entitled to get what they want.

There is good and bad in this shift. After all, consumers are the ones who improved the experience of childbirth. Consumers are the ones demanding user-friendly hospitals. But consumers are also the ones running up the bill on CAT scans for every back strain and sonograms for every pregnancy.

Doctors may not perform appendectomies upon request. But they increasingly fill our orders out of fear of malpractice or because it's good business. And occasionally a story comes along that points out the dangerous direction of this trend.

Consider the horrific tale of Baby K.

Baby K was born just over a year ago. Like one or two of every thousand children, she was born without a brain—permanently unconscious, without any ability to see, hear, feel.

Nearly all anencephalic babies die within days of birth. But in this case, the mother insisted—against the judgment of doctors and the hospital ethics committee—that the baby be kept alive with a ventilator.

Eventually the hospital went to court to find out if it had to continue offering life-sustaining treatment. And to the surprise of most people, the lower court said it did.

The judge ruled that refusing to treat Baby K would be discrimination against the disabled and a violation of the Americans with Disability Act. Overruling the mother would also violate her right to "bring up children" as she saw fit.

The description of Baby K as "disabled" is bizarre enough. Under this definition, a hospital or doctor could be guilty of discrimination if they refused to perform brain surgery on the baby just because she didn't have a brain. There is a difference between discrimination and medical judgment.

The mother's right to make these decisions is a tougher call. In the most famous right-to-die cases, families have come to court to force the end of treatment. Families usually operate in the best interests of the patients. In all but extreme cases, they should prevail.

This, however, is the most extreme case imaginable. The mother is, in the court's words, operating out of a "firm Christian faith that all life should be protected." But treating a baby without a brain fits every ethicist's definition of the word "futile."

The obvious costs of this futility are staggering. Every day she has been in the hospital has cost her HMO about $1,400. But there are even greater hidden costs.

If the Appeals Court doesn't overturn this case, says Boston University's George Annas, "it says that there is no role for legitimate medical judgment. If this mother gets to decide how medicine is practiced on the child, independent of any benefit to the child, we couldn't run a health care system. The health care system would be everybody gets whatever they want."

I am not nostalgic for Dr. God. But if this mother wins, the courts will be ordering doctors to be providers for consumers who are always right.

Thank you, but I am not keen on do-it-yourself medicine. I'd rather have a partner.

October 24, 1993

THE MONEY OR THE EGG?

It was the price tag that finally caught the public eye. Fifty-thousand dollars for an egg?

Not just any egg, of course. The folks who placed the ad wanted the best and the brightest egg. Excuse me, the best and the brightest and the tallest egg.

The pitch that ran in newspapers at a handful of the most prestigious colleges in America—Harvard, Yale, Stanford, MIT, etc.—specifically said: "Intelligent athletic egg donor needed for loving family." This couple special-ordered a woman over 5-feet-10 with combined SATs over 1400. In return, they were quite forthright in promising: "LARGE FINANCIAL INCENTIVE."

The only thing the would-be parents fudged was the language. Egg donor? In my dictionary a donor is someone who gives, not someone who sells. This was nothing if not a sales transaction between one woman with eggs in her basket and another woman with money in her bank account.

There had been other such ads. One registry has been advertising for fresh young eggs in college newspapers since 1992. This winter the Harvard Crimson ran an ad offering $7,500 to a "5-foot-5 or taller Caucasian, slim with dark hair, intelligent and kind." It ran another ad seeking a smaller, blonder woman with blue, green, or hazel eyes for $5,000.

Infertile couples and their organizations were always careful to describe the money as "compensation" for time, for medical appointments, for the difficulty of the procedure.

But it was the latest price tag that upped the ante, that finally made us sit up and take notice, that made it indisputably clear that we are talking about a market in human material. No less than 200 women applied for the chance to sell their DNA in return for $50,000.

Eggs in exchange for a nest egg? Until now, we've been pretty ambivalent about the genetic market. On the one hand we've offered modest payments to sperm "donors" for generations with few ethical qualms. On the other hand we have banned the sale of children. Not to mention the sale of sex.

We allow women to be "compensated" for egg removal because they help infertile couples bring a new life into the world. We don't allow people to be "compensated" for giving someone their kidney, though they might save a life.

On the one hand we say an adult woman can make her own reproductive choices. On the other hand, we look askew at "LARGE FINAN-CIAL INCENTIVES" that may unduly sway those choices.

There are some 5,000 women a year—of all heights and SAT scores—who become egg donors for less Ivy League a clientele. I don't doubt that some are altruistic. But too often it's a deal made between the different haves and have-nots.

I'm not just concerned about the line between donating and selling DNA. I'm more concerned about what we used to call the informed consent of the genetic mother.

For openers, no eggs should be exchanged without a truly informed consent form. My form would begin by telling any potential seller that we don't know what will happen in the future to the young women who are sent on a hormonal roller coaster in order to produce another couple's child. We aren't even tracking these women for potential problems like cancer.

It would also tell her that we are unsure what her rights and obligations will be to the child born of a one-night stand in a petri dish between her egg and some unknown sperm.

Does the gestational mother have the right or the obligation to pass the 5-foot-10 genius off as her genetic child? Will she, on the other hand, have the obligation to tell the child that somewhere out there is an Ivy League grad who paid off her college loan with designer genes?

And speaking of offspring, there are already "open in-vitro fertilizations" like open adoptions. It seems likely that somewhere down the road, an IVF baby will get the same rights as an adoptee. The current egg holder should know that today's donation is someday's child.

Which is the point, when you come right down to it. We've been all too casual about sperm donors and kids. Any woman who isn't ready to have a child in the world had better look long and hard at this paycheck. Somewhere in the free marketplace of people, we need rules that go beyond supply and demand.

Meanwhile, let the buyers, too, beware. On the ad, the couple placed a cute little icon of a stork delivering a baby. Guess what? Wait till you tell the kid the truth. The stork's going to sound plausible.

March 11, 1999

HELLO, DOLLY—AND MOLLY AND POLLY AND LOLLY AND FOLLY

I'm glad they started with sheep. Individuality was never the ewes' strong point. Sheep don't march to the bleat of a different drummer. Aside from the occasional black sheep, they're a pretty uniform and docile flock.

What are they bred for anyway? Lamb chops? Wool? Nursery rhymes? You might call them sheepish if you weren't trying desperately by now to block this metaphor.

Nevertheless, what a great public din followed the announcement that Dr. Ian Wilmut had a little lamb. The Scottish embryologist created the first clone of an adult mammal. He named her Dolly and then proceeded to make five more carbon copies, although we don't yet know what they were named. (Molly, Polly, Lolly, Holly and, surely, Folly?)

The bulletin about Dolly and the Five Xeroxes—is this beginning to sound like a rock group?—received the same public whine of outrage that follows other great scientific surprises that blindside us with anxiety.

"But you said . . . that we wouldn't be cloning big mammals for eons." "You said that *Jurassic Park* was sci-fi and *Multiplicity* was silly-fi." And now you are saying "Hello, Dolly."

Of course, many scientists still insist we won't be able to clone people any day soon. But the man who owns the patent for this little procedure acknowledges that "there is no reason in principle why you couldn't do it." He just adds quickly, "All of us would find that offensive."

Offensive? Call that Scottish understatement. Creepy is a better word, not to mention ethically appalling. For openers, Wilmut had to use 300 embryos to get his Dolly. He had a number of deformed offspring who died along the way.

Beyond that, it doesn't take Hollywood to imagine all sorts of ghoulish new scenarios. Cloning organ donors? Ensuring "spares" for family heirs? Buying genetic immortality?

Today bioethicists may describe self-cloning as the most narcissistic act imaginable. But before Dolly, there was some pretty strong competition for that title. Remember Robert Klark Graham, who died just last week? He was the fellow who set up the so-called Nobel sperm bank in California. As many as 218 children were born with sperm from those little narcissus bulbs.

There's also a growing private market in reproductive biology. Americans are saving thousands of extra embryos in freezers. They're selling eggs and renting wombs. They're leaving sperm behind when they go to war. And that's not counting the cryogenics customers.

If I can find any good news in the Valley of the Dollys, maybe the cloning controversy will help us get a grip on the current argument about nature vs. nurture.

Of late, it seems that our fascination with the biological basis of everything has led to a belief that DNA is destiny. In a perverse way, Dolly may force us to remember that people are not just conceived; we are raised. We are the products of our environments as well as our genes.

Despite all the master race fantasies, cloning would be a rather inefficient and dicey operation. Clones are essentially identical—though delayed—twins. Same DNA, different people.

Imagine if we'd cloned Albert Einstein, everyone's favorite genius. In late 20th century America, however, Al the Second might stay home with the kids so his Mileva could finally get her Ph.D. Or, everything being relative, he might find modern physics dull.

Imagine cloning Tiger Woods. Since you cannot also clone his entire upbringing, the Tiger Cub might take all of his golf potential and become a second-rate flutist.

As for the narcissist raising his or her real inner child? This you-clone won't have your parents, your fourth-grade teacher or the thousands of accidental experiences that made you who you are. What you might get, as a clone-parent, is an adolescent rebellion of mythic proportions.

The point is that we can clone biological potential but not real people. At 7 months, Dolly is all done. At 7 months, we've just begun.

One of the things that may or may not be built into the human DNA, but distinguishes us, is a unique sense of self. It's this very understanding that sends out warning bells at the very possibility of a Xeroxed "me." It's the quite proper instinct that now demands a universal No! Humans are not for cloning.

Science leads, but we don't have to follow. At a time when geneticists look at us as programmed bits of DNA, this flock is a reminder that we are, after all, the shepherds, not the sheep.

February 27, 1997

Well, well. And you thought that your son was a chip off the old block. That your daughter was a gal just like the gal that married her dear old dad. You ain't seen nothin' yet.

Allow me to reintroduce you to Dr. Richard Seed, a.k.a. Dickie Humanseed.

We last met this scientist and failed entrepreneur in January. It was after the birth announcement of a little sheep clone named Dolly and before a Texas millionaire put up $5 million to clone the dog Missy.

The Chicago physicist got his 15 minutes of fame by announcing that he was going to clone people. With a fine ear for the sound bite, he talked chirpily about "bouncing baby clones" and said, "Clones are going to be fun."

At the time I had trouble taking him seriously, and not just because he was described as a cross between a maverick and a wacko. Could you imagine any infertile couple taking their hopes to a doctor named Seed?

Now Seed sprouts again. He appeared at the annual meeting of the Association for Politics and the Life Sciences to announce that he was going to be his own first clone. "I have decided to clone myself first to defuse the criticism that I'm taking advantage of desperate women with a procedure that's not proven." What undesperate woman is he using to house his embryo? His own wife.

Let us remember that Dr. Seed is 69 and has already reproduced seven little seedlings, including two named Richard. As for Gloria, his third wife of 29 years? Seed describes her only as "postmenopausal." This, as a colleague says, is the new gallantry. You don't tell a woman's age, just her reproductive status.

Seed's second wife, who heard about the cloning, told a British newspaper recently: "Heaven forbid! I wouldn't let him breed tadpoles." But Gloria and Richard, who suffered some recent financial setbacks, have decided to open the ultimate Ma and Pa store.

The Seed scenario is, um, ripe with possibilities for other couples. Soon the truly devoted wife may do more than merely carry her husband's child in her womb. She may carry her husband. Or at least his identical twin.

What greater love hath any woman? Instead of giving birth to a child who bears his name, she could deliver one who bears his entire genetic code.

How many women, in the first blush of romance, wish they knew their husband as a child? Be careful what you wish for. In the Seed catalog, you could be up close and personal.

Imagine what it's like to live with the same male at various stages of his development. All across America there are women playing mother and wife to the same man. Clone-raising will allow some to fulfill their deepest fantasy—"If I could only start again with this man." It will provide others with an opportunity for bonding with their mother-in-law—"he really was an impossible child."

But in either case it will add a twist to those wonderful moments when any red-blooded mother, spying the socks on the floor, narrows her eyes and hisses at her son, "You're just like your father!"

Of course, we don't know if a woman would technically be the mother of her husband's clone. She could be simply raising her second husband. If, on the other hand, she divorces the man she married, who owns the clone? The idea is pregnant with possibilities.

As for clone child? Sooner or later, any bouncing baby clone turns into a 13-year-old sitting across the table from a male with pattern baldness, swearing he'll never be like his father. Wanna bet?

As for Gloria herself, I don't dispute her love for the good doctor. But does she actually want a houseful of little Dickies?

The same Dickie who once exclaimed, "I am proud of the fact that I was the most unpopular person at Oak Park High School"? The same Dickie who once said ruefully that he was just a "near-genius"? Who said he was "subject to continuous frustration" because he'd never win a Nobel prize?

The one thing that he has in abundance is ego. The idea man behind the Ma and Pa cloning counter acknowledges that "ego is involved with it . . . no question, ego is involved."

The one thing we can say about Seed is that he's an original. He's truly one of a kind. Dear Gloria: Let's keep it that way.

September 17, 1998

CLONE OR CLOWN

All in all it's probably not the best PR move for an atheist cult to dub its first offspring Eve. It might look as if they think they're God. Besides, the biblical, or even the Darwinian Eve was the mother of us all. The girl whose birth was trumpeted as the first-ever clone would be the daughter and identical twin of one of us.

Still, the Raelian believers and scientists get credit for their 15 minutes of fame and their half-hour on CNN. When Brigitte Boisselier, the Raelian bishop and midriff-baring CEO of Clonaid, announced that the first clone was born by Caesarean section to a 31-year-old American, she had the stage to herself for at least half a news cycle before the skeptics weighed in.

Frankly, the company established by Raelian scientists to clone humans always struck me as a dubious enterprise. Clonaid? It sounds like a cross between a rock 'n' roll fund-raiser and a nose spray.

Clonaid began life as a mailbox in the Caribbean and upgraded to a fly-infested lab in an abandoned high school in West Virginia. The scientific notes reportedly kept by a researcher didn't inspire confidence: "We went to the slaughterhouse and got some ovaries." Thankfully, this was when they were doing research on cows, not women, but you get the idea.

Boisselier's report that five of their 10 clones were successful strains credibility. Her announcement yesterday of a second clone birth breaks credibility. It took 277 tries to get one Dolly. Yet, they've produced an all-too-perfect rainbow of diversity. One lesbian mother, an Asian surrogate, and the clones of two dead babies? Where, oh, where is the partridge in the pear tree?

As for Rael and the Raelians, where do we begin? Claude Vorilhon, aka Rael, the French-born race car driver, journalist, and author of *Let's Welcome Our Fathers from Space,* met the 4-foot-tall, dark-haired, olive-skinned aliens with almond-shaped eyes near a volcano in 1973.

There, he reports, they explained how our species was cloned from theirs (hold the green skin) and would clone ourselves into immortality. We would download our personalities and memories into our adult clones and, zap, eternal life. I can't wait.

Rael is a man of apparent good humor—which you need when you dress in white space clothes, believe that Steven Spielberg stole your story for *Close Encounters,* and wear your hair in a topknot. He remembers one of the aliens saying to him, "Aren't you sorry that you didn't bring your camera?" You betcha.

It would, however, take more than a camera for credibility this time. The only way I'll believe in Eve is if I'm personally standing there when they take the blood samples and do the DNA test.

Nevertheless—you knew there would be a nevertheless—this story got our attention because today's hoax is tomorrow's possibility.

Over the past decade, one offspring at a time, we've learned that we can fool Mother Nature. From a "test-tube baby" named Louise to a little lamb named Dolly, to half a dozen other cloned critters, we've gradually created the reproductive technology of cloning.

Now all we have to do is create hundreds, probably thousands of defective embryos and fetuses, dangerous pregnancies, and genetically deformed children to get (maybe) a healthy clone. That's all, folks.

Since Dolly wobbled onto the stage in 1997, we've had plenty of folks willing and eager to experiment. Dr. Richard Seed was the first to announce that he'd clone himself and have his (post-menopausal) wife carry his little seedlings. That blessed event didn't, blessedly, happen.

Today, along with the Raelians and their little Eve project, we have two other fertility doctors claiming they have pregnant women ready to give birth to clones. Sooner or later is getting sooner.

So, yes, the story of Eve registers high on the hoax meter. After all, Clonaid was designed in the words of its vice president "to create controversy." But the alarm is, in fact, long overdue.

A spokesman for President Bush, who greeted Eve without the requisite politician's kiss, said soberly that it underscores the need for a ban on cloning. He didn't mention that our government deep-sixed just such a ban, rejecting an international agreement outlawing reproductive cloning to create humans, because it didn't also outlaw therapeutic cloning to cure diseases.

At home, a similar all-or-nothing opposition to cloning has created a congressional stalemate. Many legislators can't seem to distinguish between the promise of therapeutic cloning and the threat of reproductive cloning.

Here's what we've learned from this "dress rehearsal." We need a sharp, simple ban on cloning humans now. Leave the thornier questions of therapeutic cloning for another day.

The Raelians want us to welcome Eve into the family. I think we ought to raise Cain.

January 5, 2003

A MORAL BANKRUPTCY

L ast winter, when stories of priestly sexual abuse broke over my city, I couldn't help comparing the church scandal with the Enron scandal.

It was, admittedly, a bit of a stretch. The tower that Enron built was not literally a cathedral, although there was a good deal of (mammon) worship. The Houston company dealt in energy; the Boston archdiocese dealt in souls. Besides, it's far worse to have a child violated than a 401(k).

Still, each scandal had its cover-ups and its CEOs with shredded reputations. The citizens used the same vocabulary of betrayal. Employees and parishioners alike talked about losing their "faith."

Now, however, the analogy is nearly complete. Both stories have arrived at the same chapter in their history: Chapter 11.

It has been a year since Enron filed for bankruptcy, as protection from its creditors. It has been just a few days since the Boston archdiocese admitted that it too is considering bankruptcy, as protection from its victims.

A bankrupt Catholic Church? Are all other metaphors now officially irrelevant?

The narrative of this church sexual abuse tale moved gruesomely from Chapter 1 to Chapter 10, from sexual assaults to secret settlements, and rogue priests transferred from one parish to another like bad debts to off-shore corporations.

At some point, the outrageous became so routine that many of us began to suffer from shock fatigue. Pedophiles in Los Angeles, sexual abuse in St. Louis? What else is new?

Then Tuesday, a Boston court released another 2,200 pages of church documents as lurid as anything imagined in a 19th-century anti-papist novel. In the recorded allegations, there's the saga of one priest who beat his housekeeper and had a long affair with a woman. There's another—so hooked on cocaine he was nicknamed "the blow king of Malden"—who admitted sex with a teenager as well as with other men.

Most bizarre of all is Robert V. Meffan, a priest who enticed teenage girls preparing to become nuns into sex acts by claiming to be "the second coming of Christ." A 73-year-old now living out a comfortable retirement with his depraved delusion intact, he told a *Boston Globe* reporter, "What I was trying to show them is that Christ is human . . . I felt that by having this little bit of intimacy with them that this is what it would be like with Christ."

These documents with bureaucratic comments scribbled casually in the margins—"Problem: Little Children"—broke through the shock barrier. And so too did the litany of notes from the cardinal to the criminals that sprinkled through the record. His words, full of warmth and pastoral empathy, read like thank-you notes to torturers.

To a self-confessed gay "sex addict" who feared that one of the boys he abused had committed suicide, Cardinal Bernard Law wrote, "It is my hope that some day in the future you will return to an appropriate ministry bringing with you the wisdom which emerges from difficult experience."

To an accused priest transferred to the Army chaplaincy without any warning of sexual abuse charges, he offered fare-thee-well, "I have every confidence that you will render fine priestly service to the people who come under your care."

And to the priest who seduced girls into "intimacy," Law sent his best retirement wishes: "Without doubt over these years of generous care, the lives and hearts of many people have been touched by your sharing of the Lord's Spirit. We are truly grateful."

Against this background, what are we to say when the page turns to Chapter 11? Have a nice day?

Throughout the scandal, Catholic leaders have been both apologetic and defensive. It was a different time, they say, we didn't know then what we know now. What precisely didn't they know then? That the Rev. Robert V. Meffan was not Jesus Christ?

They also insist that the church has changed in its attitudes toward victims. How precisely has it changed, if it declares bankruptcy?

Throughout this sorry tale, one thing has dismayed loyal Catholics the most: The realization that the hierarchy defended the institution instead of defending the children. The church hunkered down to protect its moral reputation. And lost its moral authority.

Indeed, the church is not talking about bankruptcy as an admission of failure, but as a tactic to stave off lawsuits and settlements. It has no intention of "restructuring" its all-male rules and celibate regulations, but every intention of saving the old hierarchies and coffers.

In the tale of two scandals, the CEO of Enron is gone, but the CEO of the Boston archdiocese is, incredibly, still at his post. Pink slips appear regularly now on the collection plates and yet the church fathers, deep in moral debt, are deciding whether to seek financial protection against the very victims they failed to protect.

Chapter 11? They might as well close the book.

December 8, 2002

H ow do you react to a medical horror story? What is the proper etiquette of emotions that rush up from your gut to greet such a tale?

Just two weeks ago, when a Tampa surgeon cut off the wrong foot of his patient, I read the news with equal parts of bleak terror and black humor. After all, what do you say: That you want a surgeon who knows his right from his left? That you will wear one sock into the operating room?

Days later, a small item in the paper told about a Michigan woman who had the wrong breast removed. What do you say to that? That if you ever go to the hospital, you will cover your body with instructions: X marks the right spot?

These are stories that elicit anger as deep as our own vulnerability. Yet even anger wars with the truths wrapped inside cliches: Accidents happen, no one is perfect, the "human factor" includes a capacity for the most terrible of mistakes.

But this time, it's happened to one of us, to Betsy Lehman of all people. A friend, a colleague at *The Boston Globe*, a 39-year-old mother of two young daughters who had reached for the promise of a breast cancer cure in bone marrow transplant, writing, "I'm resigned to the idea of going through hell for the hope of a chance." A chance she didn't get.

I can't reduce Betsy to a paragraph. She had warmth and smarts, a fine-honed skepticism and a delicious, playful sense of humor. She had as generous a spirit as I've known.

I've been to dozens of funerals, and by now I know the ones you don't want to go to. The ones where parents bury their children. The ones where young children sit, bewildered and restless, without a mother to comfort them for the loss of their mother.

If, as the Talmud says, each person is an entire world, Betsy's death last December left a hole the size of a crater. But we chalked up this loss to bad odds, to high risks, to gawd-awful rotten luck.

Then we learned last week that it wasn't the roll of the dice. Betsy Lehman was given a fatal overdose of the anticancer medication. She was given four times the right dosage. She was given it for four days in a row.

At best, a bone marrow transplant is a crude attempt to bludgeon the cancer cells to death and save the patient. But the overdosage killed Betsy and left another woman with a devastated heart, and went undetected by whole layers of doctors, nurses, pharmacists. They missed the warning signs, the lab tests, the electrocardiogram.

What are we to say? Accidents happen?

To those of us who count ourselves her friends, this second mourning is compounded by anger. For those who didn't know Betsy, it should be compounded by fear.

There are times, when you are sick and scared, that you try to add up the things in your favor. Betsy was our personal health columnist. She had researched and written about cancer treatments, including her own. She had written about doctors, the good and the bad, the humane and the arrogant. She knew how and when a patient had to be in charge of her own care. She was by no means a slouch in the asking questions department.

Moreover, Betsy was a patient at the Dana-Farber Cancer Institute, a cutting-edge cancer hospital that gives Boston pride in its best. Add to that the fact that Betsy's husband was a scientist who worked at this hospital.

Yet it happened to her; she was still killed by carelessness. By the human errors that add up to a system's error. By a hospital whose own self-confidence may have been a fatal flaw. By an institution that never installed the computer program that might have flagged this mistake.

Accidents happen? No one is perfect?

I haven't a doubt that the people who mishandled her case, her life, are in their own pain. In journalism, Betsy's profession and mine, the worst errors we make can destroy a reputation. In medicine they destroy people. It's the stakes that differ; not the fallibility.

I keep wondering what Betsy would say. Betsy, who wanted more than anything—enough to go for broke—to see her children grow up. Betsy, who had a profound sense of justice. And a bone-deep code of fairness.

Once, standing in the hallway discussing a story—on the one hand this, on the other hand that—I told her that she had enough hands to be an octopus. It's what made her so good. She saw shades where others saw black and white.

If this had happened to anyone else, Betsy would have been mad as hell. Mad, without forgetting that no system is really mistake-proof, no hospital human-error-proof. Mad anyway.

So what do you say? In December, when Betsy died without a trace of cancer left in her body, the world lost her generosity. In March we lost something else in short supply. A huge portion of trust.

March 29, 1995

A KIDNEY FOR THE BOSS

W ASHINGTON—Nancy Nearing gave at the office. And I do not mean the United Way. The 42-year-old Virginia mother of two gave a kidney. To her boss.

To put it as simply as she did, "I had a choice of either wringing my hands and saying, 'Oh, dear,' or doing something about it."

For six years, the technical writer had worked in Rockville, Maryland, on a computer programming team headed by Art Helms. When she heard that he was about to lose his kidneys to a genetic disease, she decided to help. But hers was a help far beyond flowers or even a pint of blood, much more than a get-well card. It was so unexpected that it ended up on Page 1 of *The Washington Post*.

Nearing's story was, no doubt, a welcome contrast from reports about Bad Samaritans that seem to dot the mediascape routinely. We are still reeling from David Cash, the University of California/Berkeley poster boy for the Bad Samaritan who had turned away while his best friend raped and killed a 7-year-old girl.

But the extraordinary tale of one kidney transplant became "news" because of what Nearing and Helms are not: family.

If the employee and boss had been sister and brother, ho hum. If they had been husband and wife, we would have hardly blinked. But Nearing's relationship to the much-respected Helms was just this: "It's such a joy to work for him."

Last year there were 3,665 transplants from live donors, and all but 153 of those came from a relative or a spouse. We expect to give—and take—at the family table. Those expectations are so high, the pressures so real, that I am told doctors will help fabricate a medical excuse for the family member who doesn't want to be a "donor."

But this story led me to wonder about how we understand all kinds of mutual exchanges in our society. Why Nearing is called "a saint" by the man who now thrives on her kidney. Why she might have been called a sinner had she refused a family member.

Today we often know our co-workers better than our cousins. It may be our friends who stay with us for better or worse, not our spouses. In sickness or in health, our children may be scattered and our neighbors on standby.

Yet in the recesses of our mind, we still retain the ancient assumptions of family first. When we search for permanence in a transient world and think about the quid pro quo of help and sacrifice, we think automatically along bloodlines.

The world is full of warning signs about gifts to and from "outsiders." Not long ago, in Minnesota, Dorothy Zauhar's brother gave a kidney to her fiance. It was a gift of love. But when the fiance turned around and married a nurse in the kidney transplant unit, the brother and sister sued.

In college newspapers, I read ads asking young women to be egg donors. What is the difference between a gift and a rip-off?

The workplace seems an equally dicey place for "gifts," fraught with mistrust and the fear of being "gypped." Many regard their workplace as a temporary way station, a Dilbert-like source of insecurity.

When Nancy Nearing gave at the office, one cynic asked me, if he fires her, does she get the kidney back? Another assured me that the only body part he would give his boss was the finger. In fact, before her extrafamilial organ was accepted, Nearing was sent to an ethicist to make sure that this was a personal gift, not a professional investment.

This cultural reticence does not mean co-workers always stay in the shallowest waters of mutual aid. Reading the new biography of Anne Frank, I am reminded that her father's employees harbored the Franks against the Nazis for two dangerous years. At the same time, we all know families—even parents—who give "freely" and then harbor bitter resentments when there is no return. They were keeping book all the time.

But it is when we step outside of the family that many of us are taught to worry about giving and receiving too much. We are warned: Neither a borrower nor a lender be. We learn to wonder which gifts come in wrapping paper and which come with strings attached?

Even Nearing and Helms, the donor and recipient, now recovering from the surgeries, seemed uncomfortable with the idea that their relationship would change. But of course, something has changed. And not just a kidney.

"For our kids," Helms's wife told the *Post* reporter, "it put a whole new perspective on life—with all this incredible goodness coming this way."

These two colleagues broke through a cultural fence of fear and family. Nancy Nearing decided to help. Sometimes it is the Good Samaritan who leads the way.

October 15, 1998

A MSTERDAM—It began with the oddest of rallying cries. People started talking about the "right to die" as if dying were not an inevitable human condition.

By the 1970s we had seen more than our share of people tied, tubed, and plugged in to a semblance of life. Gradually some began to wave the banner of patients' rights and reclaim power from medical technology and technocrats playing doctor.

But somewhere along the way the right-to-die movement went from asking about stopping treatment to asking for a doctor's help in dying. Now this is at the heart of the assisted-suicide case before the U.S. Supreme Court.

Anyone looking for hints about the direction of this debate will find them here in Holland, a country that has struggled to both allow and control doctor-assisted dying.

What began here, too, as a patients' rights movement has in some ways ceded both more power and greater burdens to doctors.

What began here, too, as an attempt to resolve the conflict that can arise between a doctor's obligations both to prolong life and relieve suffering has ended up with more conflicts left at the doctor's hand.

In Holland, euthanasia, defined as the termination of life by a doctor at the express wish of a patient, remains technically illegal. But it's permitted under state guidelines in cases of "unbearable suffering." Here, nearly 80 percent of doctors have been asked for euthanasia, but nine out of 10 requests are turned away. And while the overwhelming majority of Dutch doctors believe that it is justified in some cases, only 32 percent have actually assisted in deaths.

One of those is Herbert Cohen, an articulate family physician from Rotterdam. Retired now, he teaches others who confront this issue routinely. I ask him what question troubles doctors the most and he says, without hesitation, "Is the patient suffering enough?"

The long government form that doctors are required to fill out after assisting any death asks whether "the suffering was of such a nature that he or she could experience it as intolerable." Simple enough, but as Dr. Cohen acknowledges, "There are no objective criteria for making such a judgment."

Indeed, this thoughtful, bearded elder admits that his own decisions were based on some reckoning of "how would I feel in such a situation."

Even though these judgments are made in consultation with another doctor, opponents of euthanasia are uncomfortable giving them the power of life and death. At Catholic University in Nijmegen, Henk Ten Have wondered aloud, "What is surprising to me is that people put so much trust in the medical profession."

This month in the United States, a Congress that has yet to provide health care to all children preemptively banned federal payment for "assisted suicide." But in Holland, where everyone is covered and most have a longtime family doctor, there is no evidence that doctors fulfill death wishes cavalierly.

Decisions weigh—and heavily—on Dr. Cohen's colleagues. He describes the difficult passage that begins when a patient raises the subject or when he as a doctor says, "If you ever want to talk about euthanasia, I won't blush." It is, he says, "like climbing a terrible mountain."

The burden on doctors may be even greater in countries like our own where the issue is still shrouded in secrecy, where doctors asked for help in dying cannot even talk to each other.

On my final day in Holland, Eugene Sutorius, the chief lawyer who helped push his country to the frontier of doctor-assisted death, sits at an antique table in his sleek Arnhem office and looks back over the cases of patients' rights and doctors' conflicts that have marked his career.

I ask him where it all leads, and the intense, engaged man answers my questions with his own. "Will we look back and say, at the end of the 20th century we had that euthanasia thing—but now our doctors have learned to put their weapons down and we die in peace?

"Or are we going through a cultural change to a new situation in which death will become a personal option?"

What we do know is that the long and public euthanasia debate has taken another turn. Dutch doctors are talking more fervently today about reducing suffering through palliative care. Time and again, crossing this small country, I was told the same thing: "Euthanasia should remain a possibility, but a last resort."

Indeed, that may be the best balance. And the most difficult to maintain.

March 24, 1997

May I interrupt the conversation about weapons of mass destruction for just a moment to talk about weapons of individual destruction? Can we turn our thoughts briefly from the fate of innocent civilians to the fate of convicted criminals? To the times when the logic of law leads, one step at a time, to the lunacy of law?

Such is the case of Charles Laverne Singleton, madman and resident of death row in Arkansas. Earlier this month the 8th Circuit Court ruled that Singleton could be forcibly medicated in order to make him sane enough to be executed. In a courtroom drama that turned into theater of the absurd, the judges said he must be cured to be killed.

Here are two undisputed facts about Singleton: He is a murderer, and he is psychotic.

He stabbed a grocery clerk to death in 1979, three years after the Supreme Court reinstituted the death penalty. He descended into raving, delusional mental illness in 1987, one year after the same Supreme Court ruled that states couldn't execute a crazy person.

In the case of *Ford v. Wainwright,* the justices declared it was "cruel and unusual punishment" to execute someone who was mentally incompetent—so incompetent that he didn't understand his fate or the meaning of death or why he was condemned.

The decision was welcome but the standard was so low that even Rickey Ray Rector passed the so-called Ford test in 1992—when Bill Clinton famously came off the campaign trail to authorize his death. Rector, it should be remembered, went off to his execution, leaving some of his last meal, a piece of pecan pie to have "later."

Today, the insanity defense is notoriously unsuccessful. But the courts have heard a rash of cases about mental competency, mental illness, medication, and legal rights. At this moment, Russell Eugene Weston Jr., is being forcibly medicated so that he can stand trial in the 1998 fatal shooting of two guards in the U.S. Capitol. Meanwhile, the Supreme Court has decided to hear the appeal of dentist Charles Sell, asking whether it's legal to forcibly medicate a mentally ill man so he can face a civil trial, in this case for Medicaid fraud.

This is an age when mental illness often seems like a matter of chemistry. In the judicial system, there are many reasons to force medication on a delusional defendant: How can an irrational man make rational decisions about his treatment, let alone his trial?

There are reasons to worry about it as well: What happens when a defendant comes to court "cured" and the jury sees a "different person" than the one who committed a crime?

But the ethics of treating a patient and defendant for mental illness get far more compelling when the death penalty is involved.

When Singleton first was diagnosed as psychotic—possessed by demons—he was under a stay of execution. It could be said that he was medicated for his own good. Sometimes he took the medication voluntarily, sometimes forcibly; sometimes it helped, sometimes it didn't. But when the stay was lifted and he was back on track for execution, defining "his own good" became a much dicier proposition.

In the Circuit Court opinion, one of the judges wrote that "eligibility for execution is the only unwanted consequence of the medication," as if execution were a mere side effect of the drugs like, say, dry mouth. But if it's unethical, by AMA standards, for doctors to participate in executions, how can it be ethical to treat someone if the cure is, literally, more deadly than the disease?

Singleton's case, which will be appealed to the Supreme Court, is part of the chaos and uncertainty and unease swirling around the death penalty.

In the past year, it became unconstitutional to execute the mentally retarded. But we can still execute juveniles. Since arriving in office, Attorney General John Ashcroft has ruled 28 times that local district attorneys must pursue the death penalty, against their own judgment, in the name of "consistency." But leaving office, Illinois Governor George Ryan commuted death sentences for 164 men and three women, saying, "Our capital system is haunted by the demon of error—error in determining guilt and error in determining who among the guilty deserves to die."

Much of the controversy over the death penalty is, as it should be, about guilt and innocence and error. But the way we deal with the mentally ill, the incompetent, strikes at the moral heart of the matter.

Singleton faced a bizarre choice between a lifetime sentence of insanity or the cure of a death sentence.

As for those who believe that the death penalty can be reasonable and fair? The story of Charles Laverne Singleton has ended that delusion.

February 20, 2003

T his is the question Jack Kevorkian posed at the very end of his fifth trial: "Just look at me. . . . Do you see a murderer?" He asked this as if murder were an image, not an action. As if the jury, which found him guilty Friday of second-degree murder, were just another focus group.

But what do the rest of us see when we look at Kevorkian? A medical "hit man," in the words of the prosecutor, "with a bag of poison to do his job"? A Rosa Parks or Martin Luther King, in Kevorkian's words, who put doctor-assisted death on the national agenda?

Do we see the death deliveryman who sent Tom Youk to the hereafter with a chilling "Okey-doke"? The publicity hound who handed a videotape to *60 Minutes*? The martyr of the right to die? Or the "fool" who had himself as a client during this trial?

Last November, sitting with Mike Wallace, this defrocked pathologist dared the courts to try him again: "Either they go or I go. . . . This issue has to be raised to the level where it's finally decided."

In his desire to stay in the limelight and in the face of authorities, he crossed—no, leapt—over the line from passive to active euthanasia, from assisted suicide to what some call mercy killing and others call murder.

But in the courtroom there was only one identity that mattered: whether or not Jack Kevorkian is a murderer. The irascible Kevorkian forced us, again, into a theater of legal absurdity, a place where the law disconnects from reality.

Murderer? Do you need a victim to be a murderer? Youk is described in news stories as a former race car driver as if that said something about his independent, strong will. He is shown on that infamous videotape, stricken with Lou Gehrig's disease, ready to die.

His wife denied in court, out of earshot of the jury, that the word "kill" was ever uttered. "Ugly word," she said, "Never. Never came up in conversation. Our conversation was about ending his suffering." He was afraid of dying by choking. But these arguments were not admissible.

Murderer? In the eyes of the law, the prosecutors insisted, Youk was no different from a healthy stranger shot on a street corner. And in the eyes of the law, you cannot consent to your own murder.

Of course, in closing arguments, prosecutor John Skrzynski acknowledged finally, "It would be hard for you to disregard Tom Youk's medical condition when you look at the videotapes back in the jury room . . . but his medical condition is not what is at issue here."

He said, "The law does not look at the victim and say, 'Does the victim have a quality of life that's worth protecting?' "

But there is a problem with the "eyesight" of the law. It doesn't allow for nearly as much peripheral vision as our human eyes do. The law in this case doesn't take in the background scenery of human misery; it filters out the complexity of those who would assess their own "quality of life."

I am no fan of Jack Kevorkian. Neither the man nor his methods. He has been, to put it mildly, a thorn in the side of both the law and the assisted suicide movement. I don't trust his judgment or his free-lance assessment of the 130 patients whose deaths he assisted.

Nevertheless, this was no garden variety murder. However deeply you look into them, the "eyes of the law" are too narrow for justice.

The law offered the jurors only two options: guilty or innocent. The guilty verdict—second-degree murder—may send Kevorkian to jail. He could be in jail far longer than Youk would have remained alive without him. An innocent verdict would have nullified the law on murder and left Dr. Jack on the loose with a syringe.

After Kevorkian's star turn on *60 Minutes* I contrasted our own attitude to that in Holland. Two years ago, reporting on doctor-assisted death in that small country, I learned the word "gedogen." It's how the Dutch describe the ethical gray zone for something that is illegal but allowed. In Holland, some 2.4 percent of the deaths are assisted by doctors. They don't draw the same line between active and passive euthanasia. What they do have is a very careful set of guidelines for terminally ill and suffering patients.

But here we have trouble finding a way to tolerate and circumscribe the gray zone. Kevorkian was not a "hit man." But as he admitted, "Thomas Youk's death was a result of my action."

Once again we are supposed to choose black or white: mercy or killing, guilty or innocent. Murder? What if we had guidelines instead of hard lines?

March 28, 1999

T he obituary page doesn't say how the old people died. It merely lists the causes like a coroner's report or perhaps a police blotter. Each man or woman is duly, officially, assigned a disease.

The 91-year-old man, a ski enthusiast in his youth, died of a heart ailment. The 88-year-old woman, a biographer in her prime, died of cancer. The 102-year-old man, a machine-tool executive, died of pneumonia. The closest anyone comes to dying of old age on the obituary page is the 97-year-old who died "after a long illness."

But the obits don't tell us how these people died. In pain or at peace? Surrounded by loved ones or alone? With a team of hi-technicians trying to drag them back to life or with a process we would call natural?

Even the photographs that accompany death announcements conspire to keep the reality of dying away from us. Once in a lifetime, literally, a man like essayist and biologist Dr. Lewis Thomas has his picture taken at death's door, and a stark, translucent, face illustrates his end. For the most part, however, the portraits of the dead are brimful of life.

These pages show what we know: that Americans have simply removed dying from the purview of the living. Our doctors have turned it into a disease, and we have handed the problem over to their science. Eighty percent of us now die in hospitals, and for perhaps the first time in human history it is possible to arrive at the end of a long life having never seen another person die.

But finally our aversion to the subject of dying is fading. Ten years ago, then-Governor Richard Lamm of Colorado created a furor by saying, in ill-chosen words, that the terminally ill elderly had "a duty to die" rather than hang on to machine-tethered immortality. We have to be careful, he tried to explain, that "we don't impose life on people who, in fact, are suffering beyond the ability for us to help."

That radical sentiment is almost common today. In the intervening years we've seen a political movement for "death with dignity." We've seen a textbook published on how to commit suicide. Jack Kevorkian and his supplicants have forced us to pay attention.

Just weeks ago, Bill and Hillary Clinton made death the subject of their black humor about health care reform. Playing Harry and Louise, they gasped at the realization that under the Clinton health plan "eventually we are all going to die."

And now a book starkly entitled, *How We Die*—an unlikely candidate for best-sellerdom—has risen to the top tier of the lists. Those who reach for Sherwin Nuland's book are not seeking some false comfort in his descriptions of the horsemen of death—from cancer to heart disease—and the precise ways they carry away life. They are attracted, rather, by his humanity and eloquence in the service of honesty.

Mincing no words, he writes of our desire for a swift death during sleep or a "perfect lapse into agony-free unconscious." But, he concludes, "the great majority of people do not leave life in a way they would choose."

Americans who consult with this doctor find no promises of extending the length of years through yogurt and vitamins. They find, rather, an argument about the naturalness and inevitability of aging and dying.

All this is striking proof of how the public conversation is shifting. We've gone from whispering the word cancer to talking openly about how we die.

We now share the widespread fear of prolonged, high-tech dying. Death now often comes with decisions to be made by us or for us. As Nuland writes, it is "better to know what dying is like and better to make choices that are most likely to avert the worst of it."

Indeed, his most passionate words are a personal statement: "I will not die later than I should simply for the senseless reason that a highly skilled technological physician does not understand who I am."

Finally we are coming to our senses, especially the repressed sense that dying is the inevitable last chapter. When we banish dying to hospitals and to science, we forget what Nuland writes: that "relevant event taking place at the end of our life is our death, not the attempts to prevent it."

Death is the human condition. It's not medicine's failure to cure the disease of a 102-year-old.

April 10, 1994

Connections & Missed Connections

HERE IS THE BASIC PROBLEM WITH "PLAYING HARD TO GET": IT'S THE ACTING. HOW DO YOU STOP? IF MR. RIGHT FALLS IN LOVE WITH THE ROLE YOU ARE PLAYING, DO YOU EVER KNOW IF HE LOVES YOU? IF YOU TRICK HIM, WILL YOU RESPECT HIM IN THE MORNING? AND IF HE'S ONLY IN-TERESTED IN A CHALLENGE, WHAT HAPPENS AFTER THE HONEYMOON?

—FROM "HOW TO CAPTURE MR. RIGHT," OCTOBER 31, 1996

I n those ever-so-romantic split-seconds of courtship, Rick Rockwell told his bride, "It's not fair that you didn't get to ask me all those questions, and I didn't get put on the spot." Well, I'll drink to that.

But standing there in a bridal gown and a state of shock, Darva Conger would never have thought of asking Rick, "Did you ever smack a girlfriend?" "Does your 'elevator' go all the way up to the top floor?"

This was a match made in Fox-land. When "Who Wants to Marry a Multimillionaire" ended with vows, a dismayed sociologist said that you "could hear Western civilization crumbling." The combo beauty pageant and marital stunt had grabbed a staggering audience of 23 million, including one out of every four women between the ages of 18 and 39. But Western civ has survived a lot more than this. Heck, it survived Charles and Di.

Anyone with the jaundiced eye of a practiced observer or the practiced eye of a jaundiced observer knew there would be a second act, a postnuptial disagreement. As Cher once said, "The trouble with some women is that they get all excited about nothing—and then marry him."

Still, who would have believed that while the shine was still on the $35,000 diamond ring and the bloom still on the Isuzu, and the couple still on the two-room, chaperoned honeymoon cruise, a Web site would uncover a 9-year-old restraining order from the groom's former fiancée? Her handwritten complaint said that Rockwell "threw me around and slapped and hit me in my face" and "recently said he would find me and kill me" and—oh, yes—that "his elevator doesn't go all the way to the top floor."

Now some alleged galpals and dates suggested that the, um, multimillionaire with the two broken toilets in the backyard of his 1,200-square-foot house in Encinitas, California, was a cheap date with wandering hands. Rockwell denies it all. But the folks at Fox who were counting their money—How to be a Multibillionaire!—not only canceled the return but the sequels.

Before we score one for Western civ, let's get back to reality here. There have always been arranged marriages, always been women who marry for money and men who marry for beauty. Along with modern romance we still have mail-order brides, green-card nuptials, and dating services as inquisitive as any yenta.

Admittedly, it's hard to imagine trusting Fox as a matchmaker. C-SPAN maybe, but Fox? They can't even find Ally McBeal a husband. All those weeks of checking and they didn't see the holes in the resume of a sometime stand-up comic, who once had a part in *Killer Tomatoes Strike Back!*

But the bizarre part of this story isn't in matchmaking. Nor is it the willingness of too many women to strut their stuff and promise marriage for money, fantasy, or TV exposure. It's marriage as entertainment. It's relationship TV.

In the ancient days we sent men into the coliseum to be eaten by lions for the public fun of it. Now we invite women to the green room and the altar for the fun of it.

We don't call it humiliation. We call it "reality programming." Once upon a time, *Queen for a Day* starred ordinary folks crowned with tears. Now the Jerry Springer types invite families to fall apart in public. We have women duking it out over Mr. Wrong. We have couples invited to date others and break up. We have the Jenny Jones debacle when the surprised object of a gay man's affection turned murderer.

There is one show in the works that will track the lives of 10 strangers confined to a house for 100 days. There's another that will have a cast of real people dropped on an island and voted out one by one until there's a "survivor."

What we are seeing is the hucksterism of human emotions. Once promoters got up a crowd to see Houdini get untied or watch Evel Knievel leap over a string of cars. Death-defying acts. The new extreme sport tests and toys with human emotions.

I don't know if Darva was a hoper or a gold digger. I don't know if Rick was a showoff or a dangerous phony. In this faux marriage, they came back from the cruise to two separate homes and huge stake-out crews of media.

But the creator of this show, Mike Darnell, came up with the marriage-for-money pageant after he asked himself a question, "What is it that people wish for? They want a good relationship." He put together love and money and saw more money.

Before he got into marriage, Darnell had the idea of crashing an empty 747 into the desert. This time he sent "reality programming" down in flames.

February 24, 2000

F rom time to time in the history of relationships, a creature reemerges out of the primeval muck and into the limelight proclaiming that she has the secret that will lead women into the happily-married-ever-after.

In the 1970s, she was "the total woman." This icon, hatched by Mara-bel Morgan, guaranteed nuptial nirvana to women if only they stopped "nagging" men and learned to greet them at the door in nothing but a towel. *The Total Woman* was responsible for some rather alarmed UPS drivers and one very happy publisher.

Now, in the 1990s, she is "the Rules Girl," a female who makes the Cosmo Girl look comparatively liberated. Channelers Ellen Fein and Sherrie Schneider have taken "the rules" for "capturing the heart of Mr. Right" straight from the past onto the No. 1 spot on the best-seller list.

The Rules is a veritable compost heap of do's and (mostly) don't's for a woman—oops, girl—who wants to master the fine art of womanipulation. It's a how-to book: how to make a man desperate to marry a girl just like the girl that married dear old great-granddad.

Among the 35 "time-tested secrets" are these: Don't talk to him first. Don't call him. Don't split the check. End the phone call and the date first. Don't accept a date for Saturday later than Wednesday. Let him take the lead.

All in all, the authors say upfront and repeatedly, "The purpose of The Rules is to make Mr. Right obsessed with having you as his by making yourself seem unattainable. In plain language, we're talking about playing hard to get!"

Now, my opinion on this subject is suspect. As the authors warn: "Highly educated girls have the hardest time with The Rules. They tend to think all this is beneath them." You bet.

But what this book shares with its predecessors is a stunningly low opinion of men—which in no way seems to stop women from wanting them. The Mr. Rights of *The Rules* are hopelessly driven hunter-gatherers "born to respond to a challenge." They cannot escape their destiny: "biologically, he's the aggressor."

They are also and absolutely immune to change "because men never really change." But they are, at the same time, easily conned, "conditioned," "trained," and twisted around the finger of The Rules Girl: "Do The Rules and even the biggest playboy can be yours!"

If Susan Faludi penned such a profile of the species, she would be tarred for male-bashing. But the authors' portrait of women isn't a whole lot more flattering. Without the rules, they'd be quivering, smothering, marriage-lusting losers.

This is an era that has witnessed the return of the girdle and the push-up bra (see Wonderbra). We shouldn't be surprised to see the recycling of *The Tender Trap.*

This book probably was conceived as a self-defense text for women who started out sharing dinner checks and ended up feeling exploited. In fairness, some rules—Don't date married Men—make sense. As does the sub-subtext of self-respect.

But this makeover has some bizarre contradictions for those of us who grew up breaking rules. The same Rules Girl who is informed that "men must take the lead" is also told that "men like women who are their own person." Single women are supposed to act independent. Without actually being independent. Is it any surprise that another rule is "Don't discuss the rules with your therapist"?

Here is the basic problem with "playing hard to get": It's the acting. How do you stop? If Mr. Right falls in love with the role you are playing, do you ever know if he loves you? If you trick him, will you respect him in the morning? And if he's only interested in a challenge, what happens after the honeymoon?

I wish I could introduce the Rules Girl to a friend who tells each of her daughters, "Be yourself. The only man you will scare off is your future ex-husband."

The old games were based on mistrust. This ancient hostility skids unhappily across the pages of this modern manual.

"Remember, early on in a relationship," the authors warn, "the man is the adversary (if he's someone you really like). He has the power to hurt you . . . he runs the show." But if friendship is against the rules, why play?

Of course, the beauty of a best-selling text of "time-tested secrets" is that pretty soon they're not secret. By the time Hollywood turns this text into a parody, even the dimwitted Mr. Right may figure out he's been womanipulated. In the meanwhile, there's one good piece of advice in this book.

"Before he comes to your apartment tuck this book away in your top drawer." Aw hell, put it in the wastebasket.

October 31, 1996

ver the years I have come to think of this as the plumber problem. I pick up the phone and the plumber asks, "Mrs. Levey?"

At that point, two possible responses run through my brain.

I can say, "No, I'm Ms. Goodman, although I am married to Mr. Levey and no longer married to Mr. Goodman, but by the time I was divorced and remarried, it was too late to go back to my birth name, which was, by the way, Holtz, because Goodman was my byline."

Or, I can say, "Yes."

To be frank, my answer on any given day depends on exactly how high the water is in the basement. But I offer up this brief history of plumbing, marriage, and nomenclature to make it clear that I understand the complications that can arise when one couple carries two names.

Nevertheless, I always assumed that after all these years, a younger generation of brides would leave the altar with their birth names intact. I thought that keeping your name was a leading indicator, as the economists say, of an egalitarian era.

But as I read the bumper crop of summer wedding announcements, it has become clear that one of the last things to change is name-changing. The majority of college students are female, half of the new doctors and lawyers are women, but more than 90 percent of the brides still give up their names. We have more paychecks and rights but toss out our credit cards and identities like so much rice.

In short, married women are making a name for themselves. But the name is still his. Married men are changing a lot, even diapers, but not surnames.

Wives do not take their husband's name, I am told, because men demand they do. Bridegrooms don't have to. Penn State's Laurie Scheuble, who has been studying the name phenomenon with David Johnson, her husband of 18 years, says, "Bright boys know that if they say, 'You do whatever you want, Dear,' the women are far more likely to change their name."

Women make this decision because, they have told her, it's what's done.

It's still seen as a part of marriage. Not the part that treats wives as property—the old reason women changed names—but the part that subtly and strongly makes women regard trading in their name as proof of commitment.

One glance at the wedding pages of *The New York Times,* the paper of romantic record, is a pretty good indication of the ongoing power of tradition. Wives are no longer totally disappeared under their husband's names as Mr. and Mrs. John Jones. But even now a woman who is keeping her name is treated as if she were breaking news. Or breaking norms.

Last month, for example, a Ms. Robischon, who is keeping her name, got married. So, too, Ms. Olson, who is also keeping her name.

No such editorial tagline, need I say, accompanied Mrs. Galland? No editor said "Mrs. Kirsch was giving away her birth name."

There is the social subtext to all of these public announcements: "Ms. Smith, whose marriage will never make it, is keeping her name." "Ms. Brown, a careerist who doesn't really believe in family, will keep her name."

Of course, Scheuble can tell you from her research that names can never hurt your marriage, that there is no difference in the satisfaction or duration of a marriage with one name or two. (Something else to tell the plumber?) But there is still the enormous weight of tradition coming down at precisely the moment in life when even the neurosurgeon is mystically drawn to Chantilly lace.

Yes, I know the thoroughly modern arguments for changing a name. I've heard them, done them. Why is it less patriarchal to keep a father's name than take a husband's? Shouldn't children all have the same name? One family, one name? Why confuse the teacher, let alone the plumber? But none of these explain why newlyweds don't pick a new name or why men almost never change their own. You may be certain that no editor announced to the reading public that Mr. Kirsch is keeping his name.

The truth is not only that the pull of tradition is strong but that it pulls more on women. The burden of changing traditional assumptions and relationships from the wedding bells on still rests with wives. The name is just the first thing they give or keep.

This spring a survey showed how the young are looking for "soulmates." It seems to me that the trick of marriage is not merger but negotiation, managing two I's and a we.

Maybe the real symbol is when we bring something old—ourselves—to something new—our marriages. Two first names. Two last names. One marriage.

The plumber will figure it out.

September 2, 2001

L ast June, at the very height of the wedding season, twenty something singles were asked what they wanted in a marriage partner.

These young Americans couldn't agree on the same pizza or politics. But 94 percent of them concurred that "when you marry, you want your spouse to be your soul mate, first and foremost."

The "soul mate study" caused a good deal of eye-rolling among my long-married friends. What about those days when you look across the breakfast table and soul mate is not the first image that springs to mind? How do you tell the twentysomethings about the goose bumps that arise from such passionate declarations as: "I'll do the laundry"?

Young singles weren't looking for a financial partner or even a parenting partner. They were looking for a deep, intimate, loving, and permanent super relationship. The National Marriage Project, which commissioned this survey, characterized their portrait of marriage as "emotionally deep and socially shallow."

Fast forward now to the $300 million wedding plan that the Bush administration is proposing as part of the welfare reform package. This is not a federal matchmaking service or "a national soul mate policy." It is money for programs to encourage getting and staying married.

The White House math goes like this: The families of single mothers are five times more likely to be poor than the families of married couples. Ergo, if single mothers would get and stay married, poverty would virtually disappear.

Now, let it be said right off the bat that I'm in favor of healthy, stable marriages. I don't think this is a right-wing plot to get women to stay in abusive relationships or to reassert the patriarchal family. I, too, think there's something to be said for adding realism into the romantic mix and bringing wider social supports to fragile super relationships.

But where I drop off the love and marriage horse and carriage is when wedding bells are rung as an antipoverty program. As family sociologist Frank Furstenberg puts it, the belief that marriage policy will cure poverty is "an extreme case of magical thinking."

For openers, 38 percent of all poor children already live in two-parent homes. As for single moms and dads, it's not clear whether they are poor because they are unmarried or unmarried because they are poor.

Despite all the romantic ideology, poor mothers are at a disadvantage in what sociologists unromantically call the marriage market. Two paychecks are better than one, but the men around them don't always have a paycheck. Indeed, some economists believe that the most effective marriage policy would be a jobs program for poor men.

As for men with good jobs, Stephanie Coontz of the Council on Contemporary Families muses, "Men don't go around saying, 'Gee, what's my contribution to the world today? I think I'll marry a woman to get her out of poverty.' " Studies show that they are looking for, um, soul mates with some earnings.

And while we are talking about antipoverty programs, you could argue that the BA is a better bet than the Mrs. Only 1 percent of all the single mothers with a college education and a year-round job live in poverty.

Of course, the president has not put all his hopes for reducing the welfare rolls on marriage. He is also pushing for stricter and longer work requirements on different moral grounds: "so that more Americans know the independence and dignity of work."

So on the one hand, the administration thinks dependence on welfare should be replaced with the interdependence of marriage. Or, on the other hand, with the independence of work. That's not exactly a contradiction but a tension between the values of autonomy and mutuality that every soul mate can relate to.

This tension became obvious as marriage gradually lost much of its institutional power. Marriage doesn't have the same kinship or legal permanence. It's no longer the most essential economic relationship. It's no longer even the sole acceptable child-raising unit. As those supports were shaken, we replaced them with love—and disillusionment.

The big question, says Barbara Dafoe Whitehead, a co-director of the National Marriage Project, is: "How do we get people to pick the right person and stay married?" The answer is the same whether we're talking about welfare mothers or Elizabeth Taylor: "We don't know."

It's fine to experiment with premarital counseling or couples workshops that build trust or communication skills. But the only way the administration's proposal would reduce welfare rolls is if they hired poor women to lead the workshops.

It's absurd to take $300 million from programs that actually help fight poverty—like child care or jobs—and lay them before the altar. Welfare reform and marriage? This is one knot we need to untie.

March 7, 2002

A HONEYMOON OR JAIL?

A t least nobody in Orange County, California, can say that marriage is a prison anymore. Instead, it's becoming a kind of alternative sentence.

An adult man who has impregnated a teenage girl in that county may still have his options open: He can either be a jailbird or a groom. He can have a record or a wedding band.

Talk about your *Glamour* makeovers. Over the past year or so, more than a dozen men have been transformed from accused sexual offenders, even child molesters, into desirable husbands.

Not so long ago, men were either invisible sperm donors or deadbeat dads in the debate over teenage motherhood. All the attention and all the opprobrium was focused on the girls.

Americans have only recently begun talking about the other half of the problem: males. We have learned the startling facts about the much-older partners of many teenage mothers.

We know that 400 teenagers are impregnated by men over 25 every single day. We know that 20 percent of the fathers are six or more years older than teen mothers. We know that in California, which has the highest per-capita rate of teenage pregnancy in the nation, as many as half of all teens who give birth are prior victims of sexual molestation or rape.

So we have revised the portrait of teenage mothers. Maybe they are not just sexually immoral or calculating little economists having babies for welfare checks. Maybe they are young and vulnerable.

An alliance of progressives and conservatives has turned its attention to men and agreed that it is time to dust off the old statutory rape laws. Last winter, Governor Pete Wilson warned men who had sex with minors, "That's not just wrong, not just a shame. It's a crime, a crime called statutory rape."

But in Orange County, there are some judges and social workers trying to solve the concerns of unwed motherhood and statutory rape by marrying the two together. That is, by allowing the pregnant girl to marry the statutory rapist.

During the last year, a 22-year-old man arrested for having sex with a 14-year-old girl was given court permission to marry her. Six weeks ago, a pregnant 13-year-old legally wed her 20-year-old boyfriend/child molester.

As for the 10 or so other couples who got help with their nuptials? No one knows their ages, but some of the men are said to be in their 30s.

Not surprisingly, this attempt to make a marriage out of a misdemeanor and a family out of a felony has created a furor.

In the county's social service agency, some supervisors and social workers believe that girls will be better off with fathers for their children. Others believe, as one wrote, that the men "should in fact be arrested, not rewarded with their girls' hands in marriage."

The head of the agency, Larry Leaman, maintains that the marriages are approved only under careful circumstances. In each case, it is said, both parties want to wed. Indeed, the girls have refused to testify against their older partners.

Moreover, officials try to screen out the men who want to wed only to avoid prosecution. As Leaman said, they look for "a man who is standing by the teenage mother, wanting to do the right thing, ready for a family, willing to support it."

In fairness, the alternative to this marital sentence—he may go to jail and she may go on welfare with a child—is grim. If marriage doesn't promise much hope, neither does the state. The revival of this kind of "shotgun" marriage may be a testimony to the frustration and defeat of social programs.

Even at 13, the most vulnerable girls may see men and motherhood as the best of their limited options. And they are already on the way to motherhood.

But the role of Orange County in child marriage-brokerage is on a collision course with its role as a child protector.

Statutory rape laws are based on the notion that a girl below a certain age isn't mature enough to consent to sex. How then, is she old enough to consent to marriage? Do we care only that a girl is unwed? Or that she is unprotected?

It's hard enough to ask a judge to decide which suitor should end up behind bars and which suitor should end up at the altar. It's impossible to ask the police to arrest a man as a sexual offender, even a child molester, and then attend his wedding to the victim. Pretty soon they stop enforcing the law.

Orange County officials may hope to find a handful of husbands and providers for a handful of unwed mothers with children. But in the process, they are weakening the message to men and cracking the slim defense for a whole generation of girls.

For the men, marriage may mean freedom. But for the state, it looks an awful lot like the old ball and chain.

September 12, 1996

A NEW TAKE ON DIVORCE

N EW YORK—Have you heard the one about the 95-year-old couple who went to divorce court after 70 unhappy years of marriage? The judge asked them why they hadn't split long ago. The couple said, "We were waiting for the children to die."

It's a joke that made the rounds back in the 1970s, when cultural barbs were pointed at people who stayed together "for the sake of the children." But when I recycled this oldie to lunchmates at a recent conference on marriage held by the Council on Families in America, they'd never heard it.

What does it mean when an old joke gets new laughs? That we've probably passed through an entire generation of humor, a full cycle of attitudes, a whole swing of the pendulum.

It turns out that "staying together for the sake of the children" is very much on the minds of council members—an impressive collection of scholars, think tankers and culture watchers who range politically from mid-left to mid-right. Together, they have cobbled together a report on "Marriage in America" which is also a report on unmarriage in America.

Their central point is that "the divorce revolution—the steady displacement of a marriage culture by a culture of divorce and unwed parenthood—has failed." It has failed children. And it is time to turn our attention back to strengthening marriage.

In many ways this report constitutes a brave leap into the mainstream, middle-class heart of the family matter. In the ongoing family values debate, Americans have so far pointed their collective finger at relatively easy targets like unwed mothers and disappearing dads. Indeed two of the council's members—Barbara Whitehead, who wrote the provocative "Dan Quayle was Right" piece for the *Atlantic,* and David Blankenhorn, author of *Fatherless America*—helped create that consensus.

But in sheer numbers, divorce is the chief culprit in the breakup of the family and the deteriorating well-being of children. And we have indeed been, as the report says, "curiously silent on the subject of marriage."

In an era when every other marriage ends, the extent of divorce has served to stifle us. Even Dan Quayle, in a second *Murphy Brown* speech last fall, insisted "I'm not talking about a situation where there is a divorce. . . ." His own grandmother was divorced, he demurred, as were half of his cousins. Not to mention an entire roster of "pro-family" Republican leaders from Gramm to Dole to Gingrich.

We're also silent because divorce strikes at a central conflict between two sets of American values. One is the value we place on individual freedom, on striking out and starting over, on the pursuit of happiness. The other is the value we place on commitment, building communities and stable families.

The report on marriage is unequivocally and unapologetically written from the perspective of children. The stated goal is to increase the number of children growing up with both parents.

But what's missing from this pro-marriage advocacy is the view of marriage as a relationship as well as a child-raising institution. It's worth noting that in the entire treatise, the word "love" only comes up once in a bloodless reference to "the love attachments of marriage."

At the conference, Sylvia Hewlett of the National Parenting Association acknowledged, "There is a real trade-off between adult choice and child well-being." But the report tiptoes around this trade-off by talking about divorces that "may occur simply because one partner is unhappy or because a better partner has been located."

William Galston, an outgoing member of the White House Domestic Policy Council, praised the authors of the report for having "the courage to say that middle-class parents who blithely divorce" are every bit as damaging to their children as unwed 17-year-olds. But in my experience, "blithely" is a word that people often attach to other people's divorces.

At the height of the "divorce revolution" Americans may have falsely comforted themselves with the idea that children were better off in broken than warring homes. In the counterrevolution, we can't wish away marital problems as trivial.

There is more than enough intellectual firepower among the council members to jump-start an important national conversation about marriage and how society can support it. Their laundry list of recommendations ranges from the worthy to the wishful, from a simple plea that the entertainment industry stop glamorizing infidelity to a controversial suggestion that legislators reconsider no-fault divorce laws.

But if we're to rebuild a culture of marriage that works for adults and children, we have to be as concerned with the quality as with the longevity of marriage. One of the scholars here said, "We decided to put relationships between men and women off to the next report." That may not be so easy for the men and women themselves.

April 9, 1995

You could say that Jack Welch was once larger than life. After all, as a young adult, he once looked back with disbelief at the pictures taken of his school sports teams: he never realized that he'd been so short.

Later, after divorcing his first wife—the woman who had raised the four kids while he'd been a confessed "ultimate workaholic"—Welch had another out-of-body experience. "Being single and having money," he wrote, "was like standing 6 feet 4 with a full head of hair."

GE brought good things to (his) life. For two decades, the head of General Electric had a high ride and a low golf handicap. Welch was a celebrity CEO on more magazine covers than Madonna. He was huge. "Being a CEO is the nuts!" he once wrote.

But now Jack is tumbling down.

His affair with Suzy Wetlaufer, the former editor of the *Harvard Business Review* who famously did more than interview her subject, ended Jack's second marriage. This is the wife he once described in his book, *Straight from the Gut,* as "tough, witty, and 17 years younger than I am."

Jane Welch was, in his words, "the perfect partner." A mergers and acquisitions lawyer when they met, she became a corporate wife because, in Jack's words: "I really wanted a full-time partner. . . . Jane would have to give up her career."

But once they split—two years after the prenuptial agreement ran out—Jane apparently took up her old career. In papers filed in divorce court, the retired wife listed the details of the perks that GE shareholders were paying the retired CEO.

It wasn't just the big stuff like the $15 million apartment in Manhattan, the use of the corporate jet, the limousine, and the Mercedes. They were also paying for the cheesy little stuff, from the sports tickets and satellite dishes to the laundry and toiletries.

The man whose fortune is estimated at $900 million, the man who was paid $16 million in his last year as CEO, was getting about $2.5 million a year in perks. For life.

Of course, Jack is now going around issuing some of those wonderful nonapologies, the mea-not-culpas that are the staple of public life. On *Wall Street Week* he whined that the retirement perks he negotiated in 1996 were worth less than the millions in bonuses he was offered: "I sacrificed millions of dollars."

In *The Wall Street Journal*, he renounced his perks with the drama of the Prince of Wales renouncing his rightful throne. He said, "My contract could be misportrayed as an excessive retirement package." Could be.

Well, I will leave the culpas in the hands of the SEC. But I agree that, as Welch wrote, "the world has changed during the past year."

Today, the *Economist* puts Jack Welch on its cover as a fall guy, not a superstar. He's listed, fairly or not, in the crashing pantheon of Kenneth Lay and Bernard Ebbers.

But don't forget another change. When Jane Welch went to court this time, the attention wasn't on her greed, but on his. For once it wasn't the soon-to-be ex-wife of a gazillionaire looking for big bucks from her husband who was run through the media mill. It was the corporate gazillionaire himself.

Remember the other famous GE divorce? A few years ago, when top executive Gary Wendt divorced Lorna, his wife of 30 years, it became known as the "What Is A Wife Worth Case." Gary thought Lorna should be given $10 million—all she would ever "need." Lorna thought she was "entitled" to $50 million—half—and that it wasn't about need but about partnership.

The talk back in the 1990s was about what she did to deserve "his" millions. No one questioned what he did to deserve corporate millions.

Now we have Jack and Jane. Jane was "the perfect partner" when they were married. But worth $35,000 a month when they split. The $900 million man reportedly offered her $20 million in severance. Hold the toiletries.

In this round of the battle of sexes and excesses, of love and money, the outcry wasn't about what she did to deserve postmarital welfare. But what he did to deserve postcorporate welfare. Jack was the guy who got the label: "Enough is enough."

Jack was the guru of tough love management. He once said—straight from the gut, no doubt—"Too much of American business inflicts false kindness on its employees." But it turns out that Jack didn't know from tough love.

Now a downsized Jack Welch has volunteered to teach a management course for GE. Let's just pray they don't let him teach marriage counseling.

September 19, 2002

Ever since the scandal broke over Boston, I've had a refrain running through my head: "What's celibacy got to do with it?"

It's not set to the tune of the Tina Turner rock song but of a Bach cantata.

After all, as the wind of sexual abuse shakes more priests out of the trees, it has become routine to wonder: What's behind all this? The word celibacy comes up in one story after another. Churchgoers and church-watchers repeatedly say, "We need to talk about permitting married priests."

At least one cardinal summoned to Rome, Roger Mahony of Los Angeles, said he would bring up the subject. The pope tried to head off the discussion, declaring in advance, "the value of celibacy as a complete gift of self to the Lord and his church must be carefully safeguarded." But you don't brush something off the table so firmly unless it's occupying an uncomfortable amount of space.

I don't believe celibacy causes sexual abuse any more than marriage causes divorce. Need it be said that the vast majority of priests are not predators? For that matter, an earlier and prototype pedophile in the Boston diocese, James Porter, left the priesthood, married, fathered, and still kept sexual abuse as his hobby. But at the same time, celibacy isn't irrelevant to this scandal.

The issues facing the Catholic Church have been divided into at least two parts. One is, simply and horrifically, criminal abuse of minors by a growing roster of priests. The other is a hierarchy that protected itself instead of its children, forwarding danger from one parish to another.

The first debate is about broken vows, the second about a closed, restricted circle. But the matter of a celibate priesthood may link these two.

There are theologians who say that Christian celibacy began as what Boston College's Lisa Cahill calls a "counterculture." In the first centuries after Christ, people still lived in a socially controlled framework in which they were married off and expected to reproduce for the community. Celibacy was a radical and even subversive alternative.

It wasn't until the 12th century that celibacy became mandatory for priests, in large part as a struggle over power and property. If priests could marry, they could pass land to their biological heirs, land the church wanted for itself.

But medieval protectors of the church also worried that priests were too involved in personally controlling wealth. They asked, says Cahill, "Can you be a good servant of the church if you are worried about power, wealth, political involvement?" How ironic that sounds today as the ranking prelates of a celibate church are criticized for worrying more about "power, wealth, political involvement" than about children.

There is another, deeper way in which the requirement for celibacy mirrors the rigid hierarchy that has allowed such a mess to grow. Eugene Kennedy, a former priest and author of *The Unhealed Wound: The Church and Human Sexuality,* says celibacy was and is part of a philosophical view of humanity that divides people into lower and higher parts, the physical and the spiritual.

This split, he says, "pits the flesh against the spirit and makes the soul feel imprisoned in a very tough correctional institution."

It may be "better to marry than burn" in the liturgy, but sex-as-a-fire-extinguisher is clearly second-best to virginity. In the Catholic Church the most worshipped mother is a virgin, and so are most saints. Just one married couple has been elevated to sainthood. But these two had taken and upheld a vow to live together as brother and sister.

When the church talks about a priest being called to a "higher" life, does that mean a life further away from the "lowly" body and further away from the "lowly" laity? Surely, in an all-male celibate clergy, a priest rises further and further away from women.

"I believe that the image the church took of the human person matches the image it has of itself," says Kennedy. An image of lower and higher humanity.

I am no theologian. Many priests believe that celibacy frees them to devote themselves to others beyond family. I'm sure that's true for some. And sure, too, that it isolates others.

It's the requirement—not the opportunity, but the necessity—for celibacy that narrowed the pool of priests. It's the remote, closed hierarchy that made the church soundproof.

I am told that holiness, wholeness, and health all come from the same root word. Maybe we need to redefine holiness as a wholeness of spirit and body, to expand a small up-and-down hierarchy into a wider whole. Maybe that's what celibacy has to do with it.

April 25, 2002

A nd now a word to any parent who has ever had trouble talking about sex to a child: take comfort.

Take Alex Comfort.

Yes, the very same Alex Comfort who authored and illustrated *The Joy of Sex,* a 1970s culinary trip through his quirky sexual banquet. The book was a phenomenon of biblical sales proportions.

Alex stirred the international pot of sexual liberation. But he didn't exactly do any home schooling. Sex ed for his son Nick consisted of one awkward "talk" after the son's headmaster said the boy needed to know about personal hygiene. That was about it.

This news comes from Nick Comfort himself, who has just reissued a 30th anniversary edition of *Joy,* two years after his father's death. The new *Joy* has replaced sketches of the hirsute author and his mistress/second wife with a young buff couple who look as if they jumped naked from a Calvin Klein ad. But it retains the same funky style, not to mention cooking implements, as the original.

The big news is Nick's book-tour confession that he was the unenlightened son of the sex expert. Indeed this comes just in time for our own updated look at the sex-talk gap between the current generation of parents and children.

This fall, we've had one study after another about sex, teens, and parents. The first one, from the research organization Child Trends, said that most teens aren't having sex in the afternoon or in the car but at home and at night while mom and dad are asleep on the parenting job.

The second study from the University of Minnesota said that half the moms of kids who were sexually active didn't realize it. And to boot, 45 percent of the boys and 30 percent of the girls whose moms strongly disapproved of teen sex didn't know that either. Simultaneous ignorance.

Finally, there was a survey of low-income parents for the Sex Information and Education Council of the United States which showed—again—how many more parents believe they should talk about sex than actually do.

And add these to the growing list of research that compares parents who say they've told "all" with kids who say they've been told "nothing."

It seems that we still haven't found a comfort zone in the erogenous zone.

Dr. Comfort's *Joy*-ful career as writer and illustrator and swinger began after the infamous "Sexual Official Secrets Act" had been lifted in his native Britain. It was, he once wrote, like "ripping down the Iron Curtain."

Thirty years later, a lot of us wish there were any kind of curtain, even a diaphanous veil, between teenagers and the X-rated culture. But parents are still relatively speechless.

Robert Blum, who heads the University of Minnesota study that came up with the "clueless moms" data, says that less than 4 percent of mothers are actually comfortable talking about sexual relations with kids. He guesses that fathers are worse.

"Parents aren't comfortable and kids know it," says Blum. But what's important is whether we're willing to overcome the discomfort and talk about what we saw in the paper or heard in the neighborhood.

"Parents keep asking me how to craft the one perfect sentence," says Sarah Brown of the National Campaign to Prevent Teen Pregnancy. But the issue isn't information. "Kids don't want to know the seven signs of gonorrhea but how do I say no to my boyfriend and how do I know I'm in love and let me tell you what happened at the party. Parents need to provide the values, not the biology."

Everyone who deals with teens seems to agree that the most important and toughest job is staying in connection and conversation . . . not delivering a lecture but saying what we think. Of course what we think may be a confused mix of what we did, what we're afraid of, and what we hope for our children: The Joy and the Fear of Sex. But maybe it's time we shared all that.

"A lot of parents tell me, 'I hardly ever see them. When I do I don't know whether to talk to them about the sniper, safe driving, or sex,' " says Brown. "I think we need to reacquaint parents with the job of parenting. They need to talk with young people about what they think and why." She adds, "We need to put some spine into parents."

As for comfort—Nick Comfort anyway—this decidedly nonswinging son of the sexual rebel is nevertheless a chip off the old block of a father. When asked by his 8-year-old son what sex was, he answered, "It's how men and women get on with each other."

Come to think of it, spine is about the only part of the anatomy that still isn't listed in the pages of *The Joy of Sex*.

October 27, 2002

A fter all is said and done, I'm still trying to figure out how he got away with it.

I don't mean how he got away with hawking virtue and hiding vice in public. Bill Bennett isn't the first in the crowd to pull that off.

I can't figure out how he got away with it at home.

Let me put it this way. If my husband had fed $8 million into the slot machines I might have noticed before I read it in *Newsweek* or *The Washington Monthly*.

A few days ago, some folks at the casinos dropped a dime on Bennett and passed a passel of documents to reporters. The GOP's favorite moralist defended his gambling by saying, "I don't play the milk money. I don't put my family at risk, and I don't owe anyone anything."

Anyone? Anything? Not even an explanation to the wife who shares the milk money?

When Bennett dedicated his defense of marriage, called *The Broken Hearth,* to his wife Elayne, he wrote: "And no matter what I do, Elayne keeps the hearth: warm and secure." It's pretty clear that this designated hearth-warmer—founder of a program for teenage abstinence—didn't know the extent of her husband's risk-taking with the high-rollers.

When asked, she had three memorable comments: (1) "We are financially solvent." (2) "All our bills are paid." And then the clincher: (3) "He's never going (to the casinos) again." The next day, Bennett said, "My gambling days are over." Bingo.

Never mind morality tales about vice and virtue. This is a classic fable about marriage and money.

At every altar we merge two souls into one . . . financial life. But you can count on a single hand the number of couples who arrive at that union with an economic theory of marriage.

As sociologist Pepper Schwartz says, couples talk about everything before marriage except money: "The great taboo isn't who you slept with but how much do you have in your bank account and am I entitled to it?"

The difficulties of intermarriage between the tribes of Spenders and Savers are well-known. But money is at the heart of questions about the "me" and the "us" in every marriage. It's about independence and partnership. Not to mention power and control.

We live with a cultural clash over love and money. At home we are designated partners. In the workplace we are paid as individuals.

It gets tricky when the romantic ideal of a 50–50 marriage comes up against the economic reality of 70–30 or 100–0 paycheck. Schwartz has left hundreds of interviews with one impression: "The person who is the high earner tends to think it's his or her money. 'I made it, I'm responsible for it, and I should have the veto power or the larger vote.' "

This may go unstated or even underground. Many spouses only experience the subtle power struggle when one loses a job or decides to stay home with the kids. Many only discover in divorce court that "our" money was actually "his paycheck." Some only find out who makes the decisions when the $50,000 speaking fees are fed to the one-armed bandit.

I know that every couple also needs some de-coupled dollars. Breathes there a wife who never cut the price tag off a dress before it went in the closet? A husband who never fudged how much he spent on a round of golf?

After the milk money is paid, we can afford a bit of mad money. But anything over a couple hundred dollars defies my family's definition of mad money.

In the end, it's not the little green lies that threaten the sense of union. It's the whoppers. Quick, quick, which would ring your marital betrayal meter first: Tripping over a couple of receipts for double rooms at strange motels or finding the chit for $500,000 gambled away at the Bellagio in Vegas? As Desi Arnaz would say, this spouse has some "splainin' to do."

Did you think it was odd that Bennett's *Book of Virtues* didn't mention gambling? The same man's book on marriage barely mentioned money.

As for partnership? "The greater equality between the sexes in marriage," he wrote in one throwaway line, "is one of the most significant and welcome advances of modern times." But anyone who believes Elayne co-signed his hobby must also believe that, "over 10 years, I'd say I've come out pretty close to even."

Toward the end of his marriage treatise, this gambling man did offer up one insight that proved prescient. "The truth is marriage can lead to some startling revelations." Now there's something he can bet the ranch on.

May 11, 2003

Close to Home

THERE ARE TWO WAYS TO LIVE—WIDE OR DEEP. SOONER

OR LATER WE HAVE TO DECIDE WHETHER AND WHERE

WE WANT TO LAND. WE HAVE TO CHOOSE THE PEOPLE

AND THE PLACE WE CALL HOME. WE HAVE TO CHOOSE

WHAT WE WANT TO LEARN.

—FROM "THE TRIED AND TRUE VACATION,"

SEPTEMBER 2, 1999

THE GOTTA-GO GENERATION

I t is rush hour when I pull up to my mother's apartment. I am still speeding internally through the after-work time zone. The momentum of the day is pushing me forward long after its engine has turned off.

Tonight, however, there is a job to be done, items on a list to be crossed off, a mission to be accomplished. My mother is moving, downsizing from one apartment to another, and we have all pledged to help.

My assigned task is to begin to triage the stuff of her life. To pare down and sort out which items from the past will go with her to the future. So I arrive from the office with my mind on efficiency and my eye on my watch.

Together we go through the rooms. This coat hasn't been worn in years. There is no room in the new apartment for this table. Surely, this skirt is out of style. Maybe the kids would want these dishes. Nobody uses ashtrays anymore. This lamp has got to go.

It takes a half-hour of such speeding before I notice that my mother is in a different lane, traveling at a different pace altogether. While I am urging decisions, she is telling life stories. While I am trying to finish this job and get on to the next at home, she is considering this moment in her life.

She wants to talk about the friend who gave her this scarf, about the thousand family dinners around that dining room table, about the day she bought the lamp. She wants to say goodbye to these pieces of her past, one by one, before she lets them go.

Finally seeing this, I shift gears. I slow down and sit down. And doing so, I realize how easy it is to speed through important moments without even noticing.

I have a friend whose mother says with good humor that our whole generation should wear T-shirts that read, "Gotta Go." We are forever in a rush. We do drive-by visits.

They call us the sandwich generation because so many of us are caught between parents and children, work and home. But maybe we're named after the one item on the menu made to be taken on the run.

It's not just the tasks of life that we rush through. Not just the cleaning, the shopping, the commuting, the everyday maintenance. We also manage emotions with one foot on the running board. We even short-cut the experiences of life.

This summer, a teacher I know told me a family story so over the top that it might have been penned by John Irving. Heading for the car one morning, her family discovered that their cat had been crushed by the automatic garage door.

As horrible as this was, what lingered in her mind months later was the aftermath. In their morning frenzy, they barely had time to bury the cat and less time to cry before the three of them, deeply shaken, had to race off to their jobs and classes.

We asked each other what it meant that so many people didn't have time to mourn, to feel these moments in their lives. For some reason, it made me think of Carly Simon's ironic song about our times: "Make love in the microwave/Think of all the time you save."

In the past few years, with baby boomers in the White House, I have seen another, larger image of this rush hour. Since taking office, the Clintons have lost his mother and her father. In the pace of their lives, were they allowed enough time for reflection, for the slow absorption of loss and its meaning?

This summer when Al Gore's mother was first hospitalized with a stroke and surgery, he canceled his schedule. But then he did what was required. He took his worry back to work. Gotta go.

There is a family and medical leave policy for some of us, some of the time. There are small allowances for childbirth and sickness unto death. But the traffic jam of our lives rarely makes way for everyday family problems. Nor are we, surely, expected to brake for something as routine as saying goodbye to pieces of a family home.

Tonight, however, attention will be paid. There are boxes to pack but also a life in change. There are times when the more human speed limit must be observed. When talk is slow.

I go home late and tired. But I take with me a soup pot, a dozen stories and a silver basket that was—I now know—given to my grandparents for their wedding. Someday I will tell that to the next middle-aged generation. Before they gotta go.

September 7, 1995

OUTLIVING MY FATHER

My father died when I was 24. It was much too soon. For both of us.

In the last months, this most articulate man who loved humor and debate was literally at a loss for words. In some final cruelty, cancer took his language before it took his life.

On my last visit, we didn't say much to each other. He couldn't locate the right words in the vast, jumbled dictionary of his remaining consciousness. It was if he typed "red" on a piece of paper and it came out "dog" or "she." He was cursed with knowing that.

I couldn't find the right words either. Goodbye was too simple and too terrible. I busied both of us with the comfort of daily bulletins of family life.

In the year that followed his death, on the long, flat Michigan highway between home and work, I held conversations with him in the car. The car was always a good place to talk.

I was a grown-up by every formal measure, but I often felt like a fatherless child. On those commutes, I was trying to talk with him as one adult to another. We'd never quite crossed that bridge.

This dialogue went on for a long time. In the late '60s I imagined how this veteran and I might have argued about Vietnam. In the early 1970s, I wondered how this patriarch and I would have sparred over women's liberation.

In three decades of fatherless Father's Days there have been dozens of moments when I felt the presence and absence of this family man.

Sometimes, when my daughter was a toddler, restless and affectionate, I watched her wiggle off my mother's lap and wished that she had also had this grandfather. Again and again, I felt the loss for a child who didn't know what my sister and I had known—the man whose smile graced our childhoods.

Through my adulthood he was there, at the outer edge of my vision. As the parent of a schoolchild, I would ask myself, how did he do this parenting thing? How did he get us to meet his high standards without making us fear his disapproval if we fell short? As the parent of an adolescent I wondered: How did he teach us—relentlessly at times—without sowing a rebellion?

Parents remain our touchstones—fellow travelers—even after death. They are both missing and present. So when I succeeded, I would glance sideways and see a snapshot of how my father handled success: with wry pleasure and a strong sense of the capriciousness of life.

When I failed, I would glance sideways and remember how he handled failure: with grit and perspective. He got up, put on his tie, and went back to work. "Well, it isn't cancer," he would say, until, of course, it was.

I always think of him when Father's Day comes with its offerings of greeting cards and gifts. But for me, this Father's Day is different. This year I have officially, numerically, outlived my father. I am just now older than he ever became.

I am older than my own father. I cannot tell you how oddly that rings in my middle-aged ear.

You know the questions that precocious children ask about heaven? "What happens if an old widower meets his young wife in heaven—will they both be 30 or 70?"

For me the fantasy is much more earthly. If my father and I met here and now, I would be older. If he and my husband finally met—a long-harbored wish—my husband, too, would be the older of these two men. We are the elders of the man who is my elder.

This is a passage of no small proportion. In the past year or so, when I tried to think about my future—what happens next at midlife?—I kept hitting a blank wall. It was only when my birthday came and went that I understood the nature of that dead end. What my father did at my age—to put it as bluntly as I experienced it—was die.

To outlive a parent—especially a father—is by no means my unique experience. To live beyond our parents' age is the norm. But that moment carries an unexpected echo of the original loss. The father in my memory, the man who was once out there ahead of me or beside me—this is how you do 30, 40, 50—is no longer available as a guide.

Age is an accumulation of life and loss. Adulthood is a series of lines crossed. So I pass a father threshold in middle age, just as I did at 24. From here on out, I'm on my own.

June 20, 1999

THE TRIED AND TRUE VACATION

C ASCO BAY, MAINE—We have returned to our post, holding on to the tail end of summer as it races away from us.

In front of me a scene stretches out as familiar as the face in my mirror: A tidal cove, a clam flat, a lobster boat motoring laconically from one string of traps to the next. A flock of seagulls follows the boat like oxpeckers on the backs of African cattle.

This morning the sound of the CB chatter that connects one lobsterman to another drifts up the lawn and onto the porch. And from time to time the scream of a herring gull on the roof startles me as much as a car alarm in the city.

We pick up summer here where it was left off, the way we pick up the shorts and T-shirts and baseball caps that are left to winter over in lonely chests of drawers. By now, 20 summers are strung together like lanterns along a single piece of shore line.

By September our friends are already back from places as far away as Tuscany and New Zealand. They have added the Great Barrier Reefs and the Serengeti Plains to their vacation life lists like Audubon birders boasting of a rare species.

But we have returned to this island as surely as the goldfinch and the black-crowned night heron. We do not spend the winter browsing through travel brochures. We do not make summer plans any more than do the flycatchers that migrate each year to build a nest on the exact same piece of our porch roof.

Last week on my way out of the city, a friend on his way back spotted my overflowing Bean bag. As we stood and talked about foreign ports and languages, he stopped and asked curiously, "Don't you ever want to go someplace new?" For a moment, I felt like a stick-in-this-island mud, a creature of dull habit and unimaginative routine.

But this morning, I take a fresh accounting. There are bullfrogs in the pond this summer. That's new. The purple finches that were once rare have become frequent fliers to the bird feeder, and I spotted a gannet in the bay beside the seagulls and cormorants. That's new. So are the phlox making their first personal appearance—unannounced, unplanted—in my garden.

I am not unfamiliar with travel. I have spent enough hours in enough airports to know which side I'm on in the debate over who is responsible for air rage.

From time to time I still develop a crush on a new place. Last winter I fell for Hawaii—infatuated with the exotic landscape, the people, the food. The Brazilian cardinal had it all over the red one in my Maine chestnut tree, the lush tropic trumped the granite shoreline, the warm South Pacific was more welcoming than the icy North Atlantic.

But a crush is not a marriage and I know now what I didn't know when I was young: In one way or another, we are all, inevitably, tourists. The truth is that we can't know that many places or that many people in our allotted time. Not really know them.

When we travel widely, seven cities in seven days, we are always newcomers, inevitably dwelling in the present tense. We know a snapshot—Paris in 1987, Prague in 1995, the Vineyard last year, Vancouver this year. The paradox is that we cannot actually know what is new without knowing what is past. We cannot recognize a new hairdo on someone we have just met.

There are two ways to live—wide or deep. Sooner or later we have to decide whether and where we want to land. We have to choose the people and the place we call home. We have to choose what we want to learn.

It takes time, the painter Georgia O'Keeffe once wrote, to really see a flower. It took me two or three summers to tell one berry bush from another and the best mussel beds under the seaweed. I had to spend an entire season with the trillium to know that it has a white flower in June and red berries in August. It was 20 years before an eagle was spotted over the bay! Now that is news.

So, to others, sightseeing—that strangely redundant word—may conjure up images of grand canyons and great cathedrals. But today I saw a sight on this small patch of land, a small magenta wildflower that I have never seen before. And this is how I find out what's new: by staying put.

September 2, 1999

I WORKED HARD FOR THAT
FURROWED BROW

J ust because the FDA has approved of Botox doesn't mean that I have to. In fact, since 835,000 people have already had their foreheads injected with the paralyzing fluid that keeps them from being able to frown, I figure that somebody has to frown for them.

When I first read about Botox as a cosmetic, I thought there was something vaguely charming about the idea. After all, the microbe created by the US Army to inflict botulism poisoning on our enemies was now being used for domestic and aesthetic purposes. Talk about beating your swords into tweezers.

But even before the FDA gave the green light, we heard that Botox gatherings of women had become the Tupperware parties of the 21st century. Only what's being preserved are the women, not the leftovers.

This is not, I promise you, a screed about the political incorrectness of plastic surgery or vanity. Nor is it about how beauty is only skin deep.

Over the years, my attitudes—like my jaw line—have softened toward women who choose to change their faces rather than live with them. I know there's a line between those who "need" to be "fixed" and those who don't, between those who need surgery—think burn victim—and those who need therapy—think Michael Jackson. But I'm less inclined to draw it for anyone else.

When 47-year-old Greta Van Susteren became the poster anchor for plastic surgery, I thought the criticism was way over the top. As she said, "Having plastic surgery isn't shoplifting." If it were, nearly every female-and-fifty face on TV would be behind bars. After all, most of us choose, um, some self-improvement. Where is the unacceptable point on the aesthetic slope between braces and face lifts? Aging gracefully does not mean that you have to age gray-ly. So, you tell me the cut-off between hair color and collagen.

Nevertheless.

As a woman of a certain age—the age targeted by the hefty $53 million ad campaign being launched by Allergan, the maker of Botox—every time someone I know, or watch, has some "work" done, I have a vague feeling of being deserted. It's as if they'd left a threatened neighborhood, the endangered, natural species free range, and sided with the image-makers.

Remember back when Gloria Steinem turned 40? (If you do, it's probably too late for Botox, anyway.) She said: "This is what 40 looks like." At that time it was a statement that said proudly: We are not your grand-mother's 40-year-old.

Of course, 40 never did necessarily look like Gloria. But what happens when 50 is supposed to look like 40? Does that mean the whole standard of aging has changed? Do we think 60 should look like 50? Does, say, a 70-year-old Barbara Walters actually change the future for older women on TV? Or is an older woman only accepted if she doesn't look her age?

Chemical peels. Endoscopic lifts. Microfat injections. Eyelid lifts. Face lifts. Botox marketed to women the way Viagra is to men (never mind). How long is it before looking "your age" is regarded as a slatternly failure of effort? How long before any woman who doesn't try one of the above is dismissed as someone who is "letting herself go"?

I have always loved the expression, "letting yourself go." Where do you go, when you let yourself? To the recycle bin or to freedom? On Oscar night, in a sea of nipped and tucked, siliconed and surgeried women, the only seamed faces over 50 belonged to the likes of Judi Dench, Maggie Smith, and Helen Mirren. They are all character actors. Is that where they let themselves go? Into character?

In the past few years, I have found myself looking at older women as harbingers of the future. I'm looking for energy and confidence, and yes, attractiveness. Who do I want to be when I grow up? I am sure there are young women searching for the same clues. But there's no way to find them on the Botox party masks. This is the real symbolism of Botox. It eliminates lines temporarily by paralyzing muscles. It offers an actual trade-off. You trade the ability, literally, to express your emotions—furrow that brow, crinkle that eye—for a flawless appearance. In the search for approval from others, you hide what you are feeling. Especially anger.

This seems to my cranky eye and creased eyebrow to be exactly the op-posite of my goal to become an outspoken, maybe even outrageous, laugh-out-loud, nothing-left-to-lose old lady. Spare me the Botox. I plan to remain the kind of character actor who wears her emotions, not on her sleeve or on her surgeon's bill, but on her face.

April 21, 2002

SQUIRREL SENSE

I t's 7 a.m. and Hazel is pissed.

She stands on my windowsill, front paws against the glass pane, eyes narrowed, hissing: "What the $!&% is this?"

I feel her fury even though I refuse to meet her glare, even though I studiously continue reading my paper, even though I do not speak the whiny little Squirrelese that is her native tongue.

The $!&% that has prompted her ire, is the new bird feeder, although, of course, Hazel does not see it that way. Hazel believes deeply in her gut—the primary source of any emotions attributed to her species—that this is a squirrel feeder.

Indeed, why shouldn't she? For 18 months, a daily cache of sunflower seeds flowed from a large plastic cylinder conveniently located a hop, skip, and jump from the tree that grows outside my second-story kitchen. The bottom of the container was a wooden platform for my feathered friends.

My aviary invitation list was composed of nuthatches, titmice, chickadees, finches, and sparrows. But Hazel regularly crashed this buffet line. She spent long hours sprawled on this wooden lounge dropping sunflower seeds into her mouth, rather like a Roman emperor feasting on grapes.

I watched her dine with a mixture of hostility and admiration. But when the feeder went crashing to the ground one stormy night, I replaced it with one that is, I am told, guaranteed to make life harder for her breed.

Now Hazel is pissed. She turns from me, slaps at the feeder like a punching bag, tries to embrace the swaying cylinder, and falls to the ground, only to scramble up and try again.

Here is the rub. Instead of feeling victorious this morning as my omnivorous nemesis stands defeated, I am feeling guilty. And a bit mean-spirited.

I know, I know. This is the problem with those of us who occupy the mushy left, even those who call ourselves progressives. We make lousy enemies. We are rotten at carrying grudges—except, of course, at each other—and are wimpy haters.

I ask Hazel, Do you think that Jesse Helms would have trouble evicting a squirrel from his bird feeder? Not on your life.

Would even the environmentally friendly Newt Gingrich have second thoughts that he was committing a kind of species-ism, favoring the feathered over the furry creatures? No way.

Would Rush Limbaugh admit to a grudging admiration for the nerve and gymnastic skill of this second-story burglar? Forget it.

Unaware of my internal diatribe, Hazel tries this time to walk the metal tightrope to the feeder. She slips again. Grimacing with compassion, I remember the day I named her. In the middle of a blizzard, out of seeds but not sympathy, and against my self-interest, I fed her what I had: hazelnuts.

Now, retreating cowardly to the living room, where I cannot see her frustration, I know that no right-wing think tanker would feed the enemy. But the mushy left is cursed with empathy and an ability to see the other side—even of a window pane.

I don't mean to mix politics with sunflower seeds. I have no idea of Hazel's social views, although she has a short agenda and will only grudgingly share her wealth.

Nevertheless, when I return to the kitchen some hours later, this is what I see: a small, gray squirrel dangling upside down, holding the hanger in her hind paws, circling the feeder with her front paws, burrowing her nose into the holes, happily chomping. Around her a chickadee boldly shares the meal.

The long and the short of it is that while I was worrying, she was evolving. While I was analyzing the problem, she was solving it. While I am progressive, Hazel is pure Darwinian.

When at long last she has had her fill, this most fit survivor drops back to the windowsill and the birds take up their coexisting post. Proudly standing on her own two feet, Hazel leans against the pane, staring at me smugly.

This is what we have learned. With my seed money and her resourcefulness, we'll all make it through the winter. Squirrel away that thought.

December 25, 1997

W hen I turned 50, I discovered three essential facts of middle age: periodontia, bifocals, and golf.

Golf? Did she say golf?

Let me explain. I once assumed that golf was a sport for elderly country club Republicans. The sort of men who wore green pants with whale belts and protected their clubs with fuzzy duck head covers.

Golf was Dwight David Eisenhower. My family was Adlai Stevenson.

In my 20s I thought golf was God's way of telling you that you had too much time on your hands.

In my 30s I decided that a low handicap was admissible evidence of child neglect in any custody dispute.

In my 40s, as a fairly decent tennis and squash player, I couldn't imagine hitting a ball while it was standing still. Quite frankly, it seemed unfair.

But somewhere along the way, somewhere between Bill Clinton and Big Bertha and Tiger Woods, between chiropractors and knee surgery and Advil, I had an epiphany (that's something close to a muscle spasm) that said: Golf is my next sport. To wit: my last sport. I'd better learn it now.

This was a decision aided and abetted by a quirky nine-hole golf course in Maine where people still stroll and stop to look at the view.

It was also aided and abetted by a quirky husband (more Bobby Kennedy than Adlai Stevenson) who enthusiastically gave me all his clubs. This was an act of generosity that I didn't immediately recognize for what it was. A ploy for him to get new equipment.

Now, as I approach Columbus Day weekend with a full set of clubs and big plans, I feel fully qualified at last to offer up my views on why golf begins at 50.

Yes, I know that one sign of a new and erratic duffer is the penchant for turning golf into a good walk through midlife spoiled. For reasons that remain unclear, golf has spawned more philosophical rambles than fairways.

Nobody compares tennis to life. A love game? Ken Burns and several million fans talk about baseball as the collective field of youthful dreams, but there's no senior tour on the diamonds.

Today there are, I hasten to add, some 25 million golfers and 16,010 golf courses. There are speed golfers and networking golfers and boring golfers. There is even, for reasons that escape me, a golf channel. All golf, all day long.

There is a business writer who actually correlated the handicaps of CEOs with their stock performance. And there are the very, very serious golf professionals who sit around discussing whether they should ban new improved clubs because they are making the game too easy. Say what? But from my perspective, golf is the midlife sport of choice for very different reasons. First of all, it's easier to reach your goals. In midlife, after all, it's a snap to have a handicap below your age and a score below your weight. And getting easier all the time.

Golf is like midlife because only now do you realize that the course you have set upon is governed by rules so vast, so arcane, and so arbitrary that the average person—you—will never figure it all out.

Golf is like midlife because it is absolutely unfair. As a young person, you carry the illusion that if you do your homework, study, and work overtime you'll get it all right. By middle age, you know that every time you've got it all together—work, family, putt, pitch—some piece is about to unravel. I promise you.

Golf, like midlife, is played against only one opponent: yourself. By the time you reach 50, you'd better figure out that doing well doesn't depend on others doing badly. You don't have to wish them ill. They're not the reason you are shanking the ball.

Golf is like middle age, because—ah, you knew this was coming—in these years you really do have to play it as it lays. You don't get to start everything all over again. The most you get is a mulligan. If it's an unplayable lie, everybody sympathizes, but you still have to take a penalty.

On the other hand, golf, like midlife, also offers another chance. No matter how badly you hit one ball, you can still recover on the next. Of course, no matter how well you hit one ball, you can always screw up the next.

Finally, golf is like midlife because at some time on a beautiful October day, when you are searching for a ball, or for that matter your swing, you look around and realize for the first or 50th time that in this game, you're the one keeping your own score.

October 8, 1998

HERE AND NOW WITH AUNTIE

Our conversation begins as it always does. I come for a visit and find her sitting in her chair, looking out the window. I pick up the small microphone that dangles from the newest of her hearing aids and begin the ritual.

"How are you, Auntie?" I ask, as always.

"Oh, I'm a hundred percent," she answers, as always. There is a pause while we share the echo of the ironic humor she has carried with her through life.

She says, as always, "Don't be in a rush to be 97." And I say, as always, "Well, all right, Auntie. I was going to rush, but I won't."

I sit down on the edge of the bed and take photographs out of my pocketbook. I show them to her one by one, a rogues' gallery of the nieces and nephews that she calls, happily, her "uglies." She smiles at each picture as if this were the first time she'd seen it, though in fact I have brought this stack to her many times before.

Then she says in her precise diction, "Tell me what is going on in your world?" I lean into the microphone as if it were a radio interview and tell my audience of one some stories. Where we've been. Where we're going. What we're doing. Stories that I have told her before.

Sometimes she will tell me, if I ask, tales I have heard before. Tales about a childhood in England, school in America, the longing for college, about her parents, her husband, a whole world that is now in the past.

On a good day she says, again, "I am just waiting to leave this planet. I say that philosophically, not sadly." On a bad day she asks, again, "You cannot help me exit, can you?"

We became family, Auntie and I, when she was much younger, which is to say in her 80s. I married the nephew who is more than a nephew to her—her prize, her lifeline—and—began learning.

Coming back from a family gathering one day, displaying my careful new in-law manners, I said how pleasant lunch had been. She looked up and said—not unkindly, not sharply, but directly—"I thought it was boring."

Laughing, I said to myself, "No shucking Auntie. We will be friends."

Now, we're losing her. Or rather, she is disappearing.

What she calls in her own erudite language "the diminution of my faculties" has continued in countless increments. Ears, eyes, legs. Hearing, sight, mobility. The fierce independence that characterized her life, the long walks, the daily bus trip to Burger King until she was 94. Gone, one by one, like chits she must turn in before being allowed through the door.

Her daily newspaper has given way to a large-type weekly. The names of relatives have dropped off her screen, like atrophied limbs. And then there is the rest of her memory. She lives in a narrowing time frame, a day that is repeated over again without a sense of yesterday or maybe this morning.

My husband, who shares her honesty and her humor, calls her life "Groundhog Day," after the movie about a man destined to endlessly repeat one day. Yet we are still her students. In her presence, we learn about time, about age, about letting things be what they are.

My husband will visit Auntie tomorrow, though she probably will not remember the next day that he was there. He doesn't go to chalk up a credit, just to be there.

I bring the photographs this Sunday, though she won't remember them the next. I am no longer afraid that this ritual mocks her memory loss. I judge my act by her smile.

I know now that the only way to be with Auntie is on her terms, in her time zone, in what the Zen philosophers call the now. So for a while, at her side, I am keenly aware that life is always lived in the moments. Moment by moment.

In *The New Yorker*, biographer Edmund Morris wrote recently about visiting Ronald Reagan, about trying to make small talk with a man hollowed out by the crude, cruel tool of Alzheimer's. "About six months ago, he stopped recognizing me," notes Morris. "Now I no longer recognize him."

I hope this won't happen with Auntie or to Auntie, but it may. The long ending, with its certain destination and its uncertain timetable, is a melancholy affair. We begin to miss the people they once were while they are still, not wholly, here.

But sitting beside Auntie today, a companion to her leave-taking, I no longer see it as tragic or unfair. It simply is.

February 2, 1995

C ASCO BAY, MAINE—The afternoon wind sweeps up from the cove in time to clear the uninvited mosquitoes off the ceremonial grounds. Gradually the people who have come to this island by land or air, and finally by sea, begin to collect on the rough grass beside the white tent.

As I come out of the house to join the others, a hummingbird enjoying the unexpected bounty of flower arrangements whirls away. Suddenly it occurs to me that the cat has taken off for parts unknown.

In the shimmering afternoon sun I find a place among the parents who share the informal front row. Only now do the lists, the wedding flow charts, the transportation details that rivaled D-Day, drop from my consciousness like anxiety about the weather.

Just a day ago, my daughter and I went for a walk along dirt roads brimming with lilacs. Though I am rarely at a loss for words and sometimes at an excess of words, I struggled to find something to say to the younger.

I wanted to give my woman-child some words of wisdom to wear like an amulet against and for the future. Something old, something new, even something borrowed. But everything I thought of was too much, too little, too early, too late.

So it was the daughter who said the right thing to the mother. For us, she said, marriage isn't just the next thing we do. For us, for our generation, it isn't natural or expected. It's bold. And we know that.

As we walked home together from the beach, I thought, "of course." How could this pair not know it?

They are the first of their mid-twentysomething friends to wed, the first child of their parents, the first among the grandchildren, the first among the cousins. They are even the first wedding ceremony performed by their generous and gentle friend who calls us now to bear witness to this joining.

Now, the mother of the bride, a phrase that sounds like some absurd creature fluttering anxiously in an old movie, I look around and think about boldness.

The people here are not names on some generic guest list. Together they form a village. The couple's village.

What is that old saying? It takes a village to raise a child. It's true. But villages these days are not traditional tribal zones where everyone stays in one place or even in their place.

The two young people pledged to wed are the creatures of marriages and remarriages. Their tribe was created and recreated by parents who tell themselves they are stronger at the broken places. And hope to God their children are, too.

The family trees that these two so carefully wrote out for us don't just bear aunts and uncles and cousins. They branch out through much of modern life. This morning, small half-siblings on both sides greeted each other like child anthropologists trying to devise some proper title for their relationship.

Nor do the dearly beloved gathered together share the same rituals handed down through generations. The wedding dances in their village include the hora and the polka. The attitudes run from Old Testament to New Age. The culture includes both hunters and vegetarians.

And yet these children of diverse roots have chosen to make a life together. These firsthand witnesses of disruption have chosen union. They have brought together kin and friends from diverse backgrounds and ZIP codes. They carry to this place the confidence that they are a loved center of this small world. A center that will hold.

Bold indeed.

Behind me, at opposite ends of this old, sprawling farmhouse, two young people who have optimism in their future and great holes in their jeans appear now. Through the alchemy of white lace and black tuxedo cloth they have transformed themselves into something else: A bride and a groom.

Arm in arm they walk down the makeshift aisle. Soon, through the magic of vows that include a promise to "try and understand each other" they are transformed again. Husband and wife.

Rings are exchanged, a glass is broken, a kiss is shared. As a mother who prepared for every wedding day eventuality short of a typhoon, I find myself incredibly, without a Kleenex. And here, on this ground, a new village held together by old emotions celebrates everything. Love, joy, boldness.

June 9, 1994

I went to visit Tom early in the morning, before the doctors arrived to check the growth of the cancer that had come back with lethal intent.

It was my last visit and I knew it, but the nurse stopped me at the doorway and asked me in that voice of pleasant authority: "Are you a member of the family?"

She was screening people, but I looked her in the face and without skipping a beat, I said: "I'm one of his kids." The funny part is that it was true.

I was one of Tom Winship's kids. In 1967, he had barely begun his tenure as legendary editor of *The Boston Globe*. He hired me—he adopted me—at the height of the miniskirted, counterculture, revolutionary '60s. I became one of the fully-grown reporters that he picked using the one human-resource tool he trusted: gut instinct.

Tom picked us kids, one at a time, whenever he wangled another slot. He created a community, an extended, squabbling, engaged, caffeine-high bunch of reporters for a paper that would be better than the sum of its parts, greater than any one of us.

He offered me a job I didn't want—on the women's page—at a salary $10 lower than the other paper in town. It's the best 10 bucks I never made. This exuberant, irrepressible life force, who died Thursday at 81, was the editor, the mentor, the pal, the engine behind a "writer's paper" that became world class.

How do you describe an editor and life force to those who weren't lucky enough to work for one? For the 19 years he ran the *Globe,* this man in a seersucker suit with a bow tie and suspenders would walk through the city room, slap you on the shoulder, and ask, "You havin' any fun?"

When was the last time a boss asked you that?

His old pal, Ben Bradlee, who soldiered with him as a Washington reporter in the post-World War II years, said they were both determined to make a difference and have fun doing it.

What difference does a person make? I could count the Pulitzers. I could tell you about covering civil rights and women's rights when other papers were tiptoeing around these issues.

I could tell you about his "kids" of every description who now pepper the staffs of great newspapers across this country. I could tell you about how many lifetime friendships and marriages took place under his wing and roof. But how do you describe the Greatest Generation guy with the amazing ability to keep going forward, to stay connected to the next thing?

The first time I ever had lunch with Tom, he took me to the fancy and venerable Ritz. He ordered bouillabaisse, we talked, and when the waiter came around again, he said, "Mr. Winship, can I get you anything else?" Tom turned around casually and said, "Yeah, you know, I'd like seconds." Seconds at the Ritz. I never got over it.

My irrepressible pal carried small paper cards stuck in his pockets with story ideas. Out of every 10 ideas, three were completely cockeyed. Two, as another Winship kid, Bob Turner, would say, had already been in the paper. Two more were just OK. And three would knock your socks off.

In these days, corporations run most newspapers. Editors have to go to think tanks where the managers pass out copies of *Who Moved My Cheese?* The corporations spend months working up mission statements. Everyone fills out forms about targeted goals. The editors are beholden to publishers who are beholden to stockholders. But the best of the newspaper people still believe in taking risks.

Tom was the best of them. He believed in taking on the big guys. He believed in giving it a shot—what the hell, go get 'em. Even in his alleged retirement, he believed in newspapers. He believed in himself. He believed in his kids. And as a kid who had lost my own dad far too early, I basked in the certainty that he was on my side.

Most of us kids are well into middle age now, but I say without embarrassment that I still have my stash of his "tiger notes," the scribbled words that he would send when you wrote something that tickled him. Tell the management gurus and the corporate incentive honchos and the stock-option-makers, I worked for those notes.

That last visit, I said to my old pal, "Tom, didn't we have fun?" He opened his eyes and held my hand and said as clear as a bell: "You bet we did." Before I left, he gave me a hug as he always did and said in my ear, "You were always my favorite." And I smiled because I know he loved me, and I also know without a shadow of a doubt that he said that to all us kids.

I'm not so good at loss. Who is? I know how lucky we were. But I find it totally unacceptable that I won't ever see this guy coming across the street in a straw hat to meet me for clams or sushi and his favorite main course, gossip.

Damn it, I want seconds.

March 15, 2002

WELCOME TO MY GRANDSON

BOZEMAN, MONTANA—We are watching the sunrise, my grandson and I. It's our time of day, when his sleep-deprived parents hand him over, warm and groggy.

Maybe this is why God created grandparents, I tell this newborn, who hasn't yet learned the difference between day and night, breakfast and dinner. At his stage of life and mine, our biorhythms are in predawn synchrony. As the first hints of red edge these Western mountains, we do the morning shift together.

It's been only a few days since grandparents, cousins, honorary aunts and uncles, and friends began welcoming this boy into our village. Pictures and good wishes are still traveling across the Internet tribe.

Now sitting here, I wonder if there is a grandparent pheromone or instinct that goes unmentioned in the DNA research. There must be some chemistry that turns adults with opera subscriptions and espresso machines into people who put bumper stickers on their cars that say: Ask Me About My Grandchildren.

Logan was born three weeks early into a troubled world: War brewing with Iraq. North Korea threatening nuclear weapons. Suicide bombings in Israel. I run through the cliches that fit his best of times, worst of times. I remember the Chinese curse: May you live in interesting times. Then I smile at my grandson and ask: "What was your hurry?"

When he ignores my question, I rerun the family tape to other best of/ worst of/interesting times.

I was born in 1941, just months before Pearl Harbor and before the war in Europe became the Second World War. My daughter was born in 1968 at the height of the Vietnam War, in the weeks between Martin Luther King Jr.'s and Robert Kennedy's assassinations.

Our birth years were so dismal that even the wine wasn't worth the space in a wine cellar. We too were brought into a troubled world. For my mother and myself and my daughter, birth was/is a leap of faith over fear. For us, a newborn was/ is as life-affirming as the most predictable scene in an old movie—"boil the water!"—or in the final episode of a sitcom that climaxes in a trip to the maternity ward.

From time to time, my daughter and I laughingly ask Logan what he wants to be when he grows up. Are you ready to take your SATs? His birth projects us into the future, but it also returns us to that first moment when all we really want for our children is safety. When keeping them safe is our primary job and primal emotion.

Is there a parent or grandparent who hasn't checked the breathing of a sleeping newborn? Not in this house. Nearby there is a small store of safety equipment that his parents have acquired. A car seat for the rear seat only. A stroller with a seat belt. A carrier with a sturdy strap. A monitor to hear his cry from one room to another.

There is a cache of baby books as well, indexed so a parent can find the right page in the middle of an anxious night. In the favorite of these, the authors encourage parents in ways that make babies feel that their world is a safe place.

But is it? In the paper last week, there was a story about Somali parents who hired smugglers to take their children away, to Europe, to America. They gave them away to keep them safe. Is there a pheromone that also reminds parents—and their parents—of the limits to the safety zone?

When my daughter was an infant, I used to wonder what the world would be like if we gave every world leader a single newborn to care for, hands on. Would the tender, anxious responsibility for daily survival change everything they did—or merely justify it?

When Francis Bacon wrote that children are our "hostages to fortune," he was scorning families as "impediments to great enterprises, either of virtue or mischief." But these days I read those "impediments" with a very different emotion. If those hostages to fortune make us expand the safety zone, so much the better.

After Logan's birth, I offered his family a blessing that I had learned from a friend who lived in India: "May your house be safe from tigers." My son-in-law smiled and assured me that there are no tigers near here, only bears and an occasional mountain lion.

Now the sun is over the mountains, and my grandson is sleeping. In this peaceful hour, I know that children are the real act of daring in a dangerous world. May your house be safe from tigers, little boy. And from the occasional mountain lion.

February 2, 2003

Rest Stop

THESE DAYS, IT'S POSSIBLE TO BE CITIZENS OF THE

WORLD OR NATIVES OF THE LAND. TO TOUR OR TO BE-

LONG. WE CAN APPEASE A RESTLESS DESIRE FOR A

CHANGE OF SCENE. OR WE CAN REST IN ONE PLACE AND

PAY ATTENTION TO THE SCENE AS IT CHANGES. IT'S UN-

CLEAR WHICH WAY WE WILL SEE THE MOST.

–FROM "A SENSE OF PLACE," AUGUST 1, 1993

AMERICA'S INCREDIBLE
SHRINKING VACATION

CASCO BAY, MAINE—Back in the days when Hector was a pup and the word "e-mail" was a typo, the "working vacation" was nothing more than an oxymoron. After all, you were either vacationing or working. On the job or off.

Now it's become an emblem of the American economy and George Bush, its current CEO, is spending this month as a role model on his 1,600-acre Prairie Chapel Ranch in Crawford, Texas.

This has raised the ire of the likes of Senator Robert Byrd, who thundered, "Who's watching the White House?" But it's also raised the dismay of others who watch the vacationer-in-chief conducting business and attending fund-raisers and ask, "Is he having any fun yet?"

Well, are we?

Do you remember those wonderful yesteryears when an earlier Republican president under the spell of the Maine ocean breezes came out in favor of two or three months worth of vacation? William Howard Taft said it was "necessary in order to enable one to continue his work the next year with that energy and effectiveness which it ought to have." Admittedly, the rotund Taft was a bit of a hedonist in the food department but it shows how far we've drifted on a summer tide from real vacation.

Americans have always been a touch suspicious of leisure. Our Puritan patriarchs not only famously regarded idle hands as the devil's workshop, they believed the grindstone cleared the path to salvation. We've long been wary of both the idle rich and the idle poor as threats to our democracy.

In the early 20th century a few hard-working researchers declared that a little time off was a good thing. Not surprisingly, they decided that "brain workers" needed a rest from days spent laboring in the minds, while physical workers could do without it. The idea of vacations finally caught on in the middle and working classes, but it was never codified into the law.

Now we arrive at the summer of the incredible shrinking American vacation. It's predicted that we'll take 10 percent less time off than last year, and last year was no week at the beach.

Americans have notoriously fewer vacation days than workers in any other industrialized country. While Europeans get four or five weeks paid leave by law, and even the Chinese get three weeks, we average about eight days after a year with one company and 10 days after three years. Thirteen percent of American companies offer no paid vacation at all.

Even more remarkable than how few days we get is how few we take. We essentially give back $21 million in time owed but not taken. And in an Expedia poll, one out of five workers said they feel guilty taking vacations.

So, which came first in the great vacation deprivation: the economy or the culture? Insecurity or guilt? The work ethic or the whip?

There's no doubt that a shaky economy breeds fear that any vacation could be permanent. Labor economist Barry Bluestone at Northeastern University points to a changing and insecure economy as the biggest factor. After all, he says, "We always had the Protestant work ethic. Are we more Protestant than last year? I don't think so." But then the tenured Bluestone confessed to being on a working vacation himself.

Joe Robinson, founder of a grass roots campaign to get a minimum three weeks of paid leave (www.worktolive.info), also acknowledges the role of cultural attitudes that teach "our esteem and self-worth can only come from producing and doing tasks all day."

Americans do have a stunning capacity for turning everything into work. If you don't believe that, think about the waiters everywhere who approach your table with the inevitable question: "Are you still working on that?" They make it sound as if chewing pasta was an onerous job to complete.

We not only work out, we play hard, instead of playfully. It's the spirit that turns vacations into work.

The irony is that "working vacation" came into the lingo with a wink and a nod. Now the ruse has become a reality. Fully equipped with the toys of e-mail, voice mail, cellphones, labor trumps leisure. It's the reason why 83 percent of vacationers, tethered by technology and anxiety and expectations, check in at the office.

So here we are. A working vacation means wearing boots while you carry the weight of the world on your shoulders. It means standing on the beach talking to your clients. And it means—trust me on this—sitting at a laptop looking at words on a screen instead of an ocean view.

The blessing is that we can now have a vacation without the guilt. And of course without the vacation.

As for rest, recreation, and time off? Well, fellow Americans, we're still working on that.

August 7, 2003

F rom my window, I watch the cat as he sets out on his appointed rounds. He stops to inspect the bird feeder, moves on to the asparagus bed and then, gingerly, steps around the wasp mound. Having staked out this territory, he assumes his morning post among the peony leaves.

This cat—my daughter's cat and my grandcat—arrived here weeks ago, caged and collared and thoroughly citified. He was driven up the east coast through megalopolis to the countryside where he encountered grass as a deeply suspect foreign turf.

Gradually, however, he has gone native. First the collar came off and then he shed his city manners. An encounter with a garter snake was followed by a standoff with a spaniel and, I fear, another with a mourning dove. Stalking this territory, he has now claimed it as his own.

I have watched this transformation with amusement. But this morning, it occurs to me that I have much in common with my four-pawed visitor.

I too have shed my collar—the shoes, the eyeliner, the suit—for a country uniform of baseball cap, shorts, T-shirt. I too have left the cage, the urban containers of work, office, car, for the uncontained land, sky, sea.

Moreover, like my grandcat, I have covered this small piece of the world and staked my claim over it inch by inch, year by year. Over time, I have made this territory mine the old-fashioned way: by living in it.

This morning I walk along the same road that is never quite the same. The daisies have given way to the brown-eyed Susans. The Indian paintbrush has been replaced by Queen Anne's lace.

An urban child, I grew up knowing the names of streets and shops but not the names of wildflowers. Like most adult immigrants to a new world, I will never become perfectly bilingual.

But I have learned this country the way people learn foreign languages: through total immersion. I know where to find blueberries and when to expect blackberries and the best times—maybe—to fish for mackerel. I have learned the varieties of goldenrod, the taste of wild mustard, the song of a rufous-sided towhee.

Returning to this island year after year, I have slowly added a new sense to those of touch, taste, sight, smell, sound. A sense of place.

Like most Americans, I spend much of my life in a built environment where offices and houses remain a static backdrop to the variety of humans. I live in a wide world where people skim across the surface and travel far by phones and flights and faxes.

Today, our peripheral vision is as great as the television camera. We pride ourselves on mobility. We equate that mobility with ambition, with broad horizons, with get up and go.

For my own part, I get up and go a great deal. I can tell you where the frozen yogurt stand is in the Pittsburgh airport and where every Starbucks coffee shop is in downtown Seattle. I have a modem for hotel rooms and a passport that is never out of date.

But I come here to sink into a world that too many of us skate across. I come here to remember what it's like to live deep instead of wide.

These days, it's possible to be citizens of the world or natives of the land. To tour or to belong. We can appease a restless desire for a change of scene. Or we can rest in one place and pay attention to the scene as it changes. It's unclear which way we will see the most.

On this island, in many country places, people are commonly considered newcomers until they have been here a generation. Surely we are new until we have learned which apple tree bears fruit every other year and where the poison ivy is. We are new until we have planted a tree and worried about the water well.

At some point, those of us who return, who take the course of total immersion, often discover that we have set down roots. Suddenly, on a clear Maine morning at the edge of a tidal cove, with a country cat hiding out in the peony bushes and weeds waiting in the garden, there comes a feeling of home.

On days like this what makes the most sense in this entire strange world is the sense of place.

August 1, 1993

I am suffering from what is referred to in the unmedical annals as Middle-Aged Jock syndrome.

This is a syndrome that begins at that precise moment in life when all the advice that we have hitherto followed to remain hale and hearty, fit and firm, aerobic and athletic, goes belly up on us. Or back up. Or leg up. Or, in my case, knee up.

Suddenly, body parts we never knew existed and cannot spell begin to rip, tear, inflame, and disintegrate. We discover a new verse to the old skeletal lyrics: The hip bone is connected to the thigh bone—and they are all connected to our age.

This physical betrayal, this treason on the part of the one body politic from which we had expected a modest amount of loyalty, is immediately followed by a crash course in anatomy. And, often, the verdict delivered by a much too cheerful doctor is that we can either repair our machinery or continue down the road of life like an old clunker.

The formerly unknown body part in question today is something called the meniscus. Who knew I had such a thing? Meniscus sounds like something you would find in the White Flower Farm catalog, not in your body. See the lovely yellow meniscus over there by the hibiscus.

Alas, this bit of cartilage that provides a cushion between my leg bones is unlovely. It is, moreover, torn. It is, moreover, my fault.

Middle-Aged Jock syndrome, as anyone can tell you, is often brought upon you by Middle-Aged Hubris syndrome. The onset of this particular disaster came from playing tennis with my niece, an ingrate who returned my years of affection and lessons by—what else can you expect from a lawyer?—finally beating me.

You know that ad in which the middle-aged father is whipped at hoops by his son? The one where Dad scoffs down a couple of cans of nutritional supplement—Where is the drug czar when you need him?—then goes out and beats the stuffing out of the kid?

Let us just say that in my case, the rematch didn't go quite that well.

In one fierce rally, carrying the pride of an entire generation upon my racquet, I lunged right, my knee went left, and a generation gap opened behind my kneecap. Suddenly the meniscus had a thorn.

So it is that I have arrived at my pre-op visit reading an informed consent form for what has been described to me as minor—no, check that, very minor, outpatient minor, itsy-bitsy minor, good-as-new minor—arthroscopic surgery.

Until now, as far as I understood it, arthroscopic knee surgery is this "little procedure" wherein the surgeon makes a couple of holes in your leg. One hole is for the instrument that lets him look around. The other is for the little doctor-gremlin who is sent in—Fantastic Voyage II—to snip off the torn hibiscus, uh, meniscus.

Maybe I have that a little wrong, but you get the idea.

According to my overinformed consent form, however, I am subjecting myself to the risk of everything from a blood clot to damage to my vocal cords to—oh, yes, I almost forgot—loss of bodily function or life.

This is the wonder of modern medicine. Back in the 1960s, you could have open heart surgery and be told only that "everything would be just fine." Now, after an entire generation of lawsuits and bioethicists, you go in for a knee trim and they have you sign a form saying you were warned about the danger to your teeth. (The knee bone's connected to the bicuspid?)

It reminds me of that letter to *The New England Journal of Medicine* some years ago about the two patients who were informed against their wishes about the gory details of their upcoming operations. They each immediately dropped dead of a heart attack. True.

At the same time, no overinformed consent form ever warns a patient of the doctor who took out the wrong kidney, or—my favorite of the month—the addicted anesthesiologist who kept his patients' drugs for himself.

Do I sound alarmed? No, no, not to worry. This is Middle-Aged Jock talk. At this stage of life, we exchange hot tips about anti-inflammatories the way we used to exchange phone numbers. The only decathlon event left is in the OR.

But my match awaits. I shall sign on the dotted line, sketch a DO NOT TOUCH sign on the healthy knee and give a drug test to the anesthesiologist.

If anything goes wrong, remember: Meniscus is my favorite flower.

February 20, 1997

C ASCO BAY, MAINE—The lady-slippers have finally appeared, elegant as ever and overdressed for the occasion. Their pink finery is on display between the buff of the dirt road and the gray of the stone walls that once separated seaside farmers from their neighbors.

They have arrived late, but then, everything is late this year. We say that to one another as if the weather were a schoolchild who failed to respond to the teacher's bell.

Only now are the flowers rushing to their seats, tumbling into bloom, one after another. Today we are feasting on lilacs and lupin. Irises and peonies await only a permission slip from the thermometer.

All across the island, a few species of flowers are repeated with the frequency of a quilting pattern. A single strain of iris, one clan of lupin dominate the landscape the way the name Hamilton dominates the headstones in the cemetery.

On my morning walk, I wonder whether some 19th-century peddler rowed over here with a dory full of blue iris bulbs—one variety suits all. Or did the islanders of old, like the islanders of today, pass along lupin pods and transplant the indestructible day lilies from one parent patch?

I am a novice as a naturalist. Before coming here I lived on the land as lightly as a houseplant.

A Sunday suburban farmer, I made minimum investments for maximum gain. I planted vegetables on Memorial Day for delivery before Labor Day. Like a modern CEO, I looked no further into the future of the land than the next quarterly report.

From time to time, while my daughter was growing up, I thought about planting asparagus and immediately dismissed this three-year project. All that time before dinner? I spent a whole decade believing that three years was too long to wait.

But four years ago, we dug deep into this ground and planted the gnarled and rugged asparagus whose spears we will eat tonight. Is this what they mean by putting down roots?

It may be a reverse of normal logic, but the older I get, the more I plant ahead. At 30 it was all annuals. At 40, it was perennials. Last year we planted an apple tree that now comes up to my shoulders. This year, in a fit of Maine hubris, we planted a peach tree that may not deliver until the 21st century.

And just this morning, standing by the chestnut tree, worrying again about this centenarian that looms and creaks over our house, I started to choose the site for a replacement. I must find room for its enormous size though even the most optimistic actuary tells me I won't see an infant chestnut in its towering maturity.

What was the joke George Burns used to tell audiences near the end of his life? "At my age, I don't buy green bananas." I hear people my mother's age who witness some downward trend in the young or in society, say with relief, "Well, I'm glad I won't be around to see that."

We are told that Americans live in the "now" and have trouble thinking beyond our life span. We don't landscape any further ahead than our lease or our job.

We choose fast-food trees as weedy as an ailanthus and roll out instant lawns for instant gratification. As our country ages, we are also told, we care less about the next generation of other people's children, other people's social security, other people's environment.

But I wonder if that is true. It seems to me that as more of us pass the half-century mark, as more of us see 50 years back, it's easier to see 50 years ahead. As our private future shrinks, the comprehension of the future expands.

The senior-set bumper sticker may boast that "I am spending my children's inheritance." But the desire to pass on a legacy may be as "natural" as the desire to consume it. Especially when "it" is the land.

Maybe it is easier in a limited and known place to be aware of the land's past and future. To see ourselves as the caretakers of a small and vulnerable cache of lady-slippers, to feel the link to those people—perhaps the grandparents of neighbors—who planted the stand of irises on our land. Maybe it's easy to take some special delight in reclaiming a rhubarb patch left behind by a farmer whose name may be on the deed. But surely by midlife, most of us have inherited some gratitude to the past and responsibility to the future.

A hundred years ago someone planted this chestnut tree in front of my porch. I don't know who or why. This year, I'll plant one for the next hundred years. I make my living stringing words together across a page, but planting ahead is my job.

June 15, 1997

MINDFUL OF THE UNCERTAINTY OF LIFE

Who thought up this resolution thing anyway? The whole idea of a new year is to get a clean slate and a fresh start. The icon is a baby, the calendar begins with the number one.

But what's the first assignment we get for the first of the year? To pick up our autobiography as if it were an essay left over from last semester and begin to correct it.

Let's go down the list. There is weight to be lost and weights to lift. There are cigarettes to abandon, budgets to be tightened, and an endless supply of flaws to be corrected. Happy New Year to you, too.

I don't know if it was the Puritans who popularized this ritual flogging, this universal stock-taking that sends us to the stocks. After a feast of holiday pleasure, we get a famine of repentance. It sounds like them.

Even today, the only hearts that leap in the morning after New Year's Eve belong to weight loss clinics and personal trainers. The rest of us make resolutions that read like bills that come for Christmas generosity. We correct ourselves like an overvalued stock market, stiffen our spines against the chill of a January wind, and become resolute: "firm, determined, unwavering." Have I depressed you yet?

I have been there and done this. I have treated my life like a house in need of rehab, embarked on self-improvement projects that were about as much fun—and about as successful—as stripping wallpaper off with a razor blade. I have a recycled list of resolutions to lead me onto the straight and narrow.

Now I wonder what would happen if the list wasn't about narrowing life but widening it. What about resolving to begin or enjoy rather than stop and repent?

Some years ago, when a friend of mine took a new job, she made a list of ten things she would never do. When she'd done six of them, she quit. I have told that story with delight over the years, but what if she had written down the ten things that she did want to do? How do, should, any of us measure and reconstruct our lives?

There is a phrase that's stayed with me since I first heard the traditional introduction to a will. The man had written his will, "being mindful of the uncertainty of life." This "mindfulness" had stirred him to think about what he would leave. Why not use it to think about how we live?

What if our own New Year's resolutions list was written under the same imprimatur: be mindful of the uncertainty of life?

I'm not suggesting that anyone can spend every day as if it were the last. I'm not into New Age mantras or Armageddon threats. It's an impossible and absurd burden on the psyche to live as if there were no tomorrow. I'm even wary of inspirational tales from people who suggest that cancer was the best thing that ever happened to them. That's too big a price for a wake-up call.

But an annual reminder of mindfulness? Maybe what we need are two lists. On the left side: This is What Matters to Me. On the right side: This is How I Spend My Time. In the middle, our resolution: to make the right side align with the left. To make our time matter.

This is not a marching order to Live Importantly or not at all, to Eat your Spinach and Save the World or watch out. After all, laughter matters. Dessert matters. So do sex and solitude. Joy, for that matter, is a muscle that atrophies unless you exercise it. The very word "resolute" comes from the Latin word meaning, ironically, to relax.

But it may require more "resolution" to discover and do what really matters to us than it does to get into someone else's idea of "shape." Life gets eaten away in mindless bites the way the determination for a family dinner hour is devoured by phone calls, and the promise of a Sunday off is sacrificed to e-mail and car pools.

The big hand on the clock overruns the little hand. We put off a passion for singing and placate a promised commitment to work for the environment and give the laundry precedence over the kids' bedtime reading. Mindlessly.

It is not an accident that the most popular movie of the season is an otherwise ordinary tale of a man air-shipwrecked on a desert island. *Cast Away* is a modern parable about "wasting time" in which a FedEx manager and survivalist learns the double meaning in a company pep talk. Near the end he says with irony and understanding: "Let's not commit the sin of turning our backs on time."

Make that the first resolution for a happy—mindful—New Year.

December 31, 2000

AFTER 20 YEARS OF CULTIVATION, MY GARDEN IS GROWING ME

C ASCO BAY, MAINE—On the table before me is the small crop of lupine pods that I harvested from the wild. I shell them as if they were peas and save the tiny, round seeds in a glass cup.

Tomorrow I'll plant them. It's an annual rite performed with both hubris and hope that next spring the blue flowers that grace this small island will finally take their appointed place in my landscape.

This act is, I suppose, as close as I get to playing god. Unless, that is, you count the small vegetable garden that bumps up against the bushes. On that patch my tomatoes and peppers, which are summer visitors, grow beside the hardy natives, blackberries and raspberries.

But the truth is that I come up short in the god department. A few lupine seeds may obey my command and sprout a leaf or two, but those that truly thrive have found their own way, blooming in places they have chosen for themselves, even infiltrating the day lilies that surround the porch.

In the past I would have uprooted the interlopers as I planted my seeds. Like most gardeners, I want to leave my mark on the earth. But these days, natural accidents seem to please me more than ever. After planting beans and lettuce in even rows this summer, I find myself favoring the survivors of last year's eggplant, the volunteers rising among the green peppers.

I have been coming here 20 years. A city girl by upbringing, it's been a long apprenticeship that is by no means complete. It has taken me that long to understand such a small island, to respect its nature.

Only now can I clock the cycle from strawberries to blackberries, and only now do I realize that it isn't a coincidence when the monarchs arrive with the milkweed. These days, even as I pry the lupine pods apart, I find more comfort in nature's will than in my own attempts to bend it. I find more reassurance in what the land offers up on a summer day than what I demand of it.

Maybe this is middle age mellowing, or a growing contrarian streak. All around, scientists are racing to change the very nature of nature. Companies are merrily modifying the genes of soy, altering the DNA of corn in ways that would make Dolly the cloned sheep balk before her dinner.

This summer I read that genetically modified foods are being followed by genetically modified lawns. The Scotts Co. that brought us

Miracle-Gro is working on "low mow." Eventually, they will be able to alter genes, boasts a scientist, to produce grass that won't grow—Miracle Won't Gro?—and even for grass that will glow.

The manufacturers will surely pitch their permanently stunted grass to Saturday lawn mowers and Sunday duffers. But pollen has no more respect for private property than the catbird feasting on my blueberries.

What happens if the fluorescent grass of one neighbor spreads to another lawn like a plague of plastic flamingos? What if the crew-cut grass of suburbia spreads to the prairie? The biotech opponent Jeremy Rifkin says gleefully that this is when the cry of NIMBY—not in my backyard—takes on new consumer power. But I am not so sure.

In Europe, where food is a centerpiece of culture, consumers today want to know even the name of the farmer who raised the goat that produced the cheese. The cri de coeur is "Frankenfoods."

Maybe Americans are less engaged with this debate because food often comes to us like another consumer product, transported from factory farms to corporate supermarkets to fast-food conglomerates. In preemptive ads for public opinion, biotech companies feature a family farmer. But most of us are closer in the food chain to corporate Archer Daniels Midland than to farmer Rod Gangwish.

I am no back-to-nature romantic. I don't live off this land. My milk comes from the store and my coffee from Sumatra. I pull up weeds and plant lupine.

But I'm not surprised that progress has become our bioproduct. We've spent much of human history trying to take the wildness out of the wild, struggling to make ourselves the (landscape) architects of our destiny.

We have dominated nature right down into the DNA. If some day we can create a milkweed that will bloom in December, do we then create a Christmas butterfly? Where will it end?

On an island where people know their minds and lupine know their place, I am wondering about the wisdom of lording it over nature. Sometimes, on a summer day, it's easier to live within nature.

August 13, 2000

A COMMENCEMENT DAY CONFESSION

B y now, commencement season has peaked. The sounds of pomp and circumstance are receding, the bumper crop of caps and gowns is nearly harvested, and commencement speakers are bringing their final exhortations to the campus marketplace.

By tradition, the folks who deliver the final required college lecture are people who have made "it" in the wider world. They are the designated successes, the men and women who are through with the messy business of screwing up and growing up, of making mistakes and recouping losses.

I've given my share of such speeches, though mostly to reassure the graduates that these have not, I promise, been the best years of their lives. But before the robes are packed away, I want to tell about the most, well, memorable commencement day that I ever repressed.

Back in the mid-1980s, I was invited to be the commencement speaker at the University of Pennsylvania. I was, I felt sure, the first woman to make the commencement speech on that Ivy League campus since maybe Margaret Mead.

But skating ahead of the cracking ice of working motherhood, I decided to fly down to Philadelphia on the morning of commencement. I arrived at the gate at 7 a.m. in a decaffeinated state and took my aisle seat.

Then, as we taxied away, the flight attendant welcomed us all onto the plane to Albany. Somewhere, even in the recesses of my absent mind, the word "Albany" registered, and in a full-fledged panic I was up on my feet bellowing, "ALBANY? ALBANY?"

I swear to you that I am not a person who makes scenes. Bostonians do not make scenes (except, of course, in traffic). But at that moment I did a perfect imitation of a crazy person, explaining sweatily to the attendant that there were 10,000 students, faculty, family, who would enter a stadium in Philadelphia without a commencement speaker! No woman would ever again be asked to speak there!

At that point, she said two crucial things. (1) "Miss, we can't take off until you sit down." (2) "Didn't anyone at the gate check your ticket?" Bingo! Two admissions. And so, while an entire planeload of people who wanted very badly to go to Albany glared (Where, oh where, was the paper bag to put over my head?), I literally stood my ground.

In a few minutes, and blessedly without a straitjacket, the plane taxied me back to the gate. I raced to the Philadelphia flight, prayed I would never, ever meet any of the Albany passengers again, and stopped shaking when the landing gear touched the Philadelphia runway.

I never told a soul at Penn. We "commenced" happily, and I left with my honor and my honorary degree and my secret intact. A few days ago, a graduate of that class said she remembered what I'd said at her commencement. I can't remember a thing.

But I learned again that day the thin line between success and utter disaster. The way one dumb error and one desperate recovery can change everything.

Some years later, my daughter decided that she wanted to go to Penn. Need I say that if I'd spent that day in Albany, I would never have shown my face within 100 miles of the admissions office? My daughter, by the way, met her husband there. Had I missed the plane, well. . . .

I can tell this finally without breaking into hives. But that's not the only reason I share a story for this season. You see, there has to be another moral here.

Anthropologist Mary Catherine Bateson gives adults an exercise I often think of this time of year. She asks us to compose two narratives of our life history. Narrative One? "Everything I have ever done has been heading me to where I am today." Narrative Two? "It's only after many surprises and choices, interruptions and disappointments that I have arrived somewhere I could never have anticipated." The story of life can read both ways.

Young cap-and-gown wearers often see their elders' lives as a straight line. We need to explain exactly how it works: You make plans. You have accidents. You move straight ahead. You have to take a detour. You screw up. You recover. You try hard. You get lucky.

A life that looks seamless from the outside feels like a patchwork quilt from the inside. You never just achieve something—status, success, happiness—and hold it firm. You keep composing and recomposing life.

So I hope the class of 2000 will forget all the advice that comes this year from a thousand podiums. You can't protect yourself from making mistakes in life—although I would recommend checking the sign over the doorway before you board the plane—but you can learn resilience. And if all else fails, stand up and scream.

June 11, 2000

Acknowledgments

Journalism is both a collaborative and a solitary business. You go out in the world collecting information, picking brains on deadline. Then you sit and think through your fingers on a keyboard and send your thoughts out along the electronic wire. Sooner or later those ideas land on someone's doorstop or someone's laptop.

There are many people to thank in this endeavor. First of all readers for allowing me some time over their breakfast table and some space in their daily rush. I feel as if we've been in a conversation for these twenty-five years.

Op-ed page editors are the gatekeepers of journalism, and I am grateful to 400 of them who have given me some of the most valued real estate in the business.

I also collaborated for some thirty years with friends and colleagues at the *Boston Globe* until I left that wonderful workshop for a room of my own. I thank my colleagues, lunchmates, friends at the *Globe*, especially the savviest of editorial page editors and pals, Renee Loth.

For over twenty-five years, I've been syndicated—a mafia verb if there ever was one—by the Washington Post Writers Group. Alan Shearer runs this shop with care, good humor, and a sharp eye. Alan has even let my creative grammar and penchant for inventing words like "wimpathy" not be overruled by his spell check. All these columns were edited by Alan or the wonderfully supportive Jim Hill. They saved me more times than I care to recall.

Two years ago, I was lucky enough to corral Jamie Jones to assist me in the business of telling people what I think. Jamie gathered research under deadline, switching gears as the news bulletins rushed over the electronic transom. She's done it with the grace, curiosity, and intelligence of a true wordsmith. She's had a post-graduate education in everything from Nascar to assisted suicide. Together we've shared many salads and killed only a few plants.

During this time, I took a side trail to write a book on women and friendship, *I Know Just What You Mean,* with Patricia O'Brien. Whenever I write a particularly tricky, touchy, or personal column, I pick up the phone. For being there, thanks.

My thanks also to Chuck Adams, who edited this book. And of course to my agent, Esther Newberg, the redoubtable Red Sox fan. There's always next year, Esther.

My family suffers from having a reporter in their midst who chronicles their lives. Thank you to my daughter, Katie, especially who has suffered it the longest; to my son-in-law, Soren, who married into it; to my step-daughter, Jenny, and her husband, Bart, and to the two little people who don't yet have a veto. Bless you all for still letting me come to Thanksgiving.

No one knows the stress of the column-writing business more than my husband, Bob Levey. Bob is the only person who can make me laugh at three o'clock in the morning. The life you read in these pages is shared luckily and happily with this co-conspirator.